The Islamic State in Afghanistan and Pakistan

The Islamic State in Afghanistan and Pakistan

Strategic Alliances and Rivalries

Amira Jadoon with
Andrew Mines

LYNNE
RIENNER
PUBLISHERS

BOULDER
LONDON

Published in the United States of America in 2023 by
Lynne Rienner Publishers, Inc.
1800 30th Street, Suite 314, Boulder, Colorado 80301
www.rienner.com

and in the United Kingdom by
Lynne Rienner Publishers, Inc.
Gray's Inn House, 127 Clerkenwell Road, London EC1 5DB
www.eurospanbookstore.com/rienner

Library of Congress Cataloging-in-Publication Data
Names: Jadoon, Amira, 1982– author. | Mines, Andrew, 1996– author.
Title: The Islamic State in Afghanistan and Pakistan : strategic alliances
    and rivalries / Amira Jadoon with Andrew Mines.
Description: Boulder, Colorado : Lynne Rienner Publishers, Inc., 2023. |
    Includes bibliographical references and index. | Summary: "Drawing on
    original data and newly available primary sources, explains the rise and
    resilience of IS Khorasan, an ISIS affiliate in Afghanistan and
    Pakistan"— Provided by publisher.
Identifiers: LCCN 2022043166 (print) | LCCN 2022043167 (ebook) | ISBN
    9781955055857 (hardcover) | ISBN 9781685852856 (ebook)
Subjects: LCSH: Islamic State Khorasan Province (Organization) | IS
    (Organization) | Terrorism—Afghanistan. | Terrorism—Pakistan. |
    Afghanistan—Politics and government—2001– | Pakistan—Politics and
    government—1988–
Classification: LCC HV6433.I722 J33 2023 (print) | LCC HV6433.I722
    (ebook) | DDC 363.325095491—dc23/eng/20230210
LC record available at https://lccn.loc.gov/2022043166
LC ebook record available at https://lccn.loc.gov/2022043167

British Cataloguing in Publication Data
A Cataloguing in Publication record for this book
is available from the British Library.

Printed and bound in the United States of America

The paper used in this publication meets the requirements
of the American National Standard for Permanence of
Paper for Printed Library Materials Z39.48-1992.

5 4 3 2 1

Contents

Tables and Figures

Acknowledgments

This book is a culmination of several years of extensive research on the Islamic State Khorasan (ISK), which would not have been possible without our broad support network. First and foremost, this project has benefited tremendously from the generous support of our colleagues at the Combating Terrorism Center (CTC) and the Department of Social Sciences at the US Military Academy at West Point, as well as the Program on Extremism at George Washington University. We are deeply grateful for multiple opportunities over the years to present and discuss parts of the project with a broad network of subject-matter experts, academics, and policymakers, whose insights and feedback improved our research in meaningful ways. We are also thankful to our circle of friends and family, whose support, understanding, and optimism helped us overcome any challenges and made the journey of writing this book deeply rewarding.

The research that informs the book has been influenced by meaningful feedback provided by multiple scholars and experts at various stages. We are indebted to these individuals for taking a critical eye to our work and providing constructive feedback. They include Don Rassler, Assaf Moghadam, Jason Warner, Asfandyar Mir, Craig Whiteside, Haroro J. Ingram, Tricia Bacon, and Colin Clarke.

We are also grateful to the work of brilliant reporters and researchers who study the Islamic State, Islamic State affiliates, and militancy in the Afghanistan-Pakistan region more broadly; their work has helped us to refine our ideas and approaches. Among these individuals, Abdul Sayed's support has been invaluable in many ways. Sayed was incredibly generous with his time in discussing various aspects of ISK with us, sharing insights from his fieldwork in Afghanistan, and helping us collect and analyze important primary source materials. We are also thankful for the work done on ISK by other researchers; their insights were very helpful for our own work. Among others, these include Borhan Osman, Bill Roggio, Riccardo Valle, Susannah George, Kathy Gannon, Lucas Webber, Antonio Giustozzi, Obaid Ali, Bilal Sarwary, Hassan Abbas, Amin Tarzi, and Abdul Basit. We are especially grateful to Abdul Basit for his insightful comments on our final manuscript. A plethora of locally based reporters—many of whose work was halted during and after the collapse of the former Afghan government—provided invaluable on-the-ground reporting that truly enriched our findings based on open-source information and analysis, and we thank them for their extensive coverage and dedication to their field.

Various individuals have supported our efforts to collect and analyze vast amounts of data and primary materials for our research; these include Nakissa Jahanbani, Charmaine Willis, and Muhammad al-Ubaydi. Additionally, we were supported by many outstanding research assistants, including Darren Hagan, Mikki Franklin, Kevin Laiveling, Victoria Edwards, Emma Fruchtman, Lauren Harpole, Casey Haack, Julia Lodoen, Ava Sharifi, Gleb Smirnov, Vibha Baiji, Shabir Ahmadi, and Aaron Ostrovsky.

We are especially grateful to the editorial support provided by Ayush Verma in the last stages of preparing our manuscript. We couldn't be more appreciative of Ayush's commitment and eagerness to help us cross the finish line, his editorial skills, and his genuine enthusiasm about this project. We are also grateful to our editor, Marie-Claire Antoine at Lynne Rienner Publishers, for her patience, flexibility, and feedback.

In addition to the aforementioned, Amira Jadoon would like to thank the CTC team at West Point, who have been incredibly generous and encouraging in their support for this multiyear research project. A special thanks to the CTC for providing access to unclassified documents relevant to our research, and for facilitating meetings with relevant government officials and experts. In addition to the CTC members noted earlier, Jadoon is especially grateful to the CTC leadership team (current and former): Sean Morrow, Bryan Price, Daniel Milton, and Brian Dodwell.

Amira Jadoon is very thankful to her family for their enduring support of all her professional endeavors. In particular, she is deeply grateful to her late father, Saleem Jadoon (also known as Khanji), for being a lifelong inspiration and for instilling a love for the pursuit of knowledge and the courage to persevere; to her mother, Zebunissa (also known as Ami), for her unconditional love; and to her sister, Rabia, for her unshakeable faith in Amira's goals. Last but certainly not least, Amira is thankful to her husband, Kyle McCarthy, for his boundless patience, love, and support.

Andrew Mines would like to thank the Program on Extremism team for their support, feedback, mentorship, and encouragement, particularly the program's leadership under Lorenzo Vidino, Seamus Hughes, and

Devorah Margolin. Mines would also like to thank Haroro J. Ingram and Omar Mohammed for their insights and collaboration, much of which informed the discussion and analysis of the Islamic State's methods cited within these pages.

Andrew Mines is endlessly thankful for the love and support of his mother, Jennifer, and his brothers, Timothy, Daniel, and Benjamin, whose passions and character shaped him over the years. He is also grateful to his grandmother, Nancy, his late grandfather, Richard, other family members, and his partner, Liya Khan, for her love, faith, patience, and shared strength, from a small Chicago campus all the way to the nation's capital.

1

Emergence of the Islamic State Khorasan

In the month of Dhu l-Qa'da, the soldiers of the Caliphate advanced beyond their previous locations where they gained control of new locations and defeated the enemy, with Allah's permission. Several areas have been combed of the idolatrous Taliban movement—areas in which the Taliban were present, such as the areas of Naray Obeh, Ghardi and Karkanay, as well as the area of Maydanak. With that, routes have been opened to allow the entry of the foreign fighters into the governorate, with praise to Allah. We managed to get in contact with our brothers, the war officials in the cities, and thus the soldiers of the Caliphate were able to carry out wide-ranging operations inside Pakistan—such as two operations in the city of Quetta, as well as assassinations of leaders in the governments of Afghanistan and Pakistan, and the idolatrous Taliban in various cities. We appointed an Emir of War for the Khorasan province, and we formed a military shura for the province as well, keeping in mind that the deceased brother Wali Hafiz Sa'id Khan—Allah accept him— used to oversee the military affairs of the province himself prior to that. Accordingly, military affairs in the Khorasan province have now been strengthened, with Allah's permission. We developed a new plan to protect the military camps within secure areas, and they are now protected, Allah willing. Now the brothers there, both trainers and trainees alike, are fully protected, safe, and at ease, with praise to Allah. With almighty Allah's grace, we have been able to assist the families of martyrs in the province for the first time. We have paid 10,000 rupees to each family.

In closing, we share the good news that brother Dawud, the Emir of one of the groups of the Tehrik-e-Taliban Pakistan, has pledged allegiance to the Caliph of the Muslims– Allah protect him. It is known that the brother was an official in charge of operations in the city of Karachi [Pakistan] during the era of Hakimullah Mehsud—may Allah accept him. We also share good news that the soldiers of the Caliphate are doing battle with the enemies of Allah with the utmost courage and determination. The dominion of the Caliphate is expanding day by day, with almighty Allah's permission.

—Letter from ISK to IS-Central leadership, August 8, 2016[1]

The above statement is an excerpt from a letter addressed to the "Commander of the Faithful and Caliph of the Muslims." The letter was apparently penned by the new *wali* (top leader) of the Islamic State's Khorasan province (Islamic State Khorasan [ISK]) after the death of the group's first leader, Hafiz Saeed Khan. In it, Khan's successor provides a status update to al-Baghdadi and the Islamic State's top leadership in Iraq and Syria, conveying a great sense of optimism despite recent losses. In the letter, among other items, the new *wali* heralds thirteen main accomplishments during the month of Dhu l-Qa'da (August 5, 2016–September 3, 2016), in addition to tactical advances made by ISK on the battlefield. He also notes a number of developments internal to the organization, such as receiving a new pledge of allegiance from a commander of the Tehrik-e-Taliban (TTP), identified as Dawud. The letter boasts that Dawud's support will offer ISK invaluable experience for conducting operations in Pakistan's largest city, Karachi.

Whether this report ever reached al-Baghdadi and his core leadership in Iraq and Syria (Islamic State–Central [IS-Central]) cannot be confirmed, but the letter outlines a number of key organizational developments within ISK, as well as the challenges it faced in the Afghanistan and Pakistan region one year on from its official formation. After surging onto the jihadist landscape in 2015 and despite the loss of its first leader, in mid-2016 ISK was on an upward trajectory of violence that would prove difficult to suppress. By 2018, two years after the penning of this letter, the group would gain notoriety as one of the top four most lethal militant groups in the world.[2] Three years later, in August 2021, amid the last stages of the US-led withdrawal and immediately following the Taliban's takeover of Afghanistan, ISK launched one of its most spectacular and horrific attacks ever on the Kabul airport, which left hundreds dead and wounded, including thirteen US service members. The group's relatively new leader at the time, Sanaullah Ghafari (also known as Shahab al-Muhajir), was credited by ISK's own members for orchestrating the attack as well as for the group's resurgence in 2021 and beyond. On February 7, 2022, the US Department of State announced a $10 million prize for information on al-Muhajir and anyone else involved in the Kabul airport attack.[3]

As ISK closes in on a full decade of violence and destruction, the group has managed to successfully embed itself within the region, form crucial alliances while confronting its main rival—the Afghan Taliban—and continue its campaign of violence despite intensive counterterrorism efforts.[4] However, ISK's operational activity has fluctuated significantly, largely due to losses suffered from counterterrorism operations and battles with the Afghan Taliban. By early 2020, the group was widely perceived to be a debilitated organization, and some had even declared it defeated. Yet a weakened but resilient ISK still found opportunities to sustain and even enhance its brutal reputation by conducting some of the most vicious attacks in Afghanistan to date. Against the backdrop of a delicate US-Taliban peace process, international troop withdrawals, and intra-Afghan tensions, ISK renewed and expanded its violent campaigns. In late 2021, ISK initiated the most intense and aggressive phase of its rivalry with the Taliban under the leadership of al-Muhajir, taking many by surprise. For a group that was largely considered to be defunct by 2019, ISK's notable tenacity and unwavering resolve raise a critical question and one that this book seeks to answer: What explains ISK's resiliency and continued existence?

Even during its weakest phases, ISK has still been able to reach new audiences, replenish its ranks, and perpetrate sophisticated and highly lethal attacks across the region. In May 2020, the group attacked a Doctors Without Borders maternity ward in Kabul in a Hazara Shiite community. The group's fighters targeted mothers, infants, and hospital staff, leading to the eventual closure of the clinic. In November 2020, three ISK gunmen laid siege for several hours to Afghanistan's largest university—Kabul University—killing at least nineteen people.[5] One month prior, an ISK suicide attack targeted a tutoring center in a Hazara neighborhood, leaving hundreds dead or wounded.[6] While most of ISK's violent campaigns in 2020 focused on Afghanistan, the group launched equally lethal attacks across the border in Pakistan, too. An attack in Balochistan in late 2020 killed eleven miners belonging to Pakistan's minority Shiite Hazaras, a stark reminder of the group's operational presence on both sides of the Durand Line.[7] Compared to ISK's attacks in previous years, 2020 appeared to be particularly brutal, and largely directed at civilian populations. ISK subsequently pushed forward with its strategy of stoking an outbidding war by inciting sectarian violence, setting itself back on an upward trajectory of violence throughout 2021. In 2022, the group appeared to be further emboldened, broadening its attack campaigns and expanding its recruitment efforts aggressively while also reportedly receiving new funds from IS-Central after the Kabul airport attack.[8] In April 2022, after a temporary winter season lull, ISK was linked to a series of devastating attacks across Afghanistan, to include an attack in the city of Mazar-e-Sharif on a Shiite mosque that killed and injured over ninety individuals.[9]

Today, the international community is sounding the alarm over terrorists once again using Afghanistan to plan attacks on foreign soil, and ISK is a key concern for many. Western officials issued warnings in late 2021 that ISK maintained interest in launching attacks directly against Western targets, and in March 2022 the US Department of Defense assessed that ISK could develop the capacity to conduct external operations against the United States and its allies within twelve to twenty-four months.[10] Around that time, the group also started claiming responsibility for multiple cross-border attacks in Tajikistan and Uzbekistan in April and May 2022, respectively. According to the group's own propaganda, other countries were next in its sights.

After the Taliban's takeover and collapse of the former Afghan government, ISK seems to be on a path to recovery from its heavy losses in prior years, with its ranks swelling significantly, helped in part by the release of thousands of imprisoned members during various prison breaks including the Pul-e-Charkhi prison outside of Kabul.[11] Under al-Muhajir's deft leadership throughout much of 2020–2022,[12] with Mawlawi Rajab Salahuddin (alias Mawlawi Hanas) as deputy, and Sultan Aziz Azzam as ISK's spokesperson, the group has not just retained a foothold in this new era for Afghanistan and the region, but also increased its outreach efforts to appeal to a broader audience. Since al-Muhajir's rise to the top of ISK's ranks, the number of languages featured in ISK propaganda has expanded rapidly, moving beyond traditional releases in Arabic, Pashto, and Dari to now include Urdu, Hindi, Malayalam, Uzbek, Tajik, Russian, Farsi, and English.[13] The group even released its first English-language magazine, *Voice of Khorasan,* in early 2022. A common thread across this plethora of propaganda releases is ISK's concerted efforts to undermine the legitimacy of the Taliban and criticize it for pandering to the international community in order to gain global acceptance. Within this broader campaign to delegitimize the Taliban, however, are messaging narratives that are carefully tailored to appeal to different audiences. For example, in the inaugural issue of the English-language *Voice of Khorasan* magazine, an article titled "Who Are the Taliban?" states the following:

> Currently they [the Taliban] seek to gain the pleasure of the Kuffar by doing whatever they demand of them. They have slaughtered numerous numbers of Ahlul Sunnah, closed down mosques and schools in the name of hunting down the Islamic State. . . . Numerous meetings and visits have been already made to the biggest enemies of Islam such as China, Iran and Russia. While the Taliban considers the eradication of the Uighur Muslims as an internal matter of China, the mass murders committed by the Russian, Iran regime and its proxies on the Ahlul Sunnah of Iraq and Sham is also considered something outside of their jurisdiction. Despite . . . the fact that enemies of Islam [are] slaughtering the Muslims, they [the Taliban] seek to have political and international recognition of their own needs.

Similarly, in its book published in Uzbek in early 2022, *Until When the Ignorance?* ISK criticized the Taliban for seeking alliances with Russia and Turkey, among others, decrying these engagements as an abandonment of true jihad.[14] Other unofficial ISK-affiliated propagandists have also consistently produced and distributed materials in Urdu, Hindi, and Bengali through outlets such as *Nida-e Haqq, al-Qitaal,* and *al-Burhan,* respectively, while the relatively new *Weekly Khilafat* provides translations of IS-Central's Arabic-language *al-Naba* weekly newsletters into Urdu and Hindi.[15]

To further tailor its messaging, ISK has attempted to identify and integrate specific local grievances into propaganda directed at specific audiences. The sophistication of ISK's audience segmentation features consistently in its attempts to recruit Indians, Kashmiris, Central Asians, and other audiences. For example, some of ISK's propaganda directed at Tajik militants directly threatens the Tajik government, and singles out the president of Tajikistan, Emomali Rahmon.[16] On the whole, ISK's wide-reaching propaganda campaigns shed light on the group's determination to smear the Taliban's image and standing, and on its plans to create an organization that is truly regional in scope and membership. So far, these efforts appear to have borne some fruit, which ISK frequently advertises by showcasing the diversity of nationalities among its ranks. Per ISK's own claims, the attack on a Sikh Gurudwara in Kabul in March 2020 and the August 2020 Jalalabad prison break involved Indian and Tajik perpetrators, and the attacker from the October 2021 Kunduz mosque was reportedly an Uighur Muslim.[17] Today, several years after its emergence, ISK is now widely considered to be one of the gravest security challenges to the Taliban's ability to consolidate control across the country, with the aim and the potential to exacerbate sectarian violence across the region.

Considering ISK's sustained violence amid a rapidly evolving environment, a key question about the group emerges: What factors explain ISK's rise and resilience as one of the Islamic State's most lethal, and arguably most successful, affiliates? Over the years, the group has managed to survive intense counterterrorism operations that resulted in significant territorial and human capital losses, including several governors, several hundred leadership-level members, and thousands of rank-and-file members.[18] Simply put, what explains ISK's resiliency? What enables the group not only to survive but also to threaten the future of peace and stability in Afghanistan? To answer these questions, we leverage original data on ISK's attacks and losses over the years, the group's propaganda materials released in various formats, and unclassified internal documents associated with the group retrieved from Afghanistan.

We argue that since its official formation in 2015, ISK adopted a two-pronged strategy to localize a transnational jihadist movement in the Afghanistan-Pakistan region, and generate a sustainable support base that would allow it to survive a dynamic, competitive, and challenging security environment. On one hand, ISK took advantage of the presence of myriad sectarian and antistate groups in Afghanistan and Pakistan by first establishing links with such groups, and then drawing on those connections to build and sustain its capacity over the years. ISK's alliances not only rapidly expanded its access to local expertise and logistical channels during its formative years, but also allowed the group to project power and geographical reach—garnering itself a lasting regional reputation.

On the other hand, ISK also relied on strategically provoking dominant groups in the region from the outset, especially those it considered to be nationalist in nature, as well as those that had links with state sponsors, or links with the Islamic State's global rival: al-Qaeda. ISK's strategy to harvest rivalries was critical in differentiating its brand from prevailing militant groups, and portraying itself as the sole legitimate leader of jihad. By presenting itself as a rival rather than an alliance of leading militant groups similar to the Taliban, ISK was able to position itself as the main alternative jihadist organization for both opportunistic or disgruntled individual militants, as well to entire militant factions dissenting from their core members or leaders. Without portraying other groups as illegitimate in one way or another, ISK would have likely struggled to provide a rationale for its own role in a highly competitive militant environment.

Combined with ISK's transnational jihadist narrative—which is broad enough to subsume the more parochial goals of various regional groups in South and Central Asia—ISK's two-prong strategy of forging key alliances and rivalries allowed it to exploit intra and intergroup tensions and build a diverse, continually replenishable talent pipeline. Overall, we demonstrate how ISK's strategic selection of alliances and rivalries were central to its ability to rise, overcome its losses, and resurge in 2021 and 2022, while also building a regional reputation and posing a challenge to the Afghan Taliban's consolidation of power post-2021.

ISK's Operational Environment

The Afghanistan-Pakistan region is marked by a high concentration of various militant organizations. According to a report released by the US Department of State, the region is home to one of "the highest regional concentration of terrorist groups in the world," with the Afghanistan-Pakistan border areas serving as a sanctuary to multiple terrorist and insurgent groups, including the Afghan Taliban (prior to their takeover), the Tehrik-e-Taliban Pakistan (TTP), al-Qaeda, the Haqqani Network, and the Islamic Movement of Uzbekistan (IMU). The decades-long presence of these groups continues to pose significant challenges for state control in remote areas outside of major population centers.[19] These groups have benefited from long-standing criminal networks, ranging from drug trafficking, extortion, and illicit mining to the smuggling of weapons. In other words, access to a sizable black market in both countries has facilitated militant groups' ability to survive in the region and support their operations.[20] In general, border security surrounding the Durand Line remains challenging given the tense relationship between the Pakistani and former Afghan governments, one that is characterized by deep-rooted mistrust. These challenges have persisted following the Taliban's return to power.

Militant groups in both countries target their recruitment efforts toward the region's various religious sects. In Pakistan, there are four main Sunni movements—Barelvi, Deobandi, Ahl-e-Hadees, and Jamaat-e-Islami—and several Shiite ones.[21] The Barelvis, also known as Sufis, are typically linked to devotional practices and rituals involving the shrines of Sufi saints, whereas the Deobandi school—a revivalist movement—seeks to purify Islamic practices by doing away with mystical beliefs and shrines and is committed to a "correct" interpretation of sharia (Islamic law).[22] In Afghanistan, some estimates place about 80 percent of the country's population as Sunnis and 20 percent as Shiites. The majority of the Sunni population belongs to the Hanafi school, which houses the Deobandi movement and its many militant adherents, most notably the Taliban.[23]

In general, Deobandi Islam is prevalent in the Pashtun belt on both sides of the Durand Line, which has also been influenced by Salafism over the years (also referred to as Wahhabism after its founder, Muhammad ibn Abd al-Wahhab). The rise of Salafism's influence in Afghanistan can be linked to the anti-Soviet jihad of the 1980s, in which Saudi Arabia played a notable role in "the Salafization of the Afghan mujahideen, both materially and intellectually."[24] The Islamic State and its affiliates generally subscribe to a militarized implementation of the Salafi ideology, Salafi jihadism, which forms the central basis of ISK's ideology as well. In addition to the Deobandi and Salafist movements, the Ahl-e-Hadees (also spelled Ahl-e-Hadith) movement is another Sunni reformist movement with South Asian roots that emerged in the 1870s in northern India. The movement emphasizes consulting the Quran and Hadith for guidance rather than relying on the interpretations of the various schools of Islam.[25] These three movements—Deobandi, Salafist, and Ahl-e-Hadees—among others, maintain key ideological distinctions. They are all important movements in the political-religious environment of the region, and as a result, enjoy large followings that multiple militant organizations seek to cultivate and exploit.

Dominant Militant Organizations

Pakistan has been home to a number of terrorist and insurgent organizations since the country's founding, all of which identify with different Islamic movements, including Barelvi, Deobandi, Ahl-e-Hadees, and Jamaat-e-Islami. Many of these groups also pursue varying levels of activity in Afghanistan; for some, Pakistan's neighbor offers a largely logistical resource for activities such as training, and for others it is more of a safe haven.

Perhaps the most internationally well known group after the Taliban and al-Qaeda is the TTP, also known as the Pakistani Taliban, which emerged in the tribal regions of Pakistan in 2007. The TTP has maintained a historically close relationship with the Afghan Taliban and al-Qaeda and has various splinter groups such as Jamaat-ul-Ahrar, some of which merged back with the TTP in 2020. Other groups such as Lashkar-e-Taiba, Harakat-ul-Mujahideen,

Jaish-e-Mohammed, and Hizbul Mujahideen—which have received vary-ing levels of passive or active support from Pakistan's military and intelli-gence services—remain more focused on countering Indian influence in Jammu and Kashmir, although they have evolved into a larger and more expansive militant network. Sunni sectarian groups are also present in Pakistan. Most notable is the anti-Shia group Lashkar-e-Jhangvi (LeJ), which is linked to the country's policies of Islamization and marginaliza-tion of secular democratic forces.

While some groups such as LeJ allied with ISK, others have opposed the formation of the Islamic State's regional province since its official founding in January 2015. Below is a discussion of some of the key mili-tant groups that have dominated the region's militant landscape both before and after ISK's emergence—the Afghan Taliban and the Haqqani Network, the Pakistani Taliban, and al-Qaeda. These organizations consti-tute ISK's key militant challengers despite maintaining limited links at the individual or tactical level.

The Afghan Taliban and the Haqqani Network

The United States–led invasion of Afghanistan in 2001 removed the Afghan Taliban from power, but soon paved the way for a more resilient insurgency that by 2018 was ranked as the world's deadliest militant group.[26] On August 15, 2021, the Taliban's twenty-year insurgency culminated in its takeover of Kabul, the collapse of the North Atlantic Treaty Organization (NATO)–allied Islamic Republic of Afghanistan, and the final stages of US withdrawal from Afghanistan.

After the death of the Taliban supreme leader, Mullah Akhtar Muham-mad Mansour, in a drone strike in May 2016, Mawlawi Haibatullah Akhundzada assumed leadership of the group and remains in power today.[27] Around early 2017, it was reported that Akhundzada had replaced several members of the Taliban's leadership in an attempt to consolidate his power.[28] Contrary to many narratives that portray the Taliban as a divided movement, Andrew Watkins has argued that the Taliban remained a relatively cohesive insurgent group given its leadership's efforts to retain and strengthen orga-nizational cohesion.[29] In February 2020, the Afghan Taliban signed a peace deal with the United States in Qatar, initiating a journey that would lead to intra-Afghan talks, a ceasefire, and for some, an unexpectedly swift Taliban takeover. In April 2020, the Taliban announced the appointment of Mawlavi Mahdi as the shadow district chief for Sar-e Pul province, making him the first Shiite Hazara to gain such a position of prominence,[30] although the appointment appeared to be largely symbolic and an attempt to build local legitimacy, especially given that Mahdi was killed in a Taliban raid in 2022 for rebellion. In May 2020, the son of Mullah Omar was appointed as mili-tary chief.[31] The Afghan Taliban's return to power in 2021 has given the group every incentive to strive for domestic and international legitimacy by establishing governance and security within the country. One of its first tests as the sole governing political organization in Afghanistan has been containing a highly motivated and resurgent ISK, while dealing with several other sociopolitical and economic tribulations.

Although the Afghan Taliban's goals of implementing their version of sharia and expelling United States–led coalition forces have always been tied closely to Afghanistan, the group's leadership has enjoyed sanctuary in Pakistan's Balochistan province, parts of the Federally Administered Tribal Agencies (FATA), and in Khyber Pakhtunkhwa (KPK), which has included FATA since mid-2018, with assistance from elements of the Pakistani state.[32] The Quetta Shura was formed by Taliban leaders after their fall in 2001, and until 2021 remained a government in exile, directing Taliban district administrations and provincial governors from afar.[33] The Afghan Taliban's relationship with the Pakistani state has fluctuated over the past years, and more recently the Afghan Taliban seems increasingly eager to reduce its dependence on Pakistan.[34]

The Haqqani Network—well known for its role in the Taliban's leadership, and connection to elements of the Pakistani state—was formed in 1973 by Jalaluddin Haqqani and has long been a fundamental component of the militant landscape in Afghanistan and Pakistan. The group's main areas of operations have been the southeastern Afghan provinces of Khost, Paktia and Paktika, and North Waziristan across the border in Pakistan. Jalaluddin played a key role in fighting Daud Khan's Soviet-backed regime, and prior to the formation of the Haqqani Network he studied at a Pakistan-based Deobandi madrassa called the Dar-ul-Uloom Haqqania. In the post-2001 era, the group's primary goals have been to counter Western influence and United States–led coalition forces, reestablish a Taliban regime, and oppose the implementation of democratic institutions.[35]

Jalaluddin's son, Sirajuddin Haqqani, assumed the leadership of the Haqqani Network in 2001,[36] and after the death of Mullah Omar he was appointed as second-in-command by the Taliban in July 2015.[37] Sirajuddin's position as a Taliban deputy not only solidified Haqqani influence within the Taliban but also allowed the Haqqani Network to expand its activities in Afghanistan and provide the Taliban with enhanced operational and logistical capabilities.[38] Given the Haqqani-Taliban organizational integration, many view the two groups as a single entity. In 2021, Sirajuddin became the newly appointed minister of interior of Afghanistan. He remains on the US Federal Bureau of Investigations's most-wanted list, and just prior to his appointment he was described as the "primary liaison between the Taliban and Al-Qaida" in a United Nations (UN) report.[39]

Although the Haqqani network received external support during the Soviet jihad from the US Central Intelligence Agency (CIA) and Saudi

Arabia,[40] over the proceeding decades the group established a complex financial infrastructure that uses front companies to launder money in various sectors such as real estate, car dealerships, and smuggled weapons and drugs.[41] In their seminal book on the origins of the Haqqani Network, Brown and Rassler aptly call the group the "fountainhead of jihad." As they argue, "Since the late 1970s the Haqqani network has provided a variety of state sponsors, private donors, and entrepreneur revolutionaries with a particularly valuable resource in the global economy of conflict: a platform for the delivery of violence."[42] This service has benefited the Haqqanis tremendously in terms of gaining financial and political power. The group is well known to have provided shelter to an assortment of foreign militants including Chinese Uighurs, Uzbeks, and al-Qaeda fighters. What's more, the United States and Pakistan played a critical role in enabling the Haqqani's rise because of their support for the latter's jihad against the Soviets.[43] The Haqqani's embeddedness within each country, tribal allies, and support from the United States, Saudi Arabia, and several other states uniquely positioned them to become the "richest pipeline for war material servicing the anti-Soviet conflict in the 1980s."[44] With the help of these generous funds and backing, the group established a base and supply depot at Zhawara in the province of Khost.[45]

After the 1980s, Haqqani's Zhawara base and the surrounding region became a training node for other conflicts, groups, and fighters, such as the jihad in Kashmir,[46] al-Qaeda, Uighurs, Uzbeks, and other Asian and Arab militant groups.[47] To this day, the Haqqanis provide various services to a wide range of regional and transnational militants. In July 2019, the UN noted that there still remained a close relationship between the Haqqani Network and al-Qaeda.[48] Earlier US intelligence reports noted that the Haqqani Network was one of Osama bin Laden's most important backers in South Asia, and that Sirajuddin was a member of al-Qaeda's Shura Majlis, or executive council.[49] A report by the Middle East Institute stated that al-Qaeda and the Haqqani Network financed a joint unit composed of 2,000 Haqqani Network fighters.[50] In recent years, many journalists and analysts have drawn operational links between members of the Haqqani Network and those of ISK, even though the two groups remain organizationally opposed.[51]

In sum, the Haqqani Network has survived for decades by balancing a network of relationships with the Afghan and Pakistani Taliban, al-Qaeda, and the Pakistani military, all of which have leveraged the group's capacity to deliver violence for their own purposes (and at other times to serve as interlocutors in negotiations). Since partnering with the Afghan Taliban in the 1990s, the Haqqani Network has served as an important platform for the Taliban to wield power in southeastern Afghanistan while still retaining its autonomy, and Haqqani leaders assumed key positions within the Afghan Taliban's newly formed government in 2021.[52]

The Tehrik-e-Taliban Pakistan

The Tehrik-e-Taliban Pakistan emerged as early as 2004 when groups identifying as the "Pakistani Taliban" appeared in Waziristan, although the TTP only officially coalesced in 2007.[53] The group is known to have launched some of the most vicious terrorist attacks in Pakistan's history, including its attack on an army public school in Peshawar that killed over a hundred children.

The Pakistani Taliban has maintained close relationships with several militant groups, but perhaps most notably and openly with the Afghan Taliban and al-Qaeda. TTP leaders provided the Taliban with logistical and operational support during their insurgency in Afghanistan, including the provision of suicide bombers and facilitating recruitment from Pakistan's tribal areas.[54] From the TTP's perspective, a close relationship with the Afghan Taliban provided it with vital refuge from the Pakistani army's military operations and US drone strikes in Pakistan, while boosting the TTP's own legitimacy by being linked to a cause that is popular among Pashtun tribesmen. In addition to the Afghan Taliban, al-Qaeda played an important role in TTP's ascendency in its early years. Beyond material benefits, the TTP received ideological support from al-Qaeda leadership and support for its goal of waging jihad against the Pakistani state.[55] When the US invasion of Afghanistan triggered an influx of militants from across the border into Pakistan, leaders of al-Qaeda and other Islamist groups such as the Islamic Movement of Uzbekistan recognized the TTP as *ansār*, or helpers, reinforcing the TTP's legitimacy.[56]

Years of intense campaigns by the Pakistani government, losses inflicted by the US drone program, and problems internal to the group eventually triggered the TTP's decline post-2015. Although the TTP lost considerable operational capacity over the years, the group has continued to wage a sporadic jihad against the Pakistani state. For example, the TTP conducted a series of attacks against politicians during the 2018 national elections in Pakistan, and was suspected to have used a female suicide attacker in July 2019.[57] Moreover, the designation by the United States of TTP's current leader, Noor Wali Mehsud, as a "global terrorist" in 2019, followed by the targeting of two prominent TTP leaders in Afghanistan in 2020, suggested that the group remained operational.[58]

Despite reduced operational capacity, internal disputes, breakaway factions, and defections to the Islamic State Khorasan province, the decentralized TTP continues to survive. Post-2018, the group revamped its operations and hardened its relentless war with Pakistan's security forces. In 2019 and 2020, reports that TTP militants were threatening local residents in Miranshah, North Waziristan, and Wana, South Waziristan raised concerns about a potential resurgence.[59] Perhaps most concerning, some of the well-known splinter groups linked to TTP, such as Jamaat-ul-Ahrar (JuA) and Hizbul Ahrar (HuA)—which have been responsible for deadly attacks within Pakistan—formally rejoined the TTP in August 2020 in an effort to consolidate their fight against the Pakistani state, with TTP member Noor Wali retaining the group's leadership.

Despite previous losses, a TTP revival has stirred significant concern for Pakistan. In August 2021, the TTP heralded the withdrawal of US forces from Afghanistan as a major victory for jihadist ideology and reaffirmed its support for the Afghan Taliban. The victory of the Taliban in Afghanistan and their reluctance to crack down on the TTP seemed to further embolden the group. In 2021, the group significantly accelerated its attacks in north-western Pakistan,[60] and claimed responsibility for a suicide bombing in Quetta, demonstrating its desire to expand operations.[61] In the ninth issue of its Urdu-language magazine, the TTP claimed to have conducted a total of 104 attacks in just the first three months of 2022,[62] and also announced a spring campaign targeting Pakistani security forces in April 2022. Perturbed by the TTP's rise and resolve but lacking a clear and coherent pathway to tackling the group, the Pakistani state has oscillated between kinetic operations and peace negotiations.

The TTP also resumed efforts to exploit local grievances, in particular by producing propaganda that focuses on the negative actions of the Pakistani military and Inter-Services Intelligence.[63] In March 2021, the TTP spoke out against a nonviolent march for women's rights, accusing female activists of blasphemy and obscenity in an apparent attempt to intimidate locals.[64] The group has resumed similar intimidation tactics against civilians and police in an effort to enforce its strict interpretation of sharia.[65]

The Islamic State's affiliate in Afghanistan and Pakistan emerged when the TTP was splintered, and was suffering from several internal disputes, as outlined earlier. When several TTP leaders and factions began defecting to ISK—including the entire TTP Orakzai faction and part of its Bajaur faction—ISK founding governor and former TTP commander Hafiz Saeed Khan appeared to believe that the entire TTP would be subsumed by ISK. A letter penned by Khan to IS-Central, dated June 22, 2016, states: "As for the TTP, headed by Mulla Fadlallah [Fadlullah], it is on the verge of collapsing because of the conflicts that have taken place within it. Praise to Allah. We know that it had tried to smooth out some conflicts inside the governorate, but the state of its personnel became such that they are accusing one another of being spies and agents. This is a victory Allah granted the soldiers of the Caliphate."[66]

It is unsurprising that ISK's strong anti-Pakistan narrative appealed to TTP fighters and factions, but the TTP's loyalty to the Afghan Taliban became an obstacle to complete alignment with ISK at the organizational level. For the first time, in July 2020 the TTP openly declared ISK to be a tool of the Pakistani establishment, disputing reports of its links with ISK.[67]

Al-Qaeda

In the aftermath of the 9/11 attacks, the majority of al-Qaeda fighters operating in the Afghanistan-Pakistan region were foreign-born. This dynamic is still prevalent today, and al-Qaeda has partnered with local Pakistani militant groups such as the TTP, Jaish-e-Mohammed (JeM), and LeJ to plan and execute attacks from their safe haven in Pakistan's northwestern regions.[68]

Intense counterterrorism pressure against al-Qaeda in Afghanistan and Pakistan since 9/11 resulted in the death of bin Laden[69] and the appointment of Ayman al-Zawahiri as al-Qaeda's top leader. Around the time of the Islamic State's emergence, senior al-Qaeda leaders were becoming increasingly opposed to what they perceived as al-Zawahiri's tolerance and even prioritization of "idolatrous" groups such as the Afghan Taliban at the expense of pure Salafist doctrine.[70] Nine of these al-Qaeda leaders were the first group of defectors to pledge allegiance to the Islamic State in March 2014.[71] After the official announcement of the caliphate in June 2014 and the formation of ISK in January 2015, they encouraged local Afghan and Pakistani militants to also join ISK in pursuit of global jihad.[72] According to former Afghan government senior security officials,[73] a significant proportion of ISK's founding members were al-Qaeda members. Beyond providing a major propaganda boost for the Islamic State in its global rivalry with al-Qaeda, these defections offered ISK a large number of experienced and skilled trainers and experts.[74]

The formation of a recognized Islamic State province in the Afghanistan-Pakistan region officially extended the Islamic State and al-Qaeda rivalry into South and Central Asia. However, the seeds of their rivalry were laid in the immediate years prior. When al-Qaeda's Ayman al-Zawahiri announced the creation of a new branch in South Asia in September 2014, known as al-Qaeda in the Indian Subcontinent (AQIS), many considered this to be an effort to stem the growing influence of pro–Islamic State sentiments.[75] While this view posits that fears of expanded Islamic State influence were the driving rationale for the creation of AQIS, al-Qaeda members have denied such claims. In the group's first edition of its *Resurgence* magazine, an AQIS member wrote that the "establishment of this organization is a direct result of the merger of several groups that have been engaged in Jihad in this region for several years."[76] In another edition of the magazine released in mid-2015, Adam Yahiye Gadahn, a well-known American al-Qaeda member, claimed that plans for AQIS had been finalized in mid-2013. As such, "the founding of the new branch [AQIS] had absolutely nothing to do with any perceived or presumed rivalry between al-Qaida and Islamic State."[77]

After the death of al-Baghdadi in 2019, AQIS announced an amnesty for al-Qaeda members who had joined ISK. The exact number of individuals who accepted this amnesty offer is unclear, but the policy's mere existence speaks to the intricate dynamics of the Islamic State and al-Qaeda rivalry in the region. Looking ahead, these two organizations' rivalry is likely to continue and even intensify across South and Central Asia as they compete for recruits and dominance over the global jihadist movement.

Counterterrorism and Counterinsurgency Infrastructure in Afghanistan and Pakistan

In addition to the militant landscape, the state security apparatuses in Afghanistan and Pakistan played a vital role in shaping ISK's emergence, and thus require examination.

In Afghanistan, the security forces of the former Islamic Republic of Afghanistan benefited significantly from large-scale international support for counterterrorism operations, led by the US military and its NATO allies. The NATO-led International Security Assistance Force (ISAF) provided security and engaged in combat operations across Afghanistan until 2014, at which point it transitioned primary security responsibility to the Afghan National Defense and Security Forces (ANDSF) (also known as ANSF). In 2015, NATO launched its Resolute Support Mission to train, advise, and assist the ANSF in its own combat operations, which were complemented by both joint and independent US operations. In addition to deployments of service members, the Department of Defense also employed tens of thousands of private security contractors to support the military, provide security, and train local security forces. The Central Intelligence Agency's Special Activities Division (SAD) was also present in the country, frequently partnering with the US Air Force to launch manned airstrikes and unmanned drone strikes. Special operations forces operating under Joint Special Operations Command (JSOC) worked in tandem with the CIA to lead many of the offensive combat operations against ISK in Afghanistan, occasionally in joint operations with the ANSF.[78]

ANSF capabilities were essentially split between the Ministry of Defense and the Ministry of Interior, the former of which contained the Afghan Armed Forces and the National Directorate of Security (NDS). The Afghan Armed Forces consisted of the Afghan National Army (ANA) and the Afghan Air Force (AAF), both of which held responsibility for operations against the Taliban, ISK, and other militant groups. The NDS was responsible for intelligence collection and analysis and stood up its own special forces units that worked alongside those of the ANA.[79] The NDS also housed paramilitary forces, some of which came under fire for high civilian casualty numbers in their counterterrorism operations.[80] The Ministry of Interior, on the other hand, was responsible for maintaining the Afghan National Police (ANP) and the Afghan Local Police (ALP). These police forces provided the ANSF with a number of defensive capabilities such as holding checkpoints. They also supported the NDS on counterterrorism-related arrests in urban areas. The third and more informal entity of the ANSF was the National Uprising Groups. These groups were paid for and armed by the Ministries of Defense and Interior in coordination with the Independent Directorate of Local Governance (IDLG), which was responsible for providing security and capacity-building services at the local level. National Uprising Groups were oftentimes used in remote areas inaccessible to the ANSF and ALP in order to hold territory previously seized from ISK.

Prior to the fall of the Islamic Republic, counterterrorism operations in Afghanistan usually featured US drone strikes and Special Forces raids, often in tandem with ANSF operations. The international troop withdrawal has created much uncertainty surrounding the future of counter-ISK operations in Taliban-ruled Afghanistan, especially the extent to which the over-the-horizon counterterrorism posture of the United States will be effective next to the Taliban's own efforts to contain ISK.

In Pakistan, operations against jihadist groups accelerated in 2005. Around this time, the country faced a rise in Islamic militancy and a revived Baloch insurgency, in part the products of Pakistan's partnership with the United States in the global war on terrorism. The TTP's attacks against civilians, government officials, and security forces prompted major Pakistani military campaigns against the organization's strongholds in Khyber Pakhtunkhwa and FATA, while counterterrorism in Balochistan was limited to smaller search and hunt operations.[81] Pakistan's FATA (now a part of KPK) is home to seven tribal areas, six of which share a porous and contentious border with Afghanistan;[82] the region suffers from poverty and weak governance, allowing sanctuary for extremist organizations such as al-Qaeda and the Taliban. Efforts to secure the region are hampered by law enforcement and administrative vacuums, the results of antiquated, colonial-era laws that deny legal jurisdiction to local governments and basic rights to local citizens. FATA also experiences sectarian conflict between Iranian and Saudi-backed militants, exacerbated by a recent increase in Punjabi Sunni militants.[83] Districts in the Provincially Administered Tribal Areas (PATA) have suffered from violence and a separate legal system as well.[84] The Swat Valley, for example, struggled during the rise of the TTP in 2007, which was followed by largely ineffective counterinsurgency efforts[85] until a controversial peace deal was struck in 2009.[86] Archaic governance laws and an intense insurgency also affect the Balochistan region. Despite the strategic importance of its shared border with Iran and Afghanistan, the region is underdeveloped and contains ungoverned pockets that act as militant safe havens. Counterterrorism operations in Balochistan have been small-scale and led by the frontier corps, targeting Baloch insurgents, the TTP, and LeJ.[87]

Pakistan's counterterrorism and law enforcement systems are divided between the federal and provincial levels. Each province maintains its own police force and can receive support from the federal government as needed. The federal security apparatuses consist of the National Counter Terrorism Authority (NACTA), the Federal Investigation Agency (FIA), the Intelligence Bureau (IB), the Inter-Services Intelligence (ISI), and Military Intelligence and the Directorate of Military Operations. These institutions are composed of both civilians and military personnel who conduct investigations, intelligence collection and analysis, and military operations at the federal level. At the provincial level, the local police, Crime Investigation Department / Counter Terrorism Department (CID/CTD), and Special Branch also engage in investigations and intelligence operations to counter violent extremism and protect civilians. Finally, paramilitary forces such as the Frontier Constabulary, Frontier Police, Frontier Corps, and Pakistan Rangers regulate regional borders, conduct antimilitancy and antinarcotic operations,[88] and enforce security in otherwise volatile regions.

Pakistan's counterterrorism and counterinsurgency efforts can be broken down between civilian and military components. The military has conducted numerous counterinsurgency operations in the FATA and PATA regions, such as Operation Zarb-e-Azb, launched in June 2014 in North Waziristan and Khyber agencies. In other regions, counterterrorism authority has fallen on civilian institutions, such as the Pakistani police,[89] which possesses provincial counterterrorism departments (CTDs) equipped with rapid response teams and high-security prisons.[90] The Pakistani police as an institution, however, lack the capacity to lead counterterrorism operations, and given its lack of reforms, it remains highly vulnerable to corruption.

In 2013, NACTA was ratified to act as a coordinating entity between security organizations, followed by the creation of two counterterrorism frameworks—the National Internal Security Policy (NISP) and the National Action Plan (NAP). The former aimed at reforming religious schools and targeting terrorist financing, while the latter introduced twenty points relating to terrorism, extremism, and criminal justice in the wake of the horrific 2014 attack on an Army Public School in Peshawar.[91] NAP also brings civilians and the military together through provincial committees and an antiterrorism force.[92] This framework led to the reestablishment of the death penalty in Pakistan, as well as the establishment of military courts for the speedy prosecution of terrorists.[93] The 2014 Protection of Pakistan Act also gave greater authority to the military and security agencies in detaining and killing terrorists.

Counterterrorism operations in the middle and late 2000s largely targeted the TTP, al-Qaeda, and other foreign militants hiding out in FATA and KPK. The Pakistani army launched the Wanna Operation in South Waziristan in 2004 against al-Qaeda and militants from Central Asia. The Battle of Wanna was soon followed by operations in North Waziristan and later the Bajaur Agency to reclaim territory from militant groups.[94] However, it was not until the introduction of two critical counterterrorism campaigns that regional militant groups were more severely degraded: the start of the

US drone strikes campaign in 2008, which successfully led to the elimination of many top al-Qaeda and TTP militants;[95] and Zarb-e-Azb, a 2014 joint military operation that seized territory from militant groups, dismantled safe havens, and drove fighters across the border into Afghanistan.[96] More recent operations have focused on search and hunt tactics against militants and supporters around the country. In 2017, the Pakistani army began Operation Khyber IV, aimed at clearing the Rajgal Valley, which borders ISK's former strongholds in Afghanistan. Plagued by lower but persistent levels of terrorism, Pakistan released a new comprehensive National Security Policy in 2022 that sought to place a focus on human security and improving the country's socioeconomic environment.[97]

ISK's Opportunities and Challenges

The complex militant landscape and dynamic security environments in the Afghanistan-Pakistan region have presented ISK with a plethora of challenges throughout its existence. First, the sheer number of militant groups already present in the region at the time of ISK's emergence forced it to demonstrate its unique value vis-à-vis other stronger groups with long histories and deep ties in the region. If ISK failed to offer anything novel, then there would have been limited incentives for individuals to join its ranks. Second, many of the dominant groups in the region with cross-border access to safe havens, such as the Taliban and the TTP, had close ties to the Islamic State's main rival: al-Qaeda. As such, it was likely that other militant groups would view ISK's emergence as an encroachment upon their spheres of influence. Finally, ISK's direct attacks on various state actors would in turn make it the target of counterterrorism efforts by state actors that had honed their capabilities over decades of counterterrorism and counterinsurgency operations across the region.

Yet the environment within which ISK would emerge also presented the group with various potential opportunities. For one, the presence of a wide range of militant groups with interconnections and local know-how meant that ISK could recruit from an existing pool of militants and immediately benefit from local expertise. This networked approach would allow the Islamic State to not only inject its own jihadist brand in a new region, but also localize its jihad by aligning its goals with other groups and integrating local grievances and goals. Relatedly, the Islamic State's general tendency to target minorities, especially the Shiite community, aligned with the modus operandi of other sectarian groups such as Lashkar-e-Jhangvi. And despite the challenge posed by al-Qaeda, which enjoyed a hefty reputation and lengthy history in the region, the Islamic State's global jihadist rival was in a much weaker position by the end of 2014 after being targeted for years in both Afghanistan and Pakistan. As such, ISK had an opportunity to sway al-Qaeda supporters to join an ascendant global jihadist group, one that had recently declared a caliphate in Iraq and Syria and drawn tens of thousands of supporters from around the world. When news emerged about the Islamic State's plans to expand into South and Central Asia via its new affiliate, it remained unclear whether ISK would succeed in building a local support base and sufficient operational capacity, as much would depend on the appeal of its Salafist ideology and ability to outshine its rivals, tap into local resources, and survive state operations.

Central Question and Argument

The overarching question this book seeks to answer is the following: What factors explain ISK's emergence and endurance in Afghanistan and Pakistan? More specifically, what has enabled ISK to compete with preexisting spheres of influence of dominant militant groups such as the Afghan and Pakistani Taliban, *and* survive intense counterterrorism operations? Within this overarching question, we explore a subset of questions that systematically help map ISK's evolution since 2015 and develop an explanation of the factors that have facilitated this organization's survival. These are as follows:

- What are the contours of ISK's operational capacity across Afghanistan and Pakistan, and how did the organization's strategies and tactics evolve in the face of intense state-led operations?
- What insights do counterterrorism and counterinsurgency outcomes against ISK, especially its personnel losses, provide about the structure and diversity of its militant base?
- What role did ISK's rivals and alliances play in helping the organization build an enduring reputation, a diverse and "replenishable" militant base, and highly lethal operational capacity?

What explains ISK's resiliency and its unremitting ability to inflict violence and threaten local and regional security in South and Central Asia, specifically within the Afghanistan-Pakistan region? In this book, we present the argument that ISK adopted a two-pronged strategy of harvesting alliances *as well as* rivalries to pave the way for a rapid localization of the Islamic State's transnational brand in Afghanistan-Pakistan, project power, and generate a sustainable recruitment pipeline, ultimately allowing it to adapt, overcome losses, and resurge. Since its emergence, ISK has relied on a network of cross-border alliances with lethal groups to gain local expertise, recruit, and expand its violent capacity and geographical reach. Simultaneously, it has actively provoked dominant groups in the region as key rivals to differentiate itself from others, especially those considered to have state sponsors, nationalistic agendas, and links with the Islamic State's main rival: al-Qaeda. These connections not only underpinned ISK's emergence and subsequent rise in attacks and geographical reach, but also helped the organization *project* power and remain relevant at times of intense counterterrorism operations and relative weakness.

Indeed, past research indicates that militant groups often seek cooperation in pursuit of various operational benefits. Brian Phillips, for example, has shown that the higher the number of relationships a group has, the longer they exist.[98] And as Moghadam argues:

> The desire for groups to survive to expand their existing capacity—may be as important to a group's decision to seek cooperation as the imperative to survive. At the same time, while limitations in resources and know-how underlie terrorist, rebel, and other militant groups' attempts to bolster their capacities, the constant quest for attention and recognition is another critical process goal that cooperation between like-minded groups can support.[99]

Other more obvious reasons include a desire to adapt to a changing environment and establish an organization in a new environment. Factors that can contribute to cooperation between militant groups include being in a conflict zone, state sponsorship, shared lived experiences, and geographic proximity to other groups. Surely then, the Afghanistan-Pakistan region had several dynamic characteristics that were conducive to ISK's cooperation with preexisting groups. We argue that in the case of ISK, alliances and mergers with some of the deadliest groups in the region allowed the group to not only pool resources across the border, but also to extend its operations geographically and successfully strike state and civilian targets with highly lethal attacks despite experiencing heavy manpower losses. In short, ISK's alliances contributed to its capacity *and* resiliency.

While ISK's ability to forge alliances and merge with other militant factions was fundamental to its successful setup and subsequent violent trajectory, its rivalries also played a critical role in facilitating the group's continual recruitment and long-term survival. Upon its emergence, ISK intentionally provoked dominant groups in the region through direct clashes and hostile statements. As we demonstrate in this book, presenting itself as a rival rather than an ally of leading groups gave ISK an opportunity to propagate itself as an *alternative* jihadist organization, one that could integrate the narrower goals of multiple regional organizations with its transnational ones, and provide an enduring jihadist platform for new recruits and jihadist veterans.

Although research on the effects of rivalry is limited, there are some studies indicating that rivalries increase a group's longevity by driving learning and innovation, spoiling, and providing members with additional motivation to fight and deepen their bonds with each other.[100] In the case of ISK, sustained contention with dominant militant groups in the region—including substantial clashes with the Afghan Taliban—enhanced ISK's notoriety and political relevance in a crowded conflict theater.

Overall, ISK's strategic selection of alliances and rivals has been key to the expansion of its operations across Afghanistan and Pakistan, in building its reputation and providing it with a talent pipeline to continuously replenish its human capital. Both contributed to ISK's rise and endurance as one of the deadliest organizations in the world—one that is likely to challenge the Afghan Taliban's governance in the future, as well as the stability of the region.

About the Book

This book offers a systematic examination of ISK's operational capacity, as well as its manpower and territorial losses due to counterterrorism/counterinsurgency operations over the past several years.[101] Context is crucial, and we strive to provide a rigorous, data-driven accounting that spans from ISK's founding to the August 2021 Kabul airport bombing and beyond. While the Kabul airport attack stunned the world due to the devastation it left behind,[102] it also refocused attention on the very prevalent threat of ISK in a dramatically altered landscape. Moreover, the attack brought forward questions about the broader security implications of a resurgent ISK threat on the stability of Taliban-controlled Afghanistan, threats to the United States and its allies, and the security of the broader region. Understanding the future terrorist threat and human security implications associated with the survival and endurance of ISK—especially through its intensifying battle with the Afghan Taliban in 2022 and beyond—makes studying the underlying factors of the group's resilience ever more imperative.

The book demonstrates how an emerging organization relies not only on a network of operational and logistical alliances to endure, but also on strategically positioning itself as a viable alternative to dominant groups in its sphere. We map out ISK's alliances and rivals and demonstrate how both factors contributed to ISK's recruitment and propaganda, lethal capacity, and upward violent trajectory. This strategy helped ISK establish the roots it needed for short-term influence and long-term survival.

While alliances between groups have been shown to boost violent organizations' lethality,[103] much of the literature has focused on *why* and *how* terrorist alliances emerge,[104] rather than the *effects* of alliances on a group's human capital and operational capacity (i.e., a group's geographical reach, its magnitude of attacks, and its lethality).[105] Other works that focus on the effects or motivations of cooperation have shown that cooperation between groups can help militant groups overcome resource constraints, gain access to logistical resources such as joint training, expand into other regions, and also increase their lethality.

Our case study of ISK adds to these concepts in the literature by examining the overall *effects* of such cooperation on an *emergent* affiliate of a transnational movement, including the affiliate's operational capacity and its ability to survive in challenging circumstances. In addition, past literature on the effects of rivalries among terrorist groups indicates that interorganizational rivalries can result in extreme tactics[106] and escalated violence.[107] However, how rivalries impact a group's ability to survive remains relatively unexplored. As the case study of ISK demonstrates, rivalries can be critical in differentiating a group from its main competitors and attracting a steady stream of defectors from dissatisfied leaders and rank and file members.

This book, which draws on four types of sources, is uniquely positioned to assess the evolution of ISK's strategy since its inception. We conduct a parallel examination of the group's operational trends and the magnitude of counter-ISK operations, in the context of its alliances and rivalries. Insights derived from our data on ISK's operational behavior and its manpower losses demonstrate the role of alliances in sustaining its capacity for violence and the role of its rivalries in differentiating the group from dominant players and broadening its recruitment pool. By leveraging counterterrorism outcomes, including leadership decapitation of ISK, this book shows the importance of ISK's rivalries in enabling it to recruit members from competing groups on a continual basis. Additionally, the book provides an unparalleled granular and comparative view of ISK's operational behavior across Afghanistan and Pakistan, allowing us to discern similarities and differences in strategy and behavior between countries and over time.

The loss of the Islamic State's last territorial holdings in Iraq and Syria (Islamic State in Iraq and Syria [ISIS]) in March 2019 and the death of its leader, Abu Bakr al-Baghdadi, in October 2019, were significant milestones in the fight against this global violent extremist movement. Yet the potential ability of ISIS to reconstitute itself under new leaders and leverage one of its most dangerous global affiliates remains a regional and global threat. By providing insights into the operational behavior of ISK and its choice of alliances and rivals, this book highlights a multitude of important security policy implications for the growing influence of the Islamic State's ideology outside of the Middle East.

Methodology

In order to conduct a comprehensive analysis of ISK's resiliency, this book adopts a diverse, multisource approach that incorporates original datasets, primary source propaganda materials, unclassified captured documents from Afghanistan, and various secondary sources. The diversity of the sources used ensures that the analysis presented in the book is not overly reliant on any single source and presents as complete a picture as possible.

We compiled the datasets used in this book over a time period of six years that track ISK's daily operational activity and leadership losses between 2015 and 2020. These data enable a temporal and geographical analysis of ISK's attacks, geographical variation, tactics, lethality, and losses from counterterrorism operations. The data form the basis of the analysis that demonstrates ISK's ability to survive extensive counterterrorism operations and link its operational capacity and human capital to its alliances and rivals. Our data-collection efforts with regard to ISK's leadership losses also produced insights on leaders' various characteristics, including prior affiliations.

Additionally, we have relied on various primary sources as well as secondary source research to analyze ISK's ideological messages, and to map out ISK's network of alliances and rivals qualitatively. One key component of our primary source materials includes ISK's videos, audio recordings, documents, reports, and magazine articles produced and distributed by the Islamic State on social media toward target audiences and about other groups. While we mostly relied on the Islamic State's official channels such as *al-Naba* and *Amaq,* we also used propaganda materials obtained from ISK's official and unofficial sources within Afghanistan and Pakistan. Though there are limitations and challenges when drawing on militant groups' propaganda—for example, they tend to often include exaggerated claims for the sake of publicity and recruitment—they do offer insights into the evolution of the organization's goals, messages, and target audiences. Moreover, our reliance on various other sources, including original datasets drawing on media reports and captured documents in the field, mitigates the challenges associated with overreliance on a group's own propaganda materials, which may be at times purposively misleading.

We have also leveraged access to a body of unique, unclassified ISK internal correspondences and other documents ("captured materials") that were provided to the Combating Terrorism Center at West Point by US government partners in 2017. The majority of these documents relate to ISK's earlier years in Afghanistan and Pakistan (2016 and 2017) and include items such as private letters from ISK leaders and members, summaries of military operations, and documentation of governance decisions. Relevant documents from these captured materials are used to supplement our overall findings regarding ISK's ideology, its connections to IS-Central, its internal organization, and its governance. These documents are used to supplement our findings, which are drawn primarily from ISK's observable activity as captured by the original databases used in this book. Some documents are also used for illustrative purposes throughout the book. While this material is rich and insightful, readers should be aware of the limitations that surround the use of these documents, as they were collected on the battlefield in an ad hoc manner. As such, they offer a supplemental snapshot of particular dynamics at particular times in ISK's history, and we are unable to confirm the extent to which these documents represent other materials and texts that may exist.

Research Considerations

Studying covert organizations such as ISK and collecting original data often pose a wide variety of challenges, to include reporting biases, political sensitivities of state actors, or simply a lack of complete information. These issues are common to the vast majority of works in the field of terrorism studies. As such, researchers also need to mitigate issues of misinformation (incorrect or misleading information that is spread unintentionally) and disinformation (the deliberate spreading of deceptive or false information) provided by both government officials as well as militant leaders in order to influence public opinion, deceive perceived enemies, or gain other advantages through the information environment. One of our goals in using a variety of sources—ranging from primary source materials to multiple secondary sources to original data collection—was to mitigate such issues and increase the robustness of our findings. However, we do not claim to capture every nuanced detail about ISK and its interactions with other militant groups and state actors. Additionally, while we briefly touch upon other factors that played an indirect role in ISK's rise and emergence, our book focuses specifically on the role of ISK's alliances and rivalries in shaping its trajectory and survival.[108]

While we emphasize ISK's role as an Islamic State province in this book, we also acknowledge that ISK's militant base was largely formed of militants from Afghanistan, Pakistan, and elsewhere within South and Central Asia. Thus, while the book discusses ISK as an Islamic State province and provides evidence of its linkages with IS-Central in its early years, ISK can also be viewed as a "local organization" that uses the Islamic State franchise for reputational purposes and to attract funding, especially given its local recruitment base, goals, and sources of funding. These dynamics are common features of the Islamic State movement's global expansion. As such, ISK is both an Islamic State province and a local jihadist organization, in the form of an umbrella group—an amalgamation of multiple groups and networks under one organizational brand. We discuss these dynamics in greater detail in later chapters, but our key intention is nonetheless to investigate how a new entity, one that formed under the Islamic State banner in the Afghanistan-Pakistan region, leveraged relationships with local groups to create space for itself in an ultra-competitive environment.

Additionally, as researchers and observers of ISK for several years now, we are well aware of the disagreements and different views among terrorism analysts about the potential state sponsors of ISK, and about alleged linkages with groups such as the Haqqani Network. We steer away from arguing one way or the other on these points due to both a lack of consensus, and limited observable evidence at the timing of writing this book. At the same time, we do offer examples of how ISK and other militant groups have leveraged such claims against one another, providing important insights into the dynamics of intergroup competition in the region.

Lastly, the focus of our book, ISK's alliances and rivalries, does not necessarily rely on the viewpoints of ISK leaders and rank-and-file members, given that the level of analysis in our book is at the group level rather than the individual level. Having said that, our combined use of unclassified documents, ISK's various propaganda releases over the years, secondary sources, and original datasets created from multiple, credible open-source reporting provides us with ample and unique evidence to explore the key question posed within this book.

Overview of Chapters

In Chapter 2, we begin by discussing the early years of ISK's emergence in 2014–2015 in Afghanistan and Pakistan, highlighting prominent figures and factions that pledged allegiance to the group soon after its emergence. Additionally, we also discuss the roots of ISK's ideology as it links to its goals, and the importance of the "Khorasan" region for jihadist groups more broadly. Drawing on primary and secondary sources, we discuss the key themes in ISK's propaganda, its messages to local audiences, and its criticism of the Afghan government, the Pakistani army, and key regional militant organizations such as the Taliban and Lashkar-e-Taiba. We then draw on captured materials from Afghanistan to discuss ISK's connections with IS-Central. Overall, this chapter provides the background on ISK's emergence, its general approach in the region, and its ideological affinities.

In Chapter 3, we first provide a bird's-eye view of ISK's strategy at the country and organizational level in Afghanistan and Pakistan and map out the fluctuations in the group's behavior. In sum, this chapter traces the rise, decline, and resurgence of ISK. The key goal of this chapter, as it links to the central thesis of the book, is to demonstrate the rapid rise in ISK's violent campaigns, its resurgence after a period of decline, and contextualize these trends within the broader security environment. We introduce our data on ISK's operational capacity and use descriptive analysis to trace defining trends in the evolution of the group's targeting capacity and method. We also detail how these trends were similar and different across the two countries, and what this reveals about the interconnectedness of the group across the region. The chapter concludes with a data-driven analysis of ISK's revamped attack campaigns from 2020 to the present, including the group's international operational nexus.

We proceed in Chapter 4 by giving an overview of the various counterterrorism and counterinsurgency operations undertaken against ISK in Afghanistan and Pakistan since 2015, including the magnitude and nature of these operations. The goals of this chapter are threefold: the first is to depict the level of losses faced by ISK over the years, which it had to recover from; the second goal is to demonstrate changes in ISK's strategy as it adapted to intensifying pressure; and the third is to present details uncovered from our data and unclassified ISK documents about the group's leadership structure, which provides evidence of the diversity within ISK's ranks. We introduce original data specifically on ISK's leadership losses in both countries, including characteristics such as nationalities and prior affiliations as well as a novel four-tier system for understanding ISK's leadership structure and the losses incurred at various leadership levels. Throughout Chapter 4, we analyze how counterterrorism efforts affected ISK's operational capacity, geographical presence, and retaliatory behavior. Overall, we show that while counterterrorism operations constrained ISK's geographical presence and total number of attacks, they did little to contain ISK's ability to conduct highly destructive attacks.

Building on the analysis in Chapters 3 and 4, we analyze in Chapter 5 how ISK's strategic choices in selecting *alliances* and *mergers* helped boost its operational capacity and ability to endure in a difficult environment. We map out ISK's various operational and logistical alliances with a host of militant groups, providing brief backgrounds on each of these groups, the nature of their relationship with ISK, and the underlying motivations behind such intergroup linkages. By examining one of ISK's longest-lasting operational alliances, Lashkar-e-Jhangvi, we demonstrate how this relationship boosted ISK's lethality and geographical reach.

In Chapter 6, we analyze how ISK's strategic choices of *rivals* helped the group differentiate itself from dominant players and build a diverse militant base, which it continually replenished to sustain itself. We map out ISK's key rivals in the region—focusing on groups that ISK has publicly denounced and criticized—and provide an assessment of the factors underpinning such rivalries. We leverage the cases of the Afghan Taliban and Lashkar-e-Taiba, as well as our data on targeting efforts against ISK members in Afghanistan-Pakistan, and Jammu and Kashmir to show how ISK was able to recruit experienced militants from its rivals.

We conclude in Chapter 7 by reviewing the key findings and thesis of the book and provide an overview of the medium- to long-term security implications of the existence and persistence of ISK. We discuss security implications in terms of the present and future political and socioeconomic environment of Afghanistan, and in the surrounding region. We also discuss key developments in ISK's activity in 2022 and provide a brief assessment of the likely trajectory of the Islamic State movement's influence and capacity in the region going forward.

Notes

1. Internal ISK document, Combating Terrorism Center Library.
2. Institute for Economics and Peace, *Global Terrorism Index 2019*.
3. Lalzoy, "US State Department Offers $10M Reward."
4. Jadoon, *Allied & Lethal*.
5. Gibbons-Neff and Faizi, "Gunmen Storm Kabul University."

6. Mashal and Rahim, "Deadly Explosion Hits Kabul Tutoring Center."
7. Reuters, "Islamic State Claims Responsibility for Attack That Killed 11 in Pakistan."
8. Analytical Support and Sanctions Monitoring Team, *Twelfth Report.*
9. Constable, "Taliban Vows Crackdown on ISIS."
10. McKenzie, posture statement.
11. Jadoon, Sayed, and Mines, "The Islamic State Threat in Taliban Afghanistan."
12. Ghazi and Mashal, "29 Dead After ISIS Attack on Afghan Prison"; Jadoon, Sayed, and Mines, "The Islamic State Threat in Taliban Afghanistan."
13. Valle and Webber, "The Growth and Internationalization of Islamic State Khurasan"; Province's Media Operations; https://www.militantwire.com/p/the-growth-and-internationalization?s=r.
14. Al-Azaim Foundation, *Until When the Ignorance?*
15. Valle and Webber, "The Growth and Internationalization of Islamic State Khurasan."
16. Valle, "Islamic State Khurasan Province Threatens Uzbekistan"; Al-Azaim Foundation, *Until When the Ignorance?*
17. Islamic State, "Makers of Epic Battles Series—Khurasan Province," Islamic State (telegram); Jadoon, Sayed, and Mines, "The Islamic State Threat in Taliban Afghanistan."
18. Jadoon and Mines, "Taking Aim."
19. US Department of Defense, *Enhancing Security and Stability in Afghanistan.*
20. Jadoon and Milton, "Strength from the Shadows?"
21. Fair, *In Their Own Words,* p. 11.
22. Puri, "The Past and Future of Deobandi Islam."
23. Osman, *Bourgeois Jihad.*
24. Ibid.
25. Fair, *In Their Own Words,* p. 11.
26. Institute for Economics and Peace, *Global Terrorism Index 2019.*
27. BBC News, "Taliban Leader Mullah Akhtar Mansour Killed."
28. Reuters, "Afghan Taliban's New Chief Replaces 24 'Shadow' Officials."
29. Watkins, *Taliban Fragmentation.*
30. "Taliban Appoints First Shia Hazara As Shadow District."
31. "Taliban Appoints New Leader in Military Leadership Following Recent Upheavals."
32. Giustozzi, *Koran Kalashnikov and Laptop;* Fair, *In Their Own Words,* p. 233.
33. Siddique, "Understanding the Afghan Taliban's Leadership"; Nadim, "The Quiet Rise of the Quetta Shura."
34. Bacon, "Slipping the Leash?"
35. Brown and Rassler, *Fountainhead of Jihad.*
36. United Nations Security Council, "Sirajuddin Jallaloudine Haqqani."
37. Dreazen, "The Taliban's New Number 2."
38. US Department of Defense, *Enhancing Security and Stability in Afghanistan.*
39. Analytical Support and Sanctions Monitoring Team, *Twelfth Report.*
40. Davis, "Foreign Combatants in Afghanistan."
41. Stanford University, "Mapping Militant Organizations: Haqqani Network"; Institute for the Study of War, *Afghanistan Report 6.*
42. Brown and Rassler, *Fountainhead of Jihad,* pp. 107.
43. Although US support for the group ended in the early 1990s, the Pakistani state has continued to view the group as a strategic asset. See Brown and Rassler, *Fountainhead of Jihad.*
44. Brown and Rassler, *Fountainhead of Jihad.*
45. Ibid.

46. Jamal, *Shadow War,* p. 110; Brown and Rassler, *Fountainhead of Jihad.*

47. Brown and Rassler, *Fountainhead of Jihad.*

48. United Nations, "Letter from Chair of the Security Council Committee Pursuant to Resolutions 1267 (1999), 1989 (2011) and 2253 (2015) Concerning Islamic State in Iraq and the Levant (Da'esh), al-Qaida, and Associated Individuals, Groups, Undertakings, and Entities, Addressed to the President of the Security Council," July 15, 2019; Mackenzie Institute, *Haqqani Network.*

49. Joscelyn and Roggio, "The Taliban's New Leadership Is Allied with al-Qaeda."

50. Middle East Institute, *Afghanistan's Terrorism Challenge.*

51. Gohel, "The Taliban Are Far Closer to the Islamic State Than They Claim."

52. Brown and Rassler, *Fountainhead of Jihad.*

53. Fair, *In Their Own Words,* pp. 14–15.

54. Jadoon, *The Evolution and Potential Resurgence of the Tehrik-i-Taliban Pakistan.*

55. Smith, "The Tangled Web of Taliban and Associated Movements," pp. 31–38.

56. Semple, "The Taliban Movement."

57. See Khan, "14 Days Before Elections"; Reuters, "Female Suicide Bomber Kills Eight in Northwest Pakistan."

58. Kermani, Yousafzai, and Mehsud, "Kabul Taliban."

59. Pazir, "TTP Warns Against Playing Music, Women Going Out Alone in Miramshah"; Wazir, "Pamphlet Warns Police to Leave S. Waziristan in Three Days."

60. Jadoon, *The Evolution and Potential Resurgence of the Tehrik-i-Taliban Pakistan.*

61. Ibid.

62. Jadoon, "The Untenable TTP-Pakistan Negotiations."

63. Jadoon, *The Evolution and Potential Resurgence of the Tehrik-i-Taliban Pakistan,* p. 13.

64. Ibid., p. 14.

65. Ibid., p. 14.

66. Internal ISK document, Combating Terrorism Center Library.

67. Umar Media, "The TTP Statement Against the Unjust UN Report About the TTP."

68. Congressional Research Service, *Al-Qaeda Rebuilding in Pakistan.*

69. For details, see Mir, "What Explains Counterterrorism Effectiveness?"

70. Sayed, "Why Islamic State Khurasan Poses an Indigenous Threat."

71. Rassler, "Situating the Emergence of the Islamic State Khorasan."

72. Ash-Shamali, "Al-Qaidah of Waziristan."

73. Abdul Sayed's interviews with two senior Afghan security officials, September and November 2021, as cited in Jadoon, Sayed, and Mines, "The Islamic State Threat in Taliban Afghanistan." According to these interviewees, al-Qaeda members' defections to ISK provided it with highly skilled trainers and experts who constituted a significant proportion (estimated to be one-third by the interviewees) of ISK's founding military, explosive, media, and administrative officials and commanders.

74. Jadoon, Sayed, and Mines, "The Islamic State Threat in Taliban Afghanistan."

75. Bennett, "A Comeback for al-Qaeda in the Indian Subcontinent?"

76. As-Sahab Media, *Resurgence* 1. For more details, see Reed, "Al-Qaeda in the Indian Subcontinent."

77. As-Sahab Media, *Resurgence* 2. Adam Yahiye Gadahn, a US citizen, was killed in April 2015, and was a prominent member of al-Qaeda. See Botelho and Ellis, "Adam Gadahn, American Mouthpiece for al-Qaeda, Killed."

78. Jadoon and Mines, *Broken but Not Defeated.*

79. The NDS model is based off of—and has a working partnership with—the CIA, and also benefits from limited detachments.

80. For further discussion on the structure and authority of the ANSF, see Mogelson, "The Shattered Afghan Dream of Peace"; Purkiss and Feroz, "CIA-Backed Afghan Unit Accused of Atrocities Is Able to Call in Air Strikes."

81. Hussain, "Pakistan's Achievements in War on Terror but at What Cost?"

82. Nawaz, "FATA-A Most Dangerous Place."

83. Ibid.

84. International Crisis Group, *Pakistan: Countering Militancy in PATA.*

85. McKelvey, "A Return to Hell in Swat: Foreign Policy."

86. Shah, "Malakand Announces Nizam-e-Adl Implementation."

87. Hussain, "Pakistan's Achievements in War on Terror but at What Cost?"

88. Abbas, "Transforming Pakistan's Frontier Corps."

89. Tariq and Rani, *An Appraisal of Pakistan's Anti-Terrorism Act.*

90. Khan, "Double Game."

91. International Crisis Group, *Revisiting Counter-Terrorism Strategies in Pakistan.*

92. Ibid.

93. Zahid, "Counter Terrorism Policy Measures."

94. Hussain, "Pakistan's Achievements in War on Terror but at What Cost?"

95. Jones and Fair, *Counterinsurgency in Pakistan.*

96. Hussain, "Pakistan's Achievements in War on Terror but at What Cost?"

97. Akhtar, "Pakistan's New National Security Policy."

98. Phillips, "Terrorist Group Cooperation and Longevity."

99. Moghadam, *Nexus of Global Jihad.*

100. Phillips, "Enemies with Benefits?"

101. To the best of our knowledge, there are only two books that examine IS presence in South Asia, which pose questions very different from ours as laid out in this proposal.

102. Shivaram and Pruitt-Young, "The Attack Outside Kabul Airport."

103. Horowitz and Potter, "Allying to Kill."

104. Moghadam, *Nexus of Global Jihad;* Bacon, *Why Terrorist Groups form International Alliances.*

105. There are a few important works in the literature that demonstrate the links between a group's alliances and its operational capacity, lethality, and longevity. For example, Assaf Moghadam, in the *Nexus of Global Jihad,* shows that terrorist cooperation includes not only organizational cooperation but also networked cooperation, which includes at least one informal terrorist actor. In *Why Terrorist Groups Form International Alliances,* Tricia Bacon examines the reasons why terrorist groups form international alliances and in particular alliance hubs, despite the risks associated with such partnerships such as infiltration and betrayals. While Bacon's book assesses when and why international alliances occur, Moghadam's book assesses how these groups collaborate.

106. Bloom, *Dying to Kill.*

107. Chenoweth, "Democratic Competition and Terrorist Activity"; Conrad and Greene, "Differentiation and the Severity of Terrorist Attacks"; Nemeth, "The Effect of Competition on Terrorist Group Operations."

108. ISK's alliances and rivalries as mapped within this book are not presented as absolute and rigid, and it is likely there were contentious issues and disagreements even within ISK's alliances with other groups. It is also possible that in some instances, ISK may have collaborated with militants affiliated with its rivals. Such tactical agreements or disagreements are not uncommon within and across militant groups, and may result in short-term fluctuations in intergroup relationships or disputes at the individual level.

2

Ideology and Goals

And in spite of the ongoing crusade . . . we bring the mujahidin the good
news of the Islamic State's expansion to Khorasan. Indeed, the mujahidin
from amongst the soldiers of the Khilafah have fulfilled the conditions
and met the requirements for the declaration of Wilayat Khorasan.

—Official statement by deceased Islamic State
spokesman Abu Muhammad al-Adnani[1]

In late 2014, reports first emerged about Islamic State representatives holding meetings with local militant commanders regarding the establishment
of a local affiliate for the movement. The group they established would
come to be known as one of the Islamic State's deadliest affiliates worldwide—the Islamic State Khorasan. About seven years later, on August 26,
2021, with the entire world closely watching the hasty and disastrous
United States–led exit from Afghanistan, a deadly ISK attack on the Kabul
International Airport cemented the group's global infamy and marked one
of the deadliest violent attacks for Afghans and US service members in a
decade. While the country and broader region had suffered many brutal ISK
attacks before, this one, in particular, stood out as well-planned, sophisticated, and designed for maximum shock value. Later that fall, the US government announced terrorist designations on four key ISK individuals,
including the group's top leader, Shahab al-Muhajir, and the leader of its
Kabul attacks and operations, Maulawi Rajab, both of whom planned and
approved the airport attack.[2]

Far from signaling the dawn of a more secure future, the Taliban's rapid
takeover of Afghanistan and the collapse of the Afghan government created

new opportunities for ISK to exploit,[3] especially to undermine the legitimacy and control of the Taliban's regime. Many dismissed the level of threat ISK posed; the group had been declared "defeated" only recently in November 2019, when Afghanistan's interior minister, Masoud Andarabi, heralded the demise of Islamic State affiliates in the country and claimed that the group had been driven from their strongholds, specifically in Nangarhar province.[4] These declarations of defeat—which have been announced on several occasions in ISK's history—belie realities on the ground. By late 2021, ISK was estimated to have a militant base of 4,000–5,000 fighters, boosted by the several prison breaks that took place before, during, and after the Taliban's takeover of Afghanistan. Some of these breakouts were the result of the chaos infused by the Taliban's rapid countrywide advance in 2021, while others were perpetrated by ISK itself. For example, in July 2020, ISK conducted a highly sophisticated attack on Nangarhar central prison in Jalalabad City, which resulted in the release of over 1,000 prisoners, including a reported 280 ISK inmates.[5] In addition, official UN reports from late 2021 warned that ISK maintained a presence in almost every province of Afghanistan.[6] The group remains locked in a deadly battle against the Taliban, which appears to be struggling to combat their old jihadi rivals,[7] as well as containing the potential threat to the United States and other Western states. After the attack on the Kabul airport, the Islamic State boasted in an editorial published in their weekly newsletter, *al-Naba,*[8] about the targeting of Americans, hoping that the attack would awaken those who were misled by the Taliban and al-Qaeda. The editorial sheds light on several of ISK's goals, including the delegitimizing of the Taliban and followers of al-Qaeda, and indicates ISK's unrelenting resolve. Excerpts from the article state:

> This blessed attack was the "biggest human loss" the American forces suffered in a decade, and made them lower their flags in mourning, which had not been done in years, even when Taliban's militia announced the killing of dozens of American soldiers over a year ago, in a blatant campaign of lies, where only the followers of al-Qaeda believed them.

> They [The Americans] were so confused, that they started talking about Khorasan Wilayah as if it only just started! This is only to hide their false claims before that they had finished it. So where are those who claimed Khorasan Wilayah was eliminated?

> Perhaps this attack will be blessed enough by God that some sleeping hearts of those who were led by the Taliban and al-Qaeda to the tunnel of distractions, will wake up and repent to join the Muslim community, and announce the continuity of jihad against all sects of kufr, specially America, which they now, according to the Doha Agreement, must protect and fight for, under the terms of counter terrorism.

While the mujahidin continue their jihad and preparation, the murtaddin [apostates] are celebrating with "independence"! From what did they become independent? Today, they are related and connected to America and the tawaghut[9] of the world more than ever, and for the Taliban, to remain in power is related directly to its behavior in "countering terrorism" and fulfilling the demands of America and coordinating with the tawaghut of Europe.

Although the world turned its attention to ISK with renewed concern in 2021, warning signs of a resurgent ISK had started to pervade in 2020 after a year of relative decline in the group's activities. In the context of the group's demonstrated resilience over the past seven years—when it not only fought the Taliban but also Afghan security forces amid US airstrikes—ISK's revival is less surprising. Understanding how ISK came to constitute a major threat to Afghanistan, the region, and potentially US interests requires tracing the origins of the group, its selection of alliances and rivalries, and finally the adaptation of its violent strategies over time.

This chapter provides an overview of ISK's initial emergence and approaches in the Afghanistan and Pakistan region, particularly between 2014 and 2017. During its early years, ISK's emergence and subsequent rise triggered a string of pledges of allegiance from a variety of local militant leaders, soon after which it unleashed a violent campaign in both Afghanistan and Pakistan.

Finding Friends in the Neighborhood

The official announcement of the Islamic State Khorasan, also known locally as Daesh, arrived in January 2015 through an audio recording via Islamic State's al-Furqan media outlet by the group's then-spokesman, Abu Muhammad al-Adnani. The intricate politicking behind the establishment of the group, however, had already started the year prior. In 2014, the now-deceased head of the Islamic State movement, Abu Bakr al-Baghdadi, reportedly assigned two of his lieutenants, Zubair al-Kuwaiti and Abu Imama al-Muhajir, to facilitate meetings with potentially cooperative individuals and groups by offering financial and logistical support. His delegation sought to encourage defections from al-Qaeda and Tehrik-e-Taliban Pakistan,[10] and several members of both organizations subsequently pledged allegiance to al-Baghdadi in March and October 2014, respectively.[11] Among others, they included the brother of famed jihadi ideologue Abu Muhammad al-Maqdisi, and several other TTP members, namely Hafiz Saeed Khan from the Orakzai Agency, Daulat Khan from the Kurram Agency, Fateh Gul Zaman from the Khyber Agency, Mufti Hassan from Peshawar, and Khalid Mansoor from Hangu, together with the TTP's former spokesman, Shahidullah Shahid.

The six TTP commanders subsequently reaffirmed their allegiance in the official announcement video released in January 2015, nominating Hafiz Saeed Khan as their leader and former Afghan Taliban commander Abdul Ra'uf Khadem as his deputy—but this time they were also joined by several others. Pledges to Hafiz Saeed Khan rolled in from Saad Emirati, a former Afghan Taliban commander; Ubaidah al-Peshwari, leader of the group al-Tawhid and Jihad in Peshawar; the deputy to Sheikh Abd al-Qadir al-Khorasani, leader of the group Abtal ul-Islam; Sheikh Muhsin, a militant commander from Afghanistan's Kunar province; another militant commander named Talha from northern Pakistan; and senior member of Pakistan's infamous Lal Majid (Red Mosque), Omar al-Mansur.[12] Because of the large portion of its founding members who were formerly a part of the TTP, ISK is often said to "find its roots" in the TTP, as well as in al-Qaeda, key members of which defected to the Islamic State and encouraged hundreds of local Afghan and Pakistani cadres to follow suit.[13] In addition to al-Qaeda and TTP militants, a number of Afghan Taliban fighters and leaders also defected to ISK, including senior commanders such as Abdul Ra'uf Khadim and ideologues such as Abdul Rahim Muslim Dost. They and other Afghan Taliban defectors were perhaps attracted by higher leadership positions in ISK, but also by ISK's ideology and goals of pursuing a much larger jihad than one limited to Afghanistan.[14] To reinforce this nascent groundswell of local support for the Islamic State movement, approximately 200 militants from IS-Central in Iraq and Syria traveled to Afghanistan to bolster ISK's strength and expertise.[15]

In Afghanistan, the Islamic State's delegation also reportedly held a meeting with the leaders of Lashkar-e-Islam (LeI). While LeI did not form a formal alliance or merger with ISK, it did reach an agreement to share a secure supply route through the former's stronghold in Khyber district, Pakistan. ISK leveraged this supply route to connect newly established bases in Afghanistan in the districts of Achin, Nazian, and Kot to logistical support channels in Pakistan.[16] A few months later, another group of fifty fighters led by Haya Khan and Waheed Khan from the Khyber-based Haji Namdar group joined ISK in Afghanistan.[17]

Shortly after its inception, ISK's ranks also expanded with the recruitment of Salafi jihadists from both Afghanistan and Pakistan, where they remain a strong minority since the expansion of Salafism under the wave of Arab foreign fighters in the 1980s.[18] Many Salafists found the concept of ISK appealing especially after the successes of the Islamic State's proto-state project in the Middle East, which at the time in 2014 and 2015 was ascendant in the global jihadist landscape and garnering worldwide attention. Some in Afghanistan and Pakistan even heralded the return of a Salafist Islamic State to their region; the "first Islamic State" of the post-colonial era, in fact, was the Islamic Emirate of Kunar, founded in 1990 by the Salafist political leader Jamil al-Rahman.[19] Taken together, the defections of TTP factions, al-Qaeda leaders and their followers, Afghan Taliban members, and Salafi fighters from various locations to include Khyber, Orakzai, Bajaur, and Mohmand agencies (now districts) in Pakistan all served to bolster ISK's initial ranks.[20]

In addition to individual level recruitment and outreach, ISK sought to form ideological, operational, and logistical alliances with various preexisting groups in the region (as we discuss in Chapter 5). The string of alliances and defections from several prominent groups, and the appointment of a former TTP leader, Hafiz Saeed Khan, as ISK's first governor, was a clear and early indication that the Islamic State's Khorasan province was intentionally designed to be a localized version of the Islamic State. In addition to building a localized organization that drew on local expertise, resources, and infrastructure, ISK's local connections were also critical to counteract perceptions of the Islamic State brand as "foreign," which led many scholars and policymakers to initially dismiss the possibility that the group could emerge as a notable threat. This myopic view is somewhat understandable not just because the Islamic State brand arrived from outside the region, but also because the Afghanistan-Pakistan region is one of the most militant saturated regions in the world. Moreover, few of the Islamic State's affiliates around the world at the time had evolved to become such deadly organizations. In Afghanistan and Pakistan—a region already inundated with militant groups of various types—was there room for another militant group to emerge and attain success?

The answer to the preceding question is obvious when we consider that ISK not only sustained its existence in Afghanistan and Pakistan over several years, but it also is considered to be one of the key threats to the stability of Afghanistan after the US withdrawal and the takeover by a Taliban regime. Back in its formative years, however, the first step in ISK's strategy was to create space for itself by attaining pledges of allegiance from several militant commanders and their factions, including defections from experienced individuals from prominent groups such as al-Qaeda, the Afghan Taliban, and the TTP, as well as mergers of entire factions.

In general, groups with overlapping ideologies or common enemies are more likely to cooperate, since joining forces can boost their capacity to fight their overlapping opponents. Antistate militant groups are typically positioned against much stronger government actors, and operational alliances (despite ideological differences) can bring significant capacity boosts to militant groups and result in their prolonged survival.[21] In the case of ISK, the group's long list of enemies and quixotic goals of expanding the Islamic State's global jihad to South and Central Asia overlapped with several other groups' goals in the region, and as such attracted a wide range of partners.[22] Scholars who have examined al-Qaeda's motivations to establish affiliates around the world argue that forming partnerships with several groups not only helped al-Qaeda expand the scope and scale of its operations, but also facilitated the dissemination of innovations.[23] Partners of transnational affiliates may not necessarily opt to merge with a group—as some TTP factions did with ISK—but may simply accept the leadership of that group while remaining organizationally distinct.[24] Other local groups may purely seek mutual operational benefits, without actually becoming an official part of the partner organization.

Such intergroup linkages were commonplace in the Afghanistan-Pakistan region for decades prior to the emergence of ISK. Groups such as the TTP or Lashkar-e-Taiba have cooperated with al-Qaeda, for example, but they are certainly not considered to be a part of al-Qaeda as they retain their own leadership structures and strategic goals. Yet their operational cooperation has yielded significant benefits for both parties. Similarly, while ISK sought to strike mergers with several TTP and IMU factions when it first emerged, it also cast a wide net to establish cooperative relationships with groups such as Lashkar-e-Jhangvi and Lashkar-e-Islam. In addition, ISK's members also cooperated at a tactical, if not organizational level with the members of other organizations such as Jamaat-ui-Ahrar and even the Haqqani Network (which is not organizationally linked with ISK).[25]

Survival is a primary driver of cooperation between terrorist groups,[26] and as we discuss in greater detail in Chapter 5, ISK's alliances have contributed to its resiliency by enabling it to establish strong roots in the local militant landscape, expand its reach, and amplify its lethality. The specific motivations of ISK's partners to align with the newcomer varied. At times, groups may have felt threatened due to internal disputes, lack of civilian support and resources, and counterterrorism and counterinsurgency operations by state actors.[27] These reasons seem to be the most relevant for TTP and IMU factions, which opted to completely merge with ISK. For others that faced relatively less internal turmoil or counterterrorism pressure such as Lashkar-e-Jhangvi, cooperation with ISK may have brought material benefits, but it also allowed both groups to extend operations against their common enemy: the Shiite minority. For such groups, another motivation could simply be to limit competition, outperform their competitors, and dominate the militant landscape.[28] Finally, for smaller groups that pledged support to ISK, cooperation could be perceived as a means to generate intangible benefits such as organizational endurance or a "sense of empowerment."[29] Ultimately, the fact that the Afghanistan-Pakistan region was already suffused with a plethora of groups with ideologies, goals, and targets that overlapped with ISK's provided the latter with the ability to find cooperative relationships across the region. In Chapter 5, we take a closer look at the nature of cooperation that existed between ISK and local groups, especially in its formative years, and discuss the possible motivations of groups to lend support to ISK, as well as how ISK benefited from its wide network of linkages with locals.

ISK's Goals, Ideology, and Propaganda

To fully appreciate the factors that contributed to the emergence and survival of ISK, it is useful to understand the significance of the so-called Khorasan region for the Islamic State movement more broadly. Why did IS-Central choose the Afghanistan-Pakistan region in the first place to set up an affiliate? What is the importance of the Khorasan region to the Islamic State's goals? There are both ideological and practical reasons for why the Khorasan region is considered to be an important node in the Islamic State's pursuit of a global caliphate.

The Islamic State's Goals in "Khorasan"

In general, "Greater Khorasan" refers to a historical region in South and Central Asia that was established by the Sasanian Empire (Iranian) around the third century. The Khorasan region lasted through the seventh century until the dawn of the Umayyad Caliphate, with its precise borders shifting over time. For the most part, since around the mid–seventh century the province of Khorasan, as drawn on maps, tended to cover modern-day northeastern Iran and parts of Turkmenistan, Uzbekistan, Tajikistan, and Afghanistan—but it did not include Pakistan or India.[30] In contrast to this historical Khorasan, ISK claims to represent a geographical area stretching across Central Asia, Pakistan, most of India, and parts of Iran.[31] These claims have been reinforced in the propaganda of IS-Central and other Islamic State affiliates, and represent an invented expansion of the historical region of Khorasan.

In January 2015, when Islamic State spokesman al-Adnani announced the expansion of the movement into Khorasan, he called on everyone in the region who professed the unity of God (*muwahhidun*) to unite and join hands under the caliphate. The use of the term *muwahhidun* is intentional; the term was theologized by Taqi al-Din ibn Taymiyyah, which came to be used for the forces under Muhammad ibn Abd al-Wahhab (died 1792).[32] As Amin Tarzi explains, "The term [*muwahhidun*] in modern Salafist thought is a rejection of the Shiis, Islamic mysticism (Sufism), the customs of veneration of saints and statuary, and any action or object that in their view brings an association with the absoluteness of the unity of God."[33] Per Tarzi, Adnani's use of the term *muwahhidun* meant that he was framing his audience as "the progeny of those who had fought against British and Russian oppression," calling on them now to join the battle against the American invaders, and implement *tawhid* (monotheism).

While for the Islamic State, the term "Khorasan" defines a geographical area, the term also carries different understandings and interpretations. In the context of Sunni Islam, the term "Khorasan" is often linked back to the Prophet Muhammad's sayings (referred to as the Hadith). According to various interpretations of these sayings, an Islamic army with black flags is prophesized to emerge from Khorasan, and the Muslim Mahdi (Messiah) is expected to lead this army to defeat the enemies of Islam.[34] Any group using the black flag—and the Islamic State is not the only one to use it—seeks to gain legitimacy for its armed struggle among Muslims. One variation of this Hadith is as follows: "Armies carrying the black flag will come from Khorasan. No power will be able to stop them and they will finally reach Eela (Aqsa Mosque in Jerusalem) where they will erect their flags."[35]

As Tarzi states, "The messianic version, whether evoked by a fringe Al-Qaeda group in Syria . . . or by ISKP, has an amplified symbolism denoting the ultimate apocalyptic battle between Islam and its enemies." The term is also tied to Abd al-Rahman bin Muslim (also known as Abu Muslim al-Khurasani), who led a revolt against the Arabic-centric Umayyad Caliphate along with his supporters from the Khorasan region, adorning black clothes and flags. Al-Khurasani's revolution, among other factors, would culminate in the near demise of the Umayyad Caliphate and the rise of the Abbasid Caliphate—the very caliphate that the Islamic State's ideologues claim to emulate. Al-Khurasani is also credited with expanding the influence of the Iranian peoples within a Muslim empire that was largely dominated by Arabs.[36] Outside of the Arab world, he is associated with both resisting Arab supremacy and also with planting the roots of Shia activism.[37] ISK's use of the term "Khorasan," as Tarzi argues, allowed both the group and the broader movement to signal to various audiences that the armies of the Messiah were gathering and that the final battle between Muslims and the enemies of Islam was nigh. Additionally, it also allowed the Islamic State to bolster its transnational narrative of rejecting state boundaries recognized by the international community. Because such interpretations of the Hadith have glorified the Khorasan region as a divinely ordained battleground, ISK views its goal of expanding the caliphate as critical to the Islamic State movement and to those it defines as part of the global Muslim community. Hafiz Saeed Khan, the first governor of ISK, referenced these dynamics in an interview, stating: "*Wilāyat Khurāsān* has great importance to Islam and the Muslims. It had once been under the authority of the Muslims, along with the regions surrounding it. The *Wilāyah*, by God's permission, is a gate to re-conquering all these regions until they are ruled once more by God's law, and so the territory of the blessed *Khilāfah* is expanded."[38]

In another propaganda release of 2015, ISK members emphasized the importance of jihad in Khorasan: "There is no doubt that God the Almighty blessed us with jihad in the land of Khorasan since a long time ago, and it is from the grace of God that we fought any disbeliever who entered the land of Khorasan. All of this is for the sake of establishing the Shariah. . . .

Know that the Islamic Caliphate is not limited to a particular country. These young men will fight against every disbeliever, whether in the west, east, south, or north."[39]

By virtue of being an official province of the Islamic State, ISK subscribes to its parent group's goals of establishing a global caliphate. Central to the Islamic State's vision of a caliphate is the acquisition of physical territories including the Khorasan province. As such, ISK's pursuit of a global Islamic State caliphate involves nullifying and ultimately eliminating national boundaries. To help achieve that goal, the group targets multiple regional state actors, and militant groups that it frames as stooges of state governments or intelligence services and differently defined out-groups in civil society. Nationalist movements such as the Taliban are framed as anticaliphate movements whose primary focus is to liberate Afghanistan from foreign "occupation" rather than to create a transnational Islamic caliphate. As such, ISK's claims on the Afghanistan-Pakistan region, as a fundamental part of the caliphate, delegitimize the very existence and purpose of groups such as the Taliban.

Practically, orienting the affiliate within the Khorasan region meant that ISK's mandate extended into the operational areas of several other militant groups, many of which have survived in the region for years and even decades, including IMU, the TTP, Lashkar-e-Jhangvi, the Afghan Taliban, and al-Qaeda, as well as several other Kashmir and India-oriented militant groups. Viewed from a different angle, however, the existence of these militant groups in the Afghanistan-Pakistan region also created opportunities for ISK by providing it with not only a militant network to tap into, but also an exploitable militant infrastructure across the region, including hideouts, ungoverned regions, black markets, and smuggling routes. Another advantage from the perspective of ISK at its outset—one that is true to many jihadist groups—was the presence of US troops, which provided a key mobilizing narrative to call for jihad against foreign invaders.[40] As such, the "Khorasan" label not only provided the Islamic State with a certain degree of jihadist legitimacy but also presented it with numerous opportunities to exploit.

Ideology

ISK's specific goals and tactics may be unique in some regard to the province and to Afghanistan and Pakistan, but as an affiliate of the Islamic State movement, it derives its legitimacy and overarching ideological principles from Islamic State–Central. The Islamic State subscribes to the ideology of Salafi jihadism, which is a revivalist movement within the Hanbali school— one of four major schools of jurisprudence in Sunni Islam and often considered to be strictly traditional. Salafi jihadism also serves as the guiding doctrine of al-Qaeda and its affiliates. In contrast, the Taliban's ideology is rooted in a separate school of jurisprudence called Hanafism, as well as in the Pashtunwali code, which is culturally rooted in the traditional lifestyles of the Pashtun people. Hanbali Islam, and certainly Salafi jihadism, is much more rigid in its adherence to the Salaf, or the first three generations of Muslims, comprising the Prophet and his companions, their followers, and their followers' followers. According to Hanbali religious doctrine, flexible interpretations of Islam that allow for judicial discretion, cultural customs, and community practices like those accepted by the Taliban are considered to be illegitimate innovations and thus deviations from Islam.

Salafism places a focus on the study of the Quran and the Hadith (sayings of the Prophet and his companions),[41] and rejects additional sources of law used by other schools of jurisprudence such as human reasoning, humanmade laws, and innovations in religious discourse and thought. As noted earlier, these approaches are typically viewed as deviant behaviors that threaten *tawhid.* Salafists also claim that their approach to Islam is the "only true and guiding interpretation of God's message."[42] As such, Salafi jihadists do not accept the legitimacy of numerous governments, especially those governing Muslim populations that do not adhere to their interpretation of the Islamic code and are thus considered to be unlawful state leaders.[43] These governments are often labeled as *taghut,* or tyrant regimes.

In general, Salafists share religious and political viewpoints, but the three main strands—purists (also referred to as quietists), politico-Salafists (or activists), and Salafi jihadists—differ in how to achieve their goals. For example, while purists are committed to attaining their objectives in a non-violent fashion such as through propagation and education, politico-Salafists believe in Islamic reforms to improve state structures.[44] Salafi jihadists, on the other hand, call for "violent action against the existing political order and for the establishment of a unitary state in the form of a caliphate."[45]

Salafi jihadism consists of five main components: jihad (holy war), *tawhid* (the oneness of God), *hakimiyya* (true Islamic government), *al-wala wal-bara* (loyalty to divine truth and disavowal of untruth and polytheism), and *takfir* (the naming of disbelievers).[46] Salafists generally seek to return to Islamic practice as it existed during the life of Prophet Muhammad and his followers, but proponents of Salafi jihadism view violent armed struggle as both a religious obligation and the only way to solve myriad sociopolitical and economic injustices. To do so, Salafi jihadists try to "awaken" Muslims to the decline of their religion in ideological, political, military, economic, and cultural terms.[47] The sources of this decline, as identified by Salafi jihadists, are the attacks and humiliation of Muslims by "Crusaders," "Zionists," and "apostates."[48] From this perspective, it is only through jihad that Muslims can redeem themselves, with martyrdom being the ultimate expression of jihad. Salafi jihadists also believe that Muslims must adhere to a puritanical version of Islam that reverts to the practices of the original followers of Prophet Muhammad to regain lost glory and respect.[49] Salafi jihadists commonly use the pejorative terms *kufar* (infidels or disbelievers), *murtadeen* (apostates), and *rafidah* (rejectionists) to label various out-groups whom they deem legitimate targets deserving of death because they do not subscribe to the extreme Salafist interpretation of Islam.

A core characteristic of Salafism is intolerance toward the rejectionist Shiite communities, an Islamic sect whose interpretation of Islamic traditions of *ijtihad* (independent reasoning), legitimate succession to the Prophet, and other views do not align with Salafist beliefs. This anti-Shia stance can be traced all the way back to the first generations after the Prophet in the seventh century C.E., but major jurisprudential scholars over the centuries such as Ibn Taymiyyah (1263–1328) and Muhammad ibn Abd al-Wahhab (1703–1792) developed the concept into a staunch religious doctrine that identified the Shia sect as a fundamental threat to Islam.[50] These scholars also provided religious justification for fighting unjust Muslim and non-Muslim rulers.[51] The core principles of jihad that constituted the main doctrine of the Salafist Awakening movement stem from Ibn Taymiyya's philosophy in particular. His rulings deemed it permissible to overthrow a ruler who does not adhere to true Islamic law, to cast the world into lands occupied by believers (*dar al-Islam,* or land of Islam) and nonbelievers (*dar al-kufar,* or land of unbelief), to promote the practice of excommunication of other Muslims, and to engage in a war against Jews and Christians.[52]

Another prominent figure to have influenced Salafist ideology is Sayyid Qutb (1906–1966), who was a member of the Muslim Brotherhood in Egypt and a strong opponent of Western values. Qutb concluded that "Arab leaders who claimed to practice Islam faithfully while allowing tidal waves of godless secularism, exploitative capitalism and the perverse, barbaric Western culture to drown their countrymen and women must be ousted."[53] Qutb viewed modern Muslim societies as reverting to *jahiliyya* (a period of ignorance preceding the Prophet and advent of Islam). He advocated for militancy, as jihad could be employed to overthrow illegitimate rulers and establish a society that is governed strictly by Islamic law. In Qutb's teachings, jihad was not defensive per se, but instead, "this movement uses the methods of preaching and persuasion for reforming ideas and beliefs; it uses physical power and jihad for abolishing the organizations and authorities of the *jahili* system which prevents people from reforming their idea and beliefs but forces them to obey erroneous ways."[54]

For the Islamic State movement and for ISK, the history of Salafi jihadism as an ideology and its application to modern society is not mere semantics; these are the ideological fault lines along which war must be waged. This ideology provides the underlying belief system that inspired tens of thousands to fight and die for the global movement, including thousands in the Afghanistan-Pakistan region. And, as this book explores throughout the chapters, Salafi jihadist ideology provides the core distinction that separates ISK from its rivals such as the Afghan Taliban.

Propaganda

To pursue its goals while adhering to a Salafi jihadist ideology, ISK has disseminated propaganda through a variety of media over the years and in a variety of languages. As other scholars have explored, the why, how, and who of ISK's propaganda campaigns are diverse.[55]

Dissemination. The group uses propaganda to spread its ideals, legitimize its actions, and intimidate its adversaries. It does so through media-based communications, in-person outreach, and violence. And its audiences include supporters within the region and outside the region, as well as engaged adversaries such as the Taliban and, previously, the Afghan government, in addition to disengaged adversaries such as identified civilian out-groups.[56] As ISK experienced fluctuations in territorial control, organizational strength, technical capacity, and strategic priorities, the narratives it broadcast shifted accordingly.

In early 2015, ISK's outreach efforts were largely focused on its core strongholds in Nangarhar, Afghanistan. Official ISK content was first published through the IS-Central's Bureau of Media,[57] and although official Islamic State materials tend to be released in Arabic first, most were also made available in local languages such as Pashto, Dari, and Urdu.[58] However, propaganda materials are not just released through IS-Central's outlets; local language media offices operate independently of IS-Central as well, including Khalid Media, al-Millat Media and Nidaa-e-Haq, and al-Qitaal. As discussed further later, media output through these channels is targeted toward local audiences and includes discussions of ISK's policies, and ideological justifications for its targeting priorities.[59] Other works written by senior ISK ideologues have been translated into local languages and often focus on the revivalist theories of Ibn Tamiyyah and Muhammad Ibn Abdul Wahab.[60] Some have even argued that ISK outmatched the Afghan Taliban in the quality and diversity of its propaganda materials.

In late 2015, the Islamic State established a radio station in eastern Nangarhar along the border with Pakistan in the Achin and Batikot Districts called *Khilafat Ghag* (Voice of the Caliphate). By early 2016, the station was providing daily broadcast services in Dari, English, and Pashto. These broadcasts—along with other propaganda materials such as films, leaflets, and statements released via social media platforms—focused on antigovernment and anti-Taliban narratives, inviting followers to join the Islamic State, interviews with the group's fighters, and religious chanting.[61] Over time, new radio reports would include interviews not just with fighters but also with local residents to discuss life under the caliphate.[62]

In a recruitment video released in Pashto in July 2015 titled "Message to Our People in Khorasan," founding governor Hafiz Saeed Khan states:

We adhere to the methodology of Prophet Mohammad peace be upon him and strive for his cause until it's fulfilled. It is for this cause we have waged jihad and we will fight until sovereignty belongs only to God and until we liberate all Muslim lands from Andualus to East Turkistan from the hegemony of disbelievers. This is our mission and we are defending ourselves against western disbelievers and their apostate's friends amongst us who work closely with Pakistani spy agency ISI, Afghan and other foreign agencies.[63]

Governance. During its early years, ISK leveraged its former territorial holdings to showcase life within its governed territories and justify its war against other militant groups more so than in later years, when the group shifted its focus more squarely on vilifying the Afghan Taliban and increasing coverage and publicity of its violent activities. In an interview with Hafiz Saeed Khan in IS-Central's English-language magazine *Dabiq* released in early 2016, the governor claimed that his group had conquered and established control in five "administrative regions," where it had set up judicial courts, offices for *hisbah* (religious police), offices for *zakāh* (charity), and others for education, worship, and public services. He also claimed to have set up divisions for administrative duties, with qualified and specialized officials appointed who were selected from the "*muhājirīn* and *ansār* in the *Wilāyah.*"[64] Khan's interview in the magazine heralds ISK's initial successes in gaining territorial control whereby they could implement an interpretation of sharia aligned with the Islamic State's ideology. As we discuss later in this chapter, ISK was also regularly reporting its activities within areas it considered to be under its jurisdiction to IS-Central.

In addition to setting up courts and other public services, ISK also began to silence those who publicly rejected its vision of law and order either through executions or by imprisoning individuals. According to Achin governor Haji Ghalib Mujahid, ISK had established private prisons in at least three areas of Nangarhar's Achin district by late summer 2015.[65] By his account, prisoners included religious leaders and tribal elders, and not just members of the Afghan Security Forces. In August 2015, it was estimated that about 300 people were in ISK's captivity.[66] At the same time it was silencing these dissenting voices, ISK was focusing much of its propaganda on propagating and legitimizing its vision of governance to appeal to local recruits for a global jihad with the Islamic State—and by extension ISK. In a twenty-three-minute audio message released in August 2015, Hafiz Saeed Khan encouraged members of other groups to defect to ISK: "I also call on all organizations to pledge allegiance to the Caliph . . . and ask the sheikhs and scholars in this regard, is there any value to these organizations after the declaration of the caliphate[?]."[67]

Deviant organizations. ISK also designed campaigns to frame its jihadist opponents as deviant entities, and to undermine state actors. These campaigns were complemented by content that highlighted the legitimacy of ISK's jihad, in which the group connected the historical significance of the Khorasan region to its transnational goal of eliminating national boundaries. The rejection of national boundaries and all actors who uphold them—state or nonstate—has been a persistent component of ISK's narrative since its inception, one that reinforced the group's ideology, identity, and appeal within the militant landscape. ISK's critique of other militant groups initially centered predominantly on the Afghan Taliban, al-Qaeda, and Kashmir-oriented militant groups such as Lashkar-e-Taiba. This feature remains true today, although as noted earlier, since the Afghan Taliban's return to power, it has received the bulk of ISK's propaganda ire.

ISK's early narratives surrounding al-Qaeda were largely dismissive. In the above audio message, Hafiz Saeed criticizes al-Qaeda for not having any substantial strength in the region, and for its preoccupation with disparaging the Islamic State and its goal of creating a caliphate.[68] Interestingly, most of ISK's propaganda criticizing al-Qaeda targeted its leader, Ayman al-Zawahiri (killed in 2022 by a US strike), whom ISK labeled an apostate for his obedience to the Afghan Taliban. At the same time, however, al-Qaeda's previous head and founder, Osama bin Laden, is frequently praised by ISK. Mirroring IS-Central propaganda narratives, ISK claims that the Islamic State and its global affiliates are the rightful inheritors of bin Laden's jihadist legacy while framing al-Zawahiri and al-Qaeda's global network as illegitimate successors.[69] ISK's focus on al-Zawahiri could be partially driven by the grievances of regionally based Arab leaders of al-Qaeda who pledged allegiance to ISK. Many al-Qaeda defectors who joined ISK early on left the former due to disagreements over ideological and organizational matters, and in particular with al-Zawahiri and his son-in-law, Abu Dujjana al-Basha, who held an influential position in al-Qaeda's central leadership.[70] The initial group of al-Qaeda leaders who helped initiate ISK seemed to be motivated by opposition to al-Zawahiri's loyalty to the Afghan Taliban and its Hanafi creed over more rigid adherence to Salafist practices.[71] They and other senior al-Qaeda defectors to the Islamic State would encourage Afghan and Pakistani militants to join ISK,[72] and their beliefs appear to have influenced ISK propaganda narratives, too.

ISK also used its *Khilafat Ghag* radio broadcasts to vilify other outgroups beyond rival militant groups and states. It has explicitly called out prominent or vocal members in society, including those within civil society organizations, the media, tribal elders, religious figures, and politicians. Propaganda campaigns to smear specific local individuals have been largely channeled through ISK's radio broadcasts, which the group perceives to be an efficacious way of condemning these individuals while reaching local populations.[73] After disbanding its radio broadcasts during a period of significant manpower and territorial losses, ISK reinstated the broadcasts around late 2020 to early 2021. An examination of a sample of these episodes from later years shows that much of the new content shifted focus to report on military advancements and to taunt and shame the Taliban for various developments including negotiating with the United States and, in ISK's words, embracing democracy. Other more recent episodes praised ISK's newest leader, Shahab al-Muhajir,[74] and announced an amnesty for former ISK members who had defected to the previous Afghan government in Kunar under pressure from their commanders.

State actors and Muslim minorities. ISK's propaganda also highlights the group's *takfiri* (excommunication of other Muslims) stance, given its adherence to the notion that all nonconforming Muslims are apostates and therefore legitimate targets. By subscribing to Salafist ideology, ISK rejects and differentiates itself from the monotheistic legitimacy of non-Salafist Muslims. By framing groups such as the Taliban as having betrayed the true Islamic cause, ISK attempts to legitimize its own existence while portraying others as worthy of excommunication.[75] Beyond the Taliban, ISK portrays all other Muslims from Hazara Shiites to the Afghan and Pakistani governments to the countries' Sufi communities as apostates. This rejectionist stance is firmly entrenched and propagated by IS-Central and by all of its global affiliates, and harkens to a key jihadist propaganda slogan, "Nine bullets for the apostate, one for the crusader," wherein apostates are excommunicated Muslims and crusaders are international forces. This slogan appears in key strategic documents from IS-Central's past and was made popular within jihadist circles by the scholar-warrior Abdullah Azzam during the anti-Soviet years.[76]

Naturally, ISK's goal of conquering the land of Khorasan means that there is no room for coexistence with any state actors, but it also makes no allowance for organizations that have links with state actors or any Muslim minority sects. As such, a large portion of ISK's propaganda also focuses on Shiite populations, where they are repeatedly referred to as *rafida*—a term used for those who rejected the first two caliphs to succeed the prophet in the seventh century C.E. In an article published in *al-Naba* in February 2018, the Islamic State discusses how the soldiers of the caliphate have been fighting the rejectionists in the "land of Khorasan."[77] The author praises and justifies ISK militants' persistent battle with Shiites, which the author claims gained strength during the US occupation of Afghanistan:

> God Almighty enabled His soldiers in Khorasan to inflict painful blows at the followers of the Twelver Shiite religion, kill hundreds of them, assassinate their heads, destroy their temples, and target their interests and

sources of power. This is in order to fulfill God's command to kill them for their polytheism and abstain from the rulings of the religion, and work to break their power that strengthened significantly under the Crusader occupation of the country that has continued for 16 years . . . with the entry of the American forces into the country by the help of the parties of the previous Afghan governments, including the rejectionist parties, which contributed under the direction of Iran, to ending the presence of the Taliban in the areas of the rejectionists. These parties became part of the system of government formed by the Crusaders and led by the tyrant Karzai and then by Ashraf Ghani, who is no less a disbeliever than his predecessor.

The article's author also assigns blame to Iran, decrying its involvement from the Islamic State's perspective:

In light of the competition between the parties of the Northern Alliance and the Pashtun apostates over money and power in Kabul and other regions, it seems that the rejectionist parties are trying to take advantage of the current situation to strengthen and consolidate their influence permanently, and seek to repeat the experience of their brothers in Lebanon, Yemen and Iraq, to gain controlling power through a scheme for the long term that Iranian tyrants planned for, and undoubtedly oversees its implementation through the Iranian intelligence and the Revolutionary Guard, which is tasked with managing such files in the apostate Iranian government. . . . In addition, there are recruiting operations now taking place within the rejectionist regions in Afghanistan for such militias, so that volunteers are sent to train in Iran, Iraq and the Levant, and then fight in the ranks of the Fatemiyoun militia or other factions associated with the Iranian Revolutionary Guard. Also, the rejectionist parties are actively supporting those militias by collecting financial donations, and through blood donation campaigns for the benefit of the wounded rejectionists in the battles of Iraq and the Levant, and perhaps Yemen as well.

Given ISK's animosity toward state actors, its propaganda also frequently features harsh criticism of the Afghan and Pakistani states. Hafiz Saeed Khan identifies state actors as the key difficulties faced by ISK during an early interview:

As for our difficulties, they are nothing but the *tāghūt* enemies of God— including "Pakistan" on one side, and "Afghanistan" on the other—standing with their armies and intelligence agencies against Islam, its *khilāfah*, and the *wilāyah* that represents it and implements its methodology in the region. These two governments attempt to create many problems in order to obstruct the *jihād* of the *wilāyah* and thereby hinder the establishment of Islam and its methodology in the region. They attempt to stop the expansion of the *khilāfah*. This is also the condition of those organizations that these two governments produce, support, or take advantage of, and to whom they extend aid, and for whom they pave the way. This leads these organizations, such as the nationalist Taliban movement, to instigate various problems in order to wage war against the *khilāfah*.[78]

Within this state-led conspiracy narrative propagated by ISK, it is the "tyrant" states of Afghanistan and Pakistan that support the group's rivals. A large portion of ISK's propaganda, therefore, focuses on delegitimizing the Afghan Taliban by linking the movement to the Pakistani state:

> Akhtar Mansour [former supreme leader of the Taliban] and his associates have strong and deep ties with Pakistani intelligence, and they live in the most important cities of Pakistan such as Islamabad, Peshawar, and Quetta. Even Akhtar Mansour's advisory council contains members from the Pakistani intelligence! On top of that, Pakistani intelligence aids him in everything he does. His ties to the Pakistani intelligence agency "ISI" became clear when its former head, the murtaddin retired general Hamid Gul, passed away several months ago—that general whom Pakistani intelligence hired to manage the "Islamic" organizations so that they would be submissive to the interests of the local and global *tawāghīt* (tyrants). When this general died, Akhtar Mansour gave the greatest condolences over his death out of loyalty to Pakistani intelligence and in recognition of everything they've done for him and for his Taliban movement.[79]

Armed with such critiques against the Afghan Taliban, ISK recruiting efforts spread to twenty-five of Afghanistan's thirty-four provinces by September 2015.[80] While we discuss ISK's rivals in more detail in Chapter 6, the preceding excerpts illustrate how ISK's opponents not only include the Pakistani and Afghan states, but also rival groups deemed to be either associated with a state actor, or simply those that did not support the global caliphate and subscribe to the Islamic State's ideology. In this manner, even though many TTP leaders have defected to ISK, organizationally the TTP remains aligned with the Afghan Taliban and al-Qaeda. As Hafiz Saeed Khan notes in his interview in *Dabiq,* "Both of the Talibans (Afghan and Pakistani Taliban) currently don't implement the Sharī'ah. . . . [T]here is no one left in the Pakistani Taliban except for corrupters. . . . For example, the Pakistani Taliban branch that follows *Fadlullāh* has given bay'ah to Akhtar Mansour. In other words, they've given *bay'ah* to the Pakistani intelligence!"[81]

Hafiz Saeed Khan also voiced his grievances that the Afghan Taliban "ignored our call and disrespected our delegation," and instead attacked ISK and impeded its progress. He explains that "ISK took the path of patience and did not intend to escalate tensions, but were striving to find a peaceful solution to the problem; however, our efforts to end the dispute were answered with extreme arrogance by these criminal elements."

Khan argues that elements linked with the Taliban began "to attack areas under Islamic Caliphate control and . . . under the leadership of Qari Yasir they surrounded 40 brothers in Kot, Nangarhar until we decided to withdraw from these areas."[82] As such, ISK's justifies its fight against the Afghan Taliban as an act of defense: "We were forced to defend ourselves, the Islamic Caliphate territory, our homes and families of the muhajideen. . . . This all happened by the order of some leaders sitting in Pakistan."[83] A fifteen-minute video produced by the official Wilayat Khorasan Media Office and released on May 31, 2015, titled "And on That Day the Believers Shall Rejoice—[Part] 1," opens with the following statement: "In late Rajab 1436 H [May 2015] some of the members of the Afghan Taliban movement, supported by the intelligence ISI network, carried out an attack on the Islamic State soldiers in Kot, Nangarhar, and started this war. However, and all praise due to God, they could not resist the Caliphate soldiers and fled."[84]

Overall, the narrative that ISK has developed and propagated in relation to the Taliban is that while ISK wanted the latter to join its efforts, the Afghan Taliban is linked to the Pakistani intelligence and thus continued to attack ISK. After the US withdrawal, ISK shifted its criticism of the Taliban to link them with the United States in the context of the peace negotiations.

The themes and narratives discussed here are not meant to be exhaustive and are intended to provide insights into how ISK incorporates its ideology and goals into its propaganda. New developments in ISK's operational environment were reflected in the group's propaganda and outreach efforts, with the why, how, and who of its propaganda campaigns shifting accordingly. ISK's initial outreach efforts were largely focused on its pockets of territorial control in Nangarhar,[85] but following territorial losses that continued through 2019, the group's propaganda mostly lacked any specific geographical references. Moreover, while ISK was focused more on propagation in its early days, it refocused its efforts following setbacks and losses on legitimization (justifying its violence and presence) and intimidation (instilling fear).[86] In more recent years, other analysts have estimated that about 97 percent of ISK's output in the eighteen months leading up to August 2021 focused on showcasing the group's military activities, the destruction associated with its attacks, and the killing of captives.[87] The group's goal in its propaganda campaigns seems to be to garner support but also to signal resolve to its opponents. However, and as we explore in later chapters, the diversity of militants featured in ISK propaganda grew increasingly diverse from 2020 to 2022, as did the languages and target audiences it reached. These shifts mark the broader reprioritization of transnationalism within ISK's strategy and offer clear signals of the group's intended trajectory in the coming months and years.

Links to IS-Central Support

Although some uncertainty remains regarding the links between IS-Central and ISK, open-source reports, as well as captured materials from Afghanistan (a sample of which we reviewed), suggest that IS-Central played an important role in aiding ISK's initial setup, as well as providing continued support and advice. Based on available evidence, IS-Central supported ISK through a range of activities, from facilitation of meetings to general and specific guidance on governing affairs to financial support.

We reviewed a collection of communications documents between IS-Central and ISK that shed light on the nature of the relationship between the two organizations during ISK's early years (2015–2017).[88] These documents show that ISK maintained regular communication with IS-Central, particularly in order to keep the latter informed of its monthly operations, output and organizational changes. For example, a memo dated July 2016 that appeared to be penned after the death of ISK's first governor,[89] Hafiz Saeed Khan, provided updates on ISK's internal organization. The letter states: "We appointed an Emir of War for the Khorasan province, and we formed a military shura for the province as well. . . . The brothers of the Khorasan province were relieved by the establishment of a Sharia committee for disputed issues, and for that reason, application of the Islamic State's methodology has been much easier. . . . We have established for the first time an office of tribes, and we have made contact with the tribes in the province."[90]

Another document from the months of August and September 2016 provides a monthly output summary, including the number and descriptions of videos and photo reports produced by ISK over the two months. The products vary from individuals' pledging allegiance and killing members of the Afghan army to a suicide bomber conducting an attack in Quetta, Pakistan.[91]

Several other documents are stamped with an "Al-Hisbah" logo (Islamic State's religious enforcement police) and appear to be intended to provide all governors of the Islamic State's various affiliates with advice.[92] One of these requests information regarding dispute resolution, cases forwarded by *hisbah* police to official judicial courts, propaganda materials distributed to the public, sermons delivered, confiscated possessions, and disciplinary measures taken.[93] Another letter dated September 8, 2015,[94] attributed to Yusuf Bin-Salih al-Arabi and addressed to the "Wali," outlines the role of *hisbah* members during military mobilizations, and how to ensure their readiness for battlefield operations.[95] Other generic Islamic State *hisbah*-stamped documents outline rules on various other topics, including distributing photos of female "sex slaves" on social media,[96] rulings on the use of satellite receivers,[97] and guidance on how to deal with "inappropriate" books, audio, and video.[98] These documents offer glimpses of the generic guidance offered by IS-Central to its affiliates, and their existence in ISK's internal documents is indicative of IS-Central's efforts to shape the latter's behavior.

ISK also frequently informed IS-Central of its operational activities, achievements, and challenges. Available documents suggest that IS-Central was particularly interested in receiving status reports on ISK military activities.[99] One such document highlights battlefield and administrative achievements and states that ISK's losses were lower compared to previous months, and proclaims the group's success in acquiring a tactical vehicle along with other weapons. The document also notes tactical withdrawals on some fronts due to Afghan and United States–led coalition operations, as well as successes on other fronts against the Taliban. Evidence from this document and others also suggests coordination of attacks across the Afghanistan-Pakistan border through contact with "war officials" in various cities such as Quetta, Pakistan. And as the above quote illustrates, ISK also kept IS-Central abreast of its administrative developments including the establishment of both a sharia committee for disputed issues and the application of Islamic law, and an office of tribes to conduct outreach and coordination with different tribes in the region.

Based on the documents examined, the group also seemed to regularly communicate its problems to IS-Central, whether they were battlefield setbacks, financial needs, internal rifts, or logistical issues. A letter penned by a self-proclaimed ISK media official named Yusuf Ahmad Khorasani asks forgiveness from an unspecified Islamic State committee for his tardiness in sending military reports. Khorasani blames his failure to do so on logistical challenges owing to the continuous bombing of ISK's leadership and media centers. He laments a series of other problems ranging from their locations being disclosed to the enemy, to lack of electricity and internet, and an inability to communicate with their "military brothers." Khorasani's letter also outlines a sparsity of available funds, saying that part of ISK's budget allocated to the media department was not currently available and prevented them from purchasing any new equipment.[100] In a separate letter, Hafiz Saeed Khan also acknowledged the group's financial problems, and pointed to the coalition's successful disruption of an ISK network in Kabul as the reason for the group's financial struggles.[101] Another letter dated June 8, 2016, from IS-Central requests alternative routes to send money to ISK such as through Dubai or Egypt in order to facilitate in-person delivery.[102]

Details within available documents also reveal that ISK was updating IS-Central on membership figures, factions and commanders that had pledged allegiance, and leadership appointments. One such document shows that ISK was initially focused on poaching commanders from the TTP, and highlights successful defections such as that of the TTP's operational commander in Karachi who pledged allegiance to ISK.[103] A letter dated June 22, 2016, from Hafiz Saeed Khan to IS-Central boasts that a number of Jamaat-ul-Ahrar members had defected to ISK,[104] while another document confirms that TTP-Bajaur from Khyber Pakhtunkhwa, Pakistan, had pledged allegiance to ISK.[105] Other letters discussed in greater detail in Chapter 4 indicate that ISK was also relaying information about internal disputes to IS-Central. These include updates on the management of dissenters who spoke out against ISK,[106] who disobeyed orders and instigated divisions,[107] and who harbored personal grudges against top ISK leadership.[108]

Collectively, the sample of documents reviewed sheds important light on how IS-Central was involved in various ways in the setup of ISK in its early years. Not only did IS-Central provide funds, guidance, and other forms of support, but it also requested to remain informed about ISK's strategy and administrative developments. The nature and depth of links between IS-Central and ISK are unclear in later years, especially following major territorial losses and the loss of multiple top leaders on both ends. Evidence from a 2018 UN report suggests that IS-Central leveraged its Khorasan province to facilitate the relocation of several key operatives.[109]

Other evidence illustrates ISK's pivot toward local fundraising streams in recent years rather than depending more singularly on IS-Central. In 2019, reports surfaced of ISK taking control of the Mazar, Dewagal, and Korengal Valleys and their forests in Kunar province, and using Chawkay district for smuggling timber between Afghanistan and Pakistan.[110] Local residents reported that approximately 20,000 trees were cut and smuggled to Pakistan annually by militant groups such as ISK, which served as the primary source of income for the district's populations.[111] Additionally, as Chapter 4 explores, IS-Central was involved in restructuring ISK's top leadership during periods of losses and decline owing to perceived deficits in leadership performance. These dynamics all point to a complex and evolving relationship between IS-Central and ISK, one that ebbs and flows depending on developments in both organizations' operational environments. What has remained relatively consistent for several years now, however, is regular praise of ISK in IS-Central's propaganda as a high-performing province, including features on its its high-profile attacks such as its prison siege in Jalalabad City in 2020 and the Kabul airport attack in August 2021.[112] ISK may or may not require as extensive support from IS-Central going forward as it received during its formative years, but both organizations continue to derive legitimacy and recruitment boosts from advertising their joint mission to establish a global caliphate. As such, both ISK and IS-Central are likely to continue projecting the narrative of a closely coordinated and supportive partnership for years to come.

The Persistent Appeal of ISK

Throughout ISK's existence, the group's extreme and Salafist ideology led many to dismiss its ability to resonate with the majority of Afghans and Pakistanis. As Borhan Osman states, "Its traditional conceptions of Islam and propaganda often fall flat with its listeners and its brutal tactics are off-putting to most Afghans who are weary after decades of war. As a result, even among those who are attracted by (parts of) their messaging, there will often be a reluctance to join."[113] Yet he argues that ISK's ideology is likely to appeal to specific populations, among them militants who may be disillusioned with their own groups. He also notes that ISK's messaging may appeal to those who are not yet members of other jihadist groups, but who may be interested in joining a transnational group like ISK, especially since the group "uses messaging that romanticizes life as a mujahidin and emphasizes the religious obligation of jihad." Potential supporters in this category include Afghan youth in urban areas. To that end, Osman argues that "the growing appeal of Salafi jihadism among Afghan youth, especially in urban areas, may explain ISKP's resilience."[114]

While recruitment of disaffected jihadists and Afghan youth may contribute to ISK's resilience, these components alone do not offer a complete explanation. They fail to capture the broader appeal of ISK's ideology outside of these two categories of supporters, as well as the opportunities presented by a region where environments change consistently and rapidly. In addition, the two trends identified above do not capture the group's persistent ability to rapidly build its operational capacity over the years and survive intense territorial and manpower losses. Rather than focus on contextually bound recruiting trends, we argue that ISK's underlying resilience stems from a broader ability to recruit from experienced jihadist groups by differentiating itself from mainstream rivals and establishing strong operational links with other groups that have allowed it to survive and thrive in the region.

As highlighted throughout this chapter, ISK's ideology, goals, propaganda, and outreach garnered substantial support across a range of actors in the region. Over the years, support for ISK has varied among militant groups, and civilians, but key pillars of its resilience have remained consistent. ISK will continue to seize opportunities to expand its recruitment and outreach, just as it did in the latter half of 2021 by exploiting renewed tensions between the Afghan Taliban and Salafist communities.[115] The scriptural and jihadist legacy of "Khorasan" and the goal of a caliphate as envisioned by the Islamic State will always appeal to some, and IS-Central is likely to continue supporting its affiliate in the region in any way it can.

Notes

1. Al-Hayat Media Center, "Say, 'Die in Your Rage!'"
2. US Government, "Sanaullah Ghafari," https://www.state.gov/taking-action-against-isis-k.
3. Watkins, "An Assessment of Taliban Rule at Three Months."
4. Reporterly, "IS-K Territorially Defeated in Afghanistan."
5. BBC News, "Islamic State Group Claims Deadly Attack on Afghanistan Prison."
6. Landay, "U.N. Envoy Says Islamic State Now Appears Present in All Afghan Provinces."
7. Blue, Gibbons-Neff, and Goldbaum, "ISIS Poses a Growing Threat to New Taliban Government in Afghanistan."

8. *Al-Naba,* "The Battle of Tawhid in Kabul."

9. Generally used to refer to unbelievers, or those who do not believe in or abide by God's guidance.

10. Iqbal, "Evolving Wave of Terrorism and Emergence of Daesh in Pakistan."

11. Rassler, "Situating the Emergence of the Islamic State of Khorasan."

12. Ibid.

13. Jadoon, Sayed, and Mines, "The Islamic State Threat in Taliban Afghanistan."

14. Sayed, "Islamic State Khorasan Province's Peshawar Seminary Attack and War."

15. Clarke, *After the Caliphate,* p. 77.

16. Iqbal, "Evolving Wave of Terrorism and Emergence of Daesh in Pakistan."

17. Ibid.

18. Farrall and Hamid, "The Arabs at War in Afghanistan."

19. Bell, "The First Islamic State: A Look Back at the Islamic Emirate of Kunar."

20. Iqbal, "Evolving Wave of Terrorism and Emergence of Daesh in Pakistan."

21. Bapat and Bond, "Alliances Between Militant Groups."

22. Bond, "Power, Identity, Credibility, and Cooperation"; Moghadam, *Nexus of Global Jihad;* Bacon, "Alliance Hubs"; Asal et al., "With Friends Like These."

23. Byman, "Buddies or Burdens?"

24. Ibid.

25. *Tolo News,* "Afghan Intelligence Tram Nabs Daesh Leader in South."

26. Bond, "Power, Identity, Credibility, and Cooperation"; Chenoweth, "Democratic Competition and Terrorist Activity"; Karmon, *Coalitions Between Terrorist Organizations.*

27. Karmon, *Coalitions Between Terrorist Organizations,* p. 25; Jackson et al., *Aptitude for Destruction.*

28. Bond, "Power, Identity, Credibility, and Cooperation."

29. Moghadam, *Nexus of Global Jihad.*

30. Tarzi, "Islamic State–Khurasan Province"; Luce, *Frontier as Process: Umayyad Khurāsān.*

31. Tarzi, "Islamic State–Khurasan Province."

32. Esposito, *Islam and Politics,* pp. 31–35.

33. Tarzi, "Islamic State–Khurasan Province," p. 122

34. For a full discussion, see Bahari and Hassan, "The Black Flag Myth."

35. See Bahari and Hassan, "The Black Flag Myth," which discusses Ahma no. 8775, Sunan al-Tirmizi no. 2269, al-Awsat no. 3560, and al-Dalail no. 6/516.

36. Tarzi, "Islamic State–Khurasan Province."

37. Ganguly and al-Istrabadi, "The Future of ISIS."

38. *Dabiq,* "Interview with the Wali of Khurasan."

39. SITE Intelligence Group, "IS' Khorasan Province Fighter Rallies Colleagues."

40. Clarke, *After the Caliphate,* pp. 78–79.

41. Meijer, *Global Islam's New Religious Movement,* p. 4.

42. Wiktorowicz, "Anatomy of the Salafi Movement."

43. Oliveti, *Terror's Source,* p. 45.

44. Wiktorowicz, "Anatomy of the Salafi Movement."

45. Haykel, "On the Nature of Salafi Thought and Action."

46. Maher, "Salafi-Jihadism: The History of an Idea."

47. Moghadam, "The Salafi-Jihad as a Religious Ideology."

48. Ibid.

49. Wiktorowicz, "Anatomy of the Salafi Movement."

50. Steinberg, "Jihadi Salafism and the Shi'is," p. 113.

51. Delong-Bas, *Wahhabi Islam,* p. 249

52. Ibid., p. 256
53. Brachman, *Global Jihadism,* 23.
54. Qutb, *Milestones,* 55.
55. "ISKP: A Threat Assessment."
56. Ibid.
57. *The New Arab,* "Islamic State Group 'Defeated' in Key Afghan Province."
58. "ISKP: A Threat Assessment."
59. Winter, "Apocalypse Later," pp. 103–221.
60. Osman, "ISKP's Battle for Minds."
61. Ghazi, "IS Radio Expands Reach in Afghanistan"; Afghanistan Journalists Center, "Outrage Grows over Government's Inaction to Stop Daesh Radio."
62. Osman, "ISKP's Battle for Minds."
63. Saeed, "Message to Our People in Khurasan."
64. *Dabiq,* "Interview with the Wali of Khurasan."
65. *Voice of America,* "Islamic State Running Prisons Inside Afghanistan."
66. Ibid.
67. Saeed, "Come Join Up with the Caliphate."
68. Ibid.
69. As-Sawarte, untitled video message.
70. According to Rassler, this group included Abu Ubayda al-Lubnani, Abu al-Muhannad al-Urduni, Abu Jarir al-Shimali (Abu Thair), Abu al-Huda al-Sudani, Abd-al-Aziz al-Maqdisi, Abdullah al-Banjabi, Abu Younis al-Kurdim, Abu A'isha al-Qurtubi, and Abu Musab al-Tadamuni. See Rassler, "Situating the Emergence of the Islamic State of Khorasan." Abu Jarir al-Shimali wrote a detailed account of these differences with Ayman al-Zawahiri and his son-in-law, Abu Dujjana al-Basha, in Islamic State Central's *Dabiq* magazine, which according to him resulted in defections to the Islamic State. For details, see ash-Shamali, "Al-Qaidah of Waziristan," pp. 40–55.
71. Sayed, "Why Islamic State Khurasan Poses an Indigenous Threat to the Afghan Taliban."
72. Ash-Shamali, "Al-Qaidah of Waziristan."
73. Osman, "ISKP's Battle for Minds."
74. Islamic State Khorasan, *Voice of the Caliphate,* episodes 43–112.
75. Ashraf, *ISIS Khorasan.*
76. Whiteside, "Nine Bullets for the Traitors, One for the Enemy."
77. *Al-Naba,* "The Rafidah Project in Khurasan."
78. *Dabiq,* "Interview with the Wali of Khurasan."
79. Ibid.
80. Raghavan, "The Islamic State Is Making These Afghans Long for the Taliban."
81. *Dabiq,* "Interview with the Wali of Khurasan."
82. Saeed, "Message to Our People in Khurasan."
83. Ibid.
84. Islamic State Khorasan, "The Day the Believers Will Rejoice: Part 1."
85. "ISKP: A Threat Assessment."
86. Ibid.
87. Ibid.
88. These documents were primary sources recovered from Afghanistan.
89. Ahmad and Torbati, "U.S. Drone Kills Islamic State Leader for Afghanistan"; ISK primary sources recovered from Afghanistan (Ref. NMEC-2017-406334).
90. ISK primary sources recovered from Afghanistan (Ref. NMEC-2017-406334).
91. NMEC-2017-301388.

92. These documents were not specifically addressed to ISK, but appeared to be generic guidelines for al-Hisbah members, which could potentially be based in Iraq and Syria or in other Islamic State provinces.

93. Internal ISK Document, Combating Terrorism Center Library.

94. Internal ISK Document, Combating Terrorism Center Library.

95. Internal ISK Document, Combating Terrorism Center Library.

96. Internal ISK Document, Combating Terrorism Center Library.

97. Internal ISK Document, Combating Terrorism Center Library.

98. Internal ISK Document, Combating Terrorism Center Library.

99. Internal ISK Document, Combating Terrorism Center Library.

100. Internal ISK Document, Combating Terrorism Center Library.

101. Internal ISK Document, Combating Terrorism Center Library.

102. Internal ISK Document, Combating Terrorism Center Library.

103. Internal ISK Document, Combating Terrorism Center Library.

104. Internal ISK Document, Combating Terrorism Center Library.

105. Internal ISK Document, Combating Terrorism Center Library.

106. Internal ISK Document, Combating Terrorism Center Library.

107. Internal ISK Document, Combating Terrorism Center Library.

108. Sayed, "Who Is the New Leader of Islamic State-Khorasan Province?"

109. Analytical Support and Sanctions Monitoring Team, *Twenty-second Report.*

110. Glinski, "Afghanistan's Forests."

111. Ibid.

112. Ghazi and Mashal, "29 Dead After ISIS Attack on Afghan Prison."

113. Osman, "ISKP's Battle for Minds."

114. Osman, *Bourgeois Jihad.*

115. For details, see, for example, the ISKP video Khalid Media, "The Guarantors Are in Panic."

3

Tracing ISK's
Operational Capacity

We managed to get in contact with our brothers, the war officials in the cities, and thus the soldiers of the Caliphate were able to carry out wide-ranging operations inside Pakistan—such as two operations in the city of Quetta—as well as assassinations of leaders in the governments of Afghanistan and Pakistan, and the idolatrous Taliban in various cities.

—Letter from ISK governor Abdul Haseeb Logari to
IS-Central leadership, August 8, 2016[1]

On Saturday, April 18, 2015, a bomb exploded at the peak of rush hour outside of a bank in Jalalabad, Nangarhar province.[2] The bomber rode his motorcycle right up to the front of the bank—where local government workers would collect their salary payments—and self-detonated, killing himself and at least thirty-three others and wounding more than 100.[3] The April 2015 bank attack in Jalalabad was quickly claimed by the Islamic State's central media outlet, *Amaq*, as the work of its newly declared regional province, ISK. It also marked the first major ISK operation in Afghanistan and Pakistan, signaling the start of intense attack campaigns that would leave thousands dead and injured in the years to come.

Almost sixteen months later, on August 8, 2016, the body of recently killed president of the Balochistan Bar Association, Bilal Anwar Kasi, was being transported to a state-run hospital in Quetta, Balochistan, when another suicide attacker struck.[4] Between seventy and ninety-four individuals were killed and over 120 were injured in the attack, which was later claimed by both ISK and Jamaat-ul-Ahrar.[5] As reflected in the letter referenced above, the August 2016 Quetta bombing, ISK's first major operation in the city, appears to have prompted Logari's boasts to the Islamic State leadership in his monthly report about ISK's operations and activities.[6] ISK's attack operations continued relatively unabated despite months of battlefield setbacks,[7] intense targeting by state security forces,[8] and the recent death of its first and founding governor, Hafiz Saeed Khan, just days prior to the August 2016 Quetta attack.[9] In fact, the group would only bolster its deadly operations in the proceeding months, which eventually resulted in ISK's rise by 2018 to one of the deadliest terrorist organizations in the world.[10] Contextualizing these trends within the broader security environment, this chapter explores the violent campaigns of ISK, and traces its infamous rise, fall, and eventual resurgence over the past several years. In doing so, we highlight the logic underpinning evolving ISK's strategies, tactics, and targets.

The Targets, Tactics, and Strategic Logic of ISK's Violent Campaigns

Since its official formation in 2015, ISK has carried out attacks in over thirty provinces across Afghanistan and Pakistan. The group's most frequent target in both countries has been government actors, including local police, military, intelligence, and judicial personnel, as well as international armed forces, diplomatic representatives, and international nongovernmental organizations (NGOs). ISK has targeted police checkpoints,[11] police academies,[12] international military bases such as Bagram Airfield,[13] international embassies,[14] and even Afghanistan's Supreme Court in Kabul.[15] The group has also tried to carry out a number of high-profile assassinations against top government leaders, including failed plots against former US secretary of defense James Mattis and NATO secretary-general Jens Stoltenberg,[16] former US chargé d'affaires in Afghanistan Ross Wilson,[17] former president of Afghanistan Ashraf Ghani,[18] and former vice president Abdul Rashid Dostum.[19] While each of these high-profile assassination attempts has failed, they nonetheless display ISK's enduring commitment to attacking the highest levels of government. In addition to targeting top military and political figures in the United States and the Afghan-allied coalition, the group also consistently targets lower-level officials, including provincial governors, prominent military commanders, and renowned judges.

But perhaps ISK's most atrocious and brutal attacks have been against civilian spaces and institutions. The group's attacks have targeted public schools and universities,[20] Afghan journalists and media buildings,[21] houses of worship and religious sites,[22] health institutions,[23] and a number of vulnerable public spaces over the years, regularly leaving dozens of civilians either dead or wounded in the wake. Some of the worst attacks have targeted religious minorities, especially Hazara and Ismaili Shiite communities, but also Sufi,[24] Sikh,[25] Christian,[26] and other minority groups in Afghanistan and Pakistan. One of the worst-hit communities of all have been Kabul's Hazara residents, who have suffered well over a thousand casualties from ISK's terrorism over the years.[27] One of the most affected communities has been the Dasht-e-Barchi settlement in western Kabul, which is home to tens of thousands of ethnic Hazaras, many of whom migrated from other provinces affected by conflict in the early 2000s.[28] While ISK's predominant targets, strictly by the numbers, have been state actors, civilians have borne the brunt of the group's brutality.

After the fall of Kabul in August 2021, ISK's highly lethal attacks on religious minorities and other civilian targets continued, but the Taliban suffered the greatest number of attacks given the shift in ISK's targeting priorities. Although ISK revamped its attacks campaign against the Taliban post–US withdrawal, the year 2021 was far from the beginning of the ISK-Taliban war.[29] Instead, it merely marked a new phase of an intergroup rivalry that dates back to ISK's founding.

ISK's attack tactics have varied substantially, but have proven to be equally vicious. Particularly during its peak years of territorial control in 2015 and 2016, the group frequently engaged in guerrilla-style assaults on police and military targets, oftentimes at convoys and checkpoints. Rocket and mortar attacks against military bases and a variety of other targets have been regularly reported since 2015, as have targeted assassinations such as those outlined above. ISK fighters have also deployed *inghimasi* attack squads semi-regularly in the past—small units of fighters equipped with light assault weapons and explosives belts or vests who try to inflict as much damage as possible before their own deaths, either by enemy fire or self-detonation.[30] These units have been responsible for some of ISK's most horrific attacks, including the attack on a Kabul maternity hospital in May 2020.[31] The most damaging tactic that ISK deploys, however, is its highly lethal suicide attacks, whether through vehicle-borne or human-borne improvised explosive devices. Around 60 percent of ISK-inflicted casualties have been victims of the group's suicide attacks.[32]

Underpinning ISK's attacks against each of its target groups is a strategic logic that the group consistently reinforces through its messaging campaigns. When it targets the state—including international forces and diplomatic personnel—ISK attempts to project its power as a militant group and signal its unrelenting resolve. The greater the number of state casualties and the higher the profile of the victims, the bolder ISK appears to a variety of audiences, especially to potential recruits and militants belonging to other groups. This is one of the reasons why ISK frequently inflates the number of casualties it claims when it attacks police and military targets in particular. Attacks on state targets are also used for provocation, intended to incite responses from Afghan and international security forces that often alienate local populations, whether through increased surveillance and harassment of civilians or immediate, sometimes erroneous, kinetic responses.[33] A glaring example is the errant US drone strike in the days after the August 2021 Kabul airport attack that left numerous civilians dead, among them seven children.[34] Perhaps most important, ISK's attacks against regional state actors are a key foundation for its rejectionist identity that differentiates it from other militant groups in the region.[35] Given its unwavering antistate and antinationalist stance, at no cost does ISK accommodate state demands, negotiate with state actors and interlocutors on its behalf for political settlements, or pursue dialogue of any kind that is not directly adversarial.

When it comes to attacking civilians, ISK's main goal is to inject the conditions of chaos that the founder of the Islamic State movement, Abu Mus'ab al-Zarqawi, and his co-strategists implemented over fifteen years ago when they formed al-Qaeda in Iraq.[36] In doing so, ISK seeks to undermine the state's capacity to protect different civilian populations (especially religious minorities) under its care, as well as civilian perceptions of the state's ability to govern. Such attacks also assist ISK with coercion and intimidation of civilian populations. For civilians reluctant to cooperate with the group, these attacks help ISK extract concessions such as financial payoffs and coerced compliance, particularly around areas where ISK has enjoyed greater territorial control and influence.[37]

Finally, ISK also uses attacks against specific civilian populations—its suicide attacks and *inghimasi* attacks in particular—to further differentiate its rejectionist brand from other jihadist groups in order to outcompete them for recruitment purposes.[38] ISK's messaging campaigns work in tandem with its attacks against civilians to establish simple in-group versus out-group dichotomies that divide the civilian population along religious sectarian lines.

Prior to the fall of the Islamic Republic of Afghanistan in 2021, ISK's attacks against the Taliban helped the former position itself as the main competitor and therefore alternative to the latter, as discussed in greater detail in Chapter 6. This strategy helped ISK's recruitment efforts substantially, especially during its startup years, but also when the Taliban took over in 2021 and started their transition back to power in Afghanistan. ISK's attacks and coordinated messaging campaigns against the Taliban worked to delegitimize the latter's claim to a jihadist legacy in Afghanistan, and instead portrayed ISK as the legitimate inheritor of that legacy.[39] These dynamics remain unchanged even after the Taliban takeover in 2021. After 2021, the same logic that underpinned ISK's attacks against the previous government and its international allies was applied to its violent campaign against Afghanistan's new rulers.

The Evolution of ISK's Targeting Capacity and Method, 2015–2019

From 2015 to 2019, ISK cemented itself as one of the preeminent militant groups in the Afghanistan-Pakistan region through its use of violence, gaining global notoriety. However, ISK's capacity to conduct attacks in its first five years was not uniform, and the group struggled to generate comparably high numbers of attacks and casualties in 2015 and in 2019. Here we provide an overview of ISK's violent trajectory in its first five years, and discuss some of the key factors that explain the broad contours of its operational trends.

Number and Lethality of Attacks over Time

Overall, ISK's total number of attacks between 2015 and 2019 in Afghanistan was three times that of its attacks in Pakistan (312 and 108, respectively). Figure 3.1 shows the total number of annual attacks in both countries, as well as the yearly variation that occurred in each. In 2015, ISK reportedly conducted twenty-three attacks in Afghanistan and twenty-one in Pakistan, the only year in which attack numbers in both countries were about equal. The year 2015 was also ISK's weakest year in terms of total

Figure 3.1 ISK's Operational Rise and Decline, 2015–2019

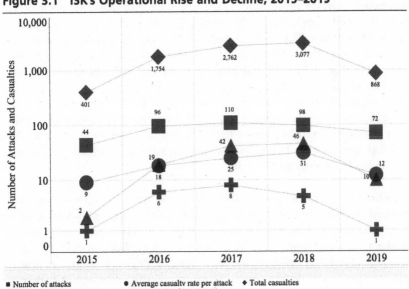

■ Number of attacks   ● Average casualty rate per attack   ◆ Total casualties
▲ Number of suicide attacks   ✦ Number of *inghimasi* attacks

Source: Author data.

numbers of attacks across both countries, although this is not necessarily surprising for a militant organization in its infancy; it usually takes time to develop the necessary logistical and personnel channels that sustain significant violent campaigns.

Divergent trajectories in Afghanistan and Pakistan, 2016–2017. In 2016, ISK's total attacks across both countries more than doubled, with attacks surging around 150 percent in Afghanistan and 86 percent in Pakistan compared to the previous year. However, whereas ISK attacks rose 77 percent in Afghanistan in 2017 to 101 attacks that year, the exact opposite occurred in Pakistan, where the group reportedly conducted only nine attacks (one-fourth of the year before), its lowest yearly number on record. Although ISK's total number of attacks in 2017 (110) was the highest of any year from 2015 to 2019, this pronounced difference between total attack numbers in Afghanistan and Pakistan cannot be disregarded. It may be the case that ISK directed the vast majority of its operational resources to Afghanistan in 2017, including resources that might otherwise have focused on attacks in Pakistan. This could possibly have been a top-down, strategic shift in the group's attack strategy, especially after the United States–led coalition's leadership decapitation strikes throughout 2015 and 2016 removed a large number of founding and integral Pakistani ISK leadership,[40] which facilitated the rapid "Afghanization" of ISK's senior leadership ranks.[41] On the other hand, ISK could have also made the decision to focus its attack campaigns in the relatively more permissive environment, where they could inflict the most damage. The Afghan security apparatus in 2017 was incredibly strained from an intensifying insurgency led by the Afghan Taliban, while the Pakistani government had managed to clamp down on multiple key ISK nodes throughout Pakistan by the end of 2016 (see Chapter 4 for more details). Overall though, the fact that ISK conducted ten times as many attacks in Afghanistan in 2017 compared to Pakistan is notable, and highlights ISK's ability to adapt its strategy to the political and militant landscapes within each country, which we discuss later in the book in greater detail.

A period of decline, 2018–2019. By 2018, total ISK attack numbers dropped slightly from 2017, with the group conducting eighty-five attacks in Afghanistan and thirteen attacks in Pakistan. Although overall attack numbers were still high—and the group was still conducting over six times as many attacks in Afghanistan as it was in Pakistan—signs of ISK's broader operational decline started to emerge. As we discuss in Chapter 4, state-led efforts to target ISK and reclaim territory in Afghanistan controlled by the group were instrumental in facilitating this broader decline.[42] By 2019, that decline was on full display. In addition to significant territorial and manpower losses, total ISK attacks across both countries fell by over 25 percent to a total of seventy-two attacks. This drop in attacks was largely driven by ISK's decline in Afghanistan; while ISK's attacks in Afghanistan almost halved from 2018 to 2019 (eighty-five to forty-six attacks), total attacks in Pakistan doubled (thirteen to twenty-six). Overall, total yearly attack numbers show the general rise and decline of ISK's operational capacity from 2015 to 2019, with diverging trends of a dramatic decline in attacks in Afghanistan by 2019 and a noticeable uptick in attacks in Pakistan from 2017 to 2019. While the contrasting trends are interesting, they may simply be a result of cross-border militant movements to evade increasing counterterrorism pressure in Afghanistan.

Persistent lethality. Total yearly attack numbers offer a key barometer of an organization's operational capacity, but they do not necessarily provide the complete picture with respect to a group's behavior, as they are only one metric of a group's strength and resolve. Additional insights can be gleaned from looking at total and average attack lethality (individuals killed and wounded) as well.[43] From 2015 to 2019, ISK's attacks on state and civilian targets left over 2,100 people killed and almost 4,700 wounded in Afghanistan, with over 800 killed and 1,200 wounded in Pakistan. Both in terms of total attack numbers and total casualties, then, ISK hit Afghanistan around three times as hard as it did Pakistan. Figure 3.1 shows the yearly evolution in ISK's total attack lethality, which follows the same general trend of rise and decline that was noted above in ISK's total attack numbers. ISK's attacks inflicted 401 casualties (154 killed, 247 wounded) across Afghanistan and Pakistan in 2015, before more than quadrupling to 1,754 casualties in 2016 (573 killed, 1,181 wounded) as the group's attacks more than doubled that year. Both data points reflect the rapid rise of ISK's operational capacity in the two years after its formation. In 2017, ISK's total lethality rose by over 57 percent to 2,762 casualties (868 killed, 1,894 wounded), just as the number of its total attacks was rising. Fourteen attacks across Balochistan,[44] Herat,[45] Kabul,[46] Sar-e Pol,[47] and Sindh[48] provinces left at least fifty casualties each, including an *inghimasi* attack on the Sardar Daud Khan Military Hospital in Kabul.[49]

However, while ISK's total attack numbers fell in 2018, the group's total lethality continued rising in 2018 to 3,077 total casualties (1,113 killed, 1,964 wounded). Again, it was in this year that ISK was ranked among the world's deadliest organizations,[50] with its attack networks managing to inflict high levels of casualties even as its total attack numbers fell. In other words, ISK's attacks became more destructive; twenty-three attacks inflicted at least fifty casualties each across Balochistan, Jowzjan, Kabul, Khyber Pakhtunkhwa, Nangarhar, and Paktia provinces, including six such attacks in Jalalabad alone. But just as ISK's total attacks in 2019 declined, so did its total lethality, which fell by 72 percent to 878 casualties (243 killed, 635 wounded). As the next chapter shows, this decline was accompanied by a general decline in ISK's territorial control and militant base, which was largely attributable to a series of successful capture or kill operations against its operatives and leadership in major urban areas such as Kabul and Jalalabad.

A closer look at ISK's country-level variation in terms of its average lethality reveals much the same dynamics as outlined above, with one notable addition. Similar to both ISK's total attacks and total casualties inflicted, the group's average lethality across Afghanistan and Pakistan followed a similar trend of rise and decline, with average lethality per attack rising steadily from about 9.1 casualties in 2015 to more than three times that in 2018, before falling by 62 percent in 2019. However, one notable addition is the massive surge in ISK's average lethality per attack in Pakistan in 2017, in which the group conducted only nine attacks but managed to kill or wound 77.6 people on average. Possible explanations for the dramatic decline in ISK's attacks in Pakistan in 2017 were discussed earlier, but the group's massive surge in lethality that year is associated with its devastating attack on the Sufi shrine of Lal Shahbaz Qalandar in Sehwan, Sindh province, which left at least ninety people dead and over 300 injured.[51] Discounting this attack, ISK's average lethality in Pakistan in 2017 was about nineteen casualties, closer to the combined yearly average of 25.1 casualties.

Attack Locations: Porous Borders and Urban Centers

Although ISK's magnitude of attacks and lethality remained much higher in Afghanistan relative to Pakistan, the group launched attacks across a large variety of geographic locations within each country—showcasing its geographical reach. The group's attacks reached targets in twenty-four provinces between 2015 and 2019, including five provinces in Pakistan and nineteen in Afghanistan.[52] Figure 3.2 depicts the geographical spread of ISK's attacks. As the figure shows, some provinces fared much worse than others. In Pakistan, the hardest-hit provinces across all five years were Balochistan (45 attacks) and Khyber Pakhtunkhwa (thirty-one attacks, or forty-one if one includes FATA), where militant activity, in general, remains high due to the presence of Baloch separatists as well as other antistate and sectarian militant groups. In Afghanistan, the hardest-hit provinces by far were Nangarhar (169 attacks) and Kabul (eighty-one attacks), which collectively accounted for 80 percent (250 of 312) of all ISK attacks in Afghanistan over the observed period. This was in part explained by the fact that ISK had established strongholds within Nangarhar since its official formation in 2015, and Kabul's densely populated areas provided numerous viable targets for militants. Aside from Jowzjan (twenty-four attacks), all of the remaining seventeen provinces in Afghanistan suffered seven or fewer

Figure 3.2   ISK Attack Locations, 2015–2019

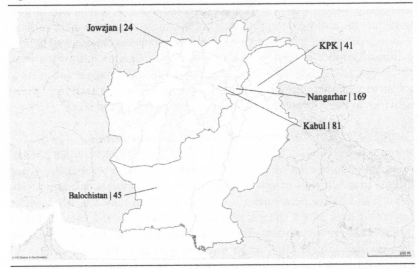

Jowzjan | 24

KPK | 41

Nangarhar | 169

Kabul | 81

Balochistan | 45

200 m

Source: Author data.

Note: Province name and total number of ISK attacks (2015–2019) listed for locations of ISK's most intense and persistent attack campaigns: Nangarhar, Kabul, Jowzjan, Khyber-Pakhtunkhwa (including FATA), and Balochistan.

attacks over the observed period. The geographic spread in terms of the number of unique provinces hit per year remained fairly consistent; after 2015, ISK managed to launch attacks in eleven to thirteen provinces from 2016 to 2019.

There are a number of reasons why these five provinces in particular— Jowzjan, Kabul, Nangarhar, Balochistan, and KPK—suffered ISK's most intense and persistent attack campaigns. First, as noted above, major urban centers such as Kabul, Jalalabad, and Quetta offer ISK and other militant groups a larger number of state and civilian targets to attack, including local minorities. Second, government counterterrorism capacity in some of these provinces has often been either strained or limited, offering a number of vulnerabilities for ISK to exploit. In some of these provinces, such as in Jowzjan and Nangarhar, tenuous government control allowed ISK to consolidate sizable territorial holdings and operational footprints at various points. In other provinces such as Balochistan, international development and investment projects—the nucleus of China's infrastructure investment in Pakistan[53]— also offered ISK opportunities to launch provocative attacks and project its transnational agenda. Third, a number of other environmental factors also played an important role, such as proximity to porous border crossings along the Durand Line between Afghanistan and Pakistan, as well as interlinked smuggling routes. However, it must be noted that ISK's selection of geographical locations overlapped with the locations of several other militant groups' operations, including Lashkar-e-Jhangvi in Balochistan, and Tehrik-e-Taliban factions in KPK. As we demonstrate in Chapter 6, a large part of ISK's operational capacity was underpinned by its strategic and tactical alliances with other groups, especially in Pakistan, which facilitated ISK's activities in these locations, helping it project its power and reach.

Target Selection: Terrorizing the State and Minorities

While it is well known that ISK targets both the state and civilian populations, an examination of ISK's target selection suggests that the group elected to attack state actors such as government officials, military installations, and police personnel more frequently than they attacked civilian targets such as public spaces, schools, and hospitals. ISK attacked state targets (221, or 53 percent) in Afghanistan and Pakistan slightly more than civilian targets (190, or 45 percent) between 2015 and 2019.[54] As Figure 3.3 shows, the difference in yearly totals (state vs. civilian) was relatively small in all years except for 2016, when ISK conducted almost twice as many attacks against state targets (fifty-nine) compared to civil-

Figure 3.3   ISK Target Selection, 2015–2019

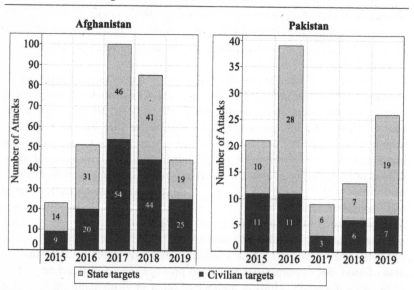

Source: Author data.

ian targets (thirty-one). This marked difference in target selection featured in both Afghanistan and Pakistan in 2016, as depicted in Figure 3.3, with Pakistan seeing a surge in attacks on state targets by 180 percent compared to the previous year.

These changes could reflect a strategic directive from ISK leadership to its networks to focus on attacking state targets. Since ISK is an antistate organization, it is possible that the group ramped up its attacks against state actors once it began to gain a footing in the region.

These shifts were likely a result of a mix of factors internal to the organization, as well as in its external environment. Given that attacking soft targets at times requires fewer resources in terms of planning requirements relative to hard targets, some of the changes in the proportion of state versus civilian targeting could be triggered by changes in counterterrorism pressure against the group in each country. Overall, ISK's attacks on civilian targets tended to result in a larger number of casualties on the whole, compared to its attacks on state targets, which could mean that the group may have elected to attack soft targets when facing increased external pressure.

Table 3.1 breaks down ISK's targets into subcategories, which were comparable in each country. The most frequent targets of ISK's attacks overall as well as broken down for both countries were members of the local police, with ninety-eight of 420 (23 percent) total attacks hitting police convoys, checkpoints, patrols, offices, training centers, and other sites. Not only did targeting the police allow ISK to provoke the state by attacking one of its core institutions, but also police targets were arguably

Table 3.1 ISK Attack Target Subcategories, 2015–2019

Target Type	Number of Attacks	Wounded	Killed	Total Casualties
Local police	98	580	345	925
Public spaces	67	1,685	728	2,413
Local government	54	1,057	573	1,630
Local military	49	221	205	426
Religious institutions	43	1,271	557	1,828
Other	40	39	99	138
Media	17	208	101	309
Unknown	14	30	18	48
Educational institutions	13	171	86	257
Foreign noncombatants	12	524	133	657
International armed forces	9	94	61	155
Health institutions	3	61	31	92
Local military and local police	1	0	10	10

Source: Author data.

easier to target compared to military installations, in part due to the fact that police forces in both countries suffered from severe inefficiencies and corruption during the observed period.

Attacks on the police inflicted the fourth-highest number of casualties, spiked by high-casualty incidents such as the attack on the Balochistan Police College in Quetta on October 24, 2016.[55] In this particular attack, three ISK-affiliated militants, all allegedly Afghan nationals,[56] entered the training center late while cadets were sleeping and opened fire, shooting many before taking hundreds of cadets hostage.[57] One of the attackers was shot by police and the other two detonated suicide belts, killing themselves and many others.[58] Many other attack plots were interdicted before they could come to fruition, including one on the Bhara Kaho Police Station in Islamabad.[59]

The next two state-target categories that saw the most attacks were government (fifty-four) and local military (forty-nine) targets, which combined left more than 2,000 casualties in the five years from 2015 to 2019. These included a variety of targeted assassinations primarily against current and former government intelligence workers,[60] but also against local politicians and prominent members of local security forces.[61] They also included larger attacks such as those against Afghanistan's Supreme Court in Kabul mentioned above,[62] as well as the Marshal Fahim National Defense University in Kabul.[63] Other state-affiliated targets included foreign noncombatants (twelve) and international armed forces (nine). ISK has also targeted diplomatic offices of Pakistan,[64] India,[65] Germany,[66] and Iraq[67] in Jalalabad and Kabul, and launched two separate attacks on Red Cross aid workers in Jowzjan in February 2017 and on the office of Save the Children in Jalalabad in January 2018, which combined left almost forty casualties.[68]

Some of ISK's worst attacks on local government targets have been against the democratic process itself, which the group staunchly opposes. Ahead of major elections in both Afghanistan and Pakistan in 2018, ISK launched a series of devastating attacks on election-related targets. On April 22, 2018, an ISK suicide attacker targeted a voter registration center in the Hazara-majority neighborhood of Dasht-e-Barchi in Kabul.[69] At least sixty were killed and 138 injured, most of whom were in a queue to receive their voter identification cards.[70] That same year, ISK targeted a procession in Kabul that included Awtar Singh Khalsa, the only Sikh candidate who planned to contest October's parliamentary elections in Afghanistan.[71] He and almost twenty others were killed in a bombing before a scheduled meeting with former President Ashraf Ghani.[72] Two weeks later, ISK claimed responsibility for a suicide bombing targeting a rally held by Siraj Raisani—candidate for the Balochistan Awami Party's (BAP) Provincial Assembly seat—in Mastung, Balochistan.[73] Raisani was killed alongside almost 150 rally-goers.[74] Then, on July 25, 2018, another ISK suicide bomber targeted a polling station in the provincial capital Quetta, killing over thirty.[75] It was a brutal months-long attacks campaign, one designed to intimidate and coerce local populations out of participating in elections, a fundamental pillar of any healthy democracy.

Ahead of attacks on local government and military targets, ISK targeted public spaces the second most frequently (sixty-seven), inflicting the most casualties by far of any target type, as noted above (2,413 total). These attacks usually targeted highly trafficked and vulnerable spaces such as markets, parks, and public transport systems, and seemed intended to garner attention and publicity. One of the first high-profile and high-casualty attacks linked to ISK, in fact, was on a bus traveling in Safoora Goth, Karachi, in May 2015 that was carrying Ismaili Shiite passengers.[76] The attack, which became known as the Safoora Goth massacre, highlights the fact that a large number of ISK attacks in public spaces have been directed at religious minorities outside their institutions and houses of worship. As noted previously, ISK adopts an extreme sectarian stance, whereby any 'Muslim' who does not subscribe to ISK's Salafi jihadist ideology is deemed to be an apostate or rejectionist, and as such, a legitimate target. In line with this approach, ISK's more recent attacks in Kabul, Herat, and Jalalabad have similarly targeted buses and minivans carrying predominantly Shiite passengers.[77]

These sectarian attacks against religious minorities in public spaces compound on top of other attacks against religious institutions; such attacks yielded the second-highest level of total casualties (1,828) compared to other types of attacks. These attacks have not just targeted Shiite houses of worship; Christians,[78] Hanafi,[79] Sufi,[80] other Sunni groups, and other religious institutions have all been targeted by ISK. Many of these attacks have inflicted tremendous loss of life, such as two separate attacks on Hanafi clerical scholars in Kabul in June and later in November 2018, which left nearly 200 casualties combined.[81] However, nearly half of ISK's attacks on religious institutions have targeted the region's Shiite communities (twenty-one, or 49 percent), including ethnic Hazaras in Afghanistan. Between 2015 and 2019, these attacks centered predominantly around Kabul, but other provinces have been hit too such as Balkh, Balochistan, Ghazni, KPK, Paktia, Punjab, Sindh, and Herat, where an attack against Shiite worshippers at the Jawadia mosque in Herat city in August 2017 left nearly a hundred dead and injured in its wake.[82]

As mentioned previously in this chapter, the Dasht-e-Barchi settlement in western Kabul, home to tens of thousands of ethnic Hazaras, has suffered consistent targeting by ISK since the group's inception. In addition to decades of political underrepresentation and discriminatory practices under the Taliban in the 1990s, the Karzai and Ghani governments, and the Taliban again after 2021, the terror inflicted by ISK has only served to shatter the community's faith in existing security guarantors.[83] The group's attacks have targeted not just Shiite and ethnic Hazara religious institutions and public spaces (including transportation), but also their media, educational, and health institutions. Hazara residents have also been targeted when gathered in public squares, exercising their right to protest peacefully.[84] On July 23, 2016, for example, a twin suicide bombing targeted protestors in Deh Mazang square, Kabul, where a crowd of mostly Hazaras had gathered to protest the Ghani government's decision to bypass their region in the development of a major power transmission project linking Afghanistan to other Central Asian states.[85] Almost a hundred protestors were killed, and hundreds more were injured.[86] The following year on December 28, 2017, an attack on the Shiite Tabayan Cultural Center in Kabul where students had gathered for a discussion forum left at least 130 dead or wounded.[87]

In sum, ISK's attempts to instigate sectarian violence go beyond the targeting of religious institutions, and instead include a broad spectrum of targets where members of the minority communities may be present. The group's attacks on other civil society sectors such as media, educational, and health organizations have also sometimes been sectarian in nature, although they are generally directed at any institution that is perceived as a product of Western influence or that goes against the principles of sharia according to ISK's ideology. Such attacks are not always high-casualty *inghimasi* and suicide operations either, but include targeted assassinations of notable figures.

Tactics: Leveraging Suicide and Inghimasi Attacks for High Lethality

ISK employed a range of violent tactics from 2015 to 2019 in order to advance its attack strategy, with suicide attacks remaining a constant throughout the years. Guerrilla-style assaults, rocket and mortar attacks, targeted assassinations, *inghimasi* attacks, and deadly suicide bombings through vehicle- and human-borne improvised explosive devices have all featured in ISK's arsenal. While certainly not a unique phenomenon within the Islamic State movement,[88] publicly known use of drone technology by ISK in Afghanistan and Pakistan to date appears to have been limited to one isolated plot. Reportedly, a university professor and four other accomplices were arrested in May 2017 by the Sindh Counter-Terrorism Department for planning to carry out targeted attacks in Karachi using improvised explosive devices (IEDs) affixed to unmanned drones on behalf of the Islamic State.[89] New technologies such as drones may have some appeal among ISK's supporters beyond this isolated case, but for now it remains an anomaly. Of much more frequent use have been the *inghimasi* and suicide attacks that are the focus of this section, given their resource-intensive preparation and highly lethal potential.

Based on statements by counterterrorism officials and previous scholarly work,[90] it appears that ISK, like its namesake in Iraq and Syria, maintained a separate department for its suicide attack operatives, what has previously been referred to as the "Martyrs' Brigade" in Iraq and other settings.[91] From 2015 to 2019, ISK is reported to have conducted at least 119 suicide attacks, as shown in Figure 3.1. The vast majority of these attacks (eighty-eight, or 74 percent) occurred in 2017 and 2018, ISK's most lethal years on record, which demonstrates ISK's reliance on suicide attacks to maintain high levels of lethality. What is striking, however, is the rapid increase in the number of ISK suicide attacks in consecutive years from 2015 (two) to 2016 (nineteen) and then 2017 (forty-two), as well as in the number of total casualties inflicted by these attacks (148 to 1,202 to 1,844, respectively). Although between 2017 and 2018, the number of reported suicide attacks rose only slightly from 2017 (forty-two) to 2018 (forty-six), associated total casualties continued to rise by significant margins (1,844 to 2,710). However, as ISK came under increased pressure from 2019 onward and lost substantial manpower and operational resources, its ability to maintain previous frequencies of suicide attacks was similarly constrained, and the number of suicide attacks fell sharply to ten attacks in 2019 (407 casualties). Overall, ISK's total suicide attack lethality far exceeded the destruction caused by other attacks; even though suicide attacks made up only about a quarter of ISK's total attacks, as shown in Table 3.2, they accounted for over 60 percent of its causalities.

The rapid rise of ISK's suicide attack capabilities is particularly concerning given the intensive training, planning, and resources required for these operations. ISK appears to have taken a number of measures to bolster its suicide attack capabilities, including implementation of plans to better protect trainers and trainees at its camps and dividing its explosives battalion into separate departments,[92] among other reforms. But in October 2017, a US airstrike destroyed a key ISK suicide martyr training camp close to its main operational stronghold in Achin, Nangarhar, killing two senior trainers in the process.[93] Despite the strike's success, ISK's total number of suicide attacks and casualties inflicted only rose the following

Table 3.2   Lethality by Tactic Type, 2015–2019

Tactic	Number of Attacks	Total Killed	Total Wounded	Total Casualties
Nonsuicide attacks	424	2,017	1,710	3,727
Suicide attacks	119	2,037	4,274	6,311

Source: Author data.

year. While such strikes can be effective in degrading the available pool of operational resources and expertise, it appears that ISK's suicide attack operations had developed beyond the point where a single strike on a training camp could alone contain the group's attack operations. Broader efforts would be necessary to fully degrade ISK's operational capacity—including its suicide attack operations—to the relatively low levels witnessed in 2019. Chapter 4 examines these dynamics in greater detail.

In addition to "traditional" suicide bombings, ISK's *inghimasi* attacks, as noted above, have become one of the group's deadliest attack tactics to date. These attacks differ from traditional suicide bombings in the sense that their success does not necessarily depend on the attackers' deaths, but the nature of the attacks make their deaths highly likely.[94] The Islamic State movement defines *inghimasi* operations as ones in which "one or more people plunge into an enemy position in which they are outnumbered, usually resulting in their death," hence the descriptive Arabic term *inghimasi* (literally "one who plunges"). One or more attackers are equipped with assault rifles and usually at least one suicide vest to detonate when the attacker becomes trapped or engaged with opposition forces, making their likely death imminent. *Inghimasi* attacks are frequently among ISK's—and the broader Islamic State movement's—most lethal and barbaric attacks. The movement divides these attacks into three categories: (1) battlefield attacks against enemy positions during clashes and ongoing battles; (2) attacks against security forces' bases and offices; and (3) attacks in civilian settings against soft targets.[95]

The attack on the Balochistan Police College in October 2016 discussed earlier in this chapter is a prime example of the second category. Each of the attackers was equipped with assault rifles, which they used to first target and kill the sentry guard before entering the grounds of the training college and firing upon cadets and trainers.[96] When Pakistani security forces arrived on the scene to engage the attackers, two of them detonated their suicide vests.[97] The March 2017 attack on the Sardar Daud Khan Military Hospital—located across the road from the former US embassy in Kabul—is an example of the third category. ISK gunmen disguised as medics stormed the hospital armed with light weapons and explosives devices after one of the attackers self-detonated at the gate, allowing the others to gain entry.[98] The attackers killed at least thirty and wounded more than sixty before entrenching themselves on the upper floors of the hospital and engaging security forces when they arrived. All of the attackers were killed after an hours-long engagement.[99]

From 2015 to 2019, ISK perpetrated at least twenty known *inghimasi* attacks. Combined, these attacks left 1,874 casualties—around seventy-two casualties per attack. The vast majority fell in ISK's peak years of 2016–2018; during its broader operational decline in 2019, the group was able to launch only one known *inghimasi* attack on a construction company in Jalalabad.[100] As other scholars have noted, *inghimasi* attacks offer tremendous propaganda value for groups like ISK,[101] serving to boost organizational morale while inflicting terror on multiple targets. These attacks also further differentiate ISK from its main militant rivals, such as the Taliban,[102] signaling a fierce rejectionist brand to potential recruits. That ISK was only able to launch one *inghimasi* attack in 2019 is indicative of the group's substantial decline in that year.

ISK's Resurgence in 2020 and 2021

After the group's period of relative decline in 2019, many Afghanistan-Pakistan observers and policymakers considered ISK to be largely defunct. On February 29, 2020, US officials and Taliban representatives signed an agreement setting out a path for the complete withdrawal of US and NATO troops from Afghanistan within a fourteen-month timeline.[103] The deal was a historic victory for the insurgents, and marked what senior Taliban representative Mohammed Naeem called "the end of the war in Afghanistan."[104] Less than one week later, on March 6, ISK attackers opened fire on a gathering of ethnic Hazaras in Kabul who were commemorating the death of famous Hazara politician Abdul Ali Mazari.[105] The former chief executive officer of Afghanistan, Abdullah Abdullah, and other politicians managed to escape unhurt, but over thirteen commemorators were killed and dozens injured in what former President Ashraf Ghani called a "crime against humanity."[106]

Later that month, on March 25, multiple ISK *inghimasi* attackers stormed a crowded Sikh temple in Kabul and opened fire.[107] At least twenty-five were killed and several more wounded before an hours-long hunt for the assailants ensued.[108] The March 2020 Sikh temple and Hazara commemoration attacks were some of the worst in months, and would ultimately signal the coming resurgence of ISK's attack campaigns following a period of relative operational decline. As the Taliban made sweeping gains nationwide and the United States–led withdrawal from Afghanistan continued into 2021, ISK would ramp up the intensity with some of its most prolific and deadly attack campaigns to date.

A New Leader in Uncertain Times

Following the attacks in March 2020, ISK focused the vast majority of its operations through April and early May on local military and police targets, the Taliban, and international armed forces stationed at Bagram Airfield in Parwan province. Most of these operations left few if any casualties, and the attacks on Bagram Airfield were confirmed by NATO officials not to have caused any casualties.[109] Then, on May 12, the group launched two massive attacks within hours of each other in one of the deadliest days of violence since the signing of the peace deal between the Taliban and the United States. In the Khewa (Kuz Kunar) district about a hundred miles east of Kabul, a suicide bomber detonated his explosives vest in the middle of a funeral ceremony where mourners had gathered to commemorate the loss of the district's police commander, Shaykh Akram, killing and wounding dozens.[110] That same day in Kabul, multiple ISK *inghimasi* fighters dressed as police officers entered a hospital run by Doctors Without Borders (MSF) in the majority Hazara Dasht-e-Barchi settlement.[111] The attackers killed over twenty—mostly nurses, mothers, and babies in the hospital's maternity ward—and wounded several more in one of the most barbaric attacks to hit Kabul in decades. Afghan special forces managed to rescue around a hundred women and children, and graphic images from the attack showed soldiers carrying a newborn baby wrapped in a blood-stained blanket from the hospital.[112]

For ISK, the May 12 attacks came at a crucial juncture; as noted above, many believed ISK to be a largely defunct organization given the decline in its attacks in 2019 compared to its peak years. As the next chapter will show in detail, ISK had hemorrhaged thousands of its members and significant territorial holdings prior to 2020. From late 2019 to early 2020, at least 1,400 ISK fighters and their families surrendered to Afghan security forces,[113] and Afghan intelligence forces arrested the group's top leader, Abdullah Orakzai, also known as Aslam Farooqi, in April 2020.[114] Farooqi's predecessor—the recently demoted Zia ul-Haq, also known as Abu Omar Khorasani[115]—was arrested shortly after Farooqi on May 11, just one day before the May 12 attacks.[116] The loss of two top leaders in short succession was a significant blow to ISK, and despite a long history of ultraviolent attacks, the violence of May 12 seemed almost desperate in its barbarity— a display of resolve in the face of crippling organizational losses and uncertainty. Even with these spectacular displays of violence, ISK once again needed to select a new leader to head the organization, and fairly quickly.

In stepped a relatively young commander and Kabul native, Sanaullah Ghafari (also known as Shahab al-Muhajir). Salafist in his ideological leanings,[117] a trained engineer, and graduate of Kabul University,[118] al-Muhajir came from a family steeped in the jihadist tradition. His family belonged to the Hizb-i-Islami Gulbuddin (HIG) party, one of the major jihadist factions that fought against US-allied forces.[119] Al-Muhajir would go on to join HIG and then later the Haqqani network, gravitating around the Haqqani's attack networks in Kabul.[120] Not long after ISK's emergence in Afghanistan, he switched allegiances and joined the group. After bolstering ISK's Kabul network—the entity responsible for some of the worst ISK attacks over its several years of existence—al-Muhajir was appointed deputy head of the Kabul cell by IS-Central, which positioned him as a senior leader in the organization more broadly.[121] As years of manpower and territorial losses forced ISK to downgrade its insurgency and focus on urban attacks (see Chapter 4), al-Muhajir's expertise in leading and coordinating urban operations, as well as his expansive social and militant networks in Kabul, ultimately made him a suitable choice to head the group,[122] revamp the group's operations, and bolster its ranks.[123] His personal connections to individuals and families with significant political influence played an important role in facilitating ISK's activities,[124] in one instance helping ISK obtain access to arms licenses from Afghan government officials.[125]

When he first assumed power after the arrests of his predecessors, there was a shroud of secrecy surrounding al-Muhajir.[126] Not much was known about the new ISK leader, and a May 2020 UN report had even speculated that a Syrian national might assume the leadership of ISK.[127] The uncertainty only mounted as months went by without al-Muhajir making his first address—and perhaps from ISK's perspective, there was little to address. As Figure 3.4 shows, attack operations were historically low, with ISK conducting only two attacks in April and three in June 2020.[128] Finally, in early July 2020, al-Muhajir made his first announcement as ISK's new leader via official IS-Central and ISK media platforms.[129] Al-Muhajir heralded a new period of militancy for the group, one defined by a strategy of urban warfare. He also vowed to aid those ISK members who were being held in security facilities run by the previous Afghan government. He offered amnesty to those who had surrendered to the former Afghan government,[130] encouraging them to appear in ISK courts, and inviting them to renew their pledges of loyalty.[131] On August 2, al-Muhajir delivered upon his promises.

Figure 3.4   ISK Attacks, 2020–2021

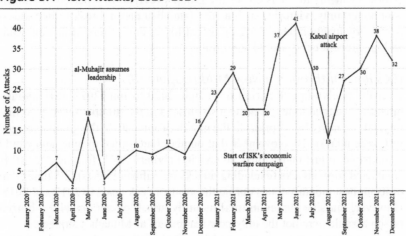

Source: Author data.

On Sunday night, a car bomb detonated outside a prison in Jalalabad City and breached the security perimeter.[132] Around ten assailants armed with assault rifles stormed into the prison, firing on prison guards, and engaging in what would become a twenty-hour gun battle that would leave twenty-nine dead, forty-eight wounded, and hundreds of inmates unaccounted for. Of the prison's approximately 1,800 inmates, about one-third were ISK militants or accused loyalists.[133] While exact numbers of escapees were difficult to verify in the immediate aftermath of the assault, later tallies would place the number of escaped ISK inmates at around 280 individuals.[134]

The attack on the Jalalabad prison in August 2020 was one of ISK's most sophisticated and ambitious attacks to date. It reinforced al-Muhajir's reputation within the organization, and among pro–Islamic State supporters across the globe. On August 3, ISK released a message from its spokesman, Sultan Aziz Azzam, trumpeting the attack's success, the bravery of ISK fighters, and the ingenuity of the group's new leader.[135] Of course, this is not to say that al-Muhajir has been solely responsible for the revival of ISK in Afghanistan. The more accurate evaluation is that ISK was able to leverage the skills of a leader in a rapidly evolving environment, one who was successful in identifying opportunities to exploit and adapt ISK's strategy and tactics to present conditions. Having already established a wide network of operational alliances while differentiating itself from dominant groups (discussed further in Chapters 5 and 6), ISK's new leader was well-positioned to exploit new opportunities stemming from an unconditional US withdrawal, the collapse of the Afghan government, and the assumption of power by an internationally isolated Taliban government. ISK's new leader successfully navigated the organization through historic lows by identifying critical elements to focus on for the group's revival. In a period of significant uncertainty, victories such as the Jalalabad prison break rallied a desperate organization hamstrung by recent losses and unsure of its new leadership. More success would soon follow.

ISK's Revival through a New Modus Operandi

Over the twelve-month period from June 2020 to June 2021, ISK's attack operations surged to levels previously unseen in the group's seven-year history, taking many by surprise. In the month of June 2020, the group managed just three attacks. By November that number had tripled to nine, and would again triple to just under thirty attacks in February 2021. In June 2021, ISK conducted forty attacks (excluding attacks on Taliban targets), 2.5 times that of its highest monthly totals during the group's peak years in 2017 and 2018. However, massive surges in total monthly attack operations and a brazen prison assault were not the only new features of al-Muhajir's strategy.

Sometime between April and May 2021, ISK issued a warning to the previous Afghan government after news surfaced that the latter was intent on repatriating ISK's captured foreign fighters to their home countries.[136] In retaliation for this proposed policy, ISK spokesman Sultan Aziz Azzam warned of an upcoming period of "economic warfare" against infrastructure targets. Then, starting in May 2021, ISK began targeting electricity pylons and oil tankers in multiple provinces including Baghlan, Kabul, Kunduz, Nangarhar, Parwan, and Samangan,[137] launching thirty-three such attacks during the three months from May to July. ISK's "economic warfare" campaign draws its inspiration from the Islamic State's insurgency in Iraq and Syria.[138] ISK and other Islamic State affiliates across the globe from Libya to Nigeria to the Philippines have deployed a similar strategy, oftentimes in coordination with IS-Central. According to the Islamic State's own propaganda, attacks targeting economic resources and other critical infrastructure can generate uncertainty within local populations, delegitimize the existing government, and also bleed opponents' resources by compelling them to expend additional resources in securing locations and targets. Starting in July 2020, attacks of this style grew increasingly common across the Islamic State's global nexus,[139] and al-Muhajir and his lieutenants led the campaign by example. ISK unleashed an economic warfare blitz in contiguous provinces from Kunduz down to Nangarhar just as the Taliban made rapid gains through military offensives across Afghanistan. But by the end of July 2021, right at the height of the United States–led withdrawal and Taliban takeover, ISK's campaign suddenly came to a halt.

On August 6, 2021, the Taliban captured the capital of Nimroz province in southern Afghanistan.[140] In a matter of days, more than ten other provincial capitals fell including Jalalabad and Nangarhar.[141] By August 15, Taliban fighters began entering Kabul—the only remaining major urban area still under the previous government's control.[142] The Taliban's swift takeover of Afghanistan surprised many including US officials and their allies, and additional US troops were deployed to aid in the orderly and safe drawdown of US and allied personnel.[143] After the fall of Kabul, evacuation efforts continued out of Hamid Karzai International Airport, strained by the thousands of Afghans attempting to flee the Taliban's new regime before the August 31 deadline. In rare photos, US service members and Taliban fighters could be seen side-by-side as they collectively oversaw the security of the evacuation.[144] As the final days of the withdrawal came closer, however, concerns grew about a potential attack amid the already chaotic atmosphere. On August 25, the US, United Kingdom, and Australian governments warned their citizens to avoid the Kabul airport due to the high threat of a terrorist attack, and US service members began urging crowds of Afghans to leave the area.[145] The next day, terror struck.

On August 26, an ISK suicide bomber named Abdul Rahman al-Logari approached Abbey Gate, one of the key airport checkpoints manned by US service members. During the Taliban takeover earlier that summer, al-Logari had escaped prison alongside more than 12,000 other prisoners including an estimated 1,800 ISK fighters.[146] Weeks later, he detonated his explosives vest in the midst of a crowd at Abbey Gate, setting off a loud explosion that brought the evacuation to a standstill.[147] At least 183 were killed including thirteen US service members,[148] the worst US casualty event in Afghanistan in a decade.[149]

Following the Kabul airport attack and the conclusion of the United States–led withdrawal days later, ISK's targeting agenda expanded and gained momentum. On October 8, 2021, one of the group's suicide bombers targeted the Shiite Said Abad mosque in Kunduz, killing or wounding nearly 200 worshippers.[150] The following week on October 15, another ISK suicide bomber targeted the Imam Bargah mosque in Kandahar—the largest of the city's Shiite mosques right in the middle of the Taliban's heartland—during prayer hours, killing or wounded at least 135 inside.[151] Since then, ISK's attacks on Afghanistan's Shiite communities have largely reverted to attacks against ethnic Hazaras and other Shiite targets in western Kabul, including multiple attacks on minibuses in November 2021,[152] one of which killed Hamid Saighani, a prominent journalist for the Ariana television network.[153]

But after the Taliban takeover, ISK turned its main operational focus to Afghanistan's new rulers. From around mid-September to the end of December 2021, ninety-seven of 127 (76 percent) ISK-claimed attacks targeted Taliban personnel and checkpoints. Around 60 percent of ISK's attacks on the Taliban occurred in Nangarhar province, where ISK previously exercised substantial territorial control.[154] Most of these attacks left small numbers of Taliban casualties, and so despite the broader surge in ISK's total attack numbers in 2021 as well as mass-casualty attacks, ISK's average casualty count per attack in 2021 (5.5) is the lowest of any year on record.[155] Overall, while ISK ramped up its attacks, these have been targeted and small operations, focused on taking out Taliban members. Even so, the group's new attack strategy has stretched the Taliban's resources thin, and harmed perceptions of their ability to contain terrorism. Targeted assassinations against civil society activists, media figures, former government personnel, community elders, and prominent voices in the Salafist community in northeast Afghanistan, in particular, have undermined the Taliban's credibility as the country's new security guarantors.[156] ISK's attacks on local Taliban units outlined above have also provoked the latter to expose its heavy-handed and draconian approach to counterinsurgency,[157] which despite mediation efforts has alienated large segments of the population through crackdowns, reprisals, mosque closures, abductions, and extrajudicial killings.[158] Toward the end of 2021, the Taliban deployed over 1,300 additional fighters to help bolster security in Nangarhar. Whether the Taliban can effectively contain ISK is an open question at the time of this book's publication, but either result will not come without serious loss of life and civilian displacement.[159]

ISK's International Operational Nexus

Around 2016–2017, the Islamic State's core media outlets began highlighting alternative destinations for its global supporters if they could not reach the so-called caliphate in Iraq and Syria.[160] One of those destinations was the Afghanistan-Pakistan region. Not long after, a young American named Naser Almadaoji was arrested in October 2018 at John Glenn International Airport in Columbus, Ohio.[161] Almadaoji, nineteen years of age, booked a flight to Astana, Kazakhstan, wherefrom he planned to be smuggled into Afghanistan to join ISK and receive training.[162] Almadaoji was not the first foreigner to try to join ISK, nor would he be the last. Individuals of over a dozen nationalities including France, China, India, and the Philippines have fought and died for ISK over the years.[163] Others, like Almadaoji, were intercepted before they could join. An Australian named Isaac El Matari allegedly made plans to join the group in 2019 before his arrest by Australian authorities,[164] and in August 2021 Taliban fighters detained two suspected British nationals allegedly attempting to link up with ISK.[165]

In addition to its ability to attract foreign fighters, ISK's role within the Islamic State movement as a node for transnational attacks had drawn scrutiny even before the Taliban's takeover. In July 2018, a UN analytical monitoring report noted the recent identification and interdiction of attack plots in Europe emanating from ISK in Afghanistan.[166] In February 2019, the former head of US Central Command, General Joseph Votel, warned that ISK had emerged as a major threat capable of carrying out attacks in the United States.[167] Another US intelligence official warned that ISK was using its members' social media accounts to acquire contacts in the United States,[168] possibly to coordinate attacks on US soil similar to the "virtual planner" strategy used by IS-Central from Syria.[169] Two months later, in April 2019, senior UN counterterrorism official Edmund Fitton-Brown raised concerns that ISK might develop a substantial external operations capability from Afghanistan,[170] concerns he echoed again in February 2020.[171] Then, in April 2020, the German government announced that it had foiled a plot to attack US and NATO facilities in Germany with a nexus both to IS-Central and to ISK.[172] According to security officials, four Tajik plotters had coordinated with two senior Islamic State leaders, one based in Syria and the other with ISK in Afghanistan.[173]

Since the Taliban's takeover, warnings of ISK's persistent transnational linkages and attack capabilities have only continued. In October 2021, Senior Pentagon official Colin Kahl warned that ISK could develop the capability to launch attacks against the United States within six to twelve months.[174] A month later, the US State and Treasury Departments announced the designations of four ISK-linked individuals as "specially designated global terrorists." They included al-Muhajir, ISK spokesman Sultan Aziz Azzam, and a senior leader in ISK's Kabul attack network named Maulawi Rajab, as well as a key international financier named Ismatullah Khalozai.[175]

Khalozai was believed to have operated both a Turkey-based hawala business and a United Arab Emirates–based financing scheme involving the sale of luxury items to help transfer and raise funds for ISK's operations. Khalozai was also accused of running human smuggling operations for ISK, including personally smuggling an ISK courier from Afghanistan into Turkey.[176]

ISK poses a persistent operational threat both in terms of transnational attacks, especially in the region, and foreign fighter recruitment. It has demonstrated the ambition and propensity to inspire international appeal, support, and action, albeit on a scale that so far has been much smaller than IS-Central in the mid-2010s. However, assessments of ISK's international operational nexus need to be addressed with healthy scrutiny. While dynamics can change rapidly—especially in an environment as permissive as ISK finds itself today—the group's external operations threat has since been revised down by US officials. By the end of 2021, the US Defense Intelligence Agency qualified earlier statements that ISK could develop an external operations capability within six to twelve months, stating:

> The DIA assessed that ISIS-K could develop directed external plots against the West, including the U.S. homeland, within the next year if the group prioritizes developing such a capability. However, the DIA assessed that ISIS-K is prioritizing attacks within Afghanistan over external operations. Regionally, ISIS-K maintains connections to fighters from countries across Central and South Asia, probably making the group a threat to U.S. interests in those countries.[177]

The Department of Defense's updated assessments placed new, important qualifications on its earlier statements. As the preceding passage highlights, there are sharp distinctions between an organization such as ISK maintaining interest in conducting external operations, and prioritizing those operations for development over other strategic focuses. If ISK were to develop external operations capabilities on a scale similar to the Islamic State during its peak years from 2014 to 2016, it would likely need to emulate three important qualities that made IS-Central so successful. These qualities could in turn provide key benchmarks for assessing ISK's external operations capabilities going forward.

First, IS-Central developed an independent external operations wing that it staffed with "virtual planners"—foreign nationals who networked recruits in the United States, United Kingdom, Europe, and elsewhere across the globe.[178] These virtual planners not only encouraged and facilitated recruits' travel and attack plotting, but also engaged in direct plotting.[179] One unit nicknamed by the US Federal Bureau of Investigation (FBI) as "The Legion" involved around a dozen virtual planners[180]—most of them English-speaking Western nationals—who operated out of Islamic State–held territory in Raqqa, Syria.[181] The group's most prominent operative, a British national named Junaid Hussain, held a celebrity status within the Islamic State movement before his death in a drone strike in July 2015.[182] His successor, Siful Sujan, was responsible for coordinating the only publicly known Islamic State–funded plot in the United States at the time.[183] Maintaining a substantive network with dedicated external operations focus such as "The Legion" would be a critical element of any major ISK external attacks capacity, one that could move beyond inspiring attacks to directly plotting them. As of the time of writing, no such network is known to exist on a scale even close to that of "The Legion."

Second, IS-Central developed a comprehensive mobilization infrastructure to facilitate the travel and processing of foreign recruits who tried to join the group in Syria and Iraq.[184] Newly arrived recruits were placed in indoctrination camps and filtered into groups based on their primary language.[185] After that, they would receive weapons and explosives training, and some would be asked to join external operations units such as those outlined earlier.[186] Afghanistan today is a much more inhospitable environment for prospective foreign fighters owing to the Taliban's commitments to the international community,[187] but perhaps more importantly due to the Taliban's own self-interest in containing ISK. While visibility into ISK's activities has declined significantly since the fall of Kabul, there is little evidence to suggest that ISK has either the capacity or the risk appetite to stand up a major foreign fighter processing hub on the same scale as IS-Central and potentially risk exposing itself to Afghan Taliban fighters and over-the-horizon strikes.[188] That said, the group has cleared and established routes for foreign fighters to pass into friendly ISK custody in the past. Recall the excerpt from captured ISK correspondences detailed at the very start of this book: "Several areas have been combed of the idolatrous Taliban movement— areas in which the Taliban were present, such as the areas of Naray Obeh, Ghardi and Karkanay, as well as the area of Maydanak. With that, routes have been opened to allow the entry of the foreign fighters into the governorate, with praise to Allah."[189] If ISK were to expand on past efforts and build out an IS-Central-styled foreign fighter processing infrastructure, it would provide a risky signal that ISK is not only succeeding in its transnational recruiting agenda, but comfortable enough in its strategic posture to risk exposing members to targeting by various state and nonstate actors.

And third, IS-Central developed a formidable media production and dissemination apparatus to reach a global audience.[190] The group released content in well over thirty languages, cohered and coordinated through its Central Media Directorate in Iraq and Syria.[191] Potential foreign recruits were shown videos of fighters who looked like them and spoke their languages, engaged in heroic acts on the battlefield and in Islamic State–controlled cities.[192] As former senior US counterterrorism official Alberto Fernandez noted, "By spring of 2014, the focus of Islamic State propaganda finally shifts away from rival Islamist factions and internecine squabbles and starts to target a wider audience."[193] By contrast, ISK's media capacities since its inception have been much more limited and the group is focused on reaching local populations through narratives that target and delegitimize the Taliban in particular.[194] Since 2020, however, ISK has increasingly highlighted the diverse identities of regional fighters who conducted attacks on behalf of the group,[195] including Indian nationals who perpetrated the Sikh temple attack in Kabul in March 2020 and the August 2020 Jalalabad prison-break operations,[196] and a Uighur Muslim who perpetrated the October 2021 Kunduz mosque bombing.[197] ISK appears to be deepening its strategy of regional recruitment, including among Central Asians, Indians, Chinese, and Kashmir-based militants.[198] Whether the group is able to meaningfully expand its recruitment pool beyond the immediate region in the coming months and years remains to be seen, but two important transnational narratives will continue to shape those efforts. The first is a staunchly anti-Taliban platform that paints ISK's rival as a puppet of a greater international conspiracy led by the United States, Russia, China, and other countries against "true believers." The second is the historical draw of the Afghanistan-Pakistan region outlined in Chapter 2 as the lands from which the Messiah's army will emerge, and as the legacy of jihadist heroes who expelled foreign invaders.

The Rise, Fall, and Resurgence of ISK's Operational Capacity

Over the seven years from 2015 to 2021, ISK pursued a comprehensive attack operations strategy that was consistently reinforced through the group's messaging campaigns. In that same time period, ISK's operational capacity has gone through serious ebbs and flows, but the group's resilience ultimately led to its resurgence. Overall yearly attack numbers and total casualties inflicted by ISK attacks rose steadily from 2015 to 2018 before falling sharply in 2019 and then resurging just as sharply from 2020 to 2021. Total yearly numbers of districts affected by ISK attacks have followed a similar pattern, as have other metrics including the use of deadly tactics such as suicide bombings and *inghimasi* operations.

The majority of ISK's operational focus has been on Afghanistan, where the group conducted three times as many attacks as it did in Pakistan, taking advantage of the weaker socioeconomic and political environment within the country. The damage, trauma, and loss of life inflicted in both countries, however, cannot be chalked up to tallies alone. Of the total provinces between both countries that suffered ISK attacks from 2015 to 2021, the worst-hit regions in Pakistan were Balochistan (fifty-one) and Khyber-Pakhtunkhwa (fifty-eight attacks) provinces (both of which share a border with Afghanistan and have the presence of various militant groups),[199] while the worst hit in Afghanistan were Nangarhar (443), Kabul (182), and Jowzjan (fifty-one) provinces, which includes the most recent wave of ISK's targeted campaign against the Taliban.

Over the course of seven years, ISK attacked state targets slightly more than civilian targets in both countries, but the most frequent targets were members of local police forces (161 attacks), followed by attacks on local government (128) and military targets (118). To undermine the state system as a whole, ISK specifically singled out pro-democratic targets such as election rallies, political candidates, and voter registration centers for some of its most destructive suicide bombings, as well as targets affiliated with foreign democratic governments such as diplomats and humanitarian organizations. Religious institutions and gatherings of the region's minorities, including Christian, Hanafi, Sufi, other Sunni groups, and Zikri (Mahdavia) communities, have suffered tremendously at the hands of ISK, but Shiite communities in both countries have suffered the most, particularly Afghanistan's ethnic Hazaras. In addition to houses of worship, ISK has targeted these communities in public spaces including transportation, markets, and parks, as well as in their media, educational, and health institutions.

A broad spectrum of targeting tactics underpinned ISK's comprehensive attack operations strategy. Guerrilla-style assaults, rocket and mortar attacks, remote IED explosions, targeted assassinations, suicide bombings through vehicle- and human-borne IEDs, and deadly *inghimasi* operations have all featured in those tactics. Suicide attacks in particular remained a prominent tactic that accounted for the majority of casualties inflicted by ISK in both countries. Most notable was the rapid increase in the number of suicide attacks the group conducted from 2015 to 2017, and the increasingly lethal impact of those attacks. The *inghimasi* operations undertaken by the group were just as, if not more, lethal on average. As time went on, these *inghimasi* operations grew more sophisticated, eventually culminating in one of the most complex prison-break operations of any Islamic State affiliate worldwide.

After a dramatic downturn in its attack operations in 2019, ISK turned a new page under the leadership of Shahab al-Muhajir in 2020—demonstrating its resilience and determination to stay relevant. Despite his relatively young age, al-Muhajir's prior militant training, expansive local connections and expertise, and experience at the helm of ISK's Kabul attack network before his appointment as the group's top leader appears to have left him more than qualified to revamp the group's operational capacity. The reversal of ISK's fortunes under al-Muhajir highlights an important advantage available to the group by nature of its location within the Afghanistan-Pakistan region. The fact that ISK is based in one of the world's most militant saturated regions provides it with ample opportunity to recruit from a large pool of experienced militants, which we discuss in more detail later in this book. Although the specter of a truly transnational operational nexus has yet to come to fruition at the time of writing, ISK's new insurgency against the Taliban regime and continued attacks on civilian targets has so far proven incredibly draining for Afghanistan's new rulers, who are struggling to transition to a legitimate state actor, provide human security, and avert debilitating humanitarian crises.[200]

Overall, the evolution of ISK's operational strategy and tactics as discussed in this chapter demonstrates the group's tenacity and ability to prolong its survival in the region. Recent developments, along with ISK's violent campaigns over time, strongly indicate that ISK is unlikely to be neutralized in the immediate future as it continues to battle state actors while intimidating civilian populations. In the next chapter, we provide an overview of intense state-led military operations against the group and associated costs for ISK, which further show the extent of the losses that ISK had to recover from in order to make a comeback in later years.

Notes

1. Internal ISK document, Combating Terrorism Center Library.
2. Popalzai and Mehsud, "ISIS Militant Bomber on Motorbike Kills 33 at Bank in Afghanistan."
3. Sherzad, "Afghan Blast Kills 33."
4. BBC, "Pakistan Hospital Bomb Attack Kills Dozens in Quetta."
5. Zafar, "Quetta Weeps Again."
6. Internal ISK document, Combating Terrorism Center Library.
7. Jadoon and Mines, *Broken but Not Defeated.*
8. Ibid.
9. Gonzales, "U.S. Officials Confirm Death of Senior ISIS Leader."
10. Institute for Economics and Peace, *Global Terrorism Index 2019.*
11. Neuman, "Islamic State Claims Responsibility for Deadly Attack Aimed at Afghan Hazaras."
12. Yusafzai, "Islamic State Claims Attack on Pakistan Police Academy."
13. Lawrence, "ISIS Attack Targets US Troops at Bagram Airfield."
14. Rasmussen, "Kabul: At Least 90 Killed."
15. Popalzai and Narayan, "20 Dead in Suicide Blast Outside Afghan Supreme Court in Kabul."
16. Ward, "Terrorists Just Tried to Assassinate Defense Secretary Jim Mattis in Afghanistan."
17. Popalzai, Hansler, and Tawfeeq, "Afghanistan Foils ISIS Plan to Assassinate the Top US Envoy to Kabul."
18. George and Hassan, "Blasts Disrupt Afghan President Ashraf Ghani's Swearing-In Ceremony."
19. *Reuters,* "Islamic State Claims Suicide Bombing Targeting Afghan Vice President."
20. Gibbons-Neff and Faizi, "Gunmen Storm Kabul University, Killing at Least 19."
21. *France 24,* "Islamic State Claims Attack on State TV Station in Afghanistan."
22. BBC News, "Afghanistan War."

23. Gannon and Akhgar, "US Blames Brutal Attack on Afghan Maternity Hospital on IS."

24. Yousafzai, "Suicide Bombing at Southwest Pakistan Shrine Kills 18."

25. BBC News, "Afghanistan Blast."

26. Hashim, "Bomb and Gun Attack on Quetta Church Kills Eight."

27. Author data.

28. Akbari, "The Risks Facing Hazaras in Taliban-Ruled Afghanistan."

29. Jadoon and Mines, "The Taliban Can't Take on the Islamic State Alone."

30. Winter, "Suicide Tactics and the Islamic State."

31. Gannon and Akhgar, "US Blames Brutal Attack on Afghan Maternity Hospital on IS."

32. Author data.

33. Program on Extremism, *Mosul and the Islamic State*, episode 2, part 1, "Opportunities Lost: Democracy."

34. Liebermann and Kaufman, "US Military Releases Videos of August Drone Strike That Killed 10 Afghan Civilians."

35. Jadoon and Mines, "What Is ISIS-K?"

36. Ingram, *The Long Jihad.*

37. Jadoon, Mines, and Sayed, "The Evolving Taliban-ISK Rivalry."

38. Ibid.

39. Tarzi, "Islamic State-Khurasan Province."

40. Jadoon and Mines, "Taking Aim."

41. Jadoon, Sayed, and Mines, "The Islamic State Threat in Taliban Afghanistan."

42. Jadoon and Mines, *Broken but Not Defeated.*

43. Average attack lethality is defined as the number of individuals killed and wounded per ISK attack.

44. Hashim, "Bomb and Gun Attack on Quetta Church Kills Eight."

45. BBC News, "Herat Mosque Blast."

46. Sukhanyar and Mashal, "Twin Mosque Attacks Kill Scores in One of Afghanistan's Deadliest Weeks."

47. *Al-Jazeera*, "Officials: Taliban, ISIL Coordinated Sar-e Pul Attack."

48. BBC News, "Pakistan: IS Attack on Sufi Shrine in Sindh Kills Dozens."

49. BBC News, "Afghanistan: IS Gunmen Dressed As Medics Kill 30 at Kabul Military Hospital."

50. Institute for Economics and Peace, *Global Terrorism Index 2019.*

51. BBC News, "Pakistan: IS Attack on Sufi Shrine in Sindh Kills Dozens."

52. The following provinces have been hit by ISK attacks. In Pakistan: Balochistan, Punjab, Sindh, Khyber-Pakhtunkhwa, and the Federally Administered Tribal Areas before they were incorporated in Khyber-Pakhtunkhwa province in 2018. In Afghanistan: Baghlan, Balkh, Ghazni, Ghor, Helmand, Herat, Jowzjan, Kabul, Khost, Kunar, Kunduz, Laghman, Logar, Nangarhar, Nuristan, Paktia, Sar-e Pol, Wardak, and Zabul.

53. Bokhari and Stacey, "China Woos Pakistan Militants to Secure Belt and Road Projects."

54. Nine attacks (2 percent) were attributed to unknown targets.

55. Zafar, "61 Killed, at Least 165 Injured as Militants Storm Police Training Centre in Quetta."

56. *Dawn*, "Assailants Came from Afghanistan."

57. Saifi, Shah, and Perry, "Quetta Attack Survivor."

58. BBC News, "Quetta Attack."

59. Internal ISK document, Combating Terrorism Center Library.

60. See, for example, Faiez and Shah, "Islamic State Attacks Afghan Intelligence Compound in Kabul."

61. See, for example, Shahid, "28 Die As Senate Deputy Leader Survives Bomb Attack in Mastung."

62. Popalzai and Narayan, "20 Dead in Suicide Blast Outside Afghan Supreme Court in Kabul."

63. *Al-Jazeera*, "Afghanistan: Gunmen Attack Kabul Military Academy"; *Al-Jazeera*, "Suicide Bomber Targets Afghan Military Training Centre in Kabul."

64. Sherzad, "Islamic State Claims Suicide Attack on Pakistani Consulate in Afghan City."

65. BBC News, "Afghanistan Militants Dead in Jalalabad Attack."

66. Rasmussen, "Kabul: At Least 90 Killed by Massive Car Bomb in Diplomatic Quarter."

67. Harooni, "Islamic State Claims Responsibility for Attack on Iraqi Embassy in Kabul."

68. Dearden, "Isis 'Kills at Least Six Red Cross' Aid Workers in Afghanistan"; Popalzai, Farhat, and Berlinger, "4 Killed in ISIS Attack on Save the Children in Afghanistan."

69. BBC News, "Afghanistan: Kabul Voter Centre Suicide Attack Kills 57."

70. United Nations Assistance Mission in Afghanistan, *Protection of Civilians in Armed Conflict.*

71. *Express News*, "Avtar Singh Khalsa, Sikh Candidate for October Polls Among 20 Killed in Afghanistan Blast."

72. BBC News, "Afghanistan Blast."

73. Shahid and Salam, "128 Perish As Savage Attack on Mastung Rally Stuns Nation."

74. *Dunya News*, "BAP Candidate Siraj Raisani Among 128 killed in Mastung Suicide Blast."

75. *CBS News*, "Polling Station Attack Marks Bloody Election Day in Pakistan."

76. BBC News, "Pakistan Gunmen Kill 45 on Karachi Ismaili Shia Bus."

77. See, for example, *The National*, "Kabul Blast." See also *Reuters*, "Islamic State Claims Responsibility for Attack in Herat, Afghanistan."

78. Hashim, "Bomb and Gun Attack on Quetta Church Kills Eight."

79. Hassan, "Death Toll Rises in Suicide Bombing of Islamic Gathering in Kabul."

80. Yousafzai, "Suicide Bombing at Southwest Pakistan Shrine Kills 18."

81. Salahuddin, "Islamic State Suicide Bomber Strikes Meeting of Afghan Clerics"; Hassan, "Death Toll Rises in Suicide Bombing of Islamic Gathering in Kabul."

82. BBC News, "Herat Mosque Blast."

83. Akbari, "The Risks Facing Hazaras in Taliban-Ruled Afghanistan."

84. Ochab, "Bombings Outside a School in Afghanistan Kill over 68 People." See also Sediqi, Shalizi, and Sultan, "Newborns Among 16 Dead in Kabul Hospital Attack."

85. Harooni, "Islamic State Claims Responsibility for Kabul Attack"; Hasrat, "Over a Century of Persecution."

86. Rasmussen, "Isis Claims Responsibility for Kabul Bomb Attack on Hazara Protesters."

87. BBC News, "Afghanistan Suicide Bomb Attack."

88. Rassler, *The Islamic State and Drones.*

89. *Pakistan Today*, "LEAs Arrest Varsity Professor, Niece for ISIS Links."

90. Giustozzi, *The Islamic State in Khorasan.*

91. Kalin, "Last Letters."

92. Internal ISK document, Combating Terrorism Center Library.

93. "U.S. Airstrike Hit ISIS Suicide Training Camp in Afghanistan Leaving 40 Dead."

94. Winter, "Suicide Tactics and the Islamic State."

95. Ibid.

96. Zafar, "61 Killed, at Least 165 Injured As Militants Storm Police Training Centre in Quetta."

97. Ibid.

98. BBC News, "Afghanistan: IS Gunmen Dressed As Medics Kill 30 at Kabul Military Hospital."

99. Harooni, "Over 30 Killed As Gunmen Dressed As Medics Attack Afghan Military Hospital."

100. *France 24*, "Deadly Suicide Attack and Gun Battle Near Airport in Afghanistan."

101. Winter, "Suicide Tactics and the Islamic State."

102. Conrad and Greene, "Competition, Differentiation, and the Severity of Terrorist Attacks."

103. Qazi, "Afghanistan's Taliban, US Sign Agreement Aimed at Ending War."

104. Ibid.

105. *Al-Jazeera*, "Dozens Killed in Kabul Ceremony Attack Claimed by ISIL."

106. *Salaam Times*, "ISIS Attack Kills Dozens at Mazari Ceremony in Kabul."

107. Abed and Mashal, "Terror Attack Strikes Afghan Capital As Another City Is Locked Down for Coronavirus."

108. Dwyer, "At Least 25 People Dead After Hours-Long Attack on Sikh Complex in Kabul."

109. *Al-Jazeera*, "Five Rockets Hit US Airbase in Afghanistan."

110. *Al-Jazeera*, "Afghanistan: Deadly Suicide Attack Targets Funeral in Nangarhar."

111. BBC News, "Afghan Attack."

112. Ibid.

113. Analytical Support and Sanctions Monitoring Team, *Twenty-sixth Report.*

114. *Al-Jazeera*, "Afghan Forces Announce Arrest of Local ISIL Leader"; Human Rights Watch, "Afghanistan: Prosecute Head of ISIS-Linked Group."

115. Analytical Support and Sanctions Monitoring Team, *Twenty-fourth Report.*

116. BBC News, "IS Regional Leader Sheikh Khorasani 'Arrested in Afghanistan.'"

117. Jadoon, Sayed, and Mines, "The Islamic State Threat in Taliban Afghanistan."

118. Yousafzai and Reals, "ISIS-K Is Trying to Undermine Afghanistan's Taliban Regime."

119. Director of National Intelligence, "Hezb-e-Islami Gulbuddin (HIG)."

120. Jadoon, Sayed, and Mines, "The Islamic State Threat in Taliban Afghanistan."

121. Ibid.

122. Ibid.

123. Ibid.

124. Ibid.

125. Yousafzai and Reals, "ISIS-K Is Trying to Undermine Afghanistan's Taliban Regime."

126. Sayed, "Who Is the New Leader of Islamic State-Khorasan Province?"

127. Analytical Support and Sanctions Monitoring Team, *Eleventh Report.*

128. Author data.

129. Black Flags Media Center, "Message from Dr Shahab al-Muhajir."

130. Analytical Support and Sanctions Monitoring Team, *Twenty-sixth Report.*

131. Islamic State Khorasan, *Voice of the Caliphate*, episodes 43–45.

132. Ghazi and Mashal, "29 Dead After ISIS Attack on Afghan Prison."

133. Ibid.

134. Jadoon, Sayed, and Mines, "The Islamic State Threat in Taliban Afghanistan."

135. Black Flags Media Center, "Special Report on the Islamic State Attack on the Nangarhar Prison."

136. Azzam, "Warning."

137. US Department of Defense, Office of Inspector General, *Lead Inspector General for Operation Freedom's Sentinel, Quarterly Report, July 1, 2021–September 30, 2021, to the United States Congress.*

138. Weber, "The Islamic State's Global Campaign of 'Economic War' Targeting Infrastructure."

139. Ibid.

140. *Al-Jazeera*, "Taliban Captures Afghan Provincial Capital Zaranj."

141. Mellen, "The Shocking Speed of the Taliban's Advance."

142. Seir et al., "Taliban Sweep Into Afghan Capital After Government Collapses."

143. Burns and Boak, "Biden Orders 1,000 More Troops to Aid Afghanistan Departure."

144. Clark, "US Marines and Taliban Outside Kabul Airport."

145. Varshalomidze, Siddiqui, and Regencia, "US, Allies Warn of 'High Terror Threat' at Kabul Airport."

146. Schmidt, "U.S. Military Focusing on ISIS Cell Behind Attack at Kabul Airport."

147. Ross et al., "Sheer Chaos."

148. Hashemi et al., "American Forces Keep Up Airlift Under High Threat Warnings."

149. Ross et al., "Sheer Chaos."

150. Gibbons-Neff and Arian, "ISIS Bomber Kills Dozens at Shiite Mosque in Northern Afghanistan."

151. BBC News, "Afghanistan: Suicide Attack Hits Kandahar Mosque During Prayers."

152. *Al-Jazeera*, "Deadly Blasts Hit Afghan Capital Kabul."

153. International Federation of Journalists, "Afghanistan: Former Ariana Television Journalist Killed in Explosion."; Gul, "Bus Bombing Kills Afghan Journalist."

154. Jadoon, Sayed, and Mines, "The Islamic State Threat in Taliban Afghanistan."

155. Ibid.

156. Sayed, "The Taliban's Persistent War on Salafists in Afghanistan"; Jadoon, Sayed, and Mines, "The Islamic State Threat in Taliban Afghanistan."

157. Clarke and Schroden, "Brutally Ineffective."

158. Siddique, "Taliban Wages Deadly Crackdown on Afghan Salafists."

159. Jadoon and Mines, "The Taliban Can't Take On the Islamic State Alone."

160. Islamic State, *Dabiq.*

161. US Department of Justice, "Ohio Man Arrested and Charged with Attempting to Travel to Join ISIS."

162. Clifford and Hughes, "Afghanistan and American Jihadists."

163. Jadoon and Mines, *Broken but Not Defeated.*

164. McKinnell, "Isaac El Matari Jailed for Seven Years."

165. Harrison-Graham, "Two Suspected British Islamic State Recruits Seized by Taliban at Border"; *Arab News*, "2 Suspected British Daesh Members Arrested in Afghanistan."

166. Analytical Support and Sanctions Monitoring Team, *Twenty-second Report.*

167. Starr and Browne, "US Officials Warn ISIS' Afghanistan Branch Poses a Major Threat."

168. Ibid.

169. Meleagrou-Hitchens and Hughes, "The Threat to the United States from the Islamic State's Virtual Entrepreneurs."

170. Cruickshank, "A View from the CT Foxhole."

171. Fitton-Brown, "The Persistent Threat from the Islamic State and al-Qaeda."

172. Soliev, "The April 2020 Islamic State Terror Plot Against U.S. and NATO Military Bases in Germany."

173. Ibid.

174. Shinkman, "ISIS in Afghanistan Could Attack U.S. Within 6 Months."

175. Blinken, "Taking Action Against ISIS-K."

176. Ibid.

177. US Department of Defense, Office of Inspector General, *Lead Inspector General for Operation Freedom's Sentinel and Operation Enduring Sentinel: Quarterly Report to the United States Congress, October 1, 2021–December 31, 2021.*

178. Meleagrou-Hitchens and Hughes, "The Threat to the United States from the Islamic State's Virtual Entrepreneurs."

179. Ibid.

180. Goldman and Schmitt, "One by One, ISIS Social Media Experts Are Killed As Result of F.B.I. Program."

181. Meleagrou-Hitchens and Hughes, "The Threat to the United States from the Islamic State's Virtual Entrepreneurs."

182. Hamid, "The British Hacker Who Became the Islamic State's Chief Terror Cybercoach."

183. Hughes, "The Only Islamic State-Funded Plot in the U.S."

184. Dodwell, Milton, and Rassler, *Then and Now.*

185. Program on Extremism, *Mosul and the Islamic State.*

186. Ibid.

187. Cullison, "Inside the Hidden War Between the Taliban and ISIS."

188. Clifford and Hughes, "Afghanistan and American Jihadists."

189. Internal ISK document, Combating Terrorism Center Library.

190. Winter, *The Virtual "Caliphate."*

191. Al-Mohammad and Winter, *From Battlefront to Cyberspace.*

192. Winter, *Media Jihad.*

193. Fernandez, *Here to Stay and Growing.*

194. Jadoon and Mines, *Broken but Not Defeated.*

195. Ibid.

196. Sarkar, "The Islamic State's Increasing Focus on India."

197. Gibbons-Neff and Arian, "ISIS Bomber Kills Dozens at Shiite Mosque in Northern Afghanistan."

198. Pantucci, "Indians and Central Asians Are the New Face of the Islamic State."

199. As noted earlier, that number rises to 41 if FATA is included.

200. International Crisis Group, *Beyond Emergency Relief.*

4

Surviving State-Led Operations

Esteemed brothers, with regard to the neglect of sending the military reports to you, there has been continuous bombing on the brothers for these past three weeks. Note that the enemies have targeted the centers and leadership and the lines of ribat *[forward deployed positions], as well as bombing the media center within the* wilayat *completely destroying it with cruise missiles.*

—Letter from ISK member Yusuf Ahmad Khorasani
to an unspecified committee, December 2016[1]

The above statement to an unspecified committee apologizes for tardiness in sending the committee a batch of requested military reports. To explain himself, Khorasani cited successful efforts by the United States–led coalition and its Afghan partners in targeting multiple ISK positions, including the destruction of ISK's media center in what was the first recorded instance of US cruise missiles targeting the group.

Over the course of six years, between 2015 and 2020, heavy losses such as these would come to define ISK's fortunes in the region and disrupt its upward trajectory post-2016. Thousands of its members and hundreds of its leaders were killed or captured, or simply surrendered to government forces on both sides of the Durand Line. Its territorial aspirations were constrained and gradually diminished in that same period, as was the group's operational capacity to launch deadly attacks against state and civilian targets. Yet ISK had still managed to make a name for itself globally as a deadly organization, and as the group resurges in a new era of Taliban rule, it is just shy of marking a decade of existence in the region, despite years of significant personnel and territorial losses.

One of the key focuses of this book is to highlight the extent of ISK's organizational resilience, and the sources of that resilience. To fully appreciate ISK's resilience though, we need to understand the extent of the damage that ISK managed to absorb and eventually recover from to the degree that is now considered a renewed threat. In this chapter, we provide evidence of ISK's resilience by demonstrating the myriad state-led operations it faced and survived.

The Nature and Magnitude of Operations Against ISK

To address the broader question of ISK's resiliency, it is essential to understand the nature and magnitude of operations against the group. These aspects depended in large part on two key factors: location and targeting force capacity. In major urban areas in Afghanistan and Pakistan—from Afghan cities such as Kabul and Jalalabad to Lahore, Quetta, Karachi, and other major cities in Pakistan—both countries' counterterrorism divisions (the former government's NDS and provincial CTDs, respectively) led efforts to identify and interdict attack cells. Elsewhere in Afghanistan, ISK militants battled for territorial control against the Afghan government and the Afghan Taliban. From the group's main hubs in Nangarhar and Kunar in the northeast to isolated pockets in Jowzjan in the north, ISK was able to temporarily seize control of local villages and compete for the centers of several districts. This forced the former government of Afghanistan and its international partners to engage in campaigns that drew substantially more resources and firepower than that required to combat smaller networks and cells in major urban areas.

The other main factor to consider is the changing targeting capacity of the governments of Afghanistan and Pakistan. In areas where ISK did gain temporary territorial control, what soon followed were significant aerial barrages and raids from Afghan and US partner forces. Over time, the Afghan army and its special forces units would lead more complex operations, and significant additions and training to the Afghan air force allowed its personnel to begin conducting a greater number of air raids and even its first night sorties.[2] Undoubtedly, however, the impact of US air operations, training, and mission support dramatically augmented the targeting capacity of Afghan forces and ultimately changed the fate of ISK, or at least ushered in its decline in 2019. It is difficult to envision a scenario in which the group could have been dislodged from its core territories in such a relatively short period of time without US support. But once the most significant of ISK's force presence and operational hubs had diminished, the onus on Afghan forces to continue the battle with ISK grew. In urban areas, increased capacity and resources for the NDS in Afghanistan and provincial CTDs in Pakistan led to many successful raids on local attack cells, financial and logistical support networks, and recruitment operations. However, despite intense targeting operations on both sides of the Durand Line—from urban arrest operations to coordinated drone strikes in rural and mountainous areas—this chapter will show that while ISK adapted its strategy and tactics over time as it faced challenges, the group remained resilient and continued its violent campaigns against government and civilian targets alike, despite significant losses.

Battling for ISK's Operational Hubs

> The apostate Afghan government, with assistance from forces of the international coalition, launched a fierce attack under intense air cover, with a severe bombardment on locations of the caliphate's soldiers in the month of Shawwal. The American forces used different types of rockets on the soldiers of the caliphate, among them long-range Cruise missiles, which they have now used for the first time since the fall of the so-called Emirate. For that reason, the soldiers of the Caliphate executed a tactical insignificant withdrawal for a short period of time, in order to prevent the loss of mujahidin lives as well as those of the general Muslim public.
>
> —Letter from ISK to Abu Bakr al-Baghdadi, August 8, 2016[3]

In the above statement, seemingly written by ISK's second governor (*wali*, the group's top leader), the author highlights not only the attacks on the group's media center referenced above, but also the broader state-led campaign against ISK that forced the group to accept tactical defeats. Importantly, these included some of ISK's territorial holdings.

Consolidating power (*tamkīn*) and establishing state-like governing authority (*khilafah*) over territory is central to the broader Islamic State movement's method of insurgency.[4] It was one of the key draws for the tens of thousands of individuals who left their countries to join the core group in Iraq and Syria, and the main crux for its declaration of a so-called caliphate. These conditions also happen to be key requirements for a local Islamic State branch to be officially recognized by the group's core leadership as an official province (*wilaya*, plural *wilayat*).[5] And of the thirty provinces across Afghanistan and Pakistan where state-led operations targeted ISK, very few actually met that threshold. Of these provinces, only one stands out in particular as the group's longstanding organizational hub: Nangarhar, Afghanistan.

The northeastern provinces of Afghanistan along the border with Pakistan offered ISK a number of strategic advantages for establishing a firm operational base, none more so than Nangarhar. Located across the border from Pakistan's tribal areas,[6] Nangarhar's southern districts hug the Spin Ghar (White Mountains) range—the refuge of militant groups for decades and the site of al-Qaeda's notorious Tora Bora complex.[7] The rugged terrain here has long presented logistical challenges for Afghan and coalition forces, allowing for the free flow of militant fighters and smuggled goods over the years through access points across the mountains.[8] ISK was eventually able to capitalize on these supply avenues, as well as other illicit economies they facilitated.[9] Overall, Nangarhar sits on an entrenched operational nexus of the broader jihadist movement that developed over decades of conflict. From older groups such as al-Qaeda to newer groups such as Lashkar-e-Islam,[10] ISK found no shortage of existing militant groups to poach recruits from, and to leverage tactically for logistical support and expertise.[11]

The footholds of the Spin Ghar range lie close to both Kabul and Jalalabad,[12] two major recruitment centers for ISK and the targets for some of the group's most heinous attacks.[13] Despite its close proximity to both cities, corruption among local government elites, failure to maintain security and delivery of services,[14] and years of battling for the support of local tribes by the coalition and the Afghan Taliban left major governance gaps in the population that ISK sought to exploit.[15] In the southern areas of Nangarhar where ISK first began its outreach, the government controlled no more than one-fifth of the local districts.[16] The group's recruiters found little difficulty reaching the populations in and around Nangarhar that other jihadist groups sought out as well,[17] from hardline Pakistani madrassas just across the border to Kabul's urban neighborhoods,[18] from major nearby universities to prisons and internally displaced person (IDP) camps.[19] At the time of ISK's ascendancy, Nangarhar also played host to thousands of militants and their families who had fled Pakistani military operations and the US drone strikes campaign over the previous decade,[20] the most recent of which drove hundreds of militants across the border into Afghanistan in 2014.[21] And, as Figure 4.1 illustrates, Nangarhar would become the site of ISK's most significant personnel losses from 2015 to 2020.

State-Led Operations and Clashes with the Afghan Taliban

It was, quite simply, an environment ripe with opportunity for a burgeoning militant organization like ISK. Not long after the Islamic State's core media apparatus first recognized the movement's Khorasan province in January 2015, ISK began clashing with local pro-Taliban factions in villages across southern Nangarhar.[22] As the group continued targeting Taliban factions, displacing unaligned locals, and establishing its bases throughout the spring of 2015, the Afghan government and coalition forces gradually mustered the resources to begin a broader counterinsurgency campaign aimed at dis-

Figure 4.1   Total Reported ISK-Linked Losses in Afghanistan by Province, 2015–2020

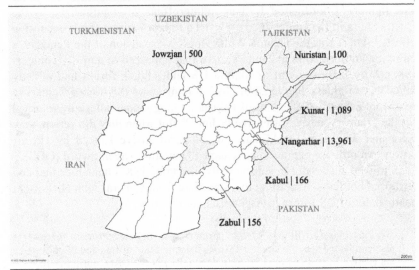

Source: Author data.
Note: Province name and total number of ISK-linked losses (2015–2020) listed for provinces with at least 100 reported losses: Jowzjan, Kabul, Kunar, Nangarhar, Nuristan, and Zabul.

lodging ISK from its core operational strongholds. The initial lag in coordinating counter-ISK operations soon wore off, and by the year's end, coalition operations had claimed just over 600 ISK-linked fatalities and around another 100 individuals captured or surrendered.[23]

US drone strikes destroyed multiple ISK positions throughout the summer of 2015 and killed scores of fighters. In some areas, however, counter-ISK operations met with less success. The resistance of the group's fighters around its main headquarters in the Mohmand Valley and nearby positions in the Pekha Valley stifled coalition gains.[24] In Nangarhar's Achin district, ISK routed local uprisings and released a notoriously gruesome video of its fighters executing elder tribal leaders by placing them on a row of explosives for detonation,[25] a barbaric display of resolve and the Islamic State's rejectionist ideology.[26] Bolstered by fresh recruits from Pakistan's tribal agencies and Afghan Taliban defectors,[27] ISK began seizing the homes of Achin residents,[28] imprisoning resisters,[29] and launching an offensive across the surrounding villages and districts with hundreds of fighters.[30] By the end of 2015, over 500 of the approximately 600 ISK-linked fatalities in Nangarhar (just over 80 percent) fell in Achin district alone.[31]

As 2016 started, the coalition's operational tempo increased, and even the logistical challenges of the cold winter months offered little respite for ISK fighters. Coordinated Taliban counteroffensives—authorized by the Quetta Shura in December 2015—played a role in limiting ISK's expansion efforts,[32] but it was the Obama White House's expansion of the Pentagon's targeting authorization in January 2016 that appeared to amplify counter-ISK efforts.[33] By the end of March, US and Afghan forces had already killed more fighters than in all of 2015, forcing some ISK-linked fighters to retreat into the tribal agencies of Pakistan, though many allegedly returned for the group's renewed offensive in June.[34] But when they did return, they were met with a major Afghan-led counteroffensive backed by US air power in a military operation codenamed Operation Green Sword (OGS).[35] OGS proved successful in substantially damaging ISK's human capital and territorial holdings. According to a statement from General John Nicholson, commander of US forces in Afghanistan at the time:

> Working closely with our Afghan partners, U.S. counterterrorism forces also conducted specific counter-ISIL-K [Islamic State of Iraq and the Levant (ISIL)–K, or ISK] operations, named GREEN SWORD, during 2016. These operations killed approximately one-third of their fighters, including Emir Hafiz Sayed Khan [ISK's top leader], and reduced the territory they hold by two-thirds. U.S. forces destroyed two dozen command and control training structures, disrupted financial support networks, and significantly reduced an ISIL-K sanctuary that existed in Nangarhar Province since early 2015 from nine to three districts.[36]

Operation Green Sword's air and ground forces were soon joined by a contingent of defensive-posture ANDSF forces aimed at dislodging ISK from its strongholds in southern Nangarhar and holding retaken positions.[37] Together, the combined joint operations delivered staggering damage, including over 2,500 reported ISK-linked fatalities in Achin and the adjacent districts of Kot and Deh Bala (just under 75 percent of all reported ISK fatalities that year).[38] Over one-third of ISK's losses reportedly came from US drone strikes, which also targeted elements of the group's infrastructure alluded to in General Nicholson's statement, including the radio station run by ISK media operatives.[39] The majority of those losses, however, were associated with Afghan-led operations.

Still, ISK proved resilient and resourceful, amassing more forces around Achin by the fall of 2016.[40] Many of its fighters took up positions around the group's strongholds in the Mohmand and Pekha Valleys—and in the heavily guarded network of caves at their entrance—after coalition forces began operations to stem ISK's weapons and personnel supply chains in early 2017.[41] To oust ISK from its valley strongholds, ANDSF and US forces launched a new military operation, Operation Hamza, in April

2017 from forward operating bases in Achin and Kot.[42] Before coalition forces entered the valleys, the United States dropped its largest nonnuclear bomb on ISK's defensive network of tunnels, and paved the way for Operation Hamza forces to continue into the valleys.[43] Soon after, ISK suffered the loss of its second top leader—Abdul Hasib Logari (Hasibullah Logari)—in a joint night raid by Afghan and US special forces.[44] As counter-ISK operations progressed through the valleys, the group scrambled to disperse into new areas while locking down its remaining holdings. To do so, ISK cashed in on its alliances with other militant groups in the area,[45] and even launched failed incursions to seize Tora Bora from the Afghan Taliban and push westward into Taliban-controlled and contested areas.[46] Still, the group continued to hemorrhage hundreds of its fighters throughout the summer,[47] and come late fall 2017, any remaining ISK positions were kept barely afloat by supply chains arriving from Pakistan's tribal areas across the border, as well as a contingent of fighters that was claimed to have been sent by the Islamic State in Iraq and Syria over the winter.[48]

Pivot to the North and Organizational Changes

As ISK cycled through successes and defeats in Nangarhar, the group's leadership took steps to move resources and personnel north into the neighboring province of Kunar,[49] which offered many of the same opportunistic conditions as did Nangarhar. ISK recruiters started outreach efforts in Kunar as early as June 2015,[50] and early reporting tracked the movement of hundreds of ISK fighters and their families as they moved northward over the following several months.[51] Increased ISK attacks on Afghan forces in Kunar were soon answered by coalition operations, and over the course of 2017, Afghan and US forces reportedly killed 152 ISK-linked individuals in the province, which was a drastic increase from the previous two years.[52] As 2018 began, Afghan forces were engaged in counter-ISK operations similar to those in Nangarhar, targeting the group's positions in the valleys at the footholds of the Hindu Kush Mountains in Kunar, as shown in Figure 4.1.[53]

In April 2018, fresh detachments of US special forces arrived to maintain the pressure further south in its Achin strongholds,[54] and succeeded in decimating the group's positions within the district's valleys by June.[55] ISK fighters tried to establish a new core stronghold in the Deh Bala district to the west,[56] but they were quickly routed.[57] The group suffered several hundred fatalities in the first half of 2018,[58] about 170 of which happened during an assault on Gurgoray village in Deh Bala by one of the largest joint Afghan-US special forces operations to date.[59] With the arrival of new Afghan territorial holding forces,[60] the reported death of another ISK top leader, Abu Saad Orakzai, in a drone strike on August 25,[61] and the failure of ISK's relocation eastward,[62] it seemed that there was nowhere for the group to go but north or into Pakistan. ISK's forces had continued fortifying themselves in valley villages in Kunar, and even tried tapping into the local timber economy for revenue.[63] But where ISK fighters went, the coalition soon followed, and throughout the summer of 2018, US drone strikes alone claimed dozens of ISK-linked fatalities.[64] As the group suffered more setbacks in both Nangarhar and Kunar in the second half of 2018 (including over 1,500 reported fatalities),[65] ISK's leadership stared down the possibility of losing their last significant holdings in Afghanistan's east before the group could reach its fifth year. At this point in time, it became imperative for ISK to adapt its strategy and tactics if it was going to survive this onslaught of state-led operations.

To adapt in the face of intense losses, IS-Central shuffled the very top of ISK's leadership structure, as well as the movement's broader strategic posture in South and Central Asia. In April 2019, then-governor of ISK Mawlawi Zia ul-Haq (Abu Omar al-Khorasani) was demoted.[66] His replacement was appointed by a visiting delegation from Iraq and Syria representing the caliph and his Delegated Committee. The change appears to have been the result of Zia ul-Haq's poor performance during his tenure overseeing ISK's setbacks in Nangarhar.[67] Not long after his ousting, ISK also underwent some structural reorganization in the region. An official Islamic State video released in May 2019 announced the restructuring of wilayat Khorasan into distinct provinces: *wilayat* Pakistan (a new province specifically in Pakistan, with the exception of Khyber Pakhtunkhwa province), *wilayat* Khorasan (now only Afghanistan and Khyber Pakhtunkhwa province in Pakistan), and wilayat Hind (Jammu and Kashmir). After both changes occurred, counter-ISK operations continued to target the group's remaining numbers in Nangarhar, but overall numbers of fatalities were not as high as in the previous three years.[68] Official estimates of the group's total force size appeared to be falling, and ISK's largest setback of 2019 was still yet to come.

Starting around November 2019, hundreds of ISK fighters and their families surrendered to Afghan authorities in Nangarhar, totaling 1,400 men, women, and children in the end.[69] Afterward, the United Nations Security Council Monitoring Team estimated the group had around 2,500 fighters remaining, 2,100 of them (over 80 percent) concentrated in Kunar.[70]

Coalition operations continued against ISK in Nangarhar and Kunar throughout 2019 and into 2020, but there were noticeable shifts in targeting tactics. As ISK experienced territorial and personnel losses in both Nangarhar and Kunar, the number of US drone strikes and ISK fatalities fell dramatically in 2019 and virtually ceased in 2020. Although Afghan Air Force strikes and operations involving Afghan ground troops gradually outpaced US drone strikes, they too declined in number. Eventually, the urgency to keep the pressure on ISK declined, as ISK's territory and force size continued to dwindle in 2019 and 2020. While ISK remained vested in reclaiming its former strongholds in Nangarhar and its secondary redoubts in Kunar, the group did not appear to have the resources to attempt to take or hold those territories just yet.

Outside of ISK's core territories in Nangarhar and Kunar, the group has struggled to build and maintain a lasting territorial presence. State-led targeting operations against ISK in Afghanistan spanned thirty provinces, but only six stand out as sites of serious ISK efforts to replicate its territorial project along the Afghanistan-Pakistan border in its formative years: Helmand in the southwest, Farah in the west, Zabul in the southeast, Takhar in the northeast, Logar in central Afghanistan, and Jowzjan in the northwest. These provincial "startups" offered ISK a number of tangible strategic advantages, as some were situated on the borders with other countries and hosted major crossing points to facilitate the transnational flow of both supplies and militants. These included fighters from Pakistan and Central Asian countries such as Tajikistan and Uzbekistan, but also fighters who came to ISK from outside the region, including the Middle East and North Africa, France, the Philippines, and elsewhere. Some of these provinces also sat on major illicit economic hubs and smuggling routes, especially drug production and distribution. Still others offered ISK the ability to tap into local recruitment from diverse talent pools, and even establish training camps overseen by its provincially appointed leadership. From a strategic perspective, the cumulative effect for ISK was the appearance of having expansive presence within the region that the group called Khorasan.[71] In reality, these were discontiguous efforts to establish beachheads that appeared to be a mix of opportunism and strategic expansion.[72]

That blend of opportunism and strategy appeared to meet in one common dynamic: ISK's efforts in all of these provinces were the result of breakaway Afghan Taliban factions or groups realigning themselves under the ISK banner, who were aggressively pursued by the Afghan Taliban after breaking away. While coalition forces played a major role in targeting ISK in multiple areas—from leadership decapitation strikes against some of ISK's top provincial leaders to Afghan army ground operations against ISK positions—Afghan Taliban pressure undoubtedly contributed to the demise of ISK territorial "startups" in several Afghan provinces. While limited pro-ISK activity has persisted in some of these provinces, the aggressive and rapid counter-ISK response from both the coalition and from the Afghan Taliban over the years effectively sealed the group's fate in each of them, except for in Jowzjan (see Chapter 6). As we discuss in Chapter 6, while ISK's strategic rivalry with the Afghan Taliban resulted in violent clashes between the two, it also helped ISK pose as an alternative to the Taliban, which ultimately contributed to its survival.

The Battle with ISK in Urban Areas

> The Americans stormed the houses of several brothers, namely the
> Uzbeks and others of our network in Kabul, and arrested them. Some of
> them had become persons wanted by the Americans. They moved to our
> areas, and hence we have suffered this financial problem. It has been
> difficult for us to receive the money from Kabul. . . . . Bear in mind, too,
> that one of the brothers who was arrested had money on him valued at
> about 80,000 USD, when the Americans stormed his house.

—Letter from ISK governor Hafiz Saeed Khan to
IS-Central leadership, June 22, 2016[73]

The above statement is from a letter apparently written by the then-governor
of ISK to IS-Central leadership. In the letter, the author provides a status
report on ISK's operations, successes, and challenges. As the letter alludes,
Afghan and international forces succeeded in raiding a number of ISK's safe
houses around Kabul in 2016. The number of raids by security forces around
the Afghan capital (as well as the number of ISK members captured or killed
in those raids) stayed relatively flat between 2015 and 2017 before spiking
in 2018 and then falling gradually in the following two years. In and around
Afghan provincial capitals elsewhere in the country (especially Jalalabad),
these same dynamics generally held true. This may have been the result of
ISK relocating assets and operational focus to major urban cities—Kabul
and Jalalabad in particular—after suffering serious territorial and manpower
losses from 2016 to 2018 as outlined earlier. Just under half of the more than
350 ISK-linked members reportedly killed or arrested in Kabul and Jalalabad from 2015 to 2020 occurred in 2018 alone. Operations against the
group's networks in urban areas tended to be the domain of Afghan intelligence, which led or partnered on the majority of raids.[74]

ISK operatives leveraged urban areas in and surrounding Kabul and
Jalalabad for several reasons. In their efforts to counter the group, Afghan
intelligence and security forces reportedly conducted well over seventy
raids and arrests between 2015 and 2020. Some of these operations aimed
to disrupt the flow of recruits leaving Kabul and Jalalabad for ISK training
camps and territorial holdings farther south in Nangarhar, especially
younger generations of Afghans drawn in by effective recruitment efforts.[75]
Several recruits were even alleged to have traveled hundreds of miles to
Jowzjan to support the group's territorial ambitions there. Afghan authorities also arrested lecturers who promoted and recruited on behalf of ISK, as
well as dozens of student supporters at universities in Kabul and Jalalabad
over the years.[76] Other operations aimed to cut off fundraising and supply
lines from Kabul in particular, where ISK fundraisers and logistics coordi-
nators sent out money, weapons, explosives, and other supplies to aid the

group's fighters in Nangarhar. By far the most intense urban counterterrorism efforts, however, were focused on interdicting attack-oriented networks that built and distributed explosive devices, and whose members planned and perpetrated violent, sectarian attacks on targets throughout Kabul, Jalalabad, and beyond.

Overall, as ISK experienced significant personnel and territorial losses in more remote areas, the group adapted its strategy to conduct more high-profile attacks in urban centers where its operatives can more easily blend into the civilian population and where high-population density venues prove to be easier targets. At its weakest, ISK appeared to recenter its strategy on urban warfare operations in order to stay relevant, and to continue its violent campaign while still disseminating its propaganda and continuing its recruitment efforts. In 2021, as ISK continued its strategy of urban warfare under its new leader, it also relaunched the propaganda radio station *Voice of the Caliphate*. In an episode aired in April 2021, one of the group's broadcasters aptly summarized ISK's new approach: "ISK no longer has the burden of protecting territories. Now our urban warriors are striking the enemy in one street of the Jalalabad or Kabul cities and then taking a nap in the next one without any fears of being arrested, or bombed from the air."[77]

Counter-ISK Operations in Pakistan

While coalition and Afghan security forces grappled with ISK's rural strongholds and urban networks, Pakistan's security forces were conducting their own operations on the other side of the border. Between 2015 and 2020, the Pakistani state reportedly captured 496 ISK-linked individuals and killed another 111. The vast majority of its counter-ISK operations were conducted by provincial police and counterterrorism departments (see Chapter 1 for more on the structure of Pakistan's security apparatus). Operations spanned around forty-one districts spread across all of Pakistan's provinces, including the tribal agencies. Earlier operations in 2015 captured almost sixty ISK supporters and networked cell members in every province except Balochistan, but by 2016 ISK's growing threat throughout the country demanded a stepped-up response.

The majority of the reported losses incurred by ISK in Pakistan occurred in 2016 (315 of 603 total members captured or killed, or 52 percent of the total), one year after the group's official formation—which may also explain the drastic fall in ISK's attacks in the country the following year. Another 134 ISK-linked individuals were captured or killed in 2017, and by 2018 the group's losses began tapering off, as did sizing estimates of its presence in Pakistan. Most of these operations occurred in major urban cities and the surrounding areas, where individuals were captured for planning attacks, possessing arms and explosives, disseminating propaganda, and facilitating the group's recruitment efforts. Pakistani security forces sought to eliminate the major resources that ISK's Pakistan-based supporters and cells provided: (1) the group's biggest source of recruitment outside of Afghanistan; (2) significant logistical and financial support; and (3) attack operations against state and civilian targets. To date, ISK (in addition to Islamic State–Pakistan, which was formed during the mid-2019 organizational reshuffle) has yet to demonstrate the capacity to hold territory anywhere in Pakistan as it did across the border in Afghanistan.[78]

Doubling Down in Punjab

As Figure 4.2 shows, the heaviest of Pakistani security forces' counter-ISK operations occured in Punjab. There, the Punjab CTD conducted at least eighty raids and arrests across the province in the observed period, capturing or killing 175 ISK-linked individuals in 2016 alone (29 percent of all ISK-linked losses in Pakistan). Many of those individuals were arrested over a single weekend in January,[79] which government officials claimed was the product of intelligence gained from a previously captured leader of the group's network in Islamabad.[80] While security forces did arrest some Pakistani citizens who were allegedly interested in joining the caliphate in Iraq and Syria,[81] it seemed that the majority of counter-ISK operations disrupted individuals and cells determined to operate within the Afghanistan-Pakistan region.[82]

Across the northern districts of Punjab, local CTDs targeted ISK recruiters who tried to build support in Pakistan's most populous province, especially among individuals affiliated with Lashkar-e-Jhangvi.[83] Between the areas in and around Lahore, Gujranwala, Sialkot, and Sargodha, the CTD captured almost 150 ISK-linked individuals and cell members in nearly fifty reported raids and arrests. Farther south in the districts of Multan and Dera Ghazi Khan, over a dozen operations led to the killing or capture of nearly forty of the group's supporters. Government forces captured another fifty+ ISK supporters in the far-north districts of Attock and Rawalpindi on the outskirts of Islamabad.[84] The success of the Punjab CTD likely stems from a number of sources, one of which might be that—when compared to other provinces—Punjab was the only one to create a new specialized counterterrorism force of thousands of officers dedicated to the National Action Plan to counter terrorism.[85] Other explanations might be the relatively higher population density of Punjab, as well as the prevalence of other groups with shared objectives such as Lashkar-e-Jhangvi and Jaish-e-Mohammed.[86]

Tackling a Dispersed ISK Network

Outside of Punjab, ISK lost about 200 supporters (about one-third of all ISK losses in Pakistan) in over fifty operations between the cities of Peshawar and Karachi, the provincial capitals of Khyber Pakhtunkhwa and

Figure 4.2 Total Reported ISK-Linked Losses in Pakistan by Province, 2015–2020

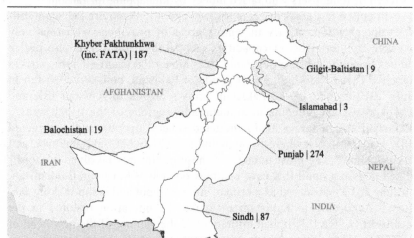

Khyber Pakhtunkhwa (inc. FATA) | 187

CHINA

Gilgit-Baltistan | 9

AFGHANISTAN

Islamabad | 3

Balochistan | 19

Punjab | 274

IRAN

NEPAL

Sindh | 87

INDIA

Source: Author data.

Note: Province name and total number of ISK-linked losses (2015–2020) listed for all provinces with data.

Sindh, respectively. In both cities, ISK enjoyed substantial financial and logistical support. In January 2016, a raid on a currency market in Peshawar led to the arrest of dozens of suspects accused of transferring funds across the border to Afghanistan to finance ISK activities.[87] After that crackdown, Peshawar police and CTD forces intermittently arrested ISK supporters and networks, including a raid that led to the arrest of a large network of twenty-four ISK members accused of coordinating attacks on government and security officials in April 2017.[88] In the southern port city of Karachi, a series of arrests in December 2015 and January 2016 took down a network of recruiters, financial facilitators, and financiers of the 2015 Karachi bus shooting earlier that year that left at least forty-five civilians dead, most of them Ismaili Shiites.[89] Among the arrestees were three women who organized a network of around twenty female recruiters and fundraisers who raised money on behalf of ISK and allegedly arranged marriages for the group's fighters.[90] The raids culminated in the arrest of the alleged orchestrator of the network and purported head of ISK in Sindh province, Umar Kathiwer.[91] Despite the network takedown, Sindh police and CTD officials were forced to keep pace with ISK as the group sustained its recruitment and fundraising operations. Officials continued to arrest local ISK recruiters,[92] including some who were receiving directions from ISK higher-ups in undisclosed locations on the border with Afghanistan,[93] as well as a cell of fundraisers who raised money by kidnapping for ransom.[94]

In only a few areas did counter-ISK operations require Pakistani military intervention, mostly in remote areas of provinces with relatively weaker counterterrorism capacities compared to the CTDs and police forces in major urban cities. Only two known Pakistani air force strikes targeted ISK-linked individuals inside of Pakistan, both of which fell in July 2017 as part of the Pakistani army's efforts to root out ISK and Lashkar-e-Islam hideouts in mountainous regions of the tribal areas.[95] Pakistani armed forces also conducted several operations that targeted ISK leadership elsewhere in the tribal areas, Khyber Pakhtunkhwa, and Balochistan.[96] The most notable of these operations involved a coordinated raid on a small ISK cave complex outside of Mastung, Balochistan, in June 2017 that served as a critical storage depot and bomb-making factory.[97] According to Pakistani officials, the operation resulted in the deaths of twelve ISK-linked militants and the capture of the new head of ISK in Sindh province, whose network was reportedly being facilitated by ISK leadership in Nangarhar.[98]

The June 2017 cave raid was one of less than ten known counter-ISK operations conducted in Balochistan over the six years following ISK's formation as shown in Figure 4.2. This is striking given that Balochistan suffered some of the highest numbers of ISK attacks, including intense suicide attacks, between 2015 and 2020. This may be the result of lower reporting of operations in the province, but it is more likely the product of relatively greater security challenges in Balochistan compared to other provinces.[99] Among other factors, these include the ongoing and intensifying Baloch separatist insurgency and frequent attacks against state and foreign government targets;[100] the tainted reputation and diminished capacity of the Balochistan police force;[101] and cooperation between ISK and militant groups such as LeJ and Jundullah that have operated in Balochistan for years.[102] Statements made by Pakistani officials after the June 2017 raid also illustrated two broader points about the group's leadership. First, it appeared that provincial efforts were being coordinated by ISK's leadership from the group's main bases in Nangarhar. Second, even after suffering networkwide disruptions and arrests of provincial leadership, ISK continued its efforts to rebuild its networks with new leadership.

These developments warrant further scrutiny, especially those regarding ISK's leadership. Leveraging our detailed data on ISK's leadership losses, including both upper and lower tier leaders, we wanted to gain insights into how the group structured itself internally, which likely contributed to its ability to continue operations despite heavy losses. In particular, we use details from ISK's reported leadership losses to develop a unique model of ISK's leadership, one that helps in understanding how ISK structured itself by geography and functions. Mapping ISK's upper- and lower-tier leadership structures and extensive losses offers us additional insights into how the group organized itself internally to survive the virtually continuous onslaught of state-led operations over the years. However, it is important to note that the tiered leadership structure that we next present is not one that is claimed by ISK; rather, it is one lens to use to understand the inner workings of the group.

ISK's Leadership Structure and Leadership Losses

We appointed an Emir of War for the Khorasan province, and we formed a military shura for the province as well. . . . The brothers of the Khorasan province were relieved by the establishment of a Sharia committee for disputed issues, and for that reason, application of the Islamic State's methodology has been much easier. . . . We have established for the first time an office of tribes, and we have made contact with the tribes in the province.

—Letter from ISK governor Abdul Hasib Logari
to IS-Central leadership, August 8, 2016[103]

The above statement appeared to be written in response to a request by the now-deceased caliph for a status update on ISK. Logari's letter provides various details of organizational developments within ISK, including, among others, the establishment of new administrative bodies and the appointment of new heads for existing bodies. Around the time of the letter's date, ISK had suffered immense manpower losses; 1,400 ISK-linked individuals were killed in the first half of 2016 alone. ISK's first governor, Hafiz Saeed Khan, had recently been killed in a US drone strike in July, and in the preceding months, the group had lost several other figures reported to hold leadership positions.

Together, these pieces of information reveal two important insights. First, ISK invested in local governance efforts by establishing administrative bodies similar to those of the Islamic State in Iraq and Syria.[104] And second, it appears that ISK remained committed to those governance efforts during periods of ascendancy despite facing significant territorial, manpower, and leadership losses.[105] ISK attempted to implement its governing rules and regulations by developing a broad structure of leadership ranks, some of whom were allocated by geographical areas of operations, while others held responsibilities over specific functions of the organization.

Of course, over time, state-led efforts as discussed above largely destroyed ISK's organizational structure and forced the group to center its resources on recruitment and urban attack campaigns rather than territorial control and administration. ISK's behavior in this regard aligns with that of the Islamic State in Iraq and Syria, which also adapted to periods of decline by relegating the size of some departments and reshuffling functional responsibilities in an adhocratic manner when faced with substantial losses.[106] ISK appears to have adopted a similar method. ISK's leadership losses when examined in the context of its rise and fall not only offer us important insights into that method in the context of the Afghanistan-Pakistan region, but also provide us with an understanding of the challenges the group had to overcome in order to survive.

Observers of ISK have traced the variation in its members' geographic location,[107] socioeconomic status,[108] nationalities,[109] prior affiliations,[110] levels of ideological commitment,[111] other militant groups within ISK's operational nexus,[112] and ISK's strategies for geographic expansion.[113] However, substantially fewer accounts of ISK's leadership structure exist, the most recognizable of which relied on interviews with ISK fighters and leaders.[114] Our account provides additional evidence of ISK's efforts to build an administrative model mirroring that of its namesake in Iraq and Syria, which, on the whole, supports the view that the Islamic State enjoyed some successes in exporting its administrative methodology to global affiliates such as ISK.[115]

There are numerous resources that collectively help us understand ISK's leadership structure, including captured materials in Afghanistan, Islamic State propaganda, open source reporting, and accounts given by various government and nongovernmental organizations. Similar to other Islamic State official provinces (or *wilayat*), ISK is led by a governor (*wali,* plural *wulut;* the term *emir/amir* is often used interchangeably), or the top leader of the group.[116] According to the Islamic State's own doctrine, governors are nominated by the province's leadership consultative council, or Shura Council, and confirmed and appointed by the caliph. The consultative council in theory has the power to remove the governor, but primarily advises him on general affairs. The Islamic State's governors also rely on various departments (*diwan,* plural *dawawīn*), such as military, education, security, and judicial, to manage and oversee the province's administrative affairs. Each of these departments or offices is led by its own appointed leader and supporting bureaucratic structures. All of these entities report to, and receive administrative support and advice from, the caliph's Delegated Committee (the top Islamic State administrative leadership body based in Iraq and Syria), as well as from the Administration of the Distant Provinces (another administrative body based in Iraq and Syria that was created to help the Delegated Committee and the caliph manage the growing number of global Islamic State provinces).[117]

In the past, ISK's governors have relied on a number of regional leaders to guide the group's territorial expansion, consolidation, and governance efforts, as well as its operational activities.[118] The deployment of regional leaders is not a phenomenon that is unique to ISK, but it does speak to the difficulties the group's governors have faced in managing dozens of operational areas dispersed throughout Afghanistan and Pakistan, especially prior to the 2019 split. Regional leaders oversee ISK's recruitment efforts and attack operations, and in turn draw on their own deputies and other local leaders to manage operations in their area of responsibility. It appears some regional leaders even appointed district-level leaders to help oversee operations within internationally recognized district boundaries and to coordinate local commanders, recruiters, and other leaders at the subdistrict level. There is evidence that regional leaders benefited from supporting representatives for some or all of ISK's major organizational departments, too.[119] In principle, these representatives seek to bolster developments in their respective administrative areas and to conform local governance efforts to ISK's broader standards and objectives. Arguably, ISK's extensive system of leadership ranks, which relied on local recruitment, helped the group sustain its operations even when it faced losses in various districts.

Drawing on our dataset on ISK's leadership losses, we developed a model to reflect the group's structure across multiple tiers, based on each reported ISK leadership loss. Our model has two important characteristics. The first is the grouping of leaders into one of four possible tiers based on the relative scope of their reported roles and activities at the time they were targeted, with Tier 1 being the largest in scope and Tier 4 being the narrowest. We identified Tier 1 leaders to be those who were appointed as ISK governors (interchangeably called emirs)—the top leadership position in the organization. Tier 2 of the leadership model consists of members of ISK's consultative council, regional leaders and their own deputies, and heads of ISK administrative departments and offices (e.g., military operations, education, recruitment and outreach, finance). Tier 3 consists strictly of district-level leaders, which as we discuss below occurred in relatively unique settings. Tier 4 consists of local leaders at the subdistrict level, including field commanders, explosives experts, judges, and other influential figures.

The second component of the model identifies whether or not the specific leader's role was geographically bound. Geographically bound leadership positions are those for which responsibilities appeared to be tied to specific areas of operation within the "Khorasan" region. Nongeographically bound positions, on the other hand, are not responsible for one area of operation alone, but oversee a key administrative function of the organization or engage in broader strategic planning and implementation of ISK's strategy across the entire province. These tend to be the most senior leadership positions within the organization, including the governor as well as his consultative council, and heads of ISK's various departments and offices. Table 4.1 provides a visual representation of our model, as well as some of the key functional responsibilities held by each leadership position based on a number of primary source materials and related analyses.[120]

Between 2015 and 2020, the number of ISK militants who held some identifiable leadership position and were reported to be killed amounted to 361, with another 287 captured, and 31 who surrendered across Afghanistan and Pakistan (679 total losses). The majority of those losses (513, or 76 percent) occurred in Afghanistan, largely in Tier 4 category, but as Figure 4.3 shows, multiple leadership tiers were targeted.

Table 4.1   Model of ISK Leadership by Tier

Tier	Position	Functional Responsibilities	Geo-Bound?
Tier 1	Governor (*wali*)	• Fill symbolic "top" role in the province • Issue general directives to ministerial departments and centers • Approve nominated leaders of ministerial departments and regional leaders • Report to the caliph and his delegated committee	No
Tier 2	Consultative Council members (Shura Council)	• Nominate/propose removal of governor to caliph and his delegated committee • Advise governor on strategic matters	
	Heads of Ministerial departments (*diwan*)	• Implement general directives from governor • Standardize implementation across regions and districts	
	Regional leaders and deputy leaders	• Implement general directives from governor • Oversee and coordinate with representatives from ministerial departments	Yes
	Regional heads of ministerial departments	• Implement department-specific directives in assigned region • Coordinate between overall head of department and regional leader	
Tier 3	District leaders and deputy leaders	• Implement directives from regional leader • Coordinate battlefield and ministerial centers within assigned district	
Tier 4	Local leaders	• Implement directives from district leader or regional leader • Coordinate operations and administrative functioning at local level	

Source: Author data, see also endnotes 116–121.

Figure 4.3 Summary of Leadership Losses by Tier and Country

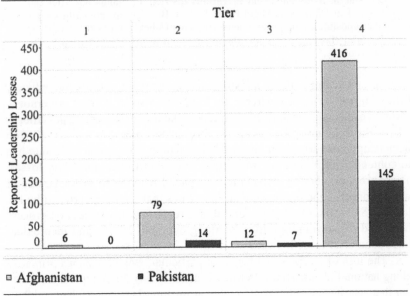

Source: Author data.

Implications of Leadership Losses

Here we provide further details on each tier of ISK's leadership model and discuss the implications of the losses within each category. In general, more information was available on leaders who fell into the higher tiers than lower tiers, but this is to be expected given the high-profile nature of their positions.

Tier 1: Governors

A letter apparently written by the Shura Council of ISK to the IS-Central Shura Council dated September 2, 2016, states:

> Greetings to you noble brothers! In your most recent letter, you ordered us to send you details about the people who want to sow discord and bring about conflict in the ranks of the mujahidin. . . . They are the ones causing conflict inside the province, and they are taking advantage of the martyrdom of Shaykh Hafiz Saeed Khan—may God accept him—the wali (Governor) of Khorasan Province. They want to sow dissension in the ranks of the mujahidin and bring about distrust inside the province between the emirs and the mujahidin, as well as interference in communication between the province and the center.[121]

Another intelligence report taken from a smart phone belonging to a member of ISK revealed the following (undated but likely drafted in 2017):

In Afghanistan, serious fighting has been erupted between two groups of the Islamic State–Khorasan in various districts of Nangarhar after the death of its Emir/*wali*, Abdul Hasib Logari. Both groups are calling each other apostates. One group wants Muawiya Uzbekistani as the successor of Abdul Hasib Logari while the other group wants Aslam Faruqi as the governor of ISK.[122]

These excerpts offer interesting snapshots of the periods immediately following two critical junctures for ISK: the loss of its first governor—Hafiz Saeed Khan—in July 2016, and then the loss of its second governor—Abdul Hasib Logari (also known as Hasibullah Logari) in April 2017. Top leadership losses triggered internal issues within ISK, which the group had to contend with in addition to experiencing significant manpower losses. There are a number of insights to be gleaned from these excerpts, one of which concerns the organizational fault lines that were exacerbated by the loss of ISK's first two top leaders. Issues regarding the succession process fomented dissension and division along national, ethnic, and ideological lines soon after these losses.

The loss of Hafiz Saeed Khan, in particular, stoked tensions primarily along national identity lines. Before his death in July 2016, reports from earlier that year had already exposed internal fractures between Afghan and Pakistani factions under his stewardship.[123] Part of the problem stemmed from disagreements over representation at senior leadership levels.[124] Because many of ISK's founding leadership and members were Pakistanis and former TTP members, ISK's Afghan constituents reportedly began to express growing frustrations with the lack of representation in key leadership positions. When coalition operations eliminated many of these founding Pakistani members between 2015 and 2016,[125] opportunities opened up for greater representation of Afghans in ISK's upper echelons. Khan's death in July 2016 offered a unique opportunity for Afghan leadership at the very top.

There is other evidence that Afghan and Pakistani factions of ISK also quarreled over increasingly limited resources,[126] as well as over ideological disputes regarding the perceived injustice of ISK's governing decisions. It appears that ISK's Afghan constituents expressed growing dismay that the organization was losing popular support because of its harsh implementation of sharia on local Afghans under its control,[127] as well as through extortive practices.[128] Those sentiments were expressed by one of ISK's founding members and the most senior ranking legal-judicial authority at the time of its formation, Abdul Rahim Muslim Dost, who also fomented rumors that then-governor Khan was being leveraged by Pakistani intelligence operatives.[129] After Khan's death, other voices of dissent appeared to echo those rumors. In the same September letter from the ISK Shura Council to the IS-Central Shura Council referenced earlier, the author decries the troubles inflicted by those rumors:

But the oppositionists, and especially Abu-Bakr Balush, mocked the order of the Wali and insisted on maintaining their corrupt stance. Abu-Bakr Balush was also detained twice by the security administration, and Umar [Mulla] was detained once, because of their poor behavior, in hopes of them letting go of their stance at that point, but instead, after they were released, they returned to their old habit. They actually raised the tenor of the conflict, and they spread false rumors about the governance of the province's affairs. They even accused the Wali of detaining members of our group and targeting some of them with drones. You know well that these kinds of rumors and lies can negatively affect the minds of the mujahidin brothers. . . . Remember too that these oppositionists used to send letters to the mujahidin outside the province ordering them not to immigrate to Khorasan Province.[130]

When coupled with other evidence from captured documents in which ISK officials lamented the ease with which coalition strikes targeted the group,[131] it is clear that successful leadership targeting dealt significant damage to organizational cohesion. And it appears that these problems plagued ISK well after Khan's successor, Abdul Hasib Logari, assumed the mantle as the group's second governor. In the wake of Logari's death in April 2017, a group of predominantly Central Asian foreign fighters led by a militant named Muawiya Uzbekistani reportedly refused to acknowledge Logari's appointed successor, Aslam Farooqi.[132] Uzbekistani's contingent appears to have been lodging accusations that Farooqi was an agent of Pakistani intelligence and even distributed pamphlets across northern Afghan provinces that smeared his name and challenged his legitimacy.[133] Beyond instigating organizational rifts, internal struggles can also have a negative effect on members' perceptions of their fallen leaders. Previous studies have found that group perceptions of fallen leaders' personalities, and especially of leaders' charisma,[134] are still being cemented postmortem.[135] Crucially, accusations such as those that were levied against both of ISK's first two governors can set up organizational roadblocks in the wake of leadership targeting, whereas reverence for martyrs can otherwise serve as a unifying and galvanizing force.

However, these dynamics also speak to the efforts that ISK exerted, aided by IS-Central, to secure the organization during delicate periods of leadership succession. Evidence discussed in this book and from other sources suggests that IS-Central leadership advised and assisted ISK in managing the latter's internal affairs when dissent and division surrounded leadership. In fact, using internal security agents to arrest dissenting voices— as the earlier-cited letter mentions—is a method IS-Central itself employed to suppress internal dissent while governing the so-called caliphate in Iraq and Syria.[136] From an organizational perspective, intensive management of dissent during succession periods is quite rational; these are critical junctures when the Islamic State movement's organizing doctrine requires the core leadership in Iraq and Syria and provincial leadership to be in lock-step.[137] And as some of the above excerpts clearly demonstrate, dissenting voices not only damaged intra-ISK cohesion, but also attempted to disrupt communications between ISK and IS-Central, as well as the two entities' underlying relationship.

These documents offer vital insights and highlight some of the various internal organizational rifts triggered by top-level leadership losses and ensuing succession disagreements. But perhaps most important, they speak to the resilience of the Islamic State's bureaucratic method. After all, ISK has experienced a dramatic rate of turnover at the top since its official founding in 2015: six governors were captured or killed through 2020—that is, the governor succession process was forced into action on average once every year for six straight years. Losing governors has not just been an occasional obstacle for ISK, it has been a defining feature of the organiza-tion. Table 4.2 provides a summary of successful coalition targeting opera-tions against ISK governors. It should be noted that these are known instances of leadership targeting that forced succession, and the table does not include other instances of leadership succession, whether known instances such as the 2019 replacement of governor Zia-ul Haq by IS-Cen-tral, or other possible instances that were not the result of capture or kill operations. There is also some disagreement around the precise timing of the killing of ISK's third governor, Abu Saeed. Overall though, the rapid turnover of ISK's leadership, the group's ability to navigate leadership changes, and its eventual resurgence under its newest leader, Shahab al-Muhajir, speak to its resilience.

A closer look at the successful targeting operations against ISK gover-nors lends additional insights. First, most of the operations against ISK's governors occurred near or in the group's former strongholds in northeast Afghanistan. This could be explained by multiple factors, but at the highest level these details support the claim that ISK used Pakistan more as a hub for recruitment, logistical, and financial support, and as a target for sectar-ian attacks rather than an operational hub for its top leadership. Second, while US air power and operational prowess played the leading role in the first four operations against ISK governors, the relative decline of ISK over time and the growing capacity of Afghan security forces allowed the latter to take the lead in subsequent operations. Afghan commandos worked alongside US forces in the complex night raid that resulted in the death of Logari in April 2017.[138] Afghan intelligence operatives led both operations that successfully captured governor Farooqi and his successor, al-Kho-rasani, in quick succession in 2020.[139] Finally, with Afghan forces and US troops now out of the picture post-August 2021, the Taliban have assumed sole responsibility for anti-ISK operations in Afghanistan. The Taliban have reportedly denied allowing the United States to conduct over-the-horizon

Table 4.2   Summary of Reported Governor (*Wali*) Losses, 2015–2020

	Losses	Targeting Forces	Targeting Methods	Result	Targeting Operation Location	Demographic Information
2015	—	—	—	—	—	—
2016	1 (Hafiz Saeed Khan)	US	Air strike	Killed	Nangarhar	Pakistani, former Pakistani Taliban
2017	2 (Abdul Hasib Logari [also known as Hasibullah Logari]; Abu Saeed Bajauri)	ANSF + US; US	Direct action raid + air support; air strike	Killed; killed	Nangarhar; Kunar	Afghan, former Afghan Taliban; Pakistani, former Pakistani Taliban
2018	1 (Abu Saad Erhabi)	US	Air strike	Killed	Nangarhar	Pakistani, former Pakistani Taliban
2019	—	—	—	—	—	—
2020	2 (Aslam Farooqi [also known as Abdallah Orakzai]; Zia-ul-Haq [also known as Abu Omar al-Khorasani])	ANSF; ANSF	Direct action raid; direct action raid	Captured; captured	Kandahar; unknown	Pakistani, former LeT and Pakistani Taliban; Afghan

Source: Author data.

counterterrorism strikes in Afghanistan (although this has not stopped the latter from conducting strikes), and declared that they can tackle ISK on their own. We explore the history and trajectory of the ISK-Taliban rivalry later in the book, but it is worth noting here that ISK's governor since mid-2020, al-Muhajir, was tasked with ensuring the organization's revival strategy in 2020 by reinvigorating its attacks in urban areas and preparing for new targeted campaigns against the Afghan Taliban, which included attacks on critical infrastructure.[140] Al-Muhajir, an alleged urban warfare expert with operational experience as a commander in the Haqqani network,[141] quickly revamped ISK's operational tempo in 2021,[142] and under his governorship, ISK looks set to resurge as one of the preeminent provinces in the Islamic State's transnational movement. He has also enjoyed the longest stretch of uninterrupted leadership over ISK in the group's history: over thirty months by the start of 2023.

Tier 2: Provincial-Level Leaders, Shura Council Members, and Regional Leaders

Frequent turnover plagued not just ISK's governors, but also its next tier of leaders. As Figure 4.3 shows, between 2015 and 2020, ninety-three high-ranking ISK leaders in the Tier 2 category were reportedly captured, killed, or surrendered to coalition forces. These included several deputy governors and known Shura Council members; forty-four reported heads of ISK administrative wings and their deputies; and forty-four reported regional heads, their deputies, and their assigned departmental/office heads.[143] It is possible that a greater number of these leaders held Shura Council positions, but given the shroud of secrecy surrounding those positions, only a few could be verified. At the time of capture/kill/surrender, a number of these leaders reportedly held multiple roles within the organization. For example, Abdul Ra'uf Khadem—one of the founding members of ISK—was reported to be both one of Hafiz Saeed Khan's first deputy governors and also the recognized head of ISK's southern branch, based in Helmand, before his death in a US drone strike in February 2015.[144]

At the time of his death, Khadem had recently led a large contingent of Taliban fighters under his command to defect and join ISK. The details of his story, as well as ISK's broader efforts in Helmand, are discussed later in the book, but available evidence shows that Khadem coordinated closely with ISK leadership in Nangarhar and IS-Central in Iraq and Syria during ISK's formation. In fact, he reportedly traveled to Iraq to consult with IS-Central leadership in October 2014, before being named Hafiz Saeed Khan's deputy in 2015, with responsibility to oversee and expand ISK's activities in Helmand and Farah provinces.[145] After his death in 2015, extant Taliban forces quickly dismantled ISK's broader efforts in Helmand.[146] Outside of ISK's main territorial hubs in northeastern Afghanistan, these same dynamics appear to have played out: reported ISK regional leaders and their deputies were killed, captured, surrendered, or forced to flee, and concerted ISK expansion efforts in those areas quickly collapsed, oftentimes immediately or within a matter of weeks.[147] Only in Jowzjan did local ISK contingents manage to hold on for a substantial period of time following the death of the original regional head, Qari Hekmat.[148] These dynamics speak to the efficacy of an ISK containment strategy in which quickly identifying and targeting regional heads is prioritized.

In Pakistan, leadership losses followed a different pattern, where thirteen of the twenty-eight reported regional heads and deputy heads were captured or killed. The majority of regional leaders in Pakistan were captured or killed in or around major cities, Lahore and Karachi in particular,

Figure 4.4 Yearly Trends in ISK Losses and Attacks Data, 2015–2020

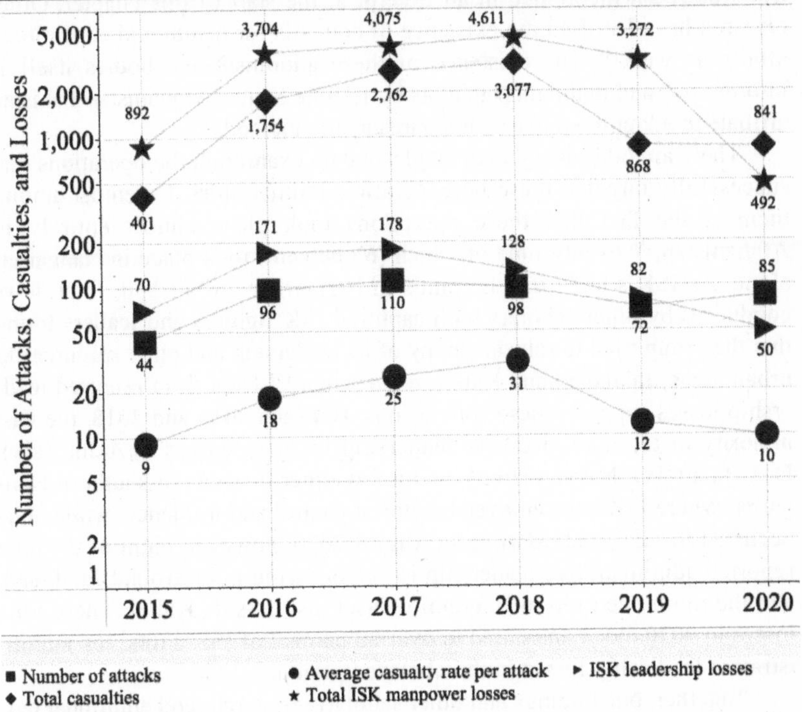

Source: Author data.

where eliminating senior ISK leadership allowed for network disruption and degradation. The nature of ISK's presence in Pakistan meant that regional leaders—who, based on available information, were assigned to entire provinces spanning multiple cities and their surrounds—were focused on recruitment, fundraising, logistics, and attack campaigns, rather than on territorial expansion.

Over the six years between 2015 and 2020, ISK lost a total of forty-four leaders reportedly holding top administrative department/office positions, as well as a few of these leaders' deputies. Available information shows that these leaders were responsible for a wide array of administrative functioning, including judicial and religious matters; intelligence and security; military training, battlefield operations, and martyrdom operations; media, proselytization, and recruitment; and logistics, information technologies, and finance. It is important to note that this list of administrative bodies is not comprehensive. We know from primary source materials that ISK established a variety of additional departments, councils, and offices such as the office of tribal outreach mentioned in an excerpt at the start of this chapter. Other research has identified the existence of councils for health and educational affairs as well.[149] The existence of these administrative bodies itself is informative, and highlights attempts by Islamic State's Afghanistan-Pakistan affiliate to adopt the movement's bureaucratic method.

There are other insights to be gleaned by examining the operations that successfully targeted these bureaucratic administrators. Foremost among them is the fact that these operations took place almost entirely in Afghanistan,[150] twenty-nine of which (66 percent) took place in Nangarhar alone. As ISK's territorial holdings in Nangarhar diminished, interviews conducted by other scholars with captured ISK fighters and leaders found that the group tried to relocate many of its leadership and other resources to urban areas, Jalalabad and Kabul in particular.[151] Data from reported leadership losses supports these conclusions. Between 2015 and 2018, the vast majority of top administrative leadership losses occurred in Achin (six), Deh Bala (six), Nazyan (four), and a few other districts in southern Nangarhar where ISK once enjoyed territorial control and influence, while none occurred in Jalalabad. Starting in August 2020, however, eight of the nine reported administrative leadership losses occurred in or around Jalalabad, and the ninth occurred in Bagrami district just outside Kabul. These nine losses in 2020 alone amounted to over 20 percent of ISK's total top administrative leadership losses in the observed period.

Together, our findings and other scholarly research lend additional evidence to the shift in ISK's strategy under its latest governor: relocate human resources to urban areas in the wake of insurmountable leadership, rank and file, and territorial losses; support organizational survival by blending in with the population; and address fundamental administrative needs through bolstered recruiting and fundraising in urban areas. As an illustrative point, the last three reported Tier 2 losses in 2020 were each reported to be heads of ISK's financial affairs.[152] Additionally, four of the fifteen total administrative leadership losses in 2020 were reportedly intelligence and security heads, all of whom were captured or killed by Afghan intelligence. The loss of key individuals responsible for the protection and security of other senior ISK leadership speaks not only to the dire straits faced by ISK in 2020, but also to the gains of previous years of coalition targeting and the progress made by Afghan security forces.

Tier 3: District-Level Leaders

We found far fewer reported instances of district-level leadership losses— that is, leaders who were reportedly assigned to oversee ISK operations in specific districts. In total, our dataset includes nineteen such leaders, seven in Pakistan and twelve in Afghanistan as shown in Figure 4.3. There are many practical reasons why leaders may have been appointed to cover specific districts. In Pakistan, the seven district-level leadership losses occurred in Rawalpindi, Gujranwala, and Karachi, three of Pakistan's most populous cities. These cities are located in Punjab and Sindh provinces; both provinces in which ISK enjoyed a broader presence across multiple, disparate localities and for which it appears to have appointed provincial-level leaders to oversee affairs. Because of the geographic spread and large population sizes of specific provinces, it would make sense for provincial-level leaders (Tier 2) to assign more localized leaders at the district level to oversee recruitment, fundraising, and attack operations. Four of the seven recorded losses were reported heads and deputy heads of recruitment in their assigned district when they were arrested by Pakistani counterterrorism police.

In Afghanistan, nearly all of the district-level leadership losses occurred in areas where ISK once exercised territorial control and influence, including eight spread across southern districts in Nangarhar. In addition to district heads of recruitment like in Pakistan, some of these leaders in Afghanistan were reportedly responsible for other functions, such as military operations, policing, and logistics. Afghan intelligence operatives led the majority of the raids that killed or captured these leaders. Interestingly, recorded losses were spread fairly evenly over the observed period (2015–2020), rather than being concentrated around the years of ISK's peak territorial control (2015–2017). It could be the case that appointing district-level leaders is not just a strategy deployed during periods of territorial control, but perhaps a more adhocratic, managerial decision used on a case-by-case basis. This would line up with other research mentioned previously, which indicates that the Islamic State in Iraq and Syria employed similar adhocratic leadership structuring decisions. Whatever the logic behind their appointment, district-level leaders did not feature heavily in our dataset relative to Tiers 2 and 4.

Tier 4: Local Leaders
Over six years, coalition and Afghan forces captured, killed, or accepted the surrender of 561 local ISK leaders, a pool of leaders we categorized as Tier 4. These lower-level leaders served in a variety of leadership functions, including recruitment, battlefield operations, attack planning, financial affairs, legal/judicial matters, military training, and other operational and administrative functions. As Figure 4.3 shows, the majority (74 percent) of those losses occurred in Afghanistan, and 66 percent occurred in the first three years of the organization's lifespan. Fewer than 5 percent of those losses occurred in 2020 when ISK's broader organizational decline was apparent.

In Afghanistan, the majority of Tier 4 leadership losses were concentrated around ISK's strongholds in Nangarhar (309, or 74 percent) and Kunar (seventy, or 17 percent). Achin district alone accounted for 117 (28 percent) of all Tier 4 losses in Afghanistan. Small, but noticeable numbers of Tier 4 leadership losses were recorded around Kabul (thirty-seven, or 9 percent) and Jalalabad (sixteen, or 4 percent), particularly after 2017. In Pakistan, the majority of Tier 4 losses occurred in Peshawar (sixty-five, or 45 percent), followed by Karachi (thirty-one, or 21 percent), Mastung (nine, or 6 percent), Gujranwala (eight, or 6 percent), Lahore (seven, or 5 percent), and Sialkot (six, or 4 percent). Almost all of the leadership losses in Peshawar occurred on a single day, when a major Pakistani federal law enforcement raid reportedly busted a large-scale financing network in which dozens of unregistered money changers were accused of transferring funds on behalf of ISK.[153] Next to Peshawar, ISK's Karachi networks in particular suffered the greatest number of low-level leadership losses, most of whom were local recruiters and financiers, and a few of whom were accused of being attack planners.

Many captured, killed, or surrendered Tier 4 leaders across Afghanistan and Pakistan reportedly came from a range of other regional militant groups. We recorded leaders who had prior affiliations with the Afghan and Pakistani Taliban—including some Haqqani network defectors—but also with al-Qaeda in the Indian Subcontinent, Tanzeem-e-Islami, Sipah-e-Sahaba Pakistan, Lashkar-e-Taiba, Jundullah, Jamaat-ul-Muslimeen, Lashkar-e-Jhangvi, and Hizb-e-Islami, among others. Leaders with such prior affiliations offer ISK a number of advantages when it comes to boosting the organization's recruiting, operational logistics, and other affairs. Many of them also end up performing multiple roles at the local level; for example, some of the leaders recorded in this dataset reportedly served not only as local recruiters for ISK but also helped the organization smuggle weapons and munitions through urban areas too.

Mapping the Evolution of ISK's Losses, Attacks, and Lethality

The previous sections examined the nature and magnitude of state-led operations against ISK and the dynamics of ISK leadership losses at multiple levels of the organization. They detailed not only the intense measures that the United States–led coalition and its Afghan partners undertook to contain the group, but also some of the internal challenges ISK faced as its territory, leadership, and rank and file were gradually degraded over the years. Across those three aspects—territory, leadership, and rank and file—the previous sections offer substantial evidence that state-led operations against ISK were successful in constraining ISK's growth. However, they leave other important questions unanswered, including how targeting operations impacted one of ISK's hallmarks as a terrorist organization: its deadly attack campaigns.

There are several ways to approach the question of how targeting operations impacted ISK's attacks. One way is to look at larger, yearly trends in total manpower and leadership losses and compare them with ISK's total number of attacks, average casualty rate (i.e., the number of individuals killed and wounded in each attack), and the group's total inflicted casualties (i.e., the total number of individuals killed and wounded) in a given year. Figure 4.4 shows those yearly changes. Overall, the data show the general growth of ISK's attack campaigns in both number, total casualties inflicted, and average casualty rate from 2015 to 2018, and then the general decline in each of those metrics from 2018 to 2020, except for the uptick in the number of ISK attacks in 2020. The data also show similar trends in ISK's total manpower losses—sequential increases from 2015 to 2018, and then a gradual decline from 2018 to 2020. While reported ISK leadership losses fluctuated slightly more than the other measures, they still show the same general arc of rise and decline overall from 2015 to 2020.

Examining these trends at the yearly level provides overarching, descriptive data for the link between ISK's losses and its attack campaigns, which generally rose together from 2015 to 2018 and then fell together from 2018 to 2020. Reorganizing the data to the monthly level offers some additional insights. At the monthly level, we found that from 2015 to 2016, the overall number of ISK attacks tended to spike randomly in one month, and were then followed by a sharp decline in attacks and an uptick in ISK personnel losses in the following month. However, that sporadic tit-for-tat trend changed in 2017. Between 2017 and 2020, both attacks, as well as the group's manpower and leadership losses, tended to surge for multiple months before falling, without a clear relationship between attacks and losses. Notably, ISK's total monthly lethality tended to spike in random, one-month bursts for all years with the exception of 2018, when the group's combined monthly lethality remained relatively high (150+ individuals injured or killed) between March and November, which marked a sustained period of highly lethal attacks.

From 2015 to 2020, months with relatively higher numbers of personnel losses tended to precede or coincide with months in which ISK-inflicted casualties were much higher. In particular, the months in which ISK governors were killed from 2015 to 2018 seemed to have a dampening effect on the number of attacks in the following months, even if lethality increased or remained the same. Although that trend ceased after 2018, it merits further examination. Did ISK respond to losing its top leaders in the past by unleashing the group's most lethal attacks? As past research shows, targeting of top leaders can often result in a backlash against civilians by foot soldiers— which may be the case for ISK as well. However, given ISK's multitier leadership structure, the effect of leadership targeting on ISK's attack tempo and lethality is a more complex phenomenon that requires a closer examination, which we review in a separate study focused specifically on the short-term effects of counter-ISK leadership targeting operations.[154] Overall, the consistent targeting of ISK's various leadership ranks, but especially its topmost ones, eventually resulted in the decline of the group's attacks, and losses of its territorial control in Afghanistan.

Surviving Counter-ISK Operations

Over the six years covered in this chapter, ISK survived immense territory, leadership, and human capital losses to the United States–led coalition and Afghan forces. Over 13,000 ISK-linked individuals were reportedly killed, about 1,600 were captured, and about 1,900 surrendered. These figures do not even account for ISK losses incurred by its strategic rivalry with the Afghan Taliban (see Chapter 6). State-led operations against ISK spanned nearly all provinces, and over 150 districts in Afghanistan and Pakistan prior to the 2019 split. Operations moved from the mountain valleys of Nangarhar and Kunar to the streets of major cities across Afghanistan and Pakistan. Major ISK efforts to exert territorial control and influence were stemmed in several provinces, sometimes quickly and sometimes because of much longer and more costly counterinsurgency campaigns. Countering the group required a massive array of targeting tactics and forces, from drone strikes, cruise missiles, the world's largest nonnuclear bomb, and complex joint special forces operations to police raids, from coordinated US and Afghan air force assets, intelligence operatives, and special forces operators to local Afghan police forces and Pakistani counterterrorism police units.

State-led operations not only contained and then whittled away at ISK over time, but also instigated internal rifts that demanded action from both ISK senior leadership and from Islamic State leadership in Iraq and Syria. Dissenters were arrested and silenced. Factions split along ethnic and national lines, vying for control and representation among ISK's top leadership when targeting operations forced the leadership succession process. That process frequently occurred at the top of the organization, with governors being captured or killed on average once per year. Hundreds of other upper-level and lower-level leaders were also targeted, which led to varying effects. Removal of regional leaders tended to lead to the quick dissolution of concerted ISK efforts in those regions outside of its core strongholds in the northeast of Afghanistan. Targeting upper-level leaders generally seemed to have constrained overall attack levels and attacks against civilians in the short term. However, state institutions were oftentimes targeted in the following week, and the months following/coinciding with governor losses were some of the deadliest months on record. Despite the notable impact of kinetic operations against ISK, the fact that the group survived these losses and began to resurge in 2021 is evidence of the organization's resilience.

In 2022, the Taliban have publicly refused to allow the United States to conduct counter-ISK operations in Afghanistan, instead insisting that they can manage the ISK threat.[155] But in the few weeks after the Taliban took over, ISK launched a new wave of deadly attacks that continued into the spring of 2022. The group targeted worshippers first in Kunduz and then in the Taliban stronghold of Kandahar, leaving well over 100 dead and 240 injured between both attacks.[156] ISK also reportedly targeted a power supply line to Kabul on October 23, temporarily leaving the city without electricity.[157] In late April 2022, after a short lull in violence, ISK was responsible for a new wave of violence where in one week alone the group conducted multiple attacks on civilian targets, including an attack on a Shiite mosque in the northern Afghan city of Mazar-e-Sharif, and another in Kunduz.[158]

ISK's recent resurgence, along with its ability to launch a deadly campaign of violence in both Afghanistan and Pakistan, and its unwavering resolve on display in the year 2022, brings us back to the important question: What explains ISK's resilience? As we demonstrate in the next two chapters, ISK's initial growth and subsequent tenacity is rooted in its ability to forge and maintain alliances and operational links with various militant groups, and aggressively position itself as a strategic rival of dominant groups such as the Taliban. ISK continues to attack Taliban personnel in the former's old stronghold of Nangarhar, launching well over 100 targeted attacks in the initial months following the latter's return to power.[159] The United States is reportedly still flying intelligence, surveillance, and reconnaissance flights over Afghanistan, and is currently looking to establish a base for over-the-horizon strike options in countries surrounding Afghanistan rather than relying on its bases in the Gulf.[160] If history is any lesson, and given ISK's strategic allies and rivals that span the region, without a broader regional approach to countering ISK that involves other regional powers coordinating and cooperating, the Taliban may not be able to contain the group alone or even with US strikes.[161]

Notes

1. Internal ISK document, Combating Terrorism Center Library.
2. Snow, Shane, and Gould, "Afghan Special Operators Partnering with US Forces More Often."
3. Internal ISK document, Combating Terrorism Center Library.
4. Ingram, *The Long Jihad.*
5. Ingram, Whiteside, and Winter, *The ISIS Reader.*
6. Now part of Khyber-Pakhtunkhwa.

7. Bergen, "The Account of How We Nearly Caught Osama bin Laden in 2001."

8. Osman, "The Islamic State in 'Khorasan.'"

9. Jadoon and Milton, "Strength from the Shadows?"

10. Osman, "With an Active Cell in Kabul, ISKP Tries to Bring Sectarianism to the Afghan War."

11. Jadoon, *Allied & Lethal.*

12. Analytical Support and Sanctions Monitoring Team, *Ninth Report.*

13. Jadoon, *Allied & Lethal.*

14. Johnson, *The Rise and Stall of the Islamic State in Afghanistan.*

15. Osman, "Descent into Chaos."

16. Johnson, *The Rise and Stall of the Islamic State in Afghanistan.*

17. Rassler, "Situating the Emergence of the Islamic State of Khorasan"; Basit, "IS Penetration in Afghanistan-Pakistan"; Tarzi, "Islamic State Khurasan Province"; Analytical Support and Sanctions Monitoring Team, *Twenty-fourth Report.*

18. Osman, "With an Active Cell in Kabul, ISKP Tries to Bring Sectarianism to the Afghan War."

19. Analytical Support and Sanctions Monitoring Team, *Tenth Report.*

20. Safdar, "Pakistan's Achievements in War on Terror but at What Cost?"

21. Ibid.

22. Johnson, *The Rise and Stall of the Islamic State in Afghanistan.* See also: Fahim, "Daesh Fighters Torch Taliban Leaders' Homes."

23. Jadoon and Mines, *Broken but Not Defeated.*

24. Osman, "The Islamic State in 'Khorasan'"; Osman, "The Battle for Mamand."

25. Reuters, "Taliban Condemns 'Brutal' Isis Video of Afghan Prisoners Being Murdered."

26. Ingram, Whiteside, and Winter, *The ISIS Reader.*

27. Johnson, *The Rise and Stall of the Islamic State in Afghanistan.*

28. Fahim, "In Nangarhar, Daesh Strengthens Its Chokehold on Achin"; Osman, Clark, and van Biljert, "Mother of All Bombs Dropped on ISKP."

29. Fahim, "Daesh Has Imprisoned 127 People in Nangarhar's Achin."

30. Fahim, "Up to 100 Daesh Militants Killed in Achin Offensive."

31. Jadoon and Mines, *Broken but Not Defeated.*

32. The Quetta Shura refers to the senior leadership council of the Afghan Taliban, which is based in the Pakistani city of Quetta in Balochistan. See Johnson, *The Rise and Stall of the Islamic State in Afghanistan.* See more in Chapter 6 on strategic rivals.

33. Lubold, "U.S. Clears Path to Target Islamic State in Afghanistan."

34. Johnson, *The Rise and Stall of the Islamic State in Afghanistan.*

35. Nicholson, "Statement for the Record on the Situation in Afghanistan."

36. Nicholson, "Department of Defense Press Briefing."

37. Ibid.

38. Jadoon and Mines, *Broken but Not Defeated.*

39. "ISIS Radio Destroyed in US Drone Strike in East of Afghanistan."

40. Zarifi, "Anti-Daesh Uprising Force Springs Into Action in Nazian."

41. Osman, "The Battle for Mamand."

42. Analytical Support and Sanctions Monitoring Team, *Ninth Report.*

43. "13 Key ISIS Leaders Killed in MOAB Bombing in East of Afghanistan"; Wellman, "Afghan Official: Death Toll from Massive US Bomb."

44. Rempfer, "Inside a Fatal Ranger Raid That killed an ISIS-K Emir in Afghanistan." The operation that killed Logari and subsequent targeting operations

are reported to have heightened ISK operational security measures and stifled the group's communications, disbursement of salaries and weapons, and operations. Giustozzi, *The Islamic State in Khorasan.*

45. Jadoon, *Allied & Lethal.*

46. Sultan, "Islamic State Say They Have Captured Afghanistan's Tora Bora Caves"; Analytical Support and Sanctions Monitoring Team, *Ninth Report.*

47. Jadoon and Mines, *Broken but Not Defeated.*

48. Zarifi, "Daesh Rebels Continue to Get Equipment."

49. Giustozzi, *The Islamic State in Khorasan.*

50. Fahim, "Islamic State Has Started Recruiting in Kunar."

51. Fahim, "Kunar Province Likely to Be Daesh Next Hideout"; *Pajhwok Afghan News,* "Daesh Families Arrive in Kunar's Sarkano District"; Salarzai, "Hundreds of Daesh Rebels Emerge in Kunar."

52. Jadoon and Mines, *Broken but Not Defeated.*

53. Marty, "The Peculiar Presence of the Islamic State in Kunar."

54. Quilty, "'Faint Lights Twinkling Against the Dark.'"

55. Forsythe, "Special Forces Soldiers Help Afghan Forces Defeat ISIS in Eastern Afghanistan."

56. Ibid.

57. Erfanyar, "Afghan, US Forces Destroy Daesh Stronghold in Nangarhar."

58. Jadoon and Mines, *Broken but Not Defeated.*

59. Forsythe, "Special Forces Soldiers Help Afghan Forces Defeat ISIS in Eastern Afghanistan."

60. Fine, Linick, and Barr, *Operation Freedom's Sentinel.*

61. Barron, "U.S. Forces Confirm Death of ISIS Leader in Afghanistan."

62. Zarifi, "Anti-Daesh Uprising Force Springs Into Action in Nazian."

63. Analytical Support and Sanctions Monitoring Team, *Ninth Report.*

64. Author data.

65. Author data.

66. Analytical Support and Sanctions Monitoring Team, *Twenty-fourth Report.*

67. Ibid.

68. Author data.

69. Analytical Support and Sanctions Monitoring Team, *Twenty-fourth Report.*

70. Ibid.

71. Tarzi, "Islamic State–Khurasan Province."

72. Giustozzi, *The Islamic State in Khorasan.*

73. Internal ISK document, Combating Terrorism Center Library.

74. Author data.

75. Osman, *Bourgeois Jihad.*

76. Ibid.

77. Islamic State Khorasan, *Voice of the Caliphate,* episode 57.

78. While this might be the result of differences in reporting in the two countries, it is more likely that ISK intentionally established its operational hubs in active conflict zones in Afghanistan, where it had a higher possibility of success.

79. Gabol, "42 IS Supporters Arrested in Punjab."

80. *The News,* "Sindh Daesh Emir Kathiyo, Islamabad Emir Amir Arrested."

81. Chaudhry, "IS Cell Busted in Sialkot, Claim Officials"; Ali, "Police Arrest 'Islamic State Inspired Militant' from Karachi."

82. *Dawn,* "Three 'Militants' Held for Plotting Attack on Shrine"

83. Gishkori, "Daesh Gradually Gaining Ground in Pakistan."

84. Author data.

85. Ahmed, "Counter-Extremism in Pakistan?"

86. Jadoon and Mines, *Broken but Not Defeated.*

87. *Khyber News,* "FIA Arrests 60 Money Changers in Peshawar for Funding Daesh"; *Express Tribune,* "FIA Raid."

88. *Khyber News,* "24 Daesh Members Involved in Several Attacks Arrested in Peshawar"; Firdous, "Da'ish Peshawar Network Dismantled, 24 Arrested."

89. For coverage of the first arrests, see Ali, "Four Well-Educated Men Held on Terrorism Charge." For coverage of the Karachi bus shooting, see BBC News, "Pakistan Gunmen Kill 45 on Karachi Ismaili Shia Bus."

90. Moosakhail, "ISIS Fundraising in Pakistan's Karachi"; *Dunya News,* "Three Women Linked to al-Qaeda, Islamic State Arrested in Karachi."

91. *Dunya News,* "Sindh IS head Ujmar Kathiwer arrested."

92. See bin Perwaiz, "'Daesh Recruiter' Arrested at Cantt Railway Station"; "FIA Arrests Daesh Recruiter from Karachi"; *Dawn,* "Three Suspected IS Militants Arrested"; Ali, "5 Suspected Daesh Terrorists Arrested in Karachi"; *Pakistan Today,* "5 Militants Arrested in Karachi."

93. *Khyber News,* "Daesh Network Active Near Pak-Afghan Border"; *The News,* "Daesh Militant Arrested from Karachi Makes Startling Revelations."

94. *Dawn,* "Investigators Find Held 'IS Men' Sent Funds to Afghanistan"; Khan, "Daesh Money Trail Traced in Pakistan"; *Times of Islamabad,* "Alleged Daesh Terror Financing Network Busted by Pakistani Agencies."

95. Shinwari, "Eight Militants Killed in New Khyber Operation."

96. Author data.

97. Syed, "Top IS Leadership Targeted in Mastung Operation"; *Dawn,* "Army Releases Details of 3-Day Mastung Operation That Targeted 'IS Facilitators.'"

98. Syed, "Top IS Leadership Targeted in Mastung Operation"; *Dawn,* "Army Releases Details of 3-Day Mastung Operation That Targeted 'IS Facilitators.'"

99. Jadoon and Mines, *Broken but Not Defeated.*

100. Abbas, "Stabilizing Pakistan Through Police Reform."

101. See Abbas, "Transforming Pakistan's Frontier Corps." See also Jamal, *Police Organisations in Pakistan;* Sahi, "Balochistan Police Facing Paucity of Senior Cops."

102. Ahmed, "Daesh Looks to Gain Foothold in Balochistan Under Ex-Karachi Cop."

103. Internal ISK document, Combating Terrorism Center Library.

104. Ingram, Whiteside, and Winter, *The ISIS Reader.*

105. Jadoon and Mines, *Broken but Not Defeated.*

106. Ingram, Whiteside, and Winter, *The ISIS Reader;* Ingram, *The Long Jihad.*

107. Analytical Support and Sanctions Monitoring Team, *Twenty-fourth Report.*

108. Osman, *Bourgeois Jihad.*

109. Johnson, *The Rise and Stall of the Islamic State in Afghanistan.*

110. See Analytical Support and Sanctions Monitoring Team, *Twenty-fourth Report.* See also US Department of Defense, *Lead Inspector General Quarterly Reports;* Ibrahimi and Akbarzadeh's, "Intra-Jihadist Conflict and Cooperation."

111. Withington, *Islamic State Wilayat Khorasan.*

112. Rassler, "Situating the Emergence of the Islamic State of Khorasan"; Jadoon, *Allied & Lethal.*

113. Giustozzi, *The Islamic State in Khorasan.*

114. Ibid.

115. Ingram, Whiteside, and Winter, "The Routinization of the Islamic State's Global Enterprise."

116. Ingram, Whiteside, and Winter, *The ISIS Reader.*

117. Ibid.

118. See also Giustozzi, *The Islamic State in Khorasan.*

119. Ibid.

120. al-Tamimi, "Archive of Islamic State Administrative Documents"; Ingram, Whiteside, and Winter, *The ISIS Reader;* Program on Extremism, "The ISIS Files."

121. Internal ISK document, Combating Terrorism Center Library.

122. Internal ISK document, Combating Terrorism Center Library.

123. Internal ISK document, Combating Terrorism Center Library.

124. Johnson, *The Rise and Stall of the Islamic State in Afghanistan.*

125. Author data.

126. Analytical Support and Sanctions Monitoring Team, *Ninth Report.* See also Giustozzi, *The Islamic State in Khorasan.*

127. Analytical Support and Sanctions Monitoring Team, *Seventh Report;* Withington, *Islamic State Wilayat Khorasan;* Global Witness, *At Any Price We Will Take the Mines;* Amiri, "Achin Residents Tell Their Stories About Life Under Daesh."

128. Amiri, "Islamic State Kills Dozens of Afghans After Foiled Sheep Theft."

129. Sayed, "The Mysterious Case of Shaikh Abdul Rahim Muslim Dost." See also internal ISK document, Combating Terrorism Center Library.

130. Internal ISK document, Combating Terrorism Center Library.

131. Internal ISK document, Combating Terrorism Center Library.

132. Internal ISK document, Combating Terrorism Center Library.

133. Internal ISK document, Combating Terrorism Center Library.

134. Ingram, "The Charismatic Leadership Phenomenon in Radical and Militant Islamism."

135. Steffens et al., "Dying for Charisma."

136. Hamming, *Al-Hazimiyya.*

137. Ingram, Whiteside, and Winter, *The ISIS Reader.*

138. Rempfer, "Inside a Fatal Ranger Raid That Killed an Emir in Afghanistan."

139. For the first operation, see *TOLO News,* "Afghan Intelligence Team Nabs Daesh Leader in South." For the second operation, see *TOLO News,* "'Key' Daesh Leaders Arrested in Kabul."

140. Jadoon, Sayed, and Mines, "The Islamic State Threat in Taliban Afghanistan."

141. Syed, "Who Is the New Leader of Islamic State-Khorasan Province?"

142. Jadoon, Sayed, and Mines, "The Islamic State Threat in Taliban Afghanistan."

143. Author data.

144. BBC News, "Afghanistan Drone Strike 'Kills IS Commander Abdul Rauf.'"

145. Osman, "The Shadows of 'Islamic State' in Afghanistan."

146. Ibid.

147. Including in Samangan, Kunduz, Baghlan, and Laghman provinces.

148. Ali, "Qari Hekmat's Island Overrun."

149. Giustozzi, *The Islamic State in Khorasan.*

150. In fact, only one operation that successfully targeted a reported administrative head occurred in Pakistan.

151. Osman, *Bourgeois Jihad;* Giustozzi, *The Islamic State in Khorasan.*

152. Author data.

153. *Khyber News,* "FIA Arrests 60 Money Changers in Peshawar for Funding Daesh."

154. Jadoon, Mines, and Milton, "Targeting Quality or Quantity?"

155. Jadoon and Mines, "The Taliban Can't Take On the Islamic State Alone."

156. For the Kunduz attack, see Raghavan and Francis, "Islamic State Claims Mosque Blast in Kunduz, Afghanistan." For the Kandahar attack, see Merhdad, Cheung, and George, "Suicide Bombers Hit Shiite Mosque in Afghanistan."

157. *Agence France-Presse,* "ISIS Claims Attack on Power Lines That Plunged Kabul into Darkness."

158. Reuters, "Deadly Blasts Claimed by Islamic State Hit Northern Afghan Cities."

159. Jadoon, Sayed, and Mines, "The Islamic State Threat in Taliban Afghanistan."

160. Desiderio and Seligman, "U.S. Intensifies Talks to Use Russian Bases for Afghan Counterterrorism Ops."

161. Jadoon and Mines, "The Taliban Can't Take On the Islamic State Alone."

5

Seeking Friends:
Alliances and Mergers

*Now then! We inform you that the Bajaur [Khyber Pakhtunkhwa, Pakistan]
Ring, one of the rings belonging to the Tehrik-e-Taliban Pakistan, under
the command of Shaykh Abu-Bakr, may Allah protect him, has pledged
allegiance to the Islamic State. We have accepted its pledge. Also note
that the number of those who have pledged allegiance to the Islamic
State, as a group or as an individual, grows day by day. We deliver this
good news to the emirs and soldiers of the Islamic Caliphate joyfully.*

—Letter from ISK governor Hafiz Saeed Khan
to IS-Central leadership, undated[1]

The above statement jubilantly reports on the latest pledge to the Islamic
State's former caliph and, by extension, ISK—this time from the TTP's
Bajaur faction. As noted in Chapter 2, TTP-Bajaur was one of a number of
groups, factions, and individuals that coalesced to form ISK's foundational
base. These militant entities collectively provided a substantial foundation
for Islamic State in the region, and bolstered the group's ranks as an increasing
number of militants were brought into ISK's fold. As this chapter shows,
support from other militant organizations would prove to be central to ISK's
rapidly increasing capacities across numerous domains, including the group's
highly lethal attack campaigns.

Since its resurgence starting in 2020, the Islamic State has continued to
make headlines across Afghanistan and Pakistan by conducting a series of
atrocious attacks, many of which not only targeted state actors but also
claimed the lives of civilians. In December 2020, the Islamic State[2] claimed a
brutal attack on 11 miners belonging to the Hazara community in Balochistan,

Pakistan, that was condemned as an "inhumane act of terrorism" by former Pakistani prime minister, Imran Khan.[3] Militants associated with ISK kidnapped the miners at night from their shared mud brick residence in the district of Bolan near the town of Mach, from where they took the captured miners to a nearby mountainous region to execute them. Six captives were found dead in a hut with their hands still tied, while the remaining five died en route to the hospital.[4] This brutal attack against the Shiite Hazara community was the result of a collaboration between one of Pakistan's deadliest sectarian organizations, Lashkar-e-Jhangvi, and ISK.[5]

Far from being an isolated event, the above attack is one of numerous over the past several years in which ISK leveraged local alliances to extend its own capacity and geographical reach. The fact that ISK leaned on LeJ is not surprising, given that LeJ is responsible for some of the most devastating sectarian attacks in Pakistan's history, and frequently targets the Shiite Hazara minority. Because of its sectarian stance, over time, the group would prove to be a natural ally for ISK, as would other groups with sectarian or antistate tendencies. While some of ISK's linkages and alliances did not endure—including those with Jamaat-ul-Ahrar and Lashkar-e-Islam—its relationship with LeJ persists.

In the years after its official formation in 2015, the Islamic State Khorasan leveraged such alliances and mergers to make its presence felt across the region by launching deadly attacks with significant geographical reach. In this chapter, we build on our discussion of ISK's alliances and mergers in the region from Chapter 2 and explore how ISK's strategic and tactical alliances played a critical role in its emergence, bolstering its capacities, and developing its resilience (as discussed in Chapters 2, 3, and 4, respectively). While other factors certainly contributed to ISK's capacity, the group's alliances and mergers not only helped localize its jihad but also helped set it up for success by building and sustaining its reputation as a lethal force.

Intergroup Cooperation: Strategic and Tactical Alliances and Mergers

A growing body of literature explores the factors that incentivize militant groups to form alliances with others, as well as the ways in which groups select their partners. Extant theories suggest that alliances are likely to emerge where groups share common ideologies, goals, and targets.[6] Generally, a common adversary can go a long way to unite disparate groups despite different ideologies and lead them to pool resources, which can facilitate groups' survival and relevance.[7] Such pooling of resources can provide groups with specific operational advantages, as it allows them to fill gaps in their expertise, skills, and resources.[8] In terms of the effects of intergroup cooperation, alliances have been directly linked to increasing groups' lethality and efficacy, especially in the face of intense counter-terrorism pressure.[9]

According to the scholar Ely Karmon, militant groups can engage in various types of cooperation: ideological, logistical, operational.[10] Ideological cooperation can take the form of verbal or written statements of support as well as formal pledges to another group. Logistical cooperation can involve several activities, including the exchange of propaganda, knowledge and information sharing, recruitment efforts, and other types of material support. Finally, operational cooperation involves groups assisting each other in any stage of conducting an attack. While it is important to be attentive to the type of cooperation between groups, it is equally important to differentiate the quality of that cooperation; to that end, it is useful to distinguish tactical alliances from strategic alliances. Strategic alliances are often considered a part of what Moghadam calls "high-end" cooperation, which tends to have a longer time horizon than tactical alliances. Strategic alliances are defined as those relationships wherein "collaborating groups share know-how and resources extensively" although they may retain their autonomous status.[11] Because partners in such alliances tend to share objectives and may cooperate in multiple domains (logistical, ideological, operational), their partnerships are generally expected to endure, which is also what makes them more dangerous. On the other hand, tactical alliances tend to be more transactional relationships, wherein groups will only cooperate in a limited domain for quick gains based on shared short-term interests. According to Moghadam, such limited partnerships can emerge "when transitory overlapping interests can result in a temporary marriage of convenience between groups that have divergent ideological orientations."[12]

Building on Karmon's domains of cooperation and Moghadam's concepts of strategic and tactical alliances, we categorize those groups that only cooperated with ISK in a single domain as tactical alliances or low-end cooperation, whereas groups cooperating with ISK in more than one domain were deemed to be engaged in high-end cooperation or strategic alliances unless they merged fully with ISK. As such, we categorized all of ISK's relationships as either mergers, strategic alliances, or tactical alliances in Table 5.1.

Out of the groups listed in Table 5.1, at least three groups were categorized as strategic alliances, and various factions merged completely with ISK. Factions that opted to merge with ISK such as TTP-Bajaur, TTP-Orakzai, and the Islamic Movement of Uzbekistan were observed or suspected to have united their leadership and members with ISK. However, groups such as Lashkar-e-Jhangvi—which formed strategic alliances by cooperating with ISK in more than one domain—were generally expected to have enduring relationships with ISK while maintaining their autonomy. ISK's relationships with groups such as the Balochistan Liberation Army

Table 5.1   Mergers and Alliances

Group	Ideological Cooperation (Pledge of Allegiance)	Logistical Cooperation (Sharing Resources)	Operational Cooperation (Linked Attacks)	Observed Relationship with ISK (Merger vs. Tactical Alliance vs. Strategic Alliance)
TTP factions (Bajaur, Orakzai, and Jundullah)	√			Merger
Islamic Movement of Uzbekistan	√	√	√	Merger
Ansar al-Mujahideen	√			Tactical
Ansar ul Khilafat Wal Jihad	√	√		Strategic
ASWJ (Sipah-e-Sahaba Pakistan)		√		Tactical
Lashkar-e-Islam		√	√	Strategic followed by rivalry
Lashkar-e-Jhangvi (al-Alami)		√	√	Strategic
Jamaat-ul-Ahrar			√	Tactical
Balochistan Liberation Army			√	Tactical

Source: Author data.

and Jamaat-ul-Ahrar are likely to be limited, sporadic, or short-lived as they are restricted to only one of the three cooperative domains.

A number of reasons explain the varying degrees of cooperation among ISK's alliances. While we do not go into extensive detail for all of these groups in this chapter, we briefly discuss some of the common characteristics among groups that opted to cooperate with ISK in some capacity. The first important factor that stands out as a prerequisite for any type of cooperation is some degree of overlapping goals and ideology. All groups that cooperated with ISK in some capacity shared its goals of implementing sharia. However, they all also belonged to the Sunni Deobandi school of thought (discussed in Chapter 1), which carries ideological distinctions to the Islamic State's Salafist ideology, but does not preclude cooperation. Second, all of these groups also shared overlapping targets with ISK, which is a key factor that provides incentives for groups to cooperate. Shared targets included the state (government and security officials) as well as various Muslim and non-Muslim minorities (most frequently the Shiite communities in the region). Third, the vast majority of groups that cooperated with ISK in more than one domain—or elected to merge with it—have been targeted by the Pakistani army in military operations, which could have provided some impetus for joining a new and ascendant jihadist group, especially one so staunchly opposed to the Pakistani state.

Groups that cooperated only in a single domain tended to have goals and targets that were different from ISK's, or their initial attempts at merging with ISK or forming deeper alliances failed due to leadership disputes. For example, even though the Balochistan Liberation Army shares a common enemy with ISK (i.e., the Pakistani state), its ethno-nationalist goals of gaining autonomy in the province of Balochistan and its lack of desire to target minorities per se directly contradict ISK's goals of eliminating national boundaries and instigating sectarian warfare. In the next sections, we provide a brief discussion of ISK's relationships with each group in Table 5.1 before turning to our key case study of the ISK-LeJ partnership.

Tehrik-e-Taliban Pakistan Factions
(Taliban Movement of Pakistan)

The TTP first emerged in 2007, when various militant factions combined under the leadership of Baitullah Mehsud to form a militant umbrella organization in response to Pakistani military operations in the FATA.[13] In the years following its emergence, the TTP established its reputation as one of Pakistan's deadliest militant organizations with close ties with al-Qaeda, the Afghan Taliban, and a host of other militant groups operating in the Afghanistan-Pakistan region. Some of its most prominent attacks include the Pakistani navy airbase attack in 2011, the Army Public School massacre in Peshawar in 2014, and an attack on Karachi's international airport in 2014.

The TTP's initial stated goals included overthrowing the Pakistani government, establishing sharia in Pakistan, and supporting the Afghan Taliban's jihad in Afghanistan when it battled coalition forces prior to taking over in 2021.[14] Operations by the Pakistani military, as well as a US drone campaign in Pakistan's northwestern regions eventually pushed many of the TTP's members into Afghanistan. Waziristan (the town of Miranshah in particular) was once considered to be the TTP's headquarters and the epicenter of terrorism by the Pakistani army. In 2014, soon after the commencement of the military operation Zarb-e-Azb, the area was mostly considered cleared of militants. However, many TTP members not only dispersed throughout Pakistan but also escaped to the border areas with Afghanistan and across the border.[15]

Around the time of ISK's emergence, the TTP was a weakened organization in terms of its operational capacity, suffering from internal fragmentation. Internal divisions and a lack of coherence, especially in the aftermath of top leader Hakimullah Mehsud's death in 2013 and his succession by the polarizing Mullah Fazlullah, only worsened infighting within the TTP.[16] In October 2014 and as explored in previous chapters, TTP-Orakzai's commander, Hafiz Saeed Khan, publicly pledged allegiance to the Islamic State, along with several other TTP commanders including Hafiz Quran of Kurram

Agency, Gul Zaman of Khyber Agency, Mufti Hassan of Peshawar, and Khalid Mansoor of the Hangu district.[17] Although at the time it was unclear if these commanders were defecting with their entire factions, those uncertainties were dispelled when subsequent large numbers of TTP members formed ISK's core organizational force.

In 2015, amid rising rumors and reports of TTP member defections to ISK, TTP spokesperson Umer Khorasani came forth to deny that the entire TTP had aligned with ISK. Instead, he publicly reaffirmed TTP's commitment to the Afghan Taliban's supreme leader, Mullah Omar (whose death was not yet widely known), and a sixty-page statement was released soon after in May 2015 criticizing the Islamic State's self-declared caliph, Abu Bakr al-Baghdadi.[18] When ISK's establishment was officially announced in January 2015, it was perhaps no surprise that a former TTP leader like Saeed Khan was selected to be the group's governor.[19] In fact in August 2016, General Nicholson noted that much of ISK's fighting force in Afghanistan—especially those based in southern Nangarhar—appeared to originate from the Orakzai Agency and had prior affiliations with the TTP chapter there.[20]

In addition to the merger of the TTP-Orakzai chapter, two other TTP factions merged with ISK: the Bajaur faction and Jundullah. The Bajaur faction's merger in 2015 was announced by its leader, who made his faction's position known publicly by pledging allegiance to the Islamic State and, by extension, loyalty to its leader in the Khorasan region, Hafiz Saeed Khan.[21] Rather than form an alliance, the Bajaur faction merged with ISK by uniting their leaders and fighters to the latter.[22] Another faction of the TTP that merged with ISK was Jundullah,[23] a notorious militant group linked to the 2004 attack on the Pakistani army's Karachi Corps commander.[24] Members of Jundullah reportedly first met with an Islamic State delegation in November 2014 in Balochistan,[25] and six days later Jundullah pledged its support to the Islamic State. The group's spokesperson, Fahad Marwat, stated, "They (Islamic State) are our brothers, and whatever plan they have we will support them."[26] In 2015 and 2016, some sources claim that ISK even attempted to merge the Iranian Jundullah with the Pakistani Jundullah, with the intention to develop a united front that could be leveraged for more widespread anti-Iran activities.[27] Prior to the emergence of ISK, Jundullah was frequently reported to target Muslim minority sects and members of other religions, with operational presence in Sindh, Balochistan, and FATA.[28] The group's sectarian stance made for a natural alignment with ISK's goals. In 2015, reports emerged that Jundullah was operationally facilitating ISK activities.[29] For example, the suicide attack on a Shiite mosque in Shikarpur, Pakistan, which killed at least sixty people, was claimed by Jundullah;[30] however, reports pointed to some degree of ISK's involvement.[31] In late 2015, Jundullah's leader, Qari Ghulam Hazrat, who was believed to be heading operations for ISK earlier in the year, was killed in an airstrike in Kunduz, Afghanistan.[32]

Perhaps in part due to its suspected links with ISK, in February 2018, the Pakistani government placed Jundullah on the first schedule of the Anti-Terrorism Act of 1997, which meant that the group's members could be prosecuted using the counterterrorism legal framework.[33] Over the following years, hundreds of TTP members continued to defect to ISK, including a number of senior commanders such as TTP spokesman Shahidullah Shahid, ISK's future governor Abdul Rahman Ghaleb, and various other commanders from the areas of Swat, Kurram Agency, and Khyber Agency.[34]

What were some of the key incentives driving TTP commanders to defect to ISK and merge their factions? This is a complex question, given that the TTP is largely locally oriented and historically has not necessarily sought to establish a transnational caliphate in line with the Islamic State's goals. There are two potential explanations, which may explain why individual TTP commanders and their supporters elected to defect to ISK. On one hand, many individuals likely joined due to ideological convictions and were genuinely motivated by the goal of pursuing a global caliphate. Context is key, and it is important to remember that at the time of 2014–2015, the Islamic State as a proto-state project in Iraq and Syria and as a global movement was ascendant, whereas al-Qaeda and the Afghan Taliban seemed to be largely underperforming in their strategic aims. It is not difficult to appreciate the appeal the Islamic State movement may have had within this context. On the other hand, other TTP members likely saw it as an opportunity for advancement, as a pathway that would allow them to improve their own standing within a new militant organization and seize nascent opportunities for leadership. Regardless of individual-level motivations, ISK's emergence occurred while the TTP was plagued with internal disagreements and splintering into numerous factions. Even at its formation, the TTP was vulnerable to such internal divisions given that it consisted of about forty Islamic and tribal factions primarily from the Federally Administered Tribal Areas[35] and KPK areas.[36] The group was also reeling from aforementioned Pakistani military operations such as Zarb-e-Azb and leadership decapitation at the hands of US drone strikes.

Scholars Abdul Sayed and Tore Hamming have also examined the role of TTP defections in building ISK's strength, offering three explanations for why the TTP became the predominant pool that ISK targeted for recruitment.[37] First, TTP's radical ideology and its increasingly sectarian stance aligned strongly with that of ISK's, more so than it did with its traditional allies—al-Qaeda and the Afghan Taliban. Second, TTP's umbrella structure and internecine fighting—which intensified after the appointment of Mullah Fazlullah as its leader—made the group's factions particularly vulnerable to ISK's attempts to poach its members. Finally, ISK's opposition to the Pakistani state, as emphasized in its various propaganda releases, aligned closely with one of the fundamental goals of TTP to undermine and attack the Pakistani government and military. As such, ISK provided TTP members with a plethora of incentives to join the new transnational Islamic State affiliate, and at the time even threatened to subsume the entire TTP. Untenable negotiations between the TTP and Pakistan today,[38] in addition to strategic divergence in the TTP's aims and those of its long-standing ally in the Afghan Taliban, have already reawakened fears of a more complete merger between the TTP and ISK in the future.[39]

Islamic Movement of Uzbekistan

The origins of the Islamic Movement of Uzbekistan are rooted in an organization formed in 1991 that aimed to overthrow the government of President Karimov, and to implement sharia in Uzbekistan. The organization was subsequently expelled from Uzbekistan, and ultimately led to the official founding of IMU in 1998. Eventually, the group developed close relationships with several regional groups, including al-Qaeda, the Afghan Taliban, and the TTP. Even though IMU always maintained its regionally focused goals of overthrowing the Uzbek government, its goals gradually became intertwined with a more transnational jihad against the West as it began to operate outside of its home base.[40] In the late 2000s, IMU was strongly suspected to have forged ties with the TTP, which may have influenced the IMU leader's subsequent call to action against the Pakistani security forces in 2008.[41]

   IMU leader Usman Ghazi rose to power around 2012 after the death of his predecessor, Abu Usman Adil, in 2012.[42] In August 2015, Ghazi pledged allegiance to al-Baghdadi soon after news emerged of the Taliban leader Mullah Omar's death.[43] Initially, Ghazi's pledge seemed to indicate an attempt to completely merge IMU with ISK, with reports emerging that Ghazi had taken hundreds of IMU members with him to join ISK, as well as publicly announcing that all IMU members would be known as ISK fighters going forward.[44] However, the Ghazi faction experienced significant setbacks when they began to clash with the Afghan Taliban under their newly adopted ISK branding in late 2015.[45] The Taliban defeated Ghazi's followers, who joined ISK fighters in Afghanistan's Zabul province, killing several key members. It is possible that rapid losses to the Taliban either discouraged further IMU defections to ISK or that some reverted back to their previous loyalties and alliances. This suspicion was reinforced in August 2016, when General Nicholson stated that although several IMU members had joined ISK, some had returned to their "original colors."[46] Indeed, upon Ghazi's death, commanders who had defected to ISK regrouped once again under the IMU branding.[47] By June 2016, this revamped IMU faction announced its loyalty to the Afghan Taliban, al-Qaeda, and other jihadist groups operating in South and Central Asia.[48] It also reminded its followers and other jihadist groups that IMU's first three leaders—Juma Namangani, Tahir Yuldashev, and Abu Usman Adil—had each pledged allegiance to the

Taliban's first supreme leader, Mullah Omar. In a clear rebuke of the Islamic State, IMU also noted that prominent al-Qaeda members and Salafi ideologues, including Abu Muhammad al Maqdisi and Abu Qatada, viewed the Islamic State's leader to be "not a caliph of Muslims but only an emir of the 'Islamic State' group."[49]

In sum, the IMU-ISK relationship is complicated, and it does seem that some IMU members may have realigned with the Taliban and al-Qaeda. However, multiple reports indicate that much of IMU—or at least the original IMU—merged with ISK and several motivators potentially explain why the former embraced the Islamic State and distanced itself from its traditional alliances. For one, IMU has always maintained a sort of a "migrant" status within the Afghanistan-Pakistan region, given that its organizational goals and roots lie in its original fight against the state of Uzbekistan. ISK's global jihad and transnational agenda of eliminating national boundaries aligned with IMU's goals, and offered it a platform within the broader jihadist landscape to continue its fight. Moreover, while the Afghan Taliban maintain mutually beneficial links with the Pakistani state and in general refrain from targeting them, ISK's hostility toward the Pakistani state and attack campaigns aligned squarely with IMU's stated objectives of waging jihad against Pakistani security forces. Additionally, the Islamic State's influence and recruitment campaign within Uzbekistan offered a convincing avenue for IMU to revive its influence within Uzbekistan.[50] Overall, IMU had multiple strategic and tactical incentives to merge with ISK as it provided IMU commanders and their followers with an enduring political platform, one that could not be offered by more ethno-nationalist oriented groups such as the Taliban.

Despite the emergence of a "new" IMU in mid-2016 that reaffirmed loyalties to al-Qaeda and the Taliban, reports started surfacing in 2017 indicating that a merger may still have occurred between ISK and IMU. In early to middle 2017, Abdul Rahman Yuldash—the son of deceased IMU leader and cofounder Tahir Yuldashev—was reportedly driving efforts to expand ISK's presence in Afghanistan, and recruiting on behalf of the Islamic State.[51] Around 2017, it was estimated that the number of Uzbeks, Tajiks, and other Central Asian fighters residing in Afghanistan ranged anywhere from 6,000 to 25,000,[52] which would offer ISK a large pool of militants to recruit to its transnational cause, especially if ISK succeeded in bringing IMU into its fold. These reports align with the analysis of IMU-linked attacks in Afghanistan and Pakistan, which show the group's declining operational capacity as an autonomous entity.[53] Between 2012 and 2018, IMU conducted a total of twelve attacks, of which eleven took place between 2012 and 2014 in Pakistan.[54] The group claimed only one attack in 2015—the abduction of thirty Hazara men in Zabul, Afghanistan.[55] Overall, IMU's declining activity post-2015 provides another indicator that the vast majority of its fighters merged with ISK, providing a boost to ISK's operational capacity and its ability to appeal to a greater pool of Central Asian fighters.

Recent ISK-claimed attacks in 2022 either on Uzbek soil or showcasing Uzbek fighters—with related Uzbek-language propaganda to match—signal the group's strategy in Taliban-ruled Afghanistan.[56] As the Taliban grow increasingly constrained by their international commitment to prevent terrorist groups from launching external attacks from Afghanistan, their relationships with externally oriented groups such as IMU are ripe for ISK to exploit. New Uzbek recruits are already in ISK's sights—whether based in Afghanistan or elsewhere—and even the "new" IMU may find itself questioning decades-long alliances with the Taliban and al-Qaeda. In 2022 and beyond, ISK's platform appears to provide the clearest path forward for IMU and Uzbek militants to achieve their goals.

Ansar-ul-Mujahideen (Helpers of the Holy Warriors)

While not much is known about the group Ansar-ul-Mujahideen (AuM), the group emerged around March 2013 and operates predominantly in Pakistan. AuM is generally affiliated with the TTP, and Uzbek fighters are reported among its ranks.[57] One of the most prominent attacks claimed by AuM was a suicide attack on a Shiite mosque in Kurram Agency in July 2013, which killed at least 57 and wounded 180 individuals.[58] The group has also been linked to attacks against Pakistani security forces, largely in North Waziristan,[59] as well as to spoiler attacks especially in 2014 when some TTP factions opted to enter negotiations with the Pakistani state.[60] While no member of AuM is known to have publicly pledged allegiance to the Islamic State, the group's name was mentioned by Shahidullah Shahid (spokesman for TTP and later ISK) in a video released in January 2015. Shahid introduced Hafez Saeed Khan as the leader of ISK in this video release, and AuM was noted as one of many groups that had pledged allegiance to the Islamic State but which could not be present in person.[61] Outside of this brief mention, however, we did not find any reports of cooperation between AuM and ISK. This could potentially mean that AuM fighters started to operate under ISK's brand, but the precise nature of the relationship between the two groups remains uncertain.

Ansar ul Khilafat Wal Jihad
(Helpers of the Caliphate and Jihad)

Ansar ul Khilfat Wal Jihad (AKWJ) has been active in Hyderabad and Karachi in Pakistan since mid-2014 and is known for its attacks against the Pakistani police.[62] AKWJ was one of the first groups to pledge allegiance to al-Baghdadi in mid-2014, and subsequently to Hafiz Saeed Khan as al-Baghdadi's appointed governor for Khorasan in 2015.[63] Per the group's own statements in 2014, AKWJ seeks to support the Islamic State's operations, which led to its announcement of a campaign called Operation Helping the Caliphate in November 2014. AKWJ's official launch statement for the campaign congratulated other groups for pledging allegiance to al-Baghdadi and declared its own support for pro-IS activities.[64] While not much else is known about how exactly the group facilitated ISK operations, members of the group stated that one of their commanders claimed that many Pakistani militants returning from the war in Syria in 2014 had joined AKWJ and that al-Baghdadi himself had approved the formation of the group.[65] According to these members, AKWJ also sought to convince other groups to pledge allegiance to the Islamic State.[66] The extent to which AKWJ has received any material or nonmaterial assistance from ISK remains unclear; however, the group seems to have provided some ideological support to ISK when it first emerged, eagerly embracing the Islamic State brand and the movement's mission in the region.

Ahle-Sunnat-wal Jamaat
(People of the Tradition and the Congregation)

Ahle-Sunnat-wal Jamaat (ASWJ) was previously known as the anti-Shia group Sipah-e-Sahaba Pakistan (SSP), a group–turned–political party that was originally formed in 1985. The SSP was founded by Maulana Haq Nawaz Jhangvi, a Deobandi cleric from the Punjabi town of Jhang in Pakistan. One of Jhangvi's goals was to create a group that would unite all Sunni sects under one banner to fight Iranian and Shiite influence, and establish a Sunni state in Pakistan.[67] Hoping to attract support and resources, the SSP appealed to Saudi Arabia, which, according to Hassan Abbas, was interested in setting up a strong Sunni terrorist base along the Pakistan-Iran border with the intention to facilitate attacks inside Iran from sanctuaries in Pakistan.[68] With Saudi financial backing, the SSP gained recruits, influence, and eventually an operational presence in Balochistan from where it began plotting complex attacks. Some of the SSP's prominent attacks include a plot to kill Iranian diplomats in Lahore, Karachi, and Multan, as well as multiple successful assassinations of Iranian diplomats.[69] Due to its links to terrorism, the group has rebranded and subsequently been banned by the Pakistani government multiple times since its formation,[70] and many of its members are suspected to have operational links with other violent groups with a shared anti-Shia ideology such as Lashkar-e-Jhangvi. These bans, while important symbolically, have proven less effective in practice, and the group has tried to rebrand as ASWJ and rebuild its status as a political party.[71] In Pakistan's largest city, Karachi, the group engages in public service provision for some of the area's poorest communities in order to garner support,[72] and 150 ASWJ candidates participated in the 2018 elections in Pakistan.[73]

In 2014, the Pakistani government in Balochistan noted that some members of ASWJ may be facilitating ISK's operations, and issued warnings of increased attacks in Balochistan and Khyber Pakhtunkhwa, especially against the Shiite community.[74] ASWJ's links with ISK largely seemed to be in the logistical realm at least in its early years, as its members were reportedly openly promoting the Islamic State in Iraq and Syria, and conducting pro–Islamic State campus rallies and sermons.[75] Given ASWJ's shift toward becoming more of a political entity, it is likely that the group intentionally limited itself to only promoting the Islamic State's brand, at least in the public domain, rather than engaging with it operationally. ASWJ's support for Islamic State activities constitutes logistical cooperation as it helped promote the movement's reputation, but little evidence currently substantiates more tangible and material links in the ASWJ–Islamic State relationship. Whether or not ASWJ is able to cement a strong status as a political party, the group will likely continue to be limited in the manner of support it can offer the Islamic State and specifically ISK. Instead, groups with fewer political constraints such as Lashkar-e-Jhangvi (which, as previously mentioned, split from the SSP in the mid 1990s) offer ISK more fruitful opportunities for expanded cooperation.

Lashkar-e-Islam (Army of Islam)

Lashkar-e-Islam represents an interesting case of a group that initially developed a strategic alliance with ISK, but whose alliance turned to rivalry likely due to fighting over resources. LeI first formed in 2004, and focused on targeting the Sunni Barelvi sect, one of Pakistan's largest religions and rival to the region's Deobandi movement.[76] A few years later around 2007, LeI started a movement to implement sharia in Pakistan's Khyber Agency, with its leader, Mangal Bagh Afridi, at the helm.[77]

Khyber Agency is an important strategic economic hub. It encompasses the Khyber Pass, a historical conduit between Pakistan and Afghanistan, and one that was used for NATO land supply lines during the US war in Afghanistan. The Khyber Pass also borders Nangarhar, which as earlier chapters explored eventually became the bastion of ISK's presence. The Pass is well known to be a hub for smuggling of various goods and provides access to weapons black markets.[78] Trade flowing through the Khyber Pass benefited LeI significantly over the years and likely contributed to its expanded political influence in the area around 2008. LeI was eventually declared an illegal organization, and the Pakistani government initiated Operation Sirat-e-Mustakeem (Operation Righteous Path) began targeting the group and other militant groups such as al-Qaeda in 2008.[79] These operations, as well as ongoing operations through 2014, compelled LeI to relocate to Nazyan district in Nangarhar, Afghanistan, as did many other militants.[80]

LeI's now-deceased leader, Mangal Bagh, was never reported to have pledged any formal support to ISK, but reports emerged of the two groups collaborating in the logistical and operational realms and even entering into a power-sharing arrangement in Nazyan district in Afghanistan.[81] LeI was also reportedly included in top-level meetings between ISK commanders and other groups such as JuA and LeJ.[82] A relationship with LeI was especially beneficial for ISK because of the former's hold over the Khyber Pass and linkages to smuggling networks. Cooperation with LeI also enabled ISK to link its operational hubs in Nangarhar, Afghanistan, to its bases in Orakzai, Pakistan.[83] In addition, the alliance between ISK and LeI allowed the former to suppress local militia commanders in Afghanistan's Achin and Nazyan districts who opposed ISK's efforts to exert control in both districts.[84] Despite their close logistical and operational cooperation, there is scant evidence of deeper ideological links between the two groups, and their relationship appears to have been largely driven by short-term mutual benefits.

LeI's relationship with ISK would eventually sour by 2017 when reports emerged that fighting had broken out between the two groups over valuable natural resources. LeI militants had occupied the wooded areas in the Achin district, which ISK attempted to take over and gain access to illegal logging revenue.[85] Various other reports indicated that the two groups continued violently clashing in Nangarhar in February 2018,[86] and ISK even released several statements on the matter through its information channels.[87] The clashes would carry into October 2018, by which time LeI claimed to have killed nineteen ISK militants in Achin and Nazyan.[88] ISK's ambitions and attempts for territorial control, which encroached upon LeI's economic turf, is the likely culprit for the two groups' alliance-turned-rivalry. Regardless of the eventual outcome of their relationship, LeI played an important role in helping ISK create space for itself across the border in Afghanistan, and leading up to their fallout LeI was known as ISK's key partner in Nangarhar during the latter's formative years.[89] Nonetheless, the case of LeI shows how even strategic alliances can quickly turn into rivalries if groups cannot resolve key issues such as resource sharing.

Jamaat-ul-Ahrar (Assembly of the Free)

Jamaat-ul-Ahrar is one of the most prominent factions that split from the TTP in August 2014 after the death of former TTP leader Hakimullah Mehsud in 2013. One of the primary drivers of JuA's decision to split was the growing animosity between the TTP's newly appointed leader, Fazlullah, and JuA's leader, Omar Khalid Khorasani, particularly regarding disputes over whether to engage in peace talks with the Pakistani state.[90] Originally, JuA was based in the Mohmand tribal agency, but subsequently relocated its operations to Nangarhar and the border region between Afghanistan and Pakistan—one of ISK's strongholds.[91] The group formed following a merger between TTP-Mohmand and the Punjabi TTP militant group Ahrar-ul-Hind.[92] During ISK's formative years, JuA leadership attempted to merge their group with ISK, and its members subsequently cooperated with ISK in the operational realm. Since its formation in 2014, JuA has remained committed to overthrowing the Pakistani government and implementing sharia in its territories.[93] The group has been linked to a number of notorious attacks, including the attack on Bacha Khan University in Khyber Pakhtunkhwa province in 2016, as well as the attack on the Army Public School in Peshawar in 2014.[94] The group was banned by the Pakistani government in 2016, and in 2017 the UN Security Council added JuA to its sanctioned list of ISIL-associated entities.[95]

Although JuA did not publicly pledge allegiance to the Islamic State, the group did provide a statement to Reuters news agency in 2016 that they respected the Islamic State and were open to assist them if necessary.[96] According to JuA's spokesman: "We respect them. If they ask us for help, we will look into it and decide."[97] Initially, JuA's leader, Omar Khorasani, seemed intent on merging his faction entirely with ISK and wrote multiple articles in JuA's *Khilafat* magazine in which he welcomed the declaration of the Islamic State's caliphate.[98] However, his demand to establish a Wilayat Hind province under his leadership was reportedly denied by IS-Central leadership, and ultimately prevented a wholesale merger.[99] As such, it is possible that any operational cooperation between the two groups likely took place at the individual member level or was merely a marriage of convenience between the groups.

Besides expressing indirect support in official statements, JuA members appear to have collaborated with ISK in an operational capacity. Several attacks were either claimed by both groups, or local authorities suspected the involvement of each group's members. For example, the targeting of four senior police officers in Quetta on July 13, 2017, was reportedly carried out by JuA, but also claimed by the Islamic State on its website.[100] According to some TTP sources, the two groups maintained a close operational relationship in Nangarhar as well.[101] Starting in early July 2020, however, the TTP announced a series of mergers with influential militant commanders in order to reconsolidate power, and one of the factions that returned to the TTP fold was JuA.[102] Therefore, the tactical alliance between JuA and ISK ultimately did not last, but like other TTP factions, JuA remains opportunistic and may explore future cooperation with ISK if the right conditions are in place, just as it has done in the past.

Balochistan Liberation Army

The Balochistan Liberation Army (BLA) has been fighting with the Pakistani state since its formation in 2000. Its goal is to create an autonomous Balochistan province separate from the Pakistani state, and it has been designated a terrorist group by Pakistan, the United Kingdom, and the United States. Although Balochistan is rich with natural resources such as gas, copper, and coal, it remains one of the poorest, least developed, and most underemployed provinces in the country, all of which drive underlying grievances that local militant groups such as the BLA seek to exploit.

Since 2006, the group has been responsible for some of the deadliest attacks in the country's history and has also been linked to the TTP. In recent years, the BLA's attacks have grown in number; the June 2020 attack on the Pakistan Stock Exchange building in Karachi was attributed to the BLA, as was an April 2021 Quetta attack that killed four people.[103] In a single week in January 2021, the group conducted two sophisticated and deadly attacks against Pakistan's security forces in Balochistan.[104]

The larger organizational goals of ISK and the BLA, along with other Baloch seperatists, diverge significantly since the latter is an ethno-separatist group rather than a jihadist insurgency. Despite divergent goals and ideologies, the two groups share a common enemy in the Pakistani state. As a result, any cooperation between the two entities is always likely to be a marriage of convenience—a tactical relationship intended to create mutual benefits for each party. Although the relationship between the BLA and ISK is far from clear, and there is a lack of evidence of any large scale cooperation, there were some early indications that their shared common enemy may have created some room for a tactical alliance, at least in the short term. An attack on a Christian community in Quetta in December 2017—which killed nine and injured about fifty-seven people—was reportedly planned and executed jointly by the BLA and ISK.[105] Such cooperation is not entirely unsurprising given that the BLA has also cooperated with other groups in the operational domain on the basis of a common target; for example, an attack on police officers in November 2017 was jointly claimed by the TTP and the BLA.[106] Despite the uncertainty surrounding the current nature of the relationship between the BLA and ISK, there is strong evidence that the BLA may have cooperated on operational matters with ISK, at least as far as both groups' activities in Balochistan are concerned. Shared interests in attacking not only the Pakistani state but also international targets—especially Chinese projects such as the China-Pakistan Economic Corridor, as well as Chinese nationals[107]—may provide key avenues of cooperation between ISK and the BLA going forward.

As the above sections demonstrate, ISK sought out alliances with numerous groups in the region that varied in quality and nature. While some groups limited their cooperation to the operational realm, others not only provided ideological support but also merged entirely with ISK. Regardless of the quality and duration of these relationships, ISK's partnerships with local groups were critical—and certainly in its early years—to help the group build its reputation in the region and bolster its operational capacity. When ISK first emerged, not only was it viewed as an external or imported brand, but it faced a highly competitive militant landscape that had long been home to its main transnational rival: al-Qaeda. Yet ISK's openness to building alliances and cooperating with groups that shared its targets and goals worked in attracting a range of opportunistic, tactical, and strategic partners. In the next section, we take a closer look at ISK's partnerships with one of Pakistan's deadliest groups, Lashkar-e-Jhangvi, to demonstrate how an alliance with this local group in particular contributed to ISK's resiliency and ultimately its ability to survive in highly challenging circumstances.

The Case of Lashkar-e-Jhangvi

Lashkar-e-Jhangvi formed in the mid-1990s, and has firmly established its reputation for being one of the deadliest sectarian groups in Pakistan. As briefly outlined in Chapter 2, LeJ has primarily targeted the country's Shiite communities, along with other religious minorities. LeJ broke off from the SSP in the mid-1990s and slowly aligned itself with the Afghan Taliban, calling for the removal of Western influences since at least 2001.[108] Named after the SSP's founder, Haq Nawaz Jhangvi, LeJ has as its express goal to continue Jhangvi's sectarian vision by conducting targeted attacks against Shiite Muslims and Iranians. In later years, LeJ would also become involved in the jihad in Kashmir, which allowed them to gain significant military training and expertise from different terrorist groups and establish links with groups such as Harkat-ul-Jihad-al-Islam and Jaish-e-Mohammed.

Despite its deeply anti-Shia ideology, LeJ's attacks are not limited to Shiite communities. In the past, the group has attacked law enforcement personnel who investigated LeJ's attacks or members, including the May 1997 murder of the senior superintendent of police in Gujranwala, Ashraf Marth, who was investigating the group's infrastructure.[109] While in its earlier years LeJ was not specifically targeted by the Pakistani state, the group was banned in 2001 and its leaders were targeted more heavily starting in 2003.[110] One of LeJ's leaders, Malik Ishaq, and his two sons were killed in July 2015 along with several other high-profile leaders during a clash with security forces.[111] The death of Ishaq came only five months after the killing of Usman Kurd, who was the leader of LeJ's Balochistan chapter.[112]

Around 2009–2010, LeJ reoriented its branding to expand its jihad under a new banner—LeJ al-Alami (LeJ International, often abbreviated as LeJ-A)—which is involved in operations outside of Pakistan.[113] This pivot toward a more transnational organizational identity made LeJ an attractive partner for regional militant groups, and although LeJ was initially established as the armed wing of the SSP, over time it evolved into the "collective armed wing of various Deobandi terrorist groups."[114] The group's reputation also proved enticing to the Islamic State's transnational agenda, and LeJ is considered to be ISK's main partner in the region. Both ISK and LeJ expend significant operational resources in Balochistan, where they mostly target the Shiite community in Quetta.[115] LeJ's deep roots in the province of Balochistan make the group even more dangerous. According to Hassan

Abbas, "LeJ has made strategic inroads into Brahui dominant areas in Balochistan as well as Sindh province. . . . Pakistani intelligence services, or some sectarian elements within it, possibly facilitated LeJ's move to Balochistan to confront Baloch nationalists, especially the BLA, around the 2007–2010 timeframe. . . . There is no evidence of an institutionalized policy, however, and the military has denied these charges vociferously."

LeJ's deep roots in the province have grown increasingly entangled with those of ISK, which maintains strongholds in certain pockets. Because of their shared ideology and sectarian targeting, ISK and LeJ have developed a deadly partnership in Balochistan, one that ISK has consistently leveraged to facilitate and strengthen its position in the region.

The Lashkar-e-Jhangvi Connection

Although LeJ never publicly pledged allegiance to the Islamic State, the group has openly expressed its willingness to cooperate and even cited examples of past cooperation with ISK. For example, LeJ spokesman Ali bin Sufyan admitted to collaborating with ISK for the October 2016 attack on a police academy in Quetta, Pakistan, which killed at least sixty individuals.[116] Additionally, there were some reports during ISK's initial emergence regarding LeJ leaders holding discussions with ISK in Saudi Arabia as well as in Afghanistan,[117] and an article in the Islamic State's weekly newspaper *al-Naba* claimed that LeJ had indeed pledged allegiance to the Islamic State.[118] There have even been some reports that LeJ received funds from IS-Central, although that relationship has not been verified.[119]

Regardless of whether LeJ formally pledged allegiance to the Islamic State or not, the two groups have reportedly been cooperating in the logistical and operational realms. Pakistani government officials and security experts frequently point to the working relationship between LeJ and ISK and often suspect them of collaborating together, especially in Balochistan.[120] In 2017, the Pakistani army released details regarding a three-day operation on a cave complex in the Splingi area of Mastung, Balochistan, in which security forces targeted Islamic State–linked commanders and fighters. The three-day operation resulted in the killing of twelve militants, reportedly including both ISK and LeJ members. An army public statement indicated that an explosives facility inside the cave was destroyed, including arms and ammunition, suicide jackets, and communication devices, shedding additional light on the operational connections between LeJ and ISK.[121]

One of the clearest examples of ISK-LeJ cooperation is a militant network known as the Pendrani group, which came to the forefront of public attention when it conducted a suicide attack in October 2015 at a Shiite mosque in Jacobabad near Shikarpur, Sindh.[122] The Islamic State claimed the attack, which killed and injured close to sixty people. Although the Pendrani group members were originally affiliated with Jaish-e-Mohammed, their leader, Abdul Hafeez Pendrani (also known as Hafeez Pandrani Brohi, an ethnic Brahui militant) later joined LeJ and his group increasingly began targeting Shiite communities in Pakistan. In February 2019, during an operation in Sibi, not far from the 2017 Splingi cave raid and October 2015 mosque bombing, Sindh police killed Abdul Hafeez Pendrani and another prominent militant named Maulvi Abdullah Brohi.[123] According to statements made by officials, Brohi and Pendrani were leading Islamic State cells in Sindh and Balochistan and were involved in several IED blasts and suicide attacks across the two provinces.[124] Pendrani was reported as being affiliated with LeJ, TTP, and JeM,[125] as well as maintaining close contact with the chief of LeJ, Asif Chotu.[126] More recently, in a May 2021 operation in Shikarpur district, local police collaborated with federal intelligence agencies to arrest three Islamic State fighters named Khalid Mahmood Pendrani (alias Amir Hamza), Usman Brohi, and Siddique Brohi.[127] Mahmood Pendrani is believed to be the brother of Abdul Hafeez and is a member of his group.[128] These linkages are further evidence that although LeJ and ISK remain autonomous and separate terrorist groups, they are interlinked, they share resources, and their cooperation is multifaceted.

Cooperation between LeJ and ISK has not been limited to Balochistan either. The militants who perpetrated the 2015 Safoora Goth massacre in Karachi—which killed about forty-five members of the Shiite Ismaili community—were linked to LeJ and the Islamic State.[129] Three years later in January 2018, Karachi police targeted and killed four militants who were connected to several terrorist incidents and reportedly affiliated with both LeJ and the Islamic State.[130] In fact, data introduced below shows that LeJ-ISK cooperation has actually seen both groups shift their attack locations to focus more heavily on Sindh province. Nonetheless, their cooperation in Balochistan—both logistical and operational—has clearly benefited from Pakistani security forces' relatively weaker capacities there compared to other provinces (as discussed in Chapter 1).

LeJ has also logistically enabled ISK in the area by facilitating pro–Islamic State recruitment. In recent interviews with scholar Hassan Abbas, Pakistani law enforcement officers voiced concerns "about the recruitment drive of ISK-LeJ-A targeting the Brahui-dominated areas,"[131] in Balochistan. These and similar concerns abound that the Islamic State, in collaboration with LeJ, will continue to leverage Brahui violent extremists such as Pendrani and his group to consolidate their own strength. Perhaps equally as concerning is that membership between ISK and LeJ seems to be becoming relatively fluid. According to a senior officer with the Sindh Counter-Terrorism Department, some ISK members in Afghanistan's Nangarhar province joined LeJ's ranks.[132] From the organizational to the individual level, linkages and cooperation between these two deadly terrorist groups have pervaded the last several years, and are likely to persist into the future.

Joint Attacks and Geographical Reach

To assess the extent to which cooperation between ISK and LeJ facilitated ISK's lethality and geographical reach, we collected data on all the joint attacks conducted by ISK and LeJ between 2015 and 2019. Figure 5.1 and Table 5.2 present the details of six attacks that were either claimed by both ISK and LeJ, or local security officials implicated both groups as being responsible. Over the same time period, ISK was linked to about 112 attacks in Pakistan,[133] which resulted in a total of 2,160 individuals killed and wounded. Out of these attacks, it may not seem striking that only six were recorded to be jointly conducted attacks with LeJ. Of course, an important caveat to keep in mind is that not all ISK-claimed attacks involving LeJ may have been reported as such in open sources. Even so, a closer examination shows that these attacks were critical in enhancing ISK's lethality. The six joint attacks—five of which were conducted in Balochistan—left just under 850 individuals reportedly killed and wounded in Pakistan, which accounts for around 40 percent of all ISK-attributed casualties in Pakistan. The magnitude of death and destruction when these two groups collaborate cannot be overstated, as shown in our discussion here of two of their most deadly joint attacks.

Figure 5.1   Locations of ISK-LeJ Collaborative Attacks, 2015–2019

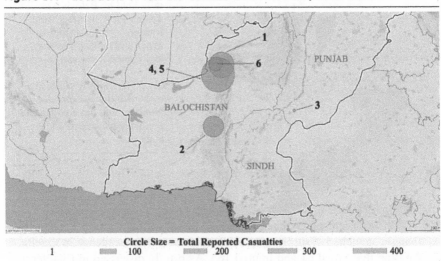

Source: Author data.
Note: Numbers on map refer to "Map Code" in first column of Table 5.2.

Table 5.2   ISK-LeJ Collaborative Attacks, 2015–2019

Map Code	Date	Location	Total Casualties	Description
1	October 24, 2016	Quetta, Balochistan	226	Attack on Balochistan police training college killed or wounded hundreds of police cadets and administrators. Attack claimed by ISK and reportedly carried out by LeJ militants.
2	November 12, 2016	Khuzdar, Balochistan	152	ISK and LeJ jointly claimed responsibility for attack on Sufi religious gathering at Shah Noorani Shrine.
3	December 30, 2016	Rahim Yar Khan, Punjab	3	Attack outside a Counter-Terrorism Department building in Punjab claimed by ISK and reportedly involved LeJ militants.
4	May 5, 2017	Mastung, Balochistan	55	ISK claimed responsibility for suicide bombing targeting convoy of deputy chairman of Senate of Pakistan, Abdul Ghafoor Haideri, which authorities also blamed on LeJ.
5	July 16, 2018	Mastung, Balochistan	329	ISK suicide bombing in Mastung targeted election rally held by Balochistan Awami Party member Siraj Raisani. Second deadliest attack in Pakistan's history, and bomber later identified as LeJ militant.
6	April 11, 2019	Hazar Ganji, Balochistan	68	ISK and LeJ jointly claimed responsibility for suicide bombing that targeted Hazara civilians gathered in local market.

Source: Author data.

On the night of October 24, 2016, Sunni militant group Lashkar-e-Jhangvi launched a surprise assault against a police academy in Quetta, Pakistan that killed 61 and injured 165. As briefly discussed in Chapter 3, over the course of the four-hour attack, three militants terrorized the sleeping cadet population with gunfire and explosives, leaving little room for an effective police response. The militants first neutralized the watchtower sentry, then stormed the barracks, and opened fire,[134] taking cadets hostage while engaging in a standoff with responding security forces. Two of the attackers detonated suicide vests in the crowded buildings,[135] resulting in the majority of the casualties. The remaining militant was killed by the military. In the aftermath of the attack, Balochistan home minister Sarfraz Bugti admitted that officials had received previous reports of terrorists entering Balochistan and planning an attack in Quetta, but the potential target was unknown.

Subsequent investigations revealed that the al-Alami faction of LeJ (LeJ-A) was responsible for carrying out the assault, while intercepted communications show that attackers received instructions from individuals within Afghanistan. The Islamic State claimed responsibility for the assault via its *Amaq* news agency, releasing photographs of the alleged gunmen. An al-Alami spokesman later confirmed that it worked together with the Islamic State to carry out this attack, but denied having direct ties to the organization.[136] The Pakistani Taliban also claimed responsibility for the attack, although this allegation remained unsubstantiated. Balochistan province is home to many separatist militant groups as well as the Pakistani Taliban; despite recent improvements to Pakistan's security posture, this attack served as a grim reminder that militant organizations will continue to pose a challenge to stability in the region.

On July 13, 2018, a suicide bomber attacked a campaign rally in Mastung, Balochistan, twelve days before Pakistan's general elections. The bombing left 149 Pakistanis dead and over 180 injured, making it the third-deadliest attack in Pakistan's history. The attack targeted Nawabzada Siraj Raisani, the Balochistan Alami Party candidate for a provincial assembly seat, who was killed in the blast. Reports indicate that the bomber made his way toward the front of the large crowd while local leaders were speaking, detonating his vest near the stage.[137] The vest contained approximately eight kilograms of explosives, as well as ball bearings and nails[138] intended to inflict maximum damage to victims' bodies. A near simultaneous suicide attack was launched at a Muttahida Majlis-e-Amal (MMA) party rally in Khyber Pakhtunkhwa province earlier that day, killing five and injuring thirty-seven.[139]

In the aftermath of the Balochistan attack, the Islamic State claimed responsibility and named the bomber by his alias Abu Bakr al-Pakistani, later identified as Hafiz Nawaz of Abbottabad.[140] Nawaz travelled to Balochistan via Afghanistan, and was affiliated with both the Islamic State and LeJ;[141] it is assumed that the two groups cooperated in the execution of the attack. The next day, security forces detained two suspects accused of housing the bomber and facilitating the devastating blast, which occurred the same day that former prime minister Nawaz Sharif returned to Pakistan to face his corruption charges. Media coverage of the attack was initially overshadowed by Sharif's dramatic return.

These events provide just two examples of lethal attacks in which ISK and LeJ collaborated. To assess how LeJ's attack patterns changed after it began collaborating with ISK, we compared LeJ's attacks in the three years prior to 2015 (the year of ISK's official formation) with its attacks in the three years after 2015. We observed a notable shift in the location of LeJ-claimed attacks in the three years after ISK's formation. In relative terms, LeJ reduced its attacks in Balochistan and Khyber Pakhtunkhwa, but intensified them in Sindh post-ISK alliance. In the 2015–2018 period, LeJ launched twenty attacks in Balochistan (a 42 percent decrease from the previous period) and twenty-three attacks in Sindh (a 187 percent increase). Thus, LeJ's relative shift away from Balochistan—while still conducting numerous attacks in the province—and increased focus on Sindh from 2015 onward overlaps with ISK's shift toward Sindh in the period from 2015 to 2017. Their collaboration seems to have continued into 2020 and 2021, including the abduction and killing of eleven Hazara miners in Balochistan mentioned at the start of this chapter.[142]

Taken together, LeJ's alliance with ISK appears to have extended into multiple domains, and constitutes a strategic rather than a tactical partnership. Their relationship has endured for several years, and not only bolstered ISK's lethality and geographical reach, but also provided it with the local know-how to establish its roots in the region, garner additional recruits, and enhance its reputation. Short of a dramatic and rapid shift in either groups' goals and targeting priorities, their alliance is likely to extend into the foreseeable future.

Islamic State Khorasan's Partnerships

The threat posed by Islamic State Khorasan has been significantly exacerbated by its mergers with various factions and splinter groups such as TTP factions and IMU, its strategic alliances with groups such as Lashkar-e-Jhangvi, and its short-term tactical alliances with groups such as Jamaat-ul-Ahrar. Even where groups such as ASWJ only provided ISK with ideological support, collaboration with local groups at all levels not only provided ISK with the required startup capital to establish itself and expand, but also allowed it to localize its jihad and bolster its operational capacity. Moreover, collaborative relationships with groups such as LeI helped ISK to establish itself territorially when it first sought control over various pockets of Nangarhar, as well as to gain access to local smuggling hubs.

Local militant groups that conduct operations in both Afghanistan and Pakistan have proven their desire and capabilities to pool resources with ISK and launch deadly attacks against common enemies, namely the Pak-

istani state, Shiite communities, and other non-Muslim minority populations. These alliances have allowed ISK to sustain greater attack lethality;
gain access to local knowledge, leadership, training, and expertise; launch
successful recruitment campaigns; and expand operations across a larger
geographic area, all despite intense targeting by state and non-state actors.
The current status of many of ISK's relationships is either unclear or in
flux. There is little evidence that ISK today maintains relationships with
groups such as LeI or JuA, but relationships can change rapidly as circumstances evolve on the ground. ISK seems to have established the most
robust and strategic partnership with LeJ, and specifically LeJ-A, which
continued at least through 2021 and most likely beyond. If history is any
indicator, ISK will be shoring up its existing alliances, rekindling lost ones,
and forging new partnerships to take on this latest phase of its evolution.
These alliances will be even more critical to ISK's strategy as it seeks to
further destabilize the region and increase its foothold.

Notes

1. Internal ISK document, Combating Terrorism Center Library.
2. Around mid-2019, the Islamic State announced the creation of Islamic State–
Pakistan and Islamic State–Hind, while retaining Islamic State Khorasan. This
largely seemed to be an organizational redesign, likely intended for ease of management. Since the creation of the Pakistani front, attacks in all of Pakistan's provinces
except for Khyber Pukhtunkhwa have been attributed to IS-Pakistan, while all attacks
in Afghanistan and Khyber Pukhtunkhwa (Pakistan) have been attributed to ISK.
3. BBC News, "Pakistan Coal Miners Kidnapped."
4. Ibid.
5. *The Nation,* "Fighting Terrorism."
6. Bond finds that groups with similar ideologies are seven times likelier to
cooperate than those with dissimilar ideologies; Bond, "Power, Identity, Credibility,
and Cooperation," p. 96. See also Moghadam, *Nexus of Global Jihad,* p. 26; Bacon,
"Alliance Hubs"; Asal et al., "With Friends Like These."
7. Bapat and Bond, "Alliances Between Militant Groups."
8. Ibid.; Cragin et al., *Sharing the Dragon's Teeth;* Jackson et al., *Aptitude for
Destruction;* Moghadam, *Nexus of Global Jihad.*
9. Bacon, *Why Terrorist Groups Form International Alliances*; Phillips, "Enemies with Benefits?"; Asal and Rethemeyer, "The Nature of the Beast."
10. Karmon, *Coalitions Between Terrorist Organizations.*
11. Moghadam, *Nexus of Global Jihad.*
12. Ibid.
13. Abbas, "A Profile of Tehrik-i-Taliban Pakistan."
14. Ibid.
15. Jadoon, "Playing Dirty to Survive."
16. Roggio, "Pakistani Taliban Name Mullah Fazlullah."
17. Basit, "IS Penetration in Afghanistan-Pakistan."
18. Joscelyn, "Pakistani Taliban Rejects."
19. Johnson, Karokhail, and Amiri, "The Islamic State in Afghanistan."
20. "Department of Defense Press Briefing by General Nicholson."

21. Khan, "TTP Bajahur Declares Allegiance to Islamic State."
22. Ibid.
23. The Jundullah group referred to in this report is a faction of the TTP, and distinct from the Iranian Jundullah movement, which operates in southeastern Iran.
24. Khan, "Pakistan Shia Mosque Blast."
25. Basit, "IS Penetration in Afghanistan-Pakistan."
26. Khan, "Jundullah Vows Allegiance to Islamic State."
27. Giustozzi, *The Islamic State in Khorasan.*
28. *Jane's Intelligence,* "Jundallah."
29. The Jundullah group referred to in this report is a faction of the TTP, and distinct from the Iranian Jundullah movement, which operates in southeastern Iran.
30. Shaikh, "At Least 60 Killed."
31. Chishti, "The ISIS Link."
32. *Afghan Zariza,* "Top Leader of Jundullah."
33. Syed, "Govt Bans Jundullah, Notification Issued."
34. Zahid, "The 'New' Militants."
35. A bill was passed by the Pakistani parliament in May 2018 to merge the Federally Administered Tribal Areas with KPK province.
36. Jamal and Ahsan, "TTP: Analyzing the Network of Terror."
37. Sayed and Hamming, "The Revival of the Pakistani Taliban."
38. Jadoon, "The Untenable TTP-Pakistan Negotiations."
39. Yousaf, "Peace Talks to Pre-empt TTP-Da'ish Nexus."
40. Mackenzie Institute, "Islamic Movement of Uzbekistan."
41. Ibid.
42. Roggio, "IMU Announces Death of Emir."
43. SITE Intelligence Group, "IMU Pledges Allegiance to IS Leader."
44. Sharipzhan, "IMU Declares It Is Now Part of the Islamic State."
45. Roggio and Weiss, "Islamic Movement of Uzbekistan Faction Emerges."
46. *Al-Jazeera,* "Afghan-Pakistan ISIL's Hafiz Saeed Khan Killed."
47. Giustozzi, "Shifting Ground."
48. Roggio and Weiss, "Islamic Movement of Uzbekistan Faction Emerges."
49. Ibid.
50. Mehl, "The Islamic Movement of Uzbekistan Opens a Door to the Islamic State."
51. Gannon, "Power Struggle Seen Within Surging Islamic State in Afghanistan"; Zahid, "Son of Slain IMU Leader."
52. Gannon, "Power Struggle Seen Within Surging Islamic State in Afghanistan."
53. Jadoon, *Allied & Lethal.*
54. Ibid.
55. BBC News, "Gunmen Seize 30 Hazara Men."
56. Valle and Webber, "ISKP's Uzbekistan-Directed Attack Bolsters Rhetoric with Deeds."
57. Rehman, "A Profile of Ahrar-ul-Hind and Ansar-ul-Mujahidin."
58. Sherazi, "'Anti-Drone' Militant Group Claims Parachinar Twin Blasts."
59. Roggio, "Ansarul Muhajideen Suicide Bomber Kills 2 Pakistani Troops."
60. Ibid.
61. *FDD's Long War Journal,* "Pakistani Taliban Splinter Group."
62. Open Source Enterprise, "Pakistan: Dawat-e-Haq Posts Images of Pro-ISIL Graffiti."
63. Rassler, "Situating the Emergence of the Islamic State of Khorasan."
64. Open Source Enterprise, "OSC Summary."

65. Giustozzi and Mangal, "Taking Shape."

66. Ibid.

67. Abbas, "A Profile of Pakistan's Lashkar-e-Jhangvi."

68. Ibid.

69. Ibid.

70. Hasan, "Pakistan bans Ahle Sunnah Wal Jamaat Islamist group."

71. Ibid.

72. Shah and Hasan, "In Pakistan, Extremist Group Expands Its Reach."

73. Anwar, "Hundreds with Terror Ties Run in Pakistan Elections."

74. *Dawn,* "IS Footprints Growing in Pakistan."

75. Rafiq, "Will the Islamic State Spread Its Tentacles to Pakistan?"; Nazish, "The Emergence of the Islamic State in Pakistan."

76. Jackson, "A Subcontinent's Sunni Schism"

77. Khattak, "Mangal Bagh and LI Marginalized in Khyber Agency."

78. Zaidi, "The Role of Lashkar-i-Islam in Pakistan's Khyber Agency."

79. Global Security, "Lashkar-e-Islami / Mangal Bagh Afridi."

80. Johnson, *The Rise and Stall of the Islamic State in Afghanistan.*

81. Osman, "The Islamic State in 'Khorasan.'"

82. Pakistan Institute for Conflict and Security Studies, *Pakistan: Security Assessment 2017.*

83. Ibid.

84. Osman, "The Islamic State in 'Khorasan.'"

85. Zerai, "ISIS, Other Militants Clash over Illegal Logging."

86. Habibzada, "IS, Lashkar-e-Islam Clash in Eastern Afghanistan."

87. Statement released via *Amaq.*

88. *Islamic Theology of Counter Terrorism,* "Lashkar-e-Islam Claims Killing 19 Islamic State Militants."

89. Osman, "The Islamic State in 'Khorasan.'"

90. Jendruck, "Pakistani Militant Groups Form New TTP Coalition."

91. United Nations, "Security Council ISIL (Da'esh) and al-Qaida Sanctions Committee Adds One Name to Its Sanctions List."

92. Shah, "Pakistan Militant Group Jamaat-ul-Ahrar Threatens Fresh Wave of Violence."

93. Roggio, "US State Department Lists Jamaat-ul-Ahrar As Terrorist Group."

94. Akbar, "TTP Names Successor to APS Mastermind Umar Mansoor."

95. United Nations, "Security Council ISIL (Da'esh) and Al-Qaida Sanctions Committee Adds One Name to Its Sanctions List."

96. Ahmed and Johnson, "Linked to Taliban and ISIS."

97. Ibid.

98. Sayed and Hamming, "The Revival of the Pakistani Taliban."

99. Sayed and Tore Hamming, "The Revival of the Pakistani Taliban."

100. Yousafzai, "Gunmen Kill Four Police in Pakistani City of Quetta."

101. Giustozzi, *The Islamic State in Khorasan.*

102. Analytical Support and Sanctions Monitoring Team, *Twenty-seventh Report,* p. 16.

103. Krishnankutty, "Help from Pakistan Taliban?"

104. Ibid.

105. Hassan, "Quetta Church Attack Planned by Daesh and BNA."

106. Ibid.

107. Fazl-e-Haider, "Pakistani Separatists Turn Their Sights on China."

108. "Chapter 6: Foreign Terrorist Organizations."

109. Abbas, "A Profile of Pakistan's Lashkar-e-Jhangvi."
110. Ibid.
111. BBC News, "Malik Ishaq."
112. Arfeen, "Usman Saifullah Kurd."
113. Shah, "Al Qaeda Linked Group Claims Kabul Suicide Attacks on Shia Pilgrims."
114. Abbas, "A Profile of Pakistan's Lashkar-e-Jhangvi."
115. Abbas, "Extremism and Terrorism Trends in Pakistan."
116. Marszal, "ISIL 'Took Part' in Quetta Attack."
117. "Jundullah Vows Allegiance to Islamic State"; Pakistan Institute for Peace Studies, *Pakistan Security Report 2017.*
118. *BBC Monitoring South Asia,* "IS Reveals Rare Details of Ties with Pakistani Militant Group Lashkar-e-Jhangvi." The IS article referenced in this report was published in the 146th edition of *al-Naba,* distributed on September 6 via IS's telegram channel.
119. Giustozzi, *The Islamic State in Khorasan.*
120. Zahid, "Lashkar-e-Jhangvi al-Alami."
121. *Dawn,* "Army Releases Details of 3-Day Mastung Operation."
122. Yusafzai, "Islamic State Claims Attack on Pakistan Police Academy."
123. Rehman, "Killing of Top ISIS Leaders in Sindh Seen As Major Blow to Group."
124. Tunio, "Two High Profile Daesh Terrorists Killed."
125. Arfeen, "The Hunt for Hafeez Brohi."
126. Ibid.
127. *Ling News,* "Did the Security Agencies Break the Terrorist Network?"
128. Ibid.
129. Zahid, "Lashkar-e-Jhangvi al-Alami."
130. Ali, "Four Militants Linked with High Profile Terror Cases."
131. Abbas, "Extremism and Terrorism Trends in Pakistan."
132. Zahid, "Lashkar-e-Jhangvi al-Alami."
133. Author data.
134. *International Business Times India,* "Pakistan: At Least 60 Killed, over 110 Injured in Quetta."
135. Yusafzai, "Islamic State Claims Attack on Pakistan Police Academy."
136. *Reuters,* "LeJ 'Collaborated with ISIS' for Quetta Attack."
137. Salam and Shahid, "128 Perish As Savage Attack on Mastung Rally Stuns Nation."
138. Ibid.
139. Ibid.
140. *Daily Pakistan Today,* "Mastung Bomber Identified."
141. Ibid.
142. *Al-Jazeera,* "Gunmen Kill Many Hazara Shia Coal Miners."

6

Making Enemies:
Strategic Rivals

*By granting of success of God Almighty, the soldiers of the Caliphate
exploded an IED on the vehicle of the apostate Taliban militia in District
4 of the city of Jalalabad yesterday, which led to its destruction and the
killing of two personnel and wounding of three others, then they
exploded a second IED on the militia's personnel after they gathered in
the place of the explosion, which led to the killing of four others and
wounding of eight with injuries. They also exploded a third IED in the
same district, on another vehicle of the militia, which led to its damage,
killing of one member and wounding of three others, and praise and
thanks be to God.*

—Islamic State's *Amaq* news agency, September 2021[1]

The above statement lays claims to multiple ISK attacks against the
Afghan Taliban in Nangarhar province following the United States withdrawal. As earlier chapters explored, this attack was one of dozens perpetrated by ISK against the Taliban in the fall of 2021 and marked the con-
tinuation of the rivalry between the two groups. While for the most part,
public attention only recently turned to this rivalry after the withdrawal,
ISK and the Afghan Taliban have been clashing with each other virtually
since the former's official formation in 2015. One question that perplexed
many was why two extreme Islamist groups would target each other
rather than cooperate?

It is not difficult to understand the logic of why ISK sought out
alliances with other militant groups, as explored in the previous chapter:
these allowed the group to build a network of local groups, which provided

critical access to relevant knowledge and skills, as well as human capital across the region. However, in addition to strategically picking its allies, ISK also positioned itself staunchly against dominant militant groups in Afghanistan and Pakistan—most prominently against the Afghan Taliban but also against some notable Kashmir-oriented groups. Perhaps the logic of why a new militant group would elect to develop intense rivalries in a region where it has no prior presence is less obvious. Wouldn't clashing with groups with long histories and connections in the region hinder ISK's ability to gain influence? While the underlying logic behind ISK's pursuit of strategic rivalries with some of the strongest militant groups in the region may not be immediately obvious, this strategy benefited ISK in important ways.

The limited literature on rivalries among militant groups suggests that the same factors that hinder groups' abilities to forge alliances can help facilitate intergroup rivalries, as can competition for the same resources. Groups can develop rivalries due to variation in their goals or if they represent different ethnic communities, but groups can also become rivals when they are seemingly identical in these aspects.[2] In the latter case, overlapping goals and co-location in the same geographical sphere can force militant groups to compete for influence and engage in outbidding wars in an effort to outperform their peers, both of which can cause an overall escalation in terrorist activities.[3] Rivalries can also serve to increase a group's longevity by invoking civilians' support, driving innovation, and eliciting spoiler attacks to disrupt any peace talks with government actors. When a group develops strategic rivalries with others, its members may be increasingly motivated to defend the group and their supporters, which in turn can enhance internal cohesion.[4]

For ISK, rivalries with some of the region's most dominant militant groups yielded many benefits, two of which stand out. First, in a crowded militant landscape where multiple groups share operational spaces and compete for resources, ISK's selection of rivals was one of the key ways that the group differentiated itself and created space for the Islamic State brand. As we discuss in this chapter, ISK largely postured against militant groups that had nationalistic goals, and those that had state backing. As explored in Chapter 2, ISK's defining ideology, goals, and supporting narratives are transnational in nature and vehemently antistate. This allowed it to attract individuals and militants to whom ISK's transnational agenda was more appealing, especially given al-Qaeda's weakened position in the region. Second, ISK's rivalries allowed the group to position itself as one of, if not the most viable alternative for militants who were dissatisfied or disgruntled with their own group or leadership. ISK's rivalries in a Taliban-controlled Afghanistan have shown to be especially fruitful. Not only has its broad jihadist platform and agenda attracted a diverse body of militants, but also ISK is perceived as one of the few organizations capable of undermining the Taliban's rule. Overall, through its rivalries, ISK has been successful at maintaining relevance, building a diverse and "replenishable" militant base, and finding "qualified" leaders and members fairly quickly, especially after significant losses. Targeting state actors and minority civilian populations alone was insufficient to distinguish its brand. Collectively then, the strategic selection of both alliances and rivalries has allowed ISK to build a unique reputation in the region, project power through conducting highly lethal attacks, maintain a robust talent pipeline, and most importantly, survive the onset of state and nonstate targeting efforts across Afghanistan and Pakistan.

The pursuit of strategic rivalries, however, did not come without costs. Even though ISK's cooperative alliances with numerous groups provided key avenues of support, the group's rivalries have forced it to expend resources clashing with groups such as the Afghan Taliban. It is possible that dominant groups could have disregarded ISK, which was only a nascent threat in 2015. Instead, the Afghan Taliban clashed violently with ISK across at least sixteen provinces between 2015 and 2020,[5] and other militant groups either supported these efforts or pursued their own fights. There are many reasons why prominent groups, and most notably the Afghan Taliban, responded aggressively to their new rival ISK, but five stand out. First, the Islamic State's goal of establishing a transnational caliphate that rejects national boundaries and acquires territories around the world—including the Afghanistan-Pakistan region—directly encroaches upon existing spheres of influence of dominant groups. Second, ISK continues to invite militants from other groups to defect and join the Islamic State, which directly threatens the human resource base of rival groups. Third, ISK's deeply sectarian, Salafi supremacist agenda interferes with the nationalist orientation and limited political goals of rival groups. Fourth, ISK's persistent focus on framing the Pakistani state as a tool of the West and therefore a priority target threatened the passive and active support provided to some regional militant groups by elements within the Pakistani state. Finally, the formation of an official Islamic State province in the Afghanistan-Pakistan region has extended the Islamic State–al-Qaeda rivalry into South and Central Asia and continues to disrupt historically deep ties between the latter and many other groups in the region.

As such, ISK's selection of strategic rivalries instigated violent intermilitant group clashes across the region, with both sides motivated out of necessity. In this chapter, we explore ISK's rivalries with the Afghan Taliban and Lashkar-e-Taiba in particular to understand the nature and extent of their animosity with ISK, and how it boosted the latter's own reputation and recruitment.

The Afghan Taliban

In the years following the 2001 US invasion of Afghanistan and the ouster of the Afghan Taliban's regime, the movement would soon reemerge as the dominant militant force in Afghanistan. From safe havens in Pakistan, the Taliban quickly coalesced an insurgency that within a few years would pose a major threat to both the new Afghan government and security forces, as well as to US soldiers across the country. Although the group's control in Afghanistan was initially obliterated in 2001 and its leaders, including Mullah Mohammed Omar, fled to Pakistan, the Taliban were able to rebuild and regroup in southern and eastern Afghanistan.[6] In part, the group's remobilization was made possible by the reorganization of senior members and development of a leadership council in the city of Quetta, Pakistan, which came to be known as the Quetta Shura. While Mullah Omar remained out of the public eye, the Quetta Shura, led by Mullah Abdul Ghani Baradar, established provincial and district governors between 2003 and 2005, as well as national commissions for various functions such as military operations, politics, and financial matters.

The movement subsequently gained access to rural districts in Afghanistan and successfully established relations with local villages.[7] At the same time, around mid-2002 senior Taliban figure Jalaluddin Haqqani—at that time head of the Haqqani network—began to remobilize his organization and infiltrate Afghanistan's Paktia and Khost provinces, ultimately setting up governance structures within select locations. Underpinning the Taliban's successful resurgence strategy were two key factors. First, the Taliban insurgency retained safe havens in Pakistan since the 2001 invasion and particularly to host the movement's main leadership structure. Scholars, government officials, and other experts around the world have since gathered substantial evidence that the Pakistani intelligence agency, Inter-Services Intelligence, formed strong ties with the movement.[8] Second, the Taliban quickly and effectively eliminated or coopted various groups and figureheads from 2007–2008 and onward that threatened their monopoly on the anti-US insurgency.[9] This second prong of the Taliban's mid-2000s resurgence strategy is a vital lesson from history, one that in part explains the movement's rapid response to counter ISK after the latter's formation.

In May 2016, as ISK was gaining momentum, US forces based in Afghanistan estimated that only 65 percent of the country's 407 districts were under government control, while the rest were either under Taliban control or contested.[10] The Afghan Taliban's strength and internal cohesion allowed the insurgency to exert control over large swathes of Afghanistan. Reports around 2017 and 2018 estimated the Taliban possessed full control over about fourteen districts, and were active in another 263, providing them leverage over millions of civilians.[11]

The Afghan Taliban's core base also fluctuated dramatically over time. Around 2014, US officials estimated the strength of the Taliban fighting force at approximately 20,000 fighters. By 2017, however, the group was estimated to be composed of around 200,000 members,[12] including around 60,000 core fighters, 90,000 fighters belonging to local militias, and tens of thousands of facilitators. Eventually, the movement would emerge as the victorious party after peace negotiations with the United States in February 2020 and the collapse of the Afghan government in 2021.[13] Back during the Islamic State's formative years, however, the Taliban were still gathering the centrifugal strength that would drive the insurgency to the seat of power a few years later.

Emergence of the Afghan Taliban and ISK Rivalry

When the Islamic State first started its regional recruitment and outreach campaign in 2014, its intentions were clear from the outset. The movement was not looking to align itself with dominant groups such as the Taliban or al-Qaeda, but would instead try to establish its brand with a separate, independent following. At the same time, ISK was not afraid to direct its recruitment efforts toward fighters in the Taliban. After all, poaching militants from the Taliban, who had years of experience fighting a sustained insurgency, was one of the most effective ways to get top talent in the region. But why would Taliban members be incentivized to defect and join forces with ISK? To poach Taliban members, as well as members from other groups, ISK had to meticulously position itself as a rival to the Taliban rather than simply another group with similar tactics and targets but perhaps grander goals. Establishing itself as one of, and eventually the main rival of the Afghan Taliban, not only allowed ISK to poach disaffected militants who lost out during the Taliban's internal leadership changes and organizational reshufflings over the years, but also from its closest allies such as factions of the Pakistani Taliban, who suddenly had an alternative to their core ally, one which was perhaps more ambitious and aggressive in its multifaceted regional ambitions.

During the period around its official formation, ISK initiated a recruitment campaign in twenty-five of Afghanistan's thirty-four provinces, with reports starting to flow in regarding the ANDSF's frequent encounters with Islamic State–affiliated fighters.[14] By 2015, it became obvious that ISK was gaining momentum, as waves of Afghan and Pakistani Taliban members continued defecting to ISK following the initial 2014 pledges.[15] Among them were a number of prominent and critical ideologues of the Afghan Taliban, including Abdul Rahim Muslim Dost and notorious military commander Saad Emirati.[16] Another senior Taliban commander, Abdul Ra'uf Khadem, was appointed as a deputy leader of ISK. Khadem was previously a detainee in Guantanamo Bay, but was transferred to Afghanistan in 2007 and,[17] upon his release, appointed as shadow governor for the Taliban in the southern Afghanistan province of Uruzgan. Khadem maintained a strong following of fighters in Helmand and Kandahar,[18] and as deputy of ISK, he set up his own unit in Helmand and Farah to attract more Taliban defectors by offering financial incentives.[19]

In addition to defections from the Taliban such as Khadem and his followers, a number of members of the Haqqani Network also defected to ISK. Reports emerged in 2016 that senior commanders in the organization had aligned with ISK, including a breakaway Taliban faction led by Mullah Rasul.[20] Saad Emirati, the senior Taliban leader noted above, was both a prominent Haqqani commander from Logar province and also subsequently a commander of his own faction of the TTP.[21] In our recorded militant losses presented in Chapter 4, dozens of mid- to senior-level Taliban commanders were noted to have swapped white Taliban flags for black Islamic State flags, well over thirty of whom were later reported killed, captured, or surrendered to United States–led Afghan forces. As we noted in Chapter 4, some of these commanders enjoyed greater success than others. For example, Qari Hekmat (Hekmatullah), a former Uzbek Taliban commander, joined his forces with ISK and came to lead the group's northern territorial project in Jowzjan province for an extended period of time.[22] Others such as Saad Emirati, who tried to establish ISK control in Logar province, were suppressed and forced to flee or rejoin the Taliban within a matter of weeks.[23] Still others such as Abdul Ra'uf Khadem were killed in US drone strikes or other targeting operations shortly after pledging support to ISK.[24] Regardless of the end result, this wave of early defections was rapid, widespread, and alarming, not just to the Taliban, but to the United States and a range of international security partners.

Initially, there were many attempts at negotiations between the Taliban and ISK through private channels to resolve tensions and violent clashes. Most groups like the Haqqani Network, which is closely tied to the Afghan Taliban, tried to stay neutral at first as long as ISK stayed out of their affairs.[25] In 2015, however, former Taliban supreme leader Akhtar Mohammad Mansour issued a public statement that warned the Islamic State against dividing the jihadist movement in Afghanistan, referring to Quranic verses that "clearly forbid Muslims from divisions, differences and internal conflicts."[26] Here is an excerpt from the letter:

> [The] Islamic Emirate, by adhering and following the abovementioned verses, from its previous jihadist experiences and understanding the environment of its society, do not consider the existence of multiple jihadist lines benefit Muslims. Because this is one of the specialties of the Afghan environment that internal conflicts and disputes always exist, if the leadership is one then this eliminates the chances of disputes and conflicts. . . . Until now, [the] Islamic Emirate has successfully eliminated all Fitnas of

disputes, conflicts, and division by having unity of lines. And now, if there are struggles to bring another line of jihad or leadership besides [the] Islamic Emirate, this will deliberately assist in providing an environment of disputes and divisions.

The statement goes on to summarize seven key points and mostly emphasizes that unity in the face of American "occupation" is crucial, that the Taliban would not interfere in ISK's affairs if they did not interfere in theirs, and that the main driver of failure is a lack of unity among Muslims defined as part of the movement.

In the end, these overtures failed to bear fruit. The Islamic State's response to Mansour's open letter came one week later, in which its former spokesman, Abu Muhammad al-Adnani, referred to the Taliban as allies of the Pakistani intelligence agencies and called on the movement to repent for its sins.[27] As the newly minted Islamic State Khorasan province started to gain momentum, both IS-Central and ISK adopted a more aggressive stance toward the Taliban, attacking the latter for receiving support from the Shiite government of Iran and framing it as a tool of the "tyrant" Pakistani state.[28] In 2015, the two groups began to clash violently in multiple areas, and it became obvious that there would not be a peaceful resolution. In 2015, ISK militants beheaded ten Taliban members in Nangarhar, which was met with a retaliatory attack by Taliban fighters against ISK militants in Mohmand Agency.[29] The cycle continued as ISK fighters responded only a week later by killing several Taliban leaders and publicizing scenes of their executions online.[30] Continued fighting between the two groups caused much destruction and displaced thousands of local families. Since these initial rounds of violence, fighting between ISK and the Taliban has continued and expanded to other provinces such as Jowzjan, where in 2018 the Taliban mobilized to recapture areas of the province controlled by Qari Hekmatullah, a former Taliban commander who defected to ISK.[31] There, too, the groups' fighting displaced thousands.[32]

The entire time, ISK continued its efforts to delegitimize the Taliban through its propaganda output. In an article in *Dabiq* titled "Interview with: The Wali of Khorasan," Hafiz Saeed Khan—the first governor of ISK— accused the Taliban of ruling by tribal customs as opposed to sharia. In the interview, Khan goes on to decry the Taliban's links to the Pakistani state: "Akhtar Mansour and his associates have strong and deep ties with Pakistani intelligence, and they live in the most important cities of Pakistan, such as Islamabad, Peshawar, and Quetta. Indeed, even Akhtar Mansour's advisory council contains members from the Pakistani intelligence! On top of that, Pakistani intelligence aids him in everything he does." His interview indicated no signs of reconciliation with the Taliban, and if anything the opposite sentiments were expressed: "The war between us and the Taliban carries on. The nationalist Taliban movement initiated the combat by attacking the *mujahhidīn*. But the *Wilāyah* repelled their aggression and the Taliban then fled many of their strategic areas."[33]

In another article in *al-Naba*, the Islamic State attempted to reframe the Taliban's fight by linking it to external actors:

> Fighting the Islamic State became a joint project between the Taliban and the infidel countries, which were terrified by the presence of the Islamic State on their borders, just as it terrified the United States of America that occupies Afghanistan. And Taliban apostates now offer fighting the Islamic State as a valuable commodity that all these coun-tries seek to obtain, and the price required in return is the opening of relationships with Taliban officials and securing political support, and possibly financial and arming support for them. Therefore, it was not surprising that the Russian Crusaders justify their open relationship with the apostate Taliban movement as being directed to fight the Islamic State, showing their fear of the deployment of its soldiers near the side of the Russian influence in Central Asia, and at the same time showing their willingness to directly intervene militarily to fight the caliphate's soldiers in the wilayat Khorasan.[34]

By the time of the Afghan government's fall in 2021, ISK and the Afghan Taliban had clashed in at least sixteen provinces across Afghanistan,[35] inflicting hundreds of casualties upon each other and killing or displacing tens of thousands of civilians as a result of their fighting.[36] After 2015, much of the ISK-Taliban rivalry became concentrated in ISK's territorial holdings in Nangarhar, Kunar, and Jowzjan. As they continued to clash, the Taliban focused on mobilizing fighters—including the movement's special forces Red Units[37]—against ISK around their main pockets of territorial control, often coinciding with US and Afghan air strikes and ground offen-sives.[38] Table 6.1 provides a summary of clashes between the Taliban and ISK between 2015 and 2020, while Figures 6.1 and 6.2 show the split between ISK versus Taliban initiated attacks over the same time period, and the geo-graphical locations of these attacks, respectively.

Table 6.1   ISK and Taliban–Initiated Attacks, 2015–2020

	2015	2016	2017	2018	2019	2020	Total
Taliban	8	13	54	72	15	7	169
Islamic State Khorasan	12	8	47	27	25	3	122
Total	20	21	101	99	40	10	291

Source: Author data.

Figure 6.1 ISK and Taliban–Initiated Attacks, 2015–2020

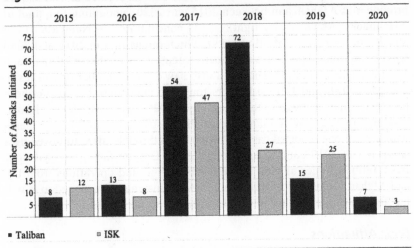

Source: Author data.

Figure 6.2 Geographical Spread of ISK-Taliban Attacks, 2015–2020

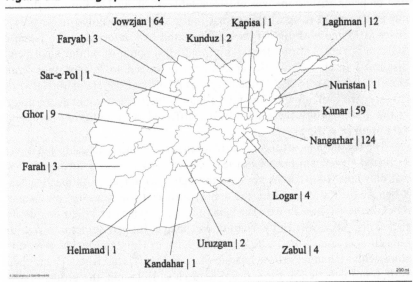

Source: Author data.
Note: Province name and total number of attacks initiated between ISK and the Taliban (2015–2020) are listed for provinces with data.

Overall, our data show that ISK and the Taliban clashed in over sixteen provinces in Afghanistan between 2015 and 2020, amounting to a total of 291 attacks. Much of the fighting was concentrated in Nangarhar (124 attacks, or 42 percent of all attacks), which intensified in 2017 and 2018 from both sides. The rest were mostly focused on Laghman, Kunar, and Jowzjan. The years 2017 and 2018 also saw a large number of clashes in Jowzjan as ISK and Taliban fighters fought to gain control in the northern province, whereas much of their fighting in 2020 was constrained to Kunar. Overall, the data show a dramatic escalation in clashes (armed engagements with at least one reported casualty) from 2016 through 2018, followed by a sharp fall in 2019 continuing through 2020. Despite facing an onslaught from Taliban forces as well as airstrikes and ground operations from US and Afghan forces, the Islamic State in Afghanistan still managed to match the Taliban in the number of attacks initiated during 2017.

Prior Affiliations

Our data on ISK leaders (including mid-tier leaders) captured or killed in Afghanistan between 2015 and 2020—as presented in Chapter 4—include individual nationalities, prior affiliations, and other demographic data, and amounts to a total of about 700 individuals who held some identifiable leadership position over the six years. Within this database, information on prior affiliations was only available on about 115 individuals, but out of these 115 at least thirty-two individuals were noted to be previously affiliated with the Afghan Taliban and had defected to the Islamic State to occupy various leadership positions, some of whom have been discussed in this book. Several others belonged to groups that were closely aligned with the Taliban such as AQIS and the Haqqani Network (twenty-two individuals). The total figure is likely higher, but as we noted in the methodology there are always difficulties in gathering complete data in these settings.

The recruitment of former Taliban members into leadership positions delivered significant benefits to ISK; for example, in some locations, ISK was only able to sustain its presence through other defecting Taliban leaders. When Abdul Ra'uf Khadem, the deputy leader of ISK who had previously rebuked the Afghan Taliban for being too temperate, was killed in a drone strike, his successor, Hafiz Wahidi, was also a Taliban defector.[39] Wahidi himself was soon killed a few months later in Helmand by the ANDSF, along with nine other fellow Islamic State militants. Had Khadem and then Wahidi not defected to carry the ISK torch in Helmand, the group's presence likely would have been nominal.

Other Taliban commanders who defected to ISK helped cement the latter's presence elsewhere in Afghanistan. Shafiq Abbass, who was killed in an airstrike in Kunar province in May 2016, was a former Taliban commander who was linked to various terrorist activities in Wata Pur district. Later in 2018, a top ISK commander in northern Afghanistan, Maulavi Habib ul-Rahman, surrendered to Afghan forces along with 250 of his fighters in order to avoid being captured by the Taliban. Rehman and his brother-in-law, Mufti Nehmat, assumed command of ISK's units in Jowzjan after the death of Qari Hekmatullah, another former Taliban commander mentioned above.[40] Both Rehman and Nehmat had previously fought in the ranks of the Taliban, but had joined ISK reportedly on the basis of the group's ideology. Collectively, these defections demonstrate that ISK's rivalry with the Taliban was critical in providing an alternative pathway for disaffected Taliban commanders and their supporters, and a force multiplier for ISK's own presence and influence in the region.

A Reinvigorated Taliban-ISK Rivalry

Since its emergence, ISK has viewed the Afghan Taliban both as its strategic rival in a saturated militant landscape, and as an ideological opponent.[41] ISK delegitimizes the Taliban's ideology and governing practices as heretical, and instead frames itself as the only legitimate jihadist actor in the region.[42] Violent attacks such as the 2021 Kabul airport attack—which left the largest number of US service member casualties in over a decade—are meant to differentiate ISK's brand from the Taliban's. But perhaps more importantly, in a post-withdrawal era, they are meant to cast doubt on the Taliban's ability to govern and provide security, while portraying ISK as a formidable force capable of challenging the Taliban. Such attacks help signal ISK's resolve to various audiences, and the collective effect of these mutually reinforcing objectives is increased longevity in the region,[43] as well as the ability to attract more recruits. While the Kabul airport attack may have come as a surprise to many, it has only heralded a renewed wave of ISK attacks and the most intense phase of the ISK– Afghan Taliban rivalry to date.

In the months following August 2021, ISK continued to launch a series of attacks on civilians, and, as previous chapters have explored, focused particularly on Shiite Hazara communities. The group became as emboldened as ever, striking the heart of Taliban territory in October 2021 when four ISK-affiliated suicide bombers targeted the Fatimiya mosque in central Kandahar, killing and injuring about 120 individuals.[44] While ISK's attacks on civilians are designed to undermine the Afghan Taliban's legitimacy, so too are the group's direct attacks on the Taliban. Encouraged by its success and the publicity garnered by its string of attacks on civilians, ISK reinvigorated its rivalry with the Taliban throughout 2021 and into 2022—placing Afghanistan's new rulers at the center of a renewed strategy. Over a single weekend in September 2021, ISK claimed responsibility for a series of blasts that targeted the Afghan Taliban in and around the city of Jalalabad,

Nangarhar, which has long been host to one of ISK's key urban networks and the source of substantial local support.[45]

Soon after, on November 2, 2021, the group perpetrated another bold attack that killed Mawlawi Hamdullah Rahmani, a senior commander responsible for the Taliban's Kabul corps, in addition to other Taliban fighters.[46] In an infographic released in Islamic State's weekly newsletter *al-Naba,* ISK reported having conducted eighteen assassinations that killed or wounded around 137 Taliban fighters, including eight commanders from October to November 2021.[47] ISK is only likely to expand its war on the Taliban for the foreseeable future, including targeting its personnel, Taliban-run infrastructure, and soft targets in Taliban-controlled areas. To do so, the group will continue to leverage its attack cells around Kabul and other cities, as well as its operational alliances with other jihadist groups.

Since its resurgence starting in 2020, ISK has ramped up its propaganda efforts to focus on its rivalry with the Taliban. Its attacks on the Taliban have been extensively featured in ISK's latest propaganda campaigns. In propaganda claims released immediately following its attacks, ISK has portrayed the Taliban not only as illegitimate due to its links with the Pakistani state—a recurring theme—but also as an incompetent collaborator of the West, one that is incapable of providing security and governance for the Afghan people. In one of its Telegram posts on August 26, 2021, following the Kabul airport bombing, ISK claimed: "History will record that these mercenary Talibs [Taliban] have become America's protectors, soldiers, protégés and spies! Is there anything more humiliating than this?!!"[48] Afterward, the Islamic State appealed to supporters of the Taliban and al-Qaeda in an *al-Naba* editorial to redress their mistakes and encouraged them to defect to ISK and embrace the "true" jihadist group.[49]

In parallel, ISK has also leveraged its propaganda to advertise the diversity of its militant base in terms of its members and attackers' ethnicities, nationalities, and prior affiliations—clearly in an effort to attract more recruits, especially from other militant groups. ISK's attacks on a Sikh temple in Kabul in March 2020 and on a prison in Jalalabad later in August 2020 both featured Indian fighters,[50] and the perpetrator of the Kunduz mosque attack in October 2021 was claimed to be an Uighur Muslim.[51] Together, attacks and subsequent propaganda claims send two key messages to various target audiences. First, the Taliban are collaborators with the West due to their peace agreement and stated intentions to support counterterrorism efforts against militant groups such as ISK. And second, ISK is the only "true" jihadist group in the region, one that is both different from the Afghan Taliban and, by extension, its partners al-Qaeda and the TTP, and that offers a viable platform for a diverse array of militants with differing objectives. These two mutually reinforcing messages have been incredibly effective in helping ISK to poach militants from the Taliban and a wide variety of groups in the region, and to further differentiate its brand in a militant saturated landscape. In addition to attracting new members more generally, ISK's messages seem designed specifically to woo marginalized Taliban members, as well as militant groups that likely partnered with the Taliban in prior years. As the Taliban continue their transition into a governing entity and distance themselves from a number of terrorist groups, and with al-Qaeda's status comparatively weakened, ISK has positioned itself as the most viable option for antistate groups such as IMU and the East Turkistan Islamic Movement (ETIM), as well as for sectarian and Kashmir-oriented groups. Similar to ISK, many of these groups such as IMU have suffered losses from state-led operations and may benefit from partnering with another jihadist group,[52] especially one with a proven track record and broad appeal. The more efficacious ISK is in undermining the Taliban, the greater its resurgence will be, and the more attractive it will seem to recruits from across the region including Central Asians, Indians, Chinese, and Kashmir-based militants. These recruits in turn help ISK to maintain its mutually beneficial alliances and forge new ones.[53]

New Channels of Recruitment Underpinned by the ISK-Taliban Rivalry

Positioning itself as the key rival to the Taliban and the region's other key transnational movement, al-Qaeda, has opened up opportunities for ISK to recruit from several other channels. First, as alluded to earlier, is among the Afghan Taliban's own members, many of whom may feel slighted by the Taliban itself for various reasons including any perceived ideological concessions following the transition to governance, or failure to dole out spoils and rewards across its broad membership. For these disaffected Afghan Taliban fighters, the obvious pathway to rebuking the Taliban would be to join ISK—its key opponent. And since the fall of Kabul in August 2021, ISK has only doubled-down on its attempts to draw additional defections from the Taliban's ranks, including through propaganda messaging and recruitment campaigns.[54] During this precarious time for the Taliban as it is trying to establish itself as a legitimate political entity to Afghans and to the international community, conceding on even minor issues of ideological purity or failing to appease the demands of its members will put it at risk of alienating supporters, potentially losing them to ISK.[55] These defections will be highly problematic for the Taliban since they can offer ISK new operational knowledge and intelligence about its rival.[56]

Second is among Afghanistan's Salafist communities, whose historic tensions with the Taliban have been exploited and leveraged by ISK.[57] After the killing of ISK's first governor, Hafiz Saeed Khan, tensions between ISK and the Taliban only intensified after Khan was eventually replaced by a cohort of Salafist scholars.[58] In fact, ISK's second governor,

Abdul Haseeb Logari, himself was a Salafist scholar. In addition, one of ISK's chief ideologues, Sheikh Jalaluddin, is an influential Salafist scholar in the Pashtun belt of Afghanistan and Pakistan.[59] Upon Logari's appointment and his subsequent implementation of a Salafist-interpreted, sharia-based system in ISK-controlled territories, a significant number of Afghan Salafists joined ISK's ranks.[60] These trends cannot be disregarded, especially as ISK continues its efforts to champion Afghanistan's Salafist communities in the northeast.[61] The abduction of the senior Afghan Salafist scholar, Shaikh Abu Obaidullah Mutawakil, from his home in Kabul on August 28, 2021, and his killing a week later stirred up fear among other Salafists that they could and would be targeted by the Taliban.[62] Fear can be a powerful motivator for driving Salafists to align themselves with ISK, and to encourage their followers to support the group as well.[63] At the same time, ISK continues to shape the discourse and direction of the broader Salafist population by assassinating prominent Salafist voices who speak out against the Islamic State. In July 2022, one of the most senior Salafist scholars and ideologues in the region—Sheikh Sardar Wali Saqib, who denounced ISK and stated his support for the Taliban—was killed in Kabul.[64] The battle for influence and support among the region's Salafists has been a defining feature of the ISK-Taliban rivalry, and that is unlikely to change in the near future.

Third are former Afghan security forces (ANDSF) members who, like some of Afghanistan's Salafists, fear being targeted or persecuted by the Taliban. Although most of these members are ideologically opposed to ISK and many fought against the group, fears of Taliban persecution and shared animosity toward Afghanistan's new rulers may incentivize small segments to fight with or otherwise support ISK. Reports in November 2021 indicated that former ANDSF members might be supporting ISK on a small scale, among them an Afghan National Army officer who oversaw weapons and ammunition distribution in Paktia province before joining ISK.[65] Both Afghan Taliban and ANDSF defectors could prove critical to ISK's capability in the medium and long term. As noted earlier, former Taliban fighters offer critical operational knowledge and intelligence about ISK's main rival—which ISK may use to continue infiltrating Taliban ranks and strike from within—whereas former ANDSF members offer expertise and training in intelligence-gathering and warfare techniques.

Fourth, and of key concern to the international community, are prospective foreign fighters and those already present in the country.[66] For current foreign fighters in the region and those who are interested in relocating to Afghanistan, ISK offers an attractive option as the strongest and most competitive jihadist group that is currently willing to take on the Afghan Taliban and pursue the goal of a transnational caliphate. The potential for foreign fighters to join the ranks of ISK may prove to be especially beneficial to the group, since their presence is empirically shown to increase militant groups' longevity, use of suicide operations, and geographic reach.[67]

Finally, ISK's strategic rivalry with the Afghan Taliban allows the group to appeal to the next generation of Afghanistan: its youth. For many younger Afghans, ISK already provided an appealing outlet for their world views. Young, urban Afghan men and women provided ISK a steady stream of support even during its years of decline, especially non-Pashtun university students.[68] According to these younger Afghans, the chief draws of ISK were frustration with the status quo, ISK's ideological purity, and the Islamic State movement's stated egalitarianism in terms of one's nationality, race, or ethnicity.[69] Similar motives have driven not just young Afghans, but also young Kashmiris and other regional youth populations toward the Islamic State.[70] As long as ISK continues to leverage these factors and its rivalry with the Afghan Taliban through recruitment campaigns targeting Afghanistan and the region's youth, the group will always find willing recruits. And for those young Afghans who will come of age during the period of humanitarian crises under the Taliban's tenure as rulers, and who will be less familiar with the Taliban's wartime insurgency appeal, ISK is likely to offer the most attractive alternative.

Lashkar-e-Taiba

Another key rival that ISK positioned itself against is Lashkar-e-Taiba (LeT), although there have been scant reports of any direct clashes between the two groups. LeT gained global notoriety in November 2008 when it conducted a series of attacks in Mumbai and laid siege to the city for more than sixty hours, killing around 166 and wounding more than 300 people.[71] But the group came into existence long before then. Most scholars place the date of Lashkar-e-Taiba formation between 1987 and 1990 as the militant armed wing of Markaz Dawat-ul Irshad (MDI), the Center for Proselytization and Preaching.[72] MDI itself was formed as a merger between Jamaat-ud-Dawa (JuD) and the militia of Zaki-ur-Rehman Lakhvi.[73]

Although the group denies its connections to LeT, JuD has long been viewed as the political and charity front of LeT, or simply as an alias of LeT. LeT/JuD is a Salafist group that falls under the Ahl-e-Hadees (Ahl-e-Hadith) movement in South Asia, which is a nineteenth-century Salafi reformist movement that originated in northern India. According to Christine Fair, LeT/JuD is "a hybrid organization: while it is most certainly jihadi, its jihad focuses upon external enemies—most notably in India, where it seeks to 'liberate' Muslims in Kashmir."[74] Unlike Deobandi groups that focus on "sectarian, anti-state and Afghan-centric causes," LeT uses propaganda and a broader narrative to focus on the threats posed by India in Kashmir, and the group's stated goal is to merge all of Kashmir with Pakistan.[75]

Most research on LeT's origins links the group to its cofounders, the infamous Abdullah Azzam and Zaki-ur-Rehman Lakhvi, who, among others, assembled a group of Ahl-e-Hadees adherents in Pakistan to fight against the Soviets in Afghanistan.[76] It is believed that JuD—under the leadership of Hafiz Muhammed Saeed—merged with Lakhvi's organization around 1986, to form the religious group known as MDI.[77] After the end of the Soviet-Afghan war, MDI/LeT members reportedly dissociated themselves from the factional fighting that ensued in order to reorient their jihad on occupied Kashmir, which has experienced political tensions and violence since the 1947 partition of India. In the early 1990s, LeT is widely believed to have formed a relationship with Pakistan's Inter-Services Intelligence, which provided the group with financial assistance and military training.[78] Although support for LeT is only one facet of a long history of Pakistani support for Kashmiri militant groups, over time the state has largely sidelined groups that failed to further a pro-Pakistan agenda, and instead chose to support more radical Islamist, pro-Pakistan groups such as Hizb-ul-Mujahideen (HM), Jaish-e-Mohammed, and LeT.[79] These three main militant outfits also have linkages among themselves, and even joined forces in 1990 to form the United Jihad Council (UJC),[80] which is still widely perceived to be supported by Pakistan's ISI.[81] LeT would go on to set up a number of training camps in Pakistan-administered Kashmir, such as the Bait ul Mujahideen and Muaskar-e-Umm ul-Qura in Muzaffarabad.[82] During this period in the 1990s, the group separated from MDI to become its own distinct militant wing, but in practice, Hafiz Saeed retained the leadership of both groups.[83]

Through its support for LeT, ISI hoped to exacerbate the conflict in Kashmir by helping the group build its military apparatus as it expanded its operations against India. To do so, scholars have argued that the Pakistani army assisted in designing the organization's training regime, and is known to co-locate security personnel at LeT training bases. With Pakistan's support, LeT emerged as the frontrunner of the jihad in Kashmir, posing a significant threat to Indian security forces in the region.[84] Over time, LeT fighters would develop a reputation as *fidayeen* attackers (individuals who died while conducting violent acts), as well as experts in making improvised explosive devices.[85] By 2005, LeT members grew increasingly involved in supporting the Afghan Taliban against the United States and Afghan forces by attacking a variety of targets, including the US base in Nuristan in 2009 and the Indian embassy in 2008.[86]

After 9/11 and the December 2001 terrorist attack on India's parliament, Pakistan came under intense international pressure to constrain militant groups operating from within its borders, which eventually resulted in the banning of LeT along with other militant groups. Although LeT's leader, Hafiz Saeed, was released just months after his arrest, MDI was officially dissolved and

LeT rebranded as JuD.[87] But the broader reorientation of LeT away from Kashmir and toward Afghanistan allowed the group to not only support the Taliban but also keep its members actively engaged in combat. In this context, LeT and a number of other organizations such as the Haqqani Network provided Pakistan leverage and influence over the jihad in Afghanistan.[88]

The Islamic State's Arrival in Jammu and Kashmir

Against this largely pro-Pakistan backdrop, the Islamic State, like its predecessor al-Qaeda, started to make a concerted effort to influence Kashmiris. In early February 2016, the Islamic State announced its intention to expand into Kashmir as part of its broader Khorasan branch,[89] around which time then–ISK governor Hafiz Saeed Khan stated in an interview for the Islamic State's *Dabiq* magazine that Kashmir fell under ISK's area of operation.[90] But penetrating the militant landscape in Jammu and Kashmir would be another tall order for the movement. Not only is the Jammu and Kashmir region—which constitutes a long-running territorial dispute between India and Pakistan and has triggered at least three wars—a highly-militarized area, but it is also already the operational grounds for three prominent militant groups—HM, LeT, and JeM. These three groups dominated the Kashmiri militant landscape at the time of the Islamic State's expansion, and all have been linked to elements of the Pakistani state. Collectively, they have each either propagated a separatist or pro-Pakistan agenda, and attempts by transnational terrorist groups to infiltrate the region and introduce a pan-Islamist ideology is still a fairly recent phenomenon.

Initially, the presence of the Islamic State in Jammu and Kashmir (ISJK) (an unofficial moniker for the group's presence in the region before the formation of the official Islamic State province, Islamic State–Hind [ISH] in 2019) seemed to be largely online. That largely online presence would slowly creep onto the streets of Kashmir during 2017, when reports started to emerge of Islamic State flags being flown in rallies and protests around the Kashmir Valley. Around mid-2017, the militant group Ansar al-Khilafah (supporters of the caliphate) in Jammu and Kashmir began disseminating pro–Islamic State propaganda materials in addition to bomb-making guides and attack manuals on Telegram.[91] Violence, although of a limited scale, would soon follow. On November 17, 2017, the Islamic State's *Amaq* news agency claimed responsibility for an attack in Srinagar that killed an Indian policeman. The militant killed in the attack, Mugees Ahmed Mir, is suspected to have been inspired by the Islamic State's online propaganda and was found wearing an Islamic State T-shirt at the time of the attack.[92] Then, in February 2018, the Islamic State issued another *Amaq* claim for an attack outside the residence of Hurriyat Party leader Fazal Haq Qureshi, who helped lead the party's mission of Kashmiri separatism.[93]

The Islamic State also claimed killing Constable Farooq Ahmad Yatoo, who was guarding Qureshi at his residence in Srinagar's Soura area.

Following these attacks, local authorities ramped up the pressure on pro–Islamic State supporters in the region. In March 2018, three militants belonging to HM were reportedly killed in an encounter with security forces in the southern district of Anantnag, Jammu and Kashmir. However, these three militants—Abu Zarr al-Hindi, Abu Barra al-Kashmiri, and Eisa Ruhollah Khatab al-Kashmiri—were identified by an Islamic State propaganda release as part of the movement, and police would later link one of them to the previous month's attack in Soura.[94] ISJK would subsequently return to its largely online status, even after the official formation of IS-Hind in May 2019, which was established to unify the numerous pro–Islamic State groups and campaigns within India and Jammu and Kashmir.[95] Although categorized as the Indian branch of the Islamic State, the group appears to be dominated by Kashmiris and has only made limited inroads into India.[96] In the early summer months of 2019, the newly minted ISH province managed to conduct only a handful of low-level attacks on security officials, and one of its senior leaders, Adil Ahmad Dass, was reportedly killed by his former comrades in LeT.[97] Then, in November 2019, four individuals were arrested by a Delhi police team deployed to Srinagar, and were later charged by India's National Investigation Agency as members of the Islamic State. Two of the individuals were reportedly in contact with ISK in Afghanistan.[98]

Additional arrests of local ISH (previously ISJK) militants occurred throughout 2020 and 2021 and served as a reminder that the Islamic State's brand and messaging had gained some traction, albeit limited, within the militant landscape in Jammu and Kashmir. In February 2020, Indian authorities claimed to bust an Islamic State cell, arresting five individuals who were suspected to be linked to ISH.[99] A few months later in August 2020, five members of ISH who reportedly had been planning an attack on an Army camp in Kashmir were arrested in the Bandipora district with Islamic State flags and weapons in their possession.[100] The following year in April 2021, Indian authorities arrested another ISH suspect identified as Malik Umair (alias Abdullah) on the Jammu-Srinagar National Highway. Umair was reportedly a commander within ISH's ranks and would be charged with planning an attack for the group in the area.[101]

While the attacks and arrests listed above are not exhaustive, it has become clear that the Islamic State—through its persistent media campaigns and now through an official province—has managed to inspire individuals in Kashmir to support the movement.[102] Although Indian police forces initially denied the existence of the Islamic State in Jammu and Kashmir, by around 2018 Indian security officials acknowledged the influence of the Islamic State in the Kashmir Valley and the potential future threat it posed. ISH did manage to match its India-focused propaganda with action, most recently on

July 11, 2022, when it targeted an Indian police patrol with pistols in Srina-gar's Lal Bazar area, leading to four casualties.[103] After the official forma-tion of ISH province in May 2019 and subsequent attacks and arrests, it became hard to dismiss the changing dynamics on the ground.

The Emergence of Rivalries in Kashmir

Pro–Islamic State online propaganda provides some insights into how the Islamic State set out to distinguish itself from preexisting militant groups in Kashmir, much as it did with ISK. The primary online channels for pro-IS propaganda materials included Ansar al-Khilafa's media wing, Al-Burhan Media, before it rebranded as ISH in 2019, in addition to ISH's monthly magazine, *Sawt al-Hind* (Voice of India) magazine, which released its first issue in 2020. Al-Burhan media published a newsletter called *al-Risalah* (The Message) in Urdu and English, which, similar to ISIS's flagship mag-azine *Dabiq*, attempted to bridge linguistic gaps and define the information space for Kashmiri jihadists and potential Indian Muslim supporters. *Sawt al-Hind* would become the Islamic State's leading magazine to galvanize pan-Indian support.[104] Through these two outlets in particular as well as others, the Islamic State took the same approach as it had in Afghanistan by positioning itself as a rival of the "old school" jihadist groups that dom-inated the Kashmiri landscape—namely Hizb-ul-Mujahideen, Jaish-e-Mohammed, and Lashkar-e-Taiba—with the latter being the most influen-tial and well resourced of them all. In its propaganda (discussed in more detail below), ISJK/ISH framed these groups as agents of the Pakistani State—a message that ran parallel to ISK's stance toward the Taliban—in order to set itself apart from existing militant groups. Such a framing of existing Kashmir-oriented militant groups seemed necessary to undermine their legitimacy, and for ISJK/ISH not only to appeal to new recruits con-sidering joining an armed group but also to poach members of other exist-ing groups. In other words, the logic of instigating rivalries in Jammu and Kashmir was similar to the logic underpinning ISK's aggressive stance toward the Taliban in Afghanistan.

When the Islamic State announced its intention to expand into Kashmir as part of its broader Khorasan branch in February 2016,[105] the pro–al-Qaeda information network, Global Islamic Media Front, announced the formation of its own affiliate in Kashmir in July 2017—Ansar Ghazwat-ul-Hind. The group was to be led by Zakir Musa, a former HM militant, and it would grow increasingly opposed to groups with separatist goals.[106] In forming its own affiliate and selecting Musa as its head, al-Qaeda, just like the Islamic State, had clearly identified and started to exploit growing expressions of discontentment among the militant milieu affiliated with HM, JeM, and LeT. This new wave of militants despised the nationalistic jihad being waged in Kashmir. Their views were made evident when Burhan Wani, a well-known commander of HM in South Kashmir, released a video calling for a "caliphate [to be] established in Kashmir," and suggested the adoption of a more pan-Islamist approach. For al-Qaeda and the Islamic State, local militants' transition away from Kashmiri separatism and toward pan-Islamism aligned with their transnational goals and agendas.[107]

A Battle of Words

As this nascent ideological divide among militants in Kashmir deepened, the only way for the Islamic State to create space for its own brand was to staunchly position itself against existing nationalistic or pro-Pakistan groups such as LeT. The movement needed to offer members of local groups that were dissatisfied with Pakistan's role in influencing the Kashmiri jihad a viable and persuasive alternative, just as ISK did with the Afghan Taliban. To support that objective, since around late 2017, the pro–Islamic State Jammu and Kashmir-focused media group *al-Qaraar* has been engaged in a social media campaign that carefully tailors its messages to enthuse its Kashmiri audience.[108] In December 2017, a pro–Islamic State Urdu-language video was shared via *al-Qaraar*'s Telegram channel using the hashtag "Wilayat Kashmir," in which a masked man claiming to represent "Mujahidin in Kashmir" pledged allegiance to the Islamic State and extended an invitation to al-Qaeda's newly formed Ansar Ghazwat-ul-Hind to join the Caliphate. In substance, he was encouraging defections to the Islamic State.[109] And similar to ISK's antistate propaganda, *al-Qaraar* released numerous posters and written documents[110] encouraging pro–Islamic State followers to target both the Indian and Pakistani armies, declaring that "those who disbelieve fight in the cause of *al-Taghoot* [the tyrants, i.e., India and Pakistan]."[111] Other posters featured pictures of purported Islamic State soldiers depicted as ISJK martyrs.

In addition to videos and pictures, ISJK/ISH supporters have also produced more substantive and lengthy materials discussing jihadist history, religious edicts, and other matters. The more detailed writings distributed by *al-Qaraar*—including "Realities of Jihad in Kashmir and Role of Pakistani Agencies," "Why We Should Leave Militant Groups in Kashmir," and "Apostasy of Syed Ali Shah Gheelani and Others"—provide deeper insights into how the Islamic State positioned itself within the Kashmiri militant landscape. Beyond *al-Qaraar*-distributed documents, some of which we discuss here, IS-Central also served as a forum to help carve out a position for the movement in Kashmir. In a 2016 issue of *Dabiq,* the Islamic State accused LeT and its leader, Hafiz Saeed, of being "apostate agents" of Pakistan who aligned their operations in Kashmir in accordance with the demands of the Pakistani state.[112] Analysis of these documents clearly shows that the Islamic State's goal was to further set itself apart from groups with links to the Pakistani state, both of which it sought to delegitimize. The first article in this issue, "Realities of Jihad in Kashmir and Role of Pakistani

Agencies," argues that the struggle in Kashmir has not been guided by true Islamic principles, but rather by Pakistan and its agents. It states: "The problem with [the] struggle in Kashmir has been that it hasn't really been free. It was not really free to be guided by Islam. . . . The thing was that this struggle was not free from the influence of Pakistan and its agencies or agents in Kashmir. Pakistan never wanted it to become a free land and be ruled by Shariah of Allah."[113] The article then goes on to draw parallels with the Soviet-Afghan war of the 1980s, in which Pakistan played a pivotal role in channeling funds to the Afghan Mujahideen. It continues:

> Let's go to the history. When Afghanistan was fighting Russia, Pakistan was open to help Afghan Mujahideen. It would receive funds from all over the world and give it to the Afghan Mujahideen. Why was that? It was not because they loved Afghanistan and wanted to see Shariah there. No. Rather it was because America wanted them to do it so that its enemy Russia would be defeated. . . . So then things changed. The same Pakistan allowed the same Americans to invade Afghanistan. . . . And today, Pakistan is helping [the] Taliban secretly because Pakistan is trying to kick India out of Afghanistan, and reduce its influence in the region. . . . But the point is that Pakistan wants [the] Taliban to remain in power in Afghanistan to counter Indian political and economic influence there. . . . Now in Kashmir, things are almost the same in the sense that Kashmir's oppression by India is being used by Pakistan to make political gains. . . . Now Pakistan never really supported Kashmir with something useful. All we were given were a few AK-47s and hand grenades. Pakistan knew and knows very well it cannot take Kashmir from India through military means. So it started playing politics. It used Kashmiris for its politics. . . . Pakistan's agents in Kashmir are used to exploiting these people of Kashmir and protests are prolonged. Pakistan always wishes that these protests must go uncontrolled. They wish there to be deaths too. This is what gives Pakistan an argument at the UN. . . . Pakistan knows it will not win the war. So it must keep Kashmir on boil. It doesn't care how many Kashmiris die or are raped. It just wants to get the land.

Finally, the article addresses Pakistan's funding of militants in Kashmir: "Know that Pakistan has invested a lot in Kashmir on borders and in funding militants etc. . . . Unless we free [the] jihad in Kashmir from Pakistan's influence, we will be treated like Afghanistan."

One of the primary motives in the article just outlined is to portray the Pakistani state as an unequivocally apostate state, a legitimate target, and a sponsor of militants in the Kashmir region in pursuit of its own motives rather than for the betterment of the Kashmiri population or implementation of sharia. True to the Islamic State's extreme sectarian stance, the article points to the presence of Shiites, Barelvis, and Hindus within Pakistan as evidence of the country's lack of interest in implementing true sharia as defined by Islamic State religious doctrine. The article concludes that Pakistan's support for the jihad in Kashmir is insincere, and although "Pakistan's agents" in Kashmir are provided with arms and funding, this is only for its own agenda.

In a document circulated by *al-Qaraar* titled "Why We Should Leave the Militant Groups in Kashmir," a pro-ISJK/ISH author seeks to clearly lay out a number of reasons for abandoning existing Kashmir oriented militant groups. But more importantly, the author clearly mentions the groups that should be abandoned because of their status as "agents" of Pakistan: "Today we see faithful Mujahideen have called for a pure jihad that is free from the taghut ['tyrant' Pakistani state] and its agents. These are very few brothers right now. We should ally with them and support their jihad instead of remaining with militant groups like HM, LeT, etc. that are slaves to Pakistan and its agents. It is time that we free our struggle from any person or country and support God's creed and the faithful Mujahideen."[114]

A third document, also released by *al-Qaraar,* shifts away from highlighting the general insincerity of Pakistan and "its agents," and moves on to naming and shaming specific Kashmiri separatist leaders such as Sayeed Ali Shah Geelani of the All Parties Hurriyat Conference (APHC). The APHC, formed in 1993, serves as a political platform for a number of diverse organizations that seek self-determination for Jammu and Kashmir.[115] Although Geelani claims to only engage in nonviolent protests, he has been accused of maintaining connections with Pakistan-funded armed militants.[116] According to the *al-Qaraar* article, Geelani is a disbeliever since he believes in democracy, seeks the judgment of the United Nations, a "false god," and considers Shiites to be Muslims. Additionally, the document criticizes Yasin Malik, the chairman of the Jammu Kashmir Liberation Front (JKLF),[117] one of the first secularist movements to seek independence for Kashmir. The naming and shaming of outspoken rival militant and political party figures is a defining trait of all Islamic State affiliates' communications strategies, and ISJK/ISH is no exception. Propaganda in this manner is designed to crowd out any space for other voices besides those representing the Islamic State and its beliefs, and figures such as Geelani and Malik have often been not only named and shamed but singled out by Islamic State affiliates around the globe for assassination.

Taken together, these three documents show that the Islamic State's key mechanism for creating space for its own brand in Kashmir, ISJK (and then ISH), was to directly delegitimize existing militant groups such as LeT, as well as other separatist parties such as APHC. While the Islamic State campaigned against a number of militant groups with links to elements within the Pakistani state, its most hostile statements seem to have been saved for LeT/JuD, whose primary goal continues to be the liberation of Indian-administered Kashmir and its mergence with Pakistan. Of all the groups targeted in ISJK/ISH's propaganda, LeT was the one that most actively sought to dismiss the notion of the Islamic State's expansion to Jammu and Kashmir, or even the idea of the broader Islamic State movement. In 2015, LeT spokesman Mehmood Shah released a statement to distance his group from the Islamic State and dismissed any links with the movement, instead emphasizing LeT's narrower goals of liberating Kashmir. Shah also claimed that any rumors of linkages between LeT and the Islamic State were mere propaganda generated by the Indian army to delegitimize the Kashmiri jihad.[118] In mid-2017, after *al-Qaraar* had disseminated more propaganda de-legitimizing LeT and reports of Islamic State flags in the Kashmir Valley had become more widespread, Shah once again condemned the Islamic State in a public statement, which was sent to a local news agency.[119] In his statement, Shah emphasized that "ISIS is an anti-Islamic terrorist organization."[120] Hafiz Saeed, the leader of LeT, himself has also labeled transnational groups such as al-Qaeda and the Islamic State as terrorist groups, which has been LeT's way of responding to criticism and also differentiating themselves from transnational groups that are not aligned with the pro-Pakistan jihadist movement.[121] LeT's political front, JuD, has also reinforced LeT's efforts to delegitimize the Islamic State. In early 2016, JuD released an open letter on its social media platforms stating that "Daesh" was harming the true cause of Islam and considered JuD to be its enemy.[122] While no clashes were generally reported, in mid-2016, JuD's spokesman, Attiqur Rahman Chohan, claimed that some of the group's members had actually been targeted in a mosque in Peshawar by the Islamic State specifically because of JuD's involvement in public rallies in Malakand, during which JuD had expressed support for the Pakistani army and had been critical of the Islamic State.[123]

Overall, one of the key features of ISJK/ISH's messaging strategy in Kashmir has been to call out groups such as LeT for their links to the Pakistani state, which is an "apostate regime" from the Islamic State's perspective. Just as the Islamic State staunchly positioned itself against the Afghan Taliban to poach members and build its own base, ISJK/ISH seeks to mirror that strategy and delegitimize the very essence of LeT's jihad, as well as other pro-Pakistan militant groups. Evidence of LeT and Islamic State members clashing in the region, however, remains limited, and most of the reported examples involve disparate, individual-level clashes between supporters of both groups. For example, in June 2019, HM chief Sayeed Salahudeen released an eight-minute video following an incident in which an ISH militant was allegedly killed by LeT in Anantnag district, southern Kashmir. Salahudeen decried the intergroup violence and called for unity among the jihadists operating in Kashmir.[124] It is possible that other one-on-one clashes between ISJK/ISH supporters and LeT have gone unreported in the past, and there are other ways to counteract one's rival that are harder to observe from a researcher's perspective when compared to direct clashes. Whatever the true extent of their past clashes, the potential for increased Islamic State–LeT intergroup violence in the future remains a distinct possibility.

Implications of the Islamic State's Rivalry with LeT

LeT and the Islamic State diverge on a number of strategic and ideological issues that have shaped their rivalry over the last several years. For LeT, the expansion of the Islamic State into Jammu and Kashmir has intruded on its sphere of influence. The Islamic State's sectarian stance and anti-Pakistan agenda stand in stark contrast to LeT's stated goals and the support it receives from elements within the Pakistani state. So too does its policy of targeting minority Muslim sects, which similarly contradicts LeT's ideological campaign to counter arguments posed by the region's Deobandi groups for justifying attacks on Pakistani civilians.[125] But perhaps most threatening to LeT/JuD has been the Islamic State's persistent attempts to poach its militants, criticize its policies, and delegitimize its very existence through recruitment and outreach efforts. Despite its operational links to al-Qaeda and the Taliban,[126] LeT's hostility toward the Islamic State's local affiliates is primarily driven by the threat they pose to its legitimacy and influence in the region. If ISK and ISH are able to successfully delegitimize LeT and its jihadist credentials, the latter's members, resources, and reputation are all on the line.

Based on this discussion then, the question that follows is whether efforts by the Islamic State to cement its rivalry with LeT and other Kashmiri oriented groups have borne any fruit? To some extent, yes, but certainly not to the extent that they have in Afghanistan and Pakistan. In 2015, the Punjab Counter Terrorism Department busted an Islamic State aligned group in the city of Sialkot, Pakistan, which it claimed to be a breakaway faction of JuD.[127] As we explored in Chapter 4, the arrests were one of many state-led operations against the Islamic State, and they offer some insights into how successful ISK and ISJK/ISH's recruitment campaigns have been. To assess whether the Islamic State's appeals to local militants in JuD/LeT to switch allegiances actually had any impact, we compiled and examined two datasets. First, we looked at the prior affiliations of a sample of militants arrested in Jammu and Kashmir by Indian forces who were suspected of being linked to the Islamic State between 2015 and 2020. Second, we looked at the prior affiliations of Islamic State militant leaders arrested, captured, or killed in Afghanistan by United States–led forces or the ANDSF, or in Pakistan by Pakistani security forces (introduced in Chapter 4).

Out of the forty-two individuals targeted in Jammu and Kashmir by Indian forces, the vast majority did not have their prior affiliations reported.

This might be because the Islamic State was their first real militant affiliation, or perhaps information on prior affiliations was not deemed important or necessary for release by local officials. However, we did note the prior affiliations of at least six individuals, which included former members of HM, Tehreek-ul-Mujhadeen, Harkat-ul-Mujahideen, and LeT. While these cases are fairly limited, the total numbers may in fact be larger, as this sample does not include LeT defectors and other militants who joined IS but who have evaded capture or death. No matter the true total, the presence of any number of LeT defectors suggests that the group's militants may have been influenced by the Islamic State's anti-LeT propaganda, and convinced to defect to ISJK/ISH or ISK. The body of one of these Islamic State-aligned individuals, a former LeT militant named Adil Ahmad Dass, was recovered by Indian authorities in June 2019 in Anantnag district after he was suspected of being targeted by other militants.[128]

Our data on ISK leaders in the second sample from Afghanistan and Pakistan included at least twenty-six militants who held some leadership status within ISK and were reported to have been previously affiliated with LeT/JuD. Perhaps the most prominent case is one of ISK's former top leaders, Aslam Farooqi, who was arrested in April 2020 by Afghan forces.[129] Farooqi, originally from the Orakzai district in Khyber Pakhtunkhwa, Pakistan, reportedly started his militant career with LeT and later joined the TTP, prior to becoming a commander within the Islamic State ranks and eventually the group's governor.[130] The presence of Islamic State militants with prior affiliations to LeT—while relatively limited, at least as far as open-source information is concerned—is nevertheless indicative of a larger trend: militants associated with the older jihadist organizations in Kashmir have been swayed to join the Islamic State either in Afghanistan or in Jammu and Kashmir, and may be persuaded to defect in the future.

Going forward, the LeT–Islamic State rivalry will continue to be shaped by the groups' divergent goals, ideologies, and messaging campaigns, but also by shifts in the broader regional security environment, especially since the Taliban's takeover in 2021. In Taliban-ruled Afghanistan, counterterrorism constraints under the previous government have largely lifted or at the very least loosened, including for LeT and other Kashmir-focused groups such as JeM. While the Taliban have publicly promised to constrain externally oriented militant groups, in practice they care more about countering ISK than containing a longstanding ally such as LeT. In fact, reports from May 2022 highlighted that LeT, in addition to JeM, still maintains multiple training camps near ISK's former strongholds in Nangarhar and Kunar.[131] These camps appear to benefit from the Taliban's protection, and in turn, LeT provides the Taliban financing and training expertise for the latter's operations, including possibly against ISK.

Given that some LeT members have defected to join ISK in the past—among them former ISK governor Aslam Farooqi—it is likely that others may follow suit in the future, especially as parts of the Taliban regime move toward forging closer ties with India, which will draw the ire of many hardline Kashmiri militants.[132] Pending any sharp decline in LeT's relationships with the Taliban, the LeT–Islamic State rivalry is likely to deepen. Short of potential future deteriorations in LeT-Taliban relations triggering more widespread LeT defections, ISJK/ISH's sustained propaganda campaigns to delegitimize key militant players in the Jammu and Kashmir landscape may continue to bring in a slow trickle of recruits.

ISK's Strategic Rivalries

In this chapter we have explored the Islamic State's efforts to instigate rivalries with two dominant players in the Afghanistan-Pakistan region, extending to Jammu and Kashmir: the Afghan Taliban and Lashkar-e-Taiba. While Islamic State's rivalries with these two groups vary in their nature and intensity, each rivalry has attempted to cast the Islamic State as the only legitimate leader of jihad in a crowded environment, and strengthened the organization via defections at the rank and file level, or at the leadership level. Moreover, defections of experienced militants have been invaluable in providing Islamic State entities in the region the local expertise and knowledge needed to attain some degree of operational success.

Tracing the nature of these rivalries, especially through propaganda campaigns, highlights the Islamic State's strategy of vilifying organizations that have links to state sponsors. In particular, the Taliban and LeT's links with the Pakistani state have provided the Islamic State ample room to delegitimize their goals and ideologies, and portray them as insincere to the true jihadist cause, if not outright traitors. Although the Islamic State has met with varying levels of success in both contexts, without these campaigns to differentiate itself from preexisting jihadist groups, individuals would have few incentives or motivations to join or defect to ISK or ISJK/ISH. As the Islamic State closes in on a full decade of operations in South and Central Asia, its approach of developing strategic rivalries is only likely to continue into the future.

Notes

1. Islamic State Attacks on Taliban in Jalalabad.
2. Phillips, "Enemies with Benefits."
3. McCormick, "Terrorist Decision Making."
4. Phillips, "Enemies with Benefits."
5. Jadoon and Mines, "The Taliban Can't Take On the Islamic State Alone."
6. Farrell, "Unbeatable."

7. Ibid.

8. Mozul, "The Quetta Shura Taliban."

9. Sayed, "Why Islamic State Khurasan Poses an Indigenous Threat to the Afghan Taliban."

10. Special Inspector General for Afghanistan Reconstruction, *October 30, 2016, Quarterly Report to the United States Congress;* Farrell, "Unbeatable."

11. Sharifi and Adamou, "Taliban 'Threaten 70% of Afghanistan.'"

12. Schroden, "Afghanistan's Security Forces Versus the Taliban."

13. Schroden, "Lessons from the Collapse of Afghanistan's Security Forces."

14. Analytical Support and Sanctions Monitoring Team, *Ninth Report.*

15. "Taliban Fighters Divert to ISIS."

16. "ISKP: A Threat Assessment."

17. Lamothe, "Meet the Shadowy Figure Recruiting for the Islamic State."

18. Ibid.

19. *Associated Press* and Gayle, "ISIS Sets Up Base in Afghanistan Less Than Three Months After British Troops Left."

20. Giustozzi, "The Transformation of the Haqqani Network."

21. Sayed and Clarke, "With Haqqanis at the Helm."

22. Ali, "Qari Hekmat's Island."

23. Osman, "The Islamic State in 'Khorasan.'"

24. Ibid.

25. Giustozzi, "Taliban and Islamic State."

26. "Letter from the Taliban to Abu Bakr al-Baghdadi From the Head of the Shura Council."

27. Osman, "The Islamic State in 'Khorasan.'"

28. "ISKP: A Threat Assessment."

29. Osman, "The Islamic State in 'Khorasan.'"

30. Osman, "The Islamic State in 'Khorasan.'"

31. Ali, "Qari Hekmat's Island"; Nordland and Ghazi, "ISIS Leader in Afghanistan Is Killed."

32. Rahim and Nordland, "Are ISIS Fighters Prisoners or Honored Guests of the Afghan Government?"

33. *Dabiq,* "An Interview: The Wali of Khorasan," pp. 49–54.

34. *Al-Naba,* "The Apostate Taliban Movement," p. 3.

35. Author data.

36. Jadoon and Mines, "The Taliban Can't Take On the Islamic State Alone."

37. Qazizai, "The Special Units Leading the Taliban's Fight Against the Islamic State."

38. Jadoon and Mines, "Taking Aim."

39. Roggio, "US Kills Islamic State's Deputy"; "ISIS Commander Killed in Afghanistan."

40. Rahim and Nordland, "Are ISIS Fighters Prisoners or Honored Guests of the Afghan Government?"

41. Jadoon, Jahanbani, and Willis, "Challenging the ISK Brand."

42. Osman, "ISKP's Battle for Minds."

43. Phillips, "Enemies with Benefits?"

44. Neuman, "Suicide Bombers Kill Nearly 50 at a Shiite Mosque in Afghanistan."

45. Berger and Khan, "Islamic State in Afghanistan Claims Responsibility."

46. Gibbons-Neff, Sahak, and Shah, "Dozens Killed in ISIS Attack on Military Hospital."

47. *Al-Naba,* "The Harvest of Wilayat Khorasan from 1 Rabi al-Awal Until 27 Rabii al-Awal."

48. "ISKP: A Threat Assessment."

49. *Al-Naba*, "The Battle of Tawhid in Kabul."

50. Bhardwaj, "2 More Indians from Kerala Suspected."

51. *South China Morning Post*, "Suicide Bombing at Afghanistan's Kunduz Mosque Kills at Least 55 Worshippers."

52. Feng, "China Taliban Afghanistan Uyghurs"; Sharipzhan, "IMU Declares It Is Now Part of the Islamic State."

53. Panucci, "Indians and Central Asians Are the New Face of the Islamic State"; Haidar and Singh, "India Unlikely to Allow Return of 4 Kerala Women."

54. "Pro-IS Eid Message Calls on Taliban Members to Join Its Ranks"

55. Bokhari, "Threatened by ISIS, the Afghan Taliban May Crack Up."

56. Mir, "Biden Didn't See the ISIS-K Threat in Afghanistan Until Too Late."

57. Sayed, "The Taliban's Persistent War on Salafists in Afghanistan."

58. Al-Khurasani, "Bright Pages for Understanding the Nationalists," pp. 757–759.

59. Other Afghan Salafist scholars who rose to prominent positions in the ISK ranks include Shaikh Maqbool (also known as Shahidullah Shahid [ISK founding spokesperson]), Shaikh Abu Saeed al-Muhajir (ISK third governor), Shaikh Abu Umar Khurasani (ISK fourth governor), Shaikh Abu Yazid Abdul Qahir Khurasani, Shaikh Qasim, and Shaikh Matiullah. For their details, see al-Khurasani, "Bright Pages for Understanding the Nationalists," pp. 757–759; al-Khurasani, "Khorasan: A Graveyard for the Crusades."

60. Sayed, "Islamic State Khorasan Province's Peshawar Seminary Attack."

61. "ISKP: A Threat Assessment"; Sayed, "Islamic State Khorasan Province's Peshawar Seminary Attack."

62. Sayed, "The Taliban's Persistent War on Salafists in Afghanistan."

63. Jalaluddin, "Why Are We Fighting Against the Taliban?"

64. Hast-e-Subh, "Wali Saqib, Head of Salafi Scholars."

65. Trofimov, "Left Behind After U.S. Withdrawal, Some Former Afghan Spies and Soldiers Turn to Islamic State."

66. Analytical Support and Sanctions Monitoring Team, *Twenty-eighth Report.*

67. Bacon, Ellis, and Milton, "Helping or Hurting?"

68. Osman, *Bourgeois Jihad.*

69. Ibid.

70. Jadoon, "An Idea or a Threat?"

71. "Mumbai Terror Attacks."

72. Fair, *In Their Own Words;* Tellis, "The Menace That Is Lashkar-e-Taiba."

73. Fair, *In Their Own Words*, p. 74.

74. Ibid.

75. Ibid., p. 71

76. Ibid., p. 75.

77. Ibid.

78. Macander, "Examining Extremism."

79. D'Souza and Routray, "Jihad in Jammu and Kashmir."

80. "United Jihad Council."

81. BBC News, "Pathankot: Kashmir-Based Militant Coalition Claims Attack."

82. Fair, *In Their Own Words*, p. 77.

83. Tankel, *Storming the World Stage.*

84. Fair, *In Their Own Words*, pp. 77–78.

85. Chalk and Fair, "Lashkar-e-Taiba Leads the Kashmiri Insurgency."

86. Subrahmanian et al., *Computational Analysis of Terrorist Groups;* Gall, *The Wrong Enemy.*

87. Center for Strategic and International Studies, "Examining Extremism."
88. Fair, *In Their Own Words*, p. 81.
89. Swami, "Islamic State threatens to Expand to Kashmir."
90. *Dabiq*, "Interview with the Wali of Khurasan."
91. *Hindustan Times*, "IS Supporters Create Kashmir Group to Step Up Presence in India."
92. Lateef, "IS Claims Zakura Attack."
93. Bhat, "Kashmir: Islamic State Claims Responsibility of Soura Attack."
94. Jameel, "3 ISIS Militants Killed in J&K's Anantnag."
95. Roul, "Islamic State Hind Province's Kashmir Campaign."
96. Ibid.
97. Ibid.
98. "Islamic State Module Busted in Jammu and Kashmir."
99. Ibid.
100. Ibid.
101. *India TV News*, "Islamic State Commander Arrested in Jammu."
102. Zahid, "Two New IS Wilayat in South Asia."
103. *Daily India*, "Kashmir Was Shaken by This Dangerous Organization."
104. Roul, "Islamic State Hind Province's Kashmir Campaign and Pan-Indian Capabilities."
105. Swami, "Islamic State Threatens to Expand to Kashmir."
106. Safi, "Kashmir Militant Leader Announced As Head of New al-Qaida–Linked Cell."
107. Qadri, "Kashmir Militant Releases Video."
108. Jadoon, "An Idea or a Threat?"
109. *BBC Urdu*, "Kashmiri Group Pledges Allegiance to Islamic State."
110. Acquired by authors through the ISJK telegram channel.
111. *Al-Taghoot* refers to the worship of a god other than Allah.
112. *Dabiq*, "The Rafidah."
113. *Al-Qaraar*, "The Realities of Jihad in Kashmir and Role of Pakistani Agencies."
114. *Al-Qaraar*, "Why We Should leave The Militant Groups in Kashmir."
115. See the All Parties Hurriyat Conference website, http://www.huriyatconference.com.
116. Buncombe, "Syed Ali Shah Geelani."
117. *Al-Qaraar*, "Apostasy of Syed Ali Shah Gheelani and Others."
118. "Nothing to Do with IS: Lashkar."
119. *Kashmir Observer*, "Lashkar Says ISIS a Terrorist Group."
120. Jadoon, Jahanbani, and Willis, "Challenging the ISK Brand."
121. Swami, "Al-Qaeda Sets Up Valley Wing."
122. *Daily Regional Times*, "Daesh Caused the Most Harm to Islam."
123. *News International*, "Case of Mosque Attack Registered."
124. *Times Now News*, "Hizbul Mujahideen Chief Calls for Truce."
125. Fair, *Fighting to the End*.
126. Ibid.
127. Chaudhry, "IS Cell Busted in Sialkot."
128. Naqash, "Adil Ahmad Dass Killing?"
129. Hamid, "NDS Commander Gives Details of Daesh Leader's Arrest."
130. Foulkes, "Aslam Farooqi."
131. Analytical Support and Sanctions Monitoring Team, *Thirteenth Report*.
132. Mir and Bacon, "India's Gamble in Afghanistan."

7

The Persistence
of ISK

The Islamic State Khorasan has persisted in South and Central Asia for several years since its official emergence in 2015. In that time, the group has managed to inflict high levels of violence in the region upon a variety of state and civilian targets while demonstrating its ability to recover from intense counterterrorism and counterinsurgency operations. In doing so, ISK has altered the security landscape in one of the most militant-saturated regions in the world, triggering new intergroup alliances and rivalries, while generating new regional security concerns.

Although ISK lost several of its topmost leaders over the years—along with numerous other mid- and lower-tier leaders and thousands of rank-and-file members—due to a focused campaign of leadership decapitation and other kinetic operations against the group, ISK managed to conduct one of its most brutal attacks yet in August 2021 as the US withdrawal was unfolding, which arrived on the heels of other spectacular attacks and prison sieges. The Kabul airport attack alone killed several US service members and heightened global concerns about the ability of the Taliban to prevent terrorism from emanating from Afghanistan. But even prior to this attack, views that ISK was largely defunct due to the losses it experienced did not match the realities of its persistent terrorist campaign. Fewer but more provocative attacks struck urban centers during the group's low-activity period, including the attack on a Doctors Without Borders maternity ward in Kabul in a Hazara Shiite community in May 2020.[1] Perhaps more so than previous attacks, the attack on the maternity ward shocked the world with its ruthlessness; among the deceased victims were mothers, infants, and medical workers. On the same day, an Islamic State suicide attacker detonated a bomb at a funeral of a local police officer in Nangarhar, which killed at least

181

thirty-two people and wounded another 132 individuals.[2] While these attacks did not necessarily imply that ISK had suddenly regained its organizational strength, they showcased a group intent on conducting increasingly brutal attacks to attract publicity and generate the environmental instability it needed to persist. The group's perseverance eventually culminated in the Kabul airport attack, which, to those observing ISK closely, did not come as a surprise.

The international publicity surrounding the Kabul airport attack, however, not only raised concerns about ISK among Western audiences, but also heightened security risks among regional governments, including Pakistan, Iran, Russia, China, India, Uzbekistan, and Tajikistan. Since the US withdrawal from Afghanistan, ISK has also intensified its war with the Taliban both in terms of its anti-Taliban propaganda and direct attacks on the group, presenting a persistent threat to the stability of Afghanistan and the well-being of its citizens. In 2022, ISK remained emboldened, further exacerbating sectarian violence and terrorism across the region, highlighting one of the group's most notable characteristics: resiliency.

Understanding the Sources of ISK's Resilience

What are ISK's sources of resilience? Within this book, we argue and demonstrate that since its emergence, ISK adopted a two-pronged strategy to localize a transnational jihadist movement in the Afghanistan-Pakistan region and build a sustainable support base that would allow it to navigate a challenging security environment. On one hand, ISK exploited the presence of a plethora of sectarian and antistate militant groups in the two countries to build cross-border alliances. On the other hand, ISK also relied on provoking rivalries with dominant groups, usually those that had nationalist agendas, links with state sponsors, or with al-Qaeda. The strategic selection of both alliances and rivalries facilitated ISK's violent trajectory, reputation, and recruitment drives, while also generating political relevance for its unique brand.

An examination of ISK's behavior over the several years following its emergence indicates that the group's overarching strategies in the region were influenced by two important factors: the political and security environments within Afghanistan and Pakistan, and the militant milieu in each country. Compared to Afghanistan, ISK faced a less permissive security environment in Pakistan. As such, within Pakistan, ISK sought opportunities to build collaborative relationships with eager militant commanders, even absorbing entire factions of other groups. As we discussed in Chapters 2 and 5, Pakistan-based militant groups have a history of strategic and tactical cooperation with other militant groups to achieve their objectives, and many of them found motivations (and common goals) to facilitate ISK's activities. As noted elsewhere in the book, the transnational jihadist narrative propagated by ISK was broad enough to subsume the more limited and local goals of other groups, allowing ISK to find common ground with them at the strategic or tactical level.

To survive in the sea of militants and tackle the challenges of the Pakistani security environment, ISK opted to foster relationships with groups that possessed locally relevant skills and knowledge, such as LeJ and Lashkar-e-Islam, while subsuming beleaguered Tehrik-e-Taliban Pakistan factions. Connecting with these groups—many of which resided along the Afghanistan-Pakistan border—also allowed ISK to exploit a porous border with pockets of safe havens in Khyber Pakhtunkhwa and Balochistan, ultimately allowing ISK to use Pakistan as a logistical hub.

How exactly did ISK's alliances facilitate ISK's survival and persistence? ISK's alliances have facilitated its emergence and survival in several ways. First, they helped in harnessing the group's reputation as a newcomer, especially when prominent militant leaders publicly pledged allegiance and merged their factions with ISK, or extended operational or logistical assistance. Groups such as LeJ, LeI, and JuA, which have a lethal reputation for conducting attacks and operating in both Afghanistan and Pakistan (or have done so in the past), directly facilitated ISK's upward violent trajectory in its early years. Operational cooperation allowed ISK to claim not only a high number of attacks in its early years but also project its presence in several provinces across the Afghanistan-Pakistan region. Because many of the groups that ISK connected with were either antistate or carried out attacks against minorities, these linkages helped ISK reinforce its goals through regular propaganda output and contributed to drawing in more recruits. Groups such as LeJ and the IMU are known to have facilitated ISK's recruitment in Balochistan and Northern Afghanistan respectively, while groups such as LeI helped ISK in connecting its bases across the Durand Line and exploring channels of smuggling.

ISK's network of alliances, however, is not the only factor that facilitated its early rise and subsequent resilience. Across the border in Afghanistan, which became ISK's main area of operations over time, ISK faced a much weaker state compared to Pakistan. However, in Afghanistan, ISK also had to contend with a much more formidable opponent that had long developed into a fierce insurgency and dominated the militant landscape: the Afghan Taliban. Here the group not only positioned itself against the Afghan government and coalition forces but also sought to delegitimize the Afghan Taliban to create opportunities for itself instead of forming a collaboration. Without having taken such an oppositional stance toward the Afghan Taliban, ISK's ideology and goals would arguably have failed to offer its potential recruits and supporters an alternative pathway for attaining their objectives. In other words, this rivalry was critical in differentiating ISK from the most dominant militant group in the region. Given the Taliban's widely known links with the Pakistani State and the Islamic State's rival, al-Qaeda, along with its nationalist (albeit Islamist) goals, ISK made efforts to frame the Taliban as an illegitimate jihadist organization, especially in contrast to its own purist ideology and goals.

To stoke this rivalry, ISK adopted an adversarial position toward the Taliban right from the beginning, engaging in violent clashes with the movement and unleashing an aggressive media campaign. The Taliban's subsequent political engagement and agreement with the United States and attempts to gain international recognition post-takeover of Kabul provided ISK with further justification to critique the movement as nationalistic in nature,[3] as well as an agent of Pakistan akin to LeT. A significant related benefit of ISK's strategic rivalries was that they incentivized numerous militants who were dissatisfied with their own organizations to join the only defiant and ascendant alternative. In a fashion similar to attracting alliances with Pakistan-oriented groups, ISK's agenda—which transcends national boundaries—served to its advantage. Militants from ISK's main rival group, the Taliban, as well as those acting under its tutelage for years, saw an opportunity to join an alternative group that could offer a more enduring jihadist platform. This became increasingly important as the Taliban sought to form a government and issued promises to the international community that it would deter and prevent terrorist groups from operating in Afghanistan.

Ultimately, by forming extensive alliances, differentiating itself from dominant militant players, and demonstrating its capacity for violence, ISK positioned itself as the group of choice for various militants. ISK's expansive network, along with its ability to draw experienced fighters from rival groups such as the TTP, the Afghan Taliban, al-Qaeda, and LeT—especially for leadership positions—allowed it to lay deep roots in the region while also developing a recruitment pipeline, all of which provided it with fertile ground to sustain the Islamic State brand.

This approach of strategically selecting alliances and rivals in the region to build operational capacity and differentiate its brand from dominant militant groups has also been observed in Jammu and Kashmir, where the Islamic State's presence is still limited (as discussed in Chapter 6). Islamic State's Jammu and Kashmir branch (ISJK) (now a part of Islamic State–Hind Province [ISH]), which was announced in early 2016, appeared to follow a similar strategy; the group positioned itself against groups such as LeT, as well as against the Indian and Pakistani states, and attempted to tap into the grievances of the Kashmiri population. In doing so, ISJK (now ISH) tries to appeal to locals, especially Kashmiri youth active on social media platforms, to abandon other local groups that it portrays as agents of Pakistan—some of which are dominated by non-Kashmiris—while infusing local forms of jihadism with transnational tones.

As noted in Chapter 4, ISK suffered a significant number of manpower losses since at least 2016, including many of its top and mid-tier leaders, which eventually culminated in the dismantling of the group's physical strongholds in Nangarhar. Despite such losses, ISK's operational trajectory shows that although the group's lethality per attack dropped over time, it continued to launch deadly attacks in both Pakistan and Afghanistan (more so in the latter) in 2019 and beyond. As the Taliban seized power in 2021 and the Afghan government collapsed, ISK emerged as the strongest group capable of standing defiant against the Afghan Taliban, ready for new recruits and a reinvigorated battle against Afghanistan's new rulers.

ISK's Evolution in a New Era

In the early months of 2021, the Biden administration promised to bring an end to America's "forever wars" while making sure that "Afghanistan does not again become a safe haven for terrorist attacks against the United States."[4] Yet there was no clear path identified as to how this goal would be achieved or a meaningful public discussion about urgent threats within Afghanistan. One actor that seldom made it to the front page in the United States was the Islamic State Khorasan. ISK made international headlines when it targeted the Kabul airport, but public attention to this resilient militant group arrived far too late. The United States and its international partners had nearly completed a full withdrawal from Afghanistan, without any residual presence in the country to manage the threat of ISK and other militant groups such as al-Qaeda.[5] A new over-the-horizon counterterrorism policy was trumpeted as the best path forward, but quickly met with its first failure when an errant drone strike in Kabul killed ten Afghan civilians, supposedly ISK militants.[6] One of those killed previously worked for an NGO focused on food security, an individual who had applied for a special immigrant visa with the intention of bringing his family to the United States.[7] A short six months later, international attention had largely moved on to the war in Ukraine, and—with the exception of intermittent appearances in the news cycle—Afghanistan and the threat of ISK largely disappeared from mainstream conversations.

Unfortunately, the threat posed by ISK remains and is likely to continue into the future, based on the group's past and current behavior, and its foreseeable trajectory. The group continues its efforts to delegitimize the Afghan Taliban and other dominant groups while maintaining diverse alliances and recruitment channels through its transnational narrative, placing the security of the region in a tenuous position. Under the steward-ship of its new leader, al-Muhajir, ISK has successfully cemented its repu-tation as the key jihadist challenger to the Taliban government. How suc-cessful the group will be in achieving its goal of weakening the Taliban's control remains unclear. However, looking ahead, a few key dynamics are likely to shape its pursuits.

The Quality of the Taliban's Governance and Control

The first factor that will influence ISK's future trajectory and tactics is the Taliban's ability to consolidate power and maintain internal cohesion. ISK alone poses a significant domestic challenge, but other armed actors also seek to upset the Taliban's consolidation efforts. Most notable among them is the National Resistance Front (NRF), led by the son of Ahmad Shah Masud, the deceased leader of the Northern Alliance that fought against the Taliban in the late 1990s and early 2000s. From its strongholds in Panjshir province, the NRF continues to launch attacks against the Taliban and leverages former Afghan government factions and security forces to pur-sue its resistance.[8] Fighting that was previously limited to pockets of the Panjshir valley spread to multiple provinces,[9] and forced the Taliban to deploy tens of thousands of fighters north to suppress the resistance move-ment.[10] Staunch anti-Taliban resistance from ISK and the NRF also has the potential to convince other armed actors that violence is a viable path for-ward, which may lead to a proliferation of armed groups and escalate the level of conflict in the country.[11]

By mid-2022, these dynamics were starting to unfold. As the 2022 spring fighting season opened, a number of new armed groups emerged to challenge the Taliban's consolidation of power, including the Afghanistan Freedom Front, the Afghanistan Islamic National and Liberation Move-ment, and others that publicized their new resistance campaigns both online and through attacks on Taliban security targets.[12] One of these groups was a breakaway Taliban faction led by an ethnic Hazara commander named Mawlawi Mehdi, who severed ties with Taliban leadership and took con-trol of Balkhab district, Sar-e Pol province, after being sidelined.[13] Reports from July 2022 indicated that the Taliban deployed nearly 8,000 fighters to counter Mehdi and his faction.[14] Diversions of Taliban fighters to counter threats posed by Mawlawi Mehdi's faction in Sar-e Pol or the NRF in Panjshir, as well as multiple other anti-Taliban fronts, all present unique security openings for ISK to exploit. If armed resistance groups continue to grow and multiply, then the risk of Afghanistan descending into another civil war increases significantly. Similar conditions of chaos facilitated the Islamic State's rise in Iraq and Syria,[15] and ISK seems intent on instigating these conditions in Afghanistan today.

Meanwhile, reports abound concerning the Taliban's struggles and failures in their role as Afghanistan's new rulers. Forced evictions,[16] violent dispersions of peaceful protests,[17] discrimination against minorities,[18] restrictive and segregationist policies against women,[19] complete lack of diverse political representation at any meaningful level,[20] and a range of other human rights abuses and civil society crackdowns are common features of the Taliban's return to power. The movement also faces multiple humanitarian crises; by May 2022, half of the Afghan population relied on humanitarian aid,[21] a record number of Afghans faced acute hunger,[22] and the long-term livelihoods of many remained unaddressed.[23] In June 2022, the country suffered from a significant earthquake, exacerbating the plight of already vulnerable communities.[24] Moreover, even in the midst of a brutal campaign by ISK, it is the Taliban themselves who have been responsible for the greatest number of violent incidents against civilians since taking power.[25] These compounding cycles of violence, humanitarian crises, and intergenerational trauma and grievances—all with the Taliban in the seat of power—present additional strategic and psychosocial levers for ISK to pull and exploit.

For their part, the Taliban have transitioned to their tenuous position of power in the movement's traditional manner. The Taliban have thus far prioritized internal cohesion above all else, capitalized on threat perceptions to mobilize fighters against real and perceived enemies, and they have maintained strategic ambiguity over ideological and governance issues.[26] These three characteristics helped to advance the Taliban's insurgency for around two decades following the 2001 US invasion; however, they now place serious constraints on the movement's ability to govern in the face of multiple humanitarian crises, tense engagements with the international community, and significant pockets of resistance. As a result, multiple fractures have occurred since their takeover in August 2021. Initial reports emerged just days after the fall of Kabul regarding a tense dispute between major Taliban factions over power-sharing decisions.[27] Additional reports from mid-2022 highlighted Taliban in-fighting over poppy cultivation and revenue allocations, clashes between Pashtun and non-Pashtun Taliban members,[28] and even full-fledged breakaways from aggrieved groups such as Mawlawi Mehdi's faction.

While prioritizing internal cohesion may have benefited the Taliban as an insurgency, continuing this strategy is likely to marginalize large segments of Afghan society—including the movement's own fighters. In the words of Taliban analyst and scholar Andrew Watkins, "If Afghanistan's compounding crises pose the Taliban with the prospect of either failing to provide for the desperate needs of the Afghan people or their own potential fragmentation, the Taliban will put their own organization first."[29]

These are all factors that ISK will be looking to exploit through its propaganda, recruitment and outreach, and alliance-building channels.

ISK's Multipronged Attack Campaigns of Destabilization

Second, how far ISK is able to advance its multipronged campaigns of destabilization will have significant bearing on the group's trajectory in the region. These campaigns are critical to the broader Islamic State movement, and hold a deeper historical context in the core heartlands of Iraq and Syria and now globally.[30] According to the movement's own insurgency doctrine, destabilization campaigns are meant to undermine existing governments and create space for Islamic State affiliates to consolidate control.[31] As explored in earlier chapters, some of ISK's 2021 attack campaigns targeted Afghan Taliban security personnel, civil society "out-groups" such as minorities, and opposing clerics, inciting retaliatory Taliban crackdowns on civilian populations. Locally tailored propaganda, proselytization, and recruiting activities worked hand-in-hand to shape the information space and garner support from local populations afflicted by or disenchanted with Taliban policies,[32] especially Salafists in northeast Afghanistan and northern Pakistan but also younger Afghans in urban areas.[33]

At the same time, economic warfare attacks against critical infrastructure targets worked to delegitimize the Taliban in the eyes of the local population. The list of targets only expanded in 2022, and foreign commercial activity,[34] humanitarian logistics corridors, and other economic targets have all either suffered from ISK's attacks or have been earmarked by the group's propagandists as targets for future attacks. Aside from delegitimizing the Taliban, ISK is also using these attacks to try to aggravate relationships between its jihadist nemesis and the international community, with the goal being an increasingly isolated and more exploitable Taliban. How advanced ISK's destabilization attack campaigns grow both in number and quality will have important implications for its ability to carve out and consolidate territorial space once more.

The Effectiveness of ISK's Recruitment and Propaganda Campaigns

Third, ISK's regional and international outreach efforts stand to further bolster its goals in the region if successful. Both prior to the Taliban's takeover and in the ensuing months, ISK leveraged its diverse militant base to attack regional countries either on their soil, on their commercial and diplomatic interests within Afghanistan, or by using fighters representing key religious and ethnic groups in their populations to perpetrate attacks. The list includes Pakistan, India, Uzbekistan, Tajikistan, Turkmenistan, Russia, Iran, and China among others as of late 2022, and ISK already flagged future attacks in its propaganda publications.[35] ISK's propaganda output itself has expanded from the traditional Arabic-, Pashto-, and Dari-language releases to more recently include Urdu, Uzbek, Tajik, Hindi, and Malayalam releases as well as a new English-language *Voice of Khorasan* magazine that debuted in January 2022.[36] Anti-Taliban and antigovernment narratives pervade each of these releases, and all are geared toward internationalizing ISK's agenda to meet the needs of as diverse a pool of recruits as possible.

The timing of these releases is also growing rapidly more responsive to current events. For example, just days after the Taliban's public announcement during bilateral discussions with India in early June 2022 that they would act against militant groups targeting Afghanistan's neighbors,[37] ISK released multiple statements, news bulletins, and videos criticizing the Taliban's engagement. These releases also decried Indian politicians for their controversial statements about the Prophet,[38] and encouraged supporters to join Islamic State–Hind Province. Shortly after, on June 18, an ISK fighter targeted a Sikh temple in Kabul, leaving several dead or wounded.[39] As ISK continues to leverage the Taliban's untenable political situation to differentiate its rejectionist brand through propaganda releases, it will also continue to try to match words with deeds. In doing so, the group is serving as a force multiplier for other regional Islamic State affiliates such as ISH in Jammu and Kashmir. The rapid expansion of ISK's regional and international outreach and parallel attack campaigns is alarming and will be one of the key drivers of its insurgency against the Taliban going forward.

Sustained Alliances and Rivalries

Finally, and undergirding all of the above dynamics, is the central thesis of this book: ISK's alliances and rivalries. If history is any indicator, ISK is likely to double down on the very pillars that helped it to cement premier status within the regional jihadist landscape and to survive intense inter-militant competition and state-led targeting operations. If the group had not positioned itself as the main rival of the Afghan Taliban and other groups with links to the Pakistani state (and in recent years the TTP), there would have been few incentives for militants belonging to other groups to abandon their prior affiliations to join ISK. And had it not strategically formed a network of alliances during its emergence and formative years, ISK would have been unlikely to build its reputation and trajectory in the first place, and would also have found it challenging to rebuild itself after experiencing heavy losses.

As the Afghan Taliban transition to a state actor, they have strong incentives to steer clear of any ties with militant groups beyond their longtime allies—the TTP and al-Qaeda—at least publicly. In this context, if the

Taliban grows increasingly constrained and al-Qaeda remains relatively subdued, local groups looking for alliances may be more likely to turn to ISK for support, especially if the latter continues to amplify its propaganda against regional state actors, target Muslim and non-Muslim minorities, and strengthen its operational capacity. Looking ahead, ISK's sustained rivalries and alliances in the region are likely to pose a significant threat to civilian populations across the region, as they have done so since its emergence several years ago. In sum, the ISK-Taliban rivalry is likely not only to continue but also to intensify, and other militant groups disaffected with the Taliban may increasingly turn to ISK as a viable option. This bodes poorly for the country as the Taliban struggle to govern in the face of country-wide humanitarian crises and widespread international recognition remains elusive.

Security and Humanitarian Implications

The security implications associated with the continued presence of the Islamic State's networked affiliate in the Afghanistan-Pakistan region, as well as its relentless war against the Taliban, are likely to impact the broader region. By virtue of being one of the Islamic State's most successful branches, ISK's goals are certainly not limited to Afghanistan or any national borders for that matter, which leaves open the possibility for the group to facilitate attacks in other countries through cooperation and inspiration. Given its focus on targeting the Shiite communities in both Afghanistan and Pakistan, the continued presence of ISK also threatens to heighten sectarian violence across the region, especially given ISK's deep links with groups such as LeJ. And as long as ISK provides a staunch Salafi jihadist platform, there remains the potential for foreign fighters from beyond the region to travel to Afghanistan to support ISK.

Beyond security concerns, key humanitarian concerns also persist as a result of ISK's war on the Taliban. Hundreds, if not thousands, of civilian casualties followed fighting between the Islamic State and the Taliban, and thousands were left internally displaced or forced to flee.[40] If the conflict between these two movements persists, tens of thousands more will likely be forced into the same fate, exacerbating already strained internal displacement, refugee, and broader migration issues in Afghanistan and its neighboring countries following the Taliban's return to power.[41] Additionally, ISK has already embarked on an economic warfare campaign in which humanitarian corridors and specific implementers are legitimate targets. If that strategy escalates further, international donors may grow less willing to provide relief, and international organizations may be less and less capable of delivering much-needed aid to specific segments of the population.

Despite the gravitas of the current situation, none of these outcomes is predetermined. Regional and international powers can and should do more to help stem the burgeoning conflict, but many—including the United States—face the intractable problem of engaging with a regime run by specially designated terrorist individuals and entities who maintain close ties to vehement foes such as al-Qaeda.[42] Beyond the political debacle of being seen as working with wanted terrorists, foreign governments have been forced to work through increasingly complex and circuitous routes around the very anti-money laundering and countering the financing of terrorism (AML/CFT) apparatuses that they themselves developed in the years after the 9/11 attacks.[43] This makes even the most straightforward missions on paper—such as the delivery of food or health supplies to Afghans—all the more difficult, and only increases the vulnerabilities of a society under attack and facing multiple crises. Although this book does not focus on the above complexities, their relevance to the ISK threat is clear and pressing.

Countering Islamic State Khorasan

What can be done, then, to counter and contain ISK? To answer that difficult question—and barring any sudden and rapid transformations within the Taliban—it is important to consider two slightly smaller but intertwined questions. The first is how the United States and international community define a "good enough" counterterrorism doctrine for Afghanistan and the region?[44] That is, what level of ISK activity are we willing to accept, and what options are available and ought to be pursued? This is the same set of questions that followed the territorial defeat of the Islamic State in Iraq and Syria, but the solution options are noticeably different. United States–led special forces operators have entered Syrian soil twice since the fall of the so-called caliphate to kill the Islamic State's top leaders.[45] Such an option is infeasible in Afghanistan today given the Taliban's stance and relationships with the United States and its partners. Analysts and policymakers have debated a range of just- (i.e., regionally based in neighboring countries), distant-, and sea-based over-the-horizon options for Afghanistan,[46] but these options largely concern the logistics of drone and manned flights in Afghan air space and are ill-suited to manage the regional expansion of a diverse, networked, and resilient militant organization such as ISK over the long term.

As we explored in Chapter 4, it took years of heavy and sustained state-led operations with major US and Afghan partner forces in-country, which at times coincided with fierce inter-militant group competition, to disrupt and degrade ISK's territorial holdings to nominal levels. The human intelligence networks, partner force capacity, in-theatre ground and air assets that drove those efforts are, for the most part, scant or nonexistent today. In their wake, other intelligence-gathering avenues through regional government agencies, cyber, open-source, and commercial and humanitarian partners need to be explored.[47] Years of counterterrorism operations have also shown that effective policing practices are key to identifying and disrupting terrorist networks.[48] To date, effective policing has been far from the Taliban's strong suit.[49] But if regional and international countries aside from the United States do consider expanding their engagement with the Taliban for pragmatic reasons, improved policing practices—particularly along shared borders—may be a viable path to pursue, especially if they lead to fewer human rights violations. At the same time, governments need to be wary about the trustworthiness of the Afghan Taliban, given their own militant makeup. Additionally, second- and third-order effects of supporting the Afghan Taliban's policing efforts need to be explored before any supporting policy is enacted.

The second question has to do with the future of US foreign policy in South and Central Asia. What would a sustainable, consistent, and responsible regional strategy look like, and how does ISK fit into that picture? Too often, US foreign policy oscillates rapidly between and even within administrations, from troop surges to drawdowns to complete withdrawals, all in rapid succession. Questions of kinetic operations and military basing are often front and center of policy discussions, at least with regards to the United States, but are they always the right conversations to lead with when approaching regional partners? How can the United States improve engagements, partnerships, and security cooperation in a holistic and forward-thinking manner with countries that have common interests to counter an aspiring Islamic State affiliate next door? The answer will vary from country to country, especially in an era of peer and near-peer competition.[50] But here the Islamic State's strength can serve as the impetus for collective action by the international community; a group that targets or threatens every country, at least in its immediate region, presents a shared security concern. A common mission to counter ISK and other regional Islamic State affiliates, similar to the sentiments that mobilized the Global Coalition to Defeat ISIS, can lead to regional and international cooperation in Afghanistan, whether or not the United States is at the helm. A compelling case must be made to not just monitor and contain, but truly disrupt and degrade ISK, rendering it politically irrelevant in the long term. And unlike with the Islamic State in Iraq and Syria, the international community should not wait until ISK has regained pockets of territorial control, especially in and around major Afghan urban centers, to sound the alarm. The alternatives to collective security cooperation—inaction or regional countries supporting a variety of proxy forces to advance their strategic aims—will likely only lead to the very conditions of instability and even civil war for which the Islamic State movement prepares and exploits.

As scholars, practitioners, and policymakers grapple with these questions, the lessons from this book show that two fundamental pillars of ISK's strengths—alliances and rivalries—should guide any formulations of a counter-strategy. Local alliances have been key to ISK's operational expansion, prowess, and survival in the past and will be going forward. Regional powers must work together to counter these groups, or at the very least disrupt intergroup links and isolate ISK. Unless its operational links with other militant groups are disrupted, ISK is likely to continue leveraging them to adapt its strategy in times of difficulty, and draw on them to bolster its own human capital and resources. Strategic rivalries allowed ISK to carve out its position as the major jihadist alternative to a so-far failing Afghan Taliban. While the Taliban government needs to carefully craft a counterterrorism approach designed to contain ISK's violence and ensure human security, regional governments can identify appropriate measures to block and disrupt ISK's outreach efforts, especially those that seek to poach militants of other groups or mobilize civilian populations against government actors.

In closing, a broader lesson from history is worth revisiting. When the Islamic State expanded across Iraq and Syria in 2014, the international community was left with two indelible impressions: that the expansion occurred rapidly and unexpectedly, and that the mobilization and pace were unprecedented. However, it was anything but so to the communities who lived through the organization's brutal years of insurgency and occupation.[51] Years later, the international community must be willing to accept that ISK possesses the ambition and growth opportunities in a permissive environment to pursue a similar outcome in the Afghanistan-Pakistan region by employing similar methods. An appreciation of this outcome as both a possible and near-term scenario is critical in order for state actors to not only anticipate ISK's future strategic, operational, and tactical behavior, but also to proactively constrain the group's trajectory.

Notes

1. Hasan and George, "Brutal Attack on Mothers and Newborns."
2. Mashal and Abed, "From Maternity Ward to Cemetery."
3. Osman, "ISKP's Battle for Minds."
4. "Interim National Security Strategic Guidance."
5. Jadoon, Mines, and Sayed, "Smaller and Smarter."
6. Liebermann and Kaufman, "US Military Releases Videos of August Drone Strike That Killed 10 Afghan Civilians."
7. "They Wanted a New Life in America."

8. Siddique, "Taliban Faces Rising Armed Resistance From Former Government Factions."

9. George and Tassal, "Inside the Taliban's Secret War in the Panjshir Valley."

10. Rasa, "NRF."

11. Clarke and Schroden, "Brutally Ineffective."

12. Farivar, "Afghan Fighting Season Ushers in New Anti-Taliban Groups."

13. Eqbal, "Taliban's Highest-Ranking Army Officer Heads to Northern Afghanistan."

14. *Hasht-e-Subh Daily,* "Mawlawi Mehdi Coherences His Forces in Balkhab."

15. Program on Extremism, "Mosul and the Islamic State, episode 4, part 2: Never Again, Silence."

16. Khalid, "An Estimated 70 Families from Andarab Forcibly Displaced by the Taliban."

17. Rasa, "Taliban Disrupts Women's Protest in Kabul."

18. Akbari, "The Risks Facing Hazaras in Taliban-Ruled Afghanistan."

19. Eqbal, "Taliban Orders Kandahar City Transportation to Not Transport Women Without a Male Chaperone." See also *Ariana News,* "Virtue and Vice Ministry Reject Claims of Ordering Gender Segregation in Restaurants"; Kermani, "Afghanistan: Policing Faces, Bodies, and Beards on Kabul Streets."

20. Akbari, "The Risks Facing Hazaras in Taliban-Ruled Afghanistan."

21. Hasan, "UNHCR: Half of Afghan Population Relies on Humanitarian Aid."

22. Schlein, "UN Says Record Number of Afghans Face Acute Hunger."

23. Bijlert, "Food Aid in a Collapsed Economy."

24. Sands and Cursino, "Afghan Earthquake: At Least 1,000 People Killed and 1,500 Injured."

25. Taylor, "Afghanistan: The Taliban Had Promised 'Amnesty for All.'"

26. Watkins, "An Assessment of Taliban Rule at Three Months."

27. Nasar, "Afghanistan: Taliban Leaders in Bust-Up at Presidential Palace."

28. *Hasht-e-Subh Daily,* "Internal Clash Between Taliban in Takhar."

29. Watkins, "An Assessment of Taliban Rule at Three Months."

30. Ingram, Whiteside, and Winter, *The ISIS Reader.*

31. Al-Hayat Media Center, "From Hijrah to Khilafah." For analysis, see Ingram's *Long Jihad* report, https://extremism.gwu.edu/sites/g/files/zaxdzs2191/f/The_Long_Jihad.pdf.

32. Valle and Firdous, "Islamic State Khorasan Propaganda Targets New Audience"; Sayed, "Why Islamic State Khurasan Poses an Indigenous Threat to the Afghan Taliban."

33. A population ISK has sought to recruit for years now. See Osman, *Bourgeois Jihad.*

34. Webber, "Islamic State's Threat to Foreign Commercial Activity in Afghanistan."

35. Valle and Firdous, "Islamic State Khorasan Propaganda Targets New Audience"; Webber, "Islamic State in Afghanistan Promises Attacks."

36. Webber, "Voice of Khorasan Magazine and the Internationalization of Islamic State's Anti-Taliban Propaganda."

37. Gupta, "Taliban to Act Against Pak LeT/JeM Terrorists in Afghanistan on Specific Intel."

38. Sayed, "Pro-ISKP Video Threatens Attacks Against Hindus in Afghanistan."

39. Akbarzai, Mehsud, and Chen, "Islamic State Says Attack on Sikh Temple Is Revenge for Prophet Insults."

40. See, for example, Fahim, "In Nangarhar, Daesh Strengthens Its Chokehold on Achin."

41. Human Rights Watch, "What's Next for Afghans Fleeing the Taliban?"

42. Mir, "Afghanistan Terrorism Challenge"; "Jihadi Movement Is Galvanized by Taliban's Takeover in Afghanistan"; Joscelyn, "Twenty Years After 9/11, Taliban and al-Qaeda Remain Inseparable."

43. Miller and Rutzen, "US Counterterrorism Measures May Block Aid to Afghans."

44. Byman, "The Good Enough Doctrine."

45. Ingram, Jadoon, and Mines, "Islamic State Leader Killed in US Raid."

46. Pettyjohn, "Over-the-Horizon Does Not Have to Mean Next Door"; Jones, "Countering a Resurgent Terrorist Threat in Afghanistan."

47. Schroden, "New Ideas for Over-the-Horizon Counterterrorism in Afghanistan,"

48. Center for Evidence Based Crime Policy, "What Works in Policing?"

49. Clarke and Schroden, "Brutally Ineffective."

50. Ingram and Mines, "The Islamic State's Second Global Pledge Campaign."

51. Program on Extremism, "Mosul and the Islamic State, episode 4, part 2: Never Again, Silence."

Glossary

al-Naba. Periodical distributed by the Islamic State.

baya. Religiously binding oath of allegiance.

Dabiq. Online magazine published by the Islamic State between July 2014 and July 2016.

Daesh. Pejorative name for the Islamic State.

emir. Literally "prince," but in jihadist terminology refers to a group's commander or leader.

ijtihad. Independent reasoning.

inghimasi. Derivation of the Arabic word *ghamasa,* "to submerge." *Inghimasi* literally means "one who plunges"; an *inghimasi* attack usually involves a perpetrator executing an attack against an enemy, expecting to be killed in the process.

IS-Central. Islamic State in Iraq and Syria.

jihad. To struggle, generally.

mujahideen. Islamic jihadist fighters.

murtadeen. Apostates.

rafidah. Rejectionists.

Salafi. One who adheres to the beliefs and practices of the Salaf, or the first three generations of Muslims, including Muhammad and his companions, their followers, and the followers of the followers.

sharia. Islamic legal system based on the teachings of the Quran and the traditions of the Prophet.

Shiite. An adherent of the Shia branch of Islam.

shura. Consultation, often used in the context of consultative leadership bodies (Shura Councils) meant to advise groups' leaders on ideological, military, governance, and other issues.

takfir. Excommunication of co-religionists.

tawhid. The oneness of God.

wali. Governor, and in the context of the Islamic State refers to the top leadership position of any officially recognized Islamic State province.

Acronyms

AAF	Afghan Air Force
AKWJ	Ansar ul Khilfat Wal Jihad
ALP	Afghan Local Police
ANA	Afghan National Army
ANDSF/ANSF	Afghan National Defense and Security Forces
ANP	Afghan National Police
APHC	All Parties Hurriyat Conference
AQIS	al-Qaeda in the Indian Subcontinent
ASWJ	Ahle-Sunnat-wal Jamaat
AuM	Ansar-ul-Mujahideen
BAP	Balochistan Awami Party
BLA	Balochistan Liberation Army
CIA	Central Intelligence Agency
CID/CTD	Crime Investigation Department / Counter Terrorism Department
CTC	Combating Terrorism Center
CTD	provincial counterterrorism department
ETIM	East Turkistan Islamic Movement
FATA	Federally Administered Tribal Agencies
FBI	Federal Bureau of Investigation
FIA	Federal Investigation Agency
HIG	Hizb-i-Islami Gulbuddin
HM	Hizb-ul-Mujahideen
HuA	Hizbul Ahrar
IB	Intelligence Bureau
IDLG	Independent Directorate of Local Governance

IDP	internally displaced person
IED	improvised explosive device
IMU	Islamic Movement of Uzbekistan
ISAF	International Security Assistance Force
ISH	Islamic State–Hind
ISHP	Islamic State–Hind Province
ISI	Inter-Services Intelligence
ISIL	Islamic State of Iraq and the Levant
ISIS	Islamic State in Iraq and Syria
ISJK	Islamic State in Jammu and Kashmir
ISK	Islamic State Khorasan
JEM	Jaish-e-Mohammed
JKLF	Jammu Kashmir Liberation Front
JSOC	Joint Special Operations Command
JuA	Jamaat-ul-Ahrar
JuD	Jamaat-ud-Dawa
KPK	Khyber Pakhtunkhwa
LeI	Lashkar-e-Islam
LeJ	Lashkar-e-Jhangvi
LeJ-A	LeJ International
LeT	Lashkar-e-Taiba
MDI	Markaz Dawat-ul Irshad
MMA	Muttahida Majlis-e-Amal
NACTA	National Counter Terrorism Authority
NAP	National Action Plan
NATO	North Atlantic Treaty Organization
NDS	National Directorate of Security
NGO	nongovernmental organization
NISP	National Internal Security Policy
NRF	National Resistance Front
OGS	Operation Green Sword
PATA	Provincially Administered Tribal Areas
SAD	Special Activities Division (CIA)
SSP	Sipah-e-Sahaba Pakistan
TTP	Tehrik-e-Taliban
UJC	United Jihad Council
UN	United Nations

Bibliography

Abbas, Hassan. "Extremism and Terrorism Trends in Pakistan: Changing Dynamics and New Challenges." *CTC Sentinel* 14:2 (2021).
———. "A Profile of Pakistan's Lashkar-e-Jhangvi." *CTC Sentinel* 2:9 (2009).
———. "A Profile of Tehrik-i-Taliban Pakistan." *CTC Sentinel* 1:2 (2008).
———, ed. *Stabilizing Pakistan Through Police Reform.* New York: Asia Society, 2012.
———. "Transforming Pakistan's Frontier Corps." *Terrorism Monitor* 5:6 (2007).
Abrahms, Max, and Jochen Meirau. "Leadership Matters: The Effects of Targeted Killings on Militant Group Tactics." *Terrorism and Political Violence* 29:5 (2017).
Abrahms, Max, and Philip Potter. "Explaining Terrorism: Leadership Deficits and Militant Group Tactics." *International Organization* 69:2 (2015).
"Afghan Attack: Babies Killed As Gunmen Storm Kabul Maternity Ward." BBC News, May 12, 2020. https://www.bbc.com/news/world-asia-52631071.
"Afghan Forces Announce Arrest of Local ISIL leader." *Al-Jazeera,* April 4, 2020. https://www.aljazeera.com/news/2020/4/4/afghan-forces-announce-arrest-of -local-isil-leader.
"Afghan Intelligence Team Nabs Daesh Leader in South: NDS." *TOLO News,* April 4, 2020. https://tolonews.com/afghanistan/afghan-intelligence-team-nabs-daesh -leader-south-nds.
"Afghan-Pakistan ISIL's Hafiz Saeed Khan Killed." *Al Jazeera,* August 13, 2016. https://www.aljazeera.com/news/2016/8/13/afghan-pakistan-isils-hafiz-saeed -khan-killed.
"Afghanistan Blast: Sikhs Among 19 Dead in Jalalabad Suicide Attack." BBC News, July 1, 2018. https://www.bbc.com/news/world-asia-44677823.
"Afghanistan Conflict: Militants in Deadly Attack on Sikh Temple in Kabul." BBC News, March 25, 2020. https://www.bbc.com/news/world-asia-52029571.
"Afghanistan: Deadly Suicide Attack Targets Funeral in Nangarhar." *Al-Jazeera,* May 12, 2020. https://www.aljazeera.com/news/2020/5/12/afghanistan-deadly -suicide-attack-targets-funeral-in-nangarhar.

"Afghanistan Drone Strike 'Kills IS Commander Abdul Rauf.'" BBC News, February 9, 2015. https://www.bbc.com/news/world-asia-31290147.

"Afghanistan: Gunmen Attack Kabul Military Academy." *Al-Jazeera,* January 29, 2018. https://www.aljazeera.com/news/2018/1/29/afghanistan-gunmen-attack -kabul-military-academy.

"Afghanistan: IS Gunmen Dressed As Medics Kill 30 at Kabul Military Hospital." BBC News, March 8, 2017. https://www.bbc.com/news/world-asia -39202525.

"Afghanistan: Kabul Voter Centre Suicide Attack Kills 57." BBC News, April 22, 2018. https://www.bbc.com/news/world-asia-43855884.

"Afghanistan Kidnap: Gunmen Seize 30 Hazara Men in Zabul." BBC News, February 24, 2015. https://www.bbc.com/news/world-asia-31600476.

"Afghanistan Militants Dead in Jalalabad Attack." BBC News, March 2, 2016. https://www.bbc.com/news/world-asia-35705774.

"Afghanistan: Suicide Attack Hits Kandahar Mosque During Prayers." BBC News, October 16, 2021. https://www.bbc.com/news/world-asia-58925863.

"Afghanistan Suicide Bomb Attack: Dozens Killed in Kabul." BBC News, December 28, 2017. https://www.bbc.com/news/world-asia-42500769.

"Afghanistan War: Kabul Mosque Blast Shatters Calm for Eid." BBC News, May 14, 2021. https://www.bbc.com/news/world-asia-57114274.

Ahmad, Jibran, and Yeganeh Torbati. "U.S. Drone Kills Islamic State Leader for Afghanistan, Pakistan: Officials." Reuters, August 12, 2016. https://www .reuters.com/article/us-afghanistan-islamicstate/u-s-drone-kills-islamic-state -leader-for-afghanistan-pakistan-officials-idUSKCN10N21L.

Ahmed, Roohan. "Daesh Looks to Gain Foothold In Balochistan Under Ex-Karachi Cop." *Samaa News,* September 18, 2019. https://www.samaaenglish .tv/news/2019/09/daesh-looks-to-gain-foothold-in-balochistan-under-ex -karachi-cop.

Ahmed, Zahid S. "Counter-Extremism in Pakistan: Success or Falling Short?" *Peace Insight,* February 16, 2017. https://www.peaceinsight.org/en/articles /counter-extremism-pakistan-success-or-falling-short/?location=pakistan &theme=conflict-prevention-early-warning.

Akbar, Ali, "TTP Names Successor to APS Mastermind Umar Mansoor." *Dawn,* October 18, 2017. https://www.dawn.com/news/1364620.

Akbari, Farkhondeh. "The Risks Facing Hazaras in Taliban-Ruled Afghanistan." *Nexus,* March 7, 2022. https://extremism.gwu.edu/risks-facing-hazaras-taliban -ruled-afghanistan.

Akbarzai, Mehsud, and Heather Chen. "Islamic State Says Attack on Sikh Temple Is Revenge for Prophet Insults." June 19, 2022. https://edition.cnn.com/2022 /06/19/asia/islamic-state-sikh-gurdwara-temple-attack-kabul-afghanistan-intl -hnk/index.html.

Akhtar, Rabia. "Pakistan's New National Security Policy." January 20, 2022. https://www.atlanticcouncil.org/blogs/southasiasource/pakistans-new-national -security-policy.

al-Adnani al-Shami A., Shaykh Abu Muhammad. "Say, Die in Your Rage." Al-Hayat Media Center, 2015.

Al-Azaim Foundation for Media Production. *Until When the Ignorance?* February 2022.

Al-Hayat Media Center. "From Hijrah to Khilafah." *Dabiq* 1 (July 2014).

al-Khurasani, Abu Saad Muhammad. *Bright pages for understanding the nationalist Taliban.* Al-Azaim Foundation for Media Production, 2021.

al-Khurasani, Abu Saad Muhammad. "Khorasan: A Graveyard for The Crusades and A Province of Jihadists." Al-Azaim Foundation for Media Production, August 29, 2021.

al-Mohammad, Asaad, and Charlie Winter. *From Battlefront to Cyberspace: Demystifying the Islamic State's Propaganda Machine.* New York: Combating Terrorism Center at West Point, 2019.

al-Tamimi, Aymenn Jawad. "Archive of Islamic State Administrative Documents." January 2015. https://www.aymennjawad.org/2015/01/archive-of-islamic-state-administrative-documents.

Ali, Imtiaz. "5 Suspected Daesh Terrorists Arrested in Karachi." *Dawn,* April 15, 2019. https://www.dawn.com/news/1476280.

———. "Four Militants Linked with High Profile Terror Cases." *Dawn,* January 13, 2018. https://www.dawn.com/news/1382684/4-militants-linked-with-high-profile-terror-cases-killed-in-karachi-police-encounter.

———. "Four Well-Educated Men Held on Terrorism Charge." *Dawn,* December 19, 2015. https://www.dawn.com/news/1227381.

———. "Police Arrest 'Islamic State Inspired Militant' from Karachi." *Dawn,* January 1, 2016. https://www.dawn.com/news/1230071.

Ali, Obaid. "Qari Hekmat's Island Overrun: Taleban Defeat 'ISKP' in Jawzjan." August 4, 2018. https://www.afghanistan-analysts.org/en/reports/war-and-peace/qari-hekmats-island-overrun-taleban-defeat-iskp-in-jawzjan.

Ali, Tariq. "Daesh Network Active Near Pak-Afghan Border: FIA." *Khyber News,* March 7, 2018. https://khybernews.tv/daesh-network-active-near-pak-afghan-border-fia.

———. "FIA Arrests Daesh Recruiter from Karachi." *Khyber News,* September 28, 2017. https://khybernews.tv/fia-arrests-daesh-recruiter-karachi.

———. "24 Daesh Members Involved in Several Attacks Arrested in Peshawar." *Khyber News,* April 7, 2017. https://khybernews.tv/24-daesh-members-involved-in-several-attacks-arrested-in-peshawar.

"Alleged Daesh Terror Financing Network Busted by Pakistani Agencies: Sources." *Times of Islamabad,* October 19, 2018. https://timesofislamabad.com/19-Oct-2018/alleged-daesh-terror-financing-network-busted-by-pakistani-agencies-sources.

Amiri, Ehsanullah. "Islamic State Kills Dozens of Afghans After Foiled Sheep Theft." *Wall Street Journal,* October 26, 2016. https://www.wsj.com/articles/islamic-state-kills-dozens-of-afghans-after-foiled-sheep-theft-1477481846.

Amiri, Sharif. "Achin Residents Tell Their Stories About Life Under Daesh." *TOLO News,* March 19, 2019. https://tolonews.com/afghanistan/achin-residents-tell-their-stories-about-life-under-daesh.

Analytical Support and Sanctions Monitoring Team. *Seventh Report of the Analytical Support and Sanctions Monitoring Team Submitted Pursuant to Resolution 2501 (2019) Concerning the Taliban and Other Associated Individuals and Entities Constituting a Threat to the Peace, Stability, and Security of Afghanistan.* New York: United Nations Security Council, 2020.

———. *Ninth Report of the Analytical Support and Sanctions Monitoring Team Pursuant to Resolution 2255 (2015) Concerning the Taliban and Other Associated Individuals and Entities Constituting a Threat to the Peace, Stability, and Security of Afghanistan.* New York: United Nations Security Council, 2018.

———. *Tenth Report of the Analytical Support and Sanctions Monitoring Team Submitted Pursuant to Resolution 2255 (2015) Concerning the Taliban and Other Associated Individuals and Entities Constituting a Threat to the Peace, Stability, and Security of Afghanistan.* New York: United Nations Security Council, 2019.

———. *Eleventh Report of the Analytical Support and Sanctions Monitoring Team Submitted Pursuant to Resolution 2368 (2017) Concerning ISIL (Da'esh), al-Qaida, and Associated Individuals and Entities.* New York: United Nations Security Council, 2020.

———. *Twelfth Report of the Analytical Support and Sanctions Monitoring Team Submitted Pursuant to Resolution 2368 (2017) Concerning ISIL (Da'esh), al-Qaida, and Associated Individuals and Entities.* New York: United Nations Security Council, 2020.

———. *Thirteenth Report of the Analytical Support and Sanctions Monitoring Team Submitted Pursuant to Resolution 2611 (2021) Concerning the Taliban and Other Associated Individuals and Entities Constituting a Threat to the Peace Stability and Security of Afghanistan.* New York: United Nations Security Council, 2022.

———. *Twenty-second Report of the Analytical Support and Sanctions Monitoring Team Submitted Pursuant to Resolution 2368 (2017) Concerning ISIL (Da'esh), al-Qaida, and Associated Individuals and Entities.* New York: United Nations Security Council, 2018.

———. *Twenty-fourth Report of the Analytical Support and Sanctions Monitoring Team Submitted Pursuant to Resolution 2368 (2017) Concerning ISIL (Da'esh), al-Qaida, and Associated Individuals and Entities.* New York: United Nations Security Council, 2019.

———. *Twenty-Sixth Report of the Analytical Support and Sanctions Monitoring Team Submitted Pursuant to Resolution 2638 (2017) Concerning ISIL (Da'esh), al-Qaida, and Associated Individuals and Entities.* New York: United Nations Security Council, 2020.

———. *Twenty-eighth Report of the Analytical Support and Sanctions Monitoring Team Submitted Pursuant to Resolution 2638 (2017) Concerning ISIL (Da'esh), al-Qaida, and Associated Individuals and Entities.* New York: United Nations Security Council, 2021.

Anwar, Madeeha. "Hundreds with Terror Ties Run in Pakistan Elections." *Voice of America,* July 24, 2018. https://www.voanews.com/a/hundreds-candidates-terror-ties-running-pakistan-elections/4498747.html.

"Apostasy of Syed Ali Shah Gheelani and Others." *Al-Qaraar,* January 2018.

"The Apostate Taliban Movement." *Al-Naba* 79 (May 2017).

Arfeen, Syed. "The Hunt for Hafeez Brohi." *Friday Times,* February 14, 2017. https://www.thefridaytimes.com/the-hunt-for-hafeez-brohi.

———. "Usman Saifullah Kurd: A Reign of Sectarian Terror." *GEO News,* February 16, 2015. https://www.geo.tv/latest/994-usman-saifullah-kurd-a-reign-of-sectarian-terror.

"Army Releases Details of 3-Day Mastung Operation That Targeted 'IS Facilitators.'" *Dawn,* June 8, 2017. https://www.dawn.com/news/1338242.

Asal, Victor, Hyun Hee Park, R. Karl Rethemeyer, and Gary Ackerman. "With Friends Like These . . . Why Terrorist Organizations Ally." *International Public Management Journal* 19:1 (2015).

Asal, Victor, and R. Karl Rethemeyer. "The Nature of the Beast: Organizational Structures and the Lethality of Terrorist Attacks." *Journal of Politics* 70:2 (2008).

Ashraf, Sarah. *ISIS Khorasan: Presence and Potential in the Afghanistan-Pakistan Region.* London: Henry Jackson Society, 2017.

Ash-Shamali, Abu Jarir. "Al-Qaidah of Waziristan." *Dabiq* 6 (2015).

"Assailants Came from Afghanistan, PM Told." *Dawn,* October 26, 2016. https://www.dawn.com/news/1292349.

Associated Press and Damien Gayle. "ISIS Sets Up Base in Afghanistan Less Than Three Months After British Troops Left." *Daily Mail Online,* January 14, 2015. https://www.dailymail.co.uk/news/article-2910420/ISIS-sets-base-Afghanistan-run-former-Guantanamo-prisoner-operating-Helmand-three-months-British-troops-left-region.html.

As-Sahab Media. *Resurgence* 1 (2014).

———. *Resurgence* 2 (2014).

As-Sawarte. Untitled nineteen-minute propaganda video. November 2021.

"Avtar Singh Khalsa, Sikh Candidate for October Polls Among 20 Killed in Afghanistan Blast." *Express News Service,* July 2, 2018. https://indianexpress.com/article/india/avtar-singh-khalsa-sikh-candidate-for-october-polls-among-20-killed-in-afghanistan-blast-5241725.

Azzam, Sultan Aziz. "Special Report on The Islamic State Attack on The Nangarhar Prison." Black Flags Media Center, August 3, 2021.

———. "Warning." Al-Azaim Foundation, April–May 2021.

Bacon, Tricia. "Alliance Hubs: Focal Points in the International Terrorist Landscape." *Perspectives on Terrorism* 8:4 (2014).

———. "Slipping the Leash? Pakistan's Relationship with the Afghan Taliban." *Survival* 60:5 (2018).

———. *Why Terrorist Groups Form International Alliances.* Pittsburgh: University of Pennsylvania Press, 2018.

Bacon, Tricia, Grace Ellis, and Daniel Milton. "Helping or Hurting? The Impact of Foreign Fighters on Militant Group Behavior." *Journal of Strategic Studies* (October 2021).

Bahari, Mustazah, and Muhammad Haniff Hassan. "The Black Flag Myth: An Analysis from Hadith Studies." *Counter Terrorist Trends and Analyses* 6:8 (2014).

"BAP Candidate Siraj Raisani Among 128 Killed in Mastung Suicide Blast." *Dunya News,* July 14, 2018. https://dunyanews.tv/en/Pakistan/447869-Ex-Balochistan-CM-Siraj-Raisani-martyed-Mastung-blast.

Bapat, Navin, and Kanisha Bond. "Alliances Between Militant Groups." *British Journal of Political Science* 42:4 (2012).

Bard, E. O'Neill. *Insurgency and Terrorism: From Revolution to Apocalypse.* Washington, DC: Potomac, 2005.

Barron, Laignee. "U.S. Forces Confirm Death of ISIS Leader in Afghanistan." *Time,* September 3, 2018. https://time.com/5385326/us-isis-leader-death-abu-saad-orakzai.

Basit, Abdul. "IS Penetration in Afghanistan-Pakistan: Assessment, Impact, and Implications." *Perspectives on Terrorism* 11:3 (2017).

"The Battle of Tawhid in Kabul." *Al-Naba* 302 (August 2021).

Bell, Kevin. "The First Islamic State: A Look Back at the Islamic Emirate of Kunar." *CTC Sentinel* 9:2 (February 2016).

Bennett, Elizabeth. "A Comeback for al-Qaeda in the Indian Subcontinent?" *Foreign Policy,* May 12, 2015.

Bergen, Peter. "The Account of How We Nearly Caught Osama bin Laden in 2001." *New Republic,* December 30, 2009. https://newrepublic.com/article/72086/the-battle-tora-bora.

Berger, Miriam, and Haq Nawaz Khan. "Islamic State in Afghanistan Claims Responsibility." *Washington Post,* September 19, 2021. https://www.washingtonpost.com/world/2021/09/19/islamic-state-khorasan-afghanistan-taliban-attacks.

Bhardwaj, Ananya. "2 More Indians from Kerala Suspected to Be Among ISIS Terrorists Who Attacked Jalalabad Jail." *The Print,* November 13, 2020. https://theprint.in/india/2-more-indians-from-kerala-suspected-to-be-among-isis-terrorists-who-attacked-jalalabad-jail/542983.

Bhat, Gulzar. "Kashmir: Islamic State Claims Responsibility of Soura Attack." *National Herald,* February 27, 2018. https://www.nationalheraldindia.com/regional/kashmir-islamic-state-claims-responsibility-of-soura-attack.

bin Perwaiz, Salis. "'Daesh Recruiter' Arrested at Cantt Railway Station." *The News,* September 29, 2017. https://www.thenews.com.pk/print/233340-Daesh-recruiter-arrested-at-Cantt-railway-station.

Bijlert, Martine van. "Food Aid in a Collapsed Economy: Relief, Tensions, and Allegations." May 23, 2022. https://www.afghanistan-analysts.org/en/reports/economy-development-environment/food-aid-in-a-collapsed-economy-relief-tensions-and-allegations.

Black Flags Media Center. "Message from Dr Shahab al-Muhajir—The New Wali of Khorasan." 2021.

———. "Special Report on the Islamic State Attack on the Nangarhar Prison." 2020.

Blinken, Antony J. "Taking Action Against ISIS-K." Washington, DC: Office of the Spokesperson, US Department of State, November 22, 2021. https://www.state.gov/taking-action-against-isis-k.

Bloom, Mia. *Dying to Kill: The Allure of Suicide Terror.* Columbia: Columbia University Press, 2005.

Blue, Victor, Thomas Gibbons-Neff, and Christina Goldbaum. "ISIS Poses a Growing Threat to New Taliban Government in Afghanistan." *New York Times,* November 3, 2021. https://www.nytimes.com/2021/11/03/world/asia/isis-afghanistan-taliban.html.

Bokhari, Farhan, and Kiran Stacey. "China Woos Pakistan Militants to Secure Belt and Road Projects." *Financial Times,* February 19, 2018. https://www.ft.com/content/063ce350-1099-11e8-8cb6-b9ccc4c4dbbb.

Bokhari, Kamran. "Threatened by ISIS, the Afghan Taliban May Crack Up." *Wall Street Journal,* August 27, 2022. https://www.wsj.com/articles/threatened-isis-afghan-taliban-rule-jihadist-islamist-pakistan-baradar-haibatullah-11630094678?mod=searchresults_pos1&page=1.

Bond, Kanisha. *Power, Identity, Credibility, and Cooperation: Examining the Development of Cooperative Arrangements Among Violent Non-State Actors.* Pittsburgh: Pennsylvania State University Press, 2010.

Borhan, Osman. *Bourgeois Jihad: Why Young, Middle-Class Afghans Join the Islamic State.* Washington, DC: US Institute of Peace, 2020.

Botelho, Greg, and Ralph Ellis. "Adam Gadahn, American Mouthpiece for al-Qaeda, Killed." April 23, 2015. https://www.cnn.com/2015/04/23/world/adam-gadahn-al-qaeda/index.html.

Brachman, Jarret M. *Global Jihadism: Theory and Practice.* Abingdon, UK: Routledge, 2008.

Brown, Vahid. "The Salafi Emirate of Kunar Between South Asia and the Arabian Peninsula." In *Pan-Islamic Connections: Transnational Networks Between South Asia and the Gulf.* ed. Christophe Jaffrelot and Laurence Louër. Oxford: Oxford University Press, 2017.

Brown, Vahid, and Don Rassler. *Fountainhead of Jihad: The Haqqani Nexus, 1973–2012.* Oxford: Oxford University Press, 2013.

Buncombe, Andrew. "Syed Ali Shah Geelani: Why Is India Afraid of This 83-Year-Old Man?" *The Independent,* March 1, 2013. https://www.independent.co.uk/voices/comment/syed-ali-shah-geelani-why-is-india-afraid-of-this-83-yearold-man-8516534.html.

Burns, Robert, and Josh Boak. "Biden Orders 1,000 More Troops to Aid Afghanistan Departure." August 15, 2021. https://apnews.com/article/joe-biden-afghanistan-4a2015be84d49c71cfe8f227a8896eae.

Byman, Daniel. "Buddies or Burdens? Understanding The al-Qaeda Relationship with Its Affiliate Organizations." *Security Studies* 23:3 (2014).

———. "The Good Enough Doctrine." *Foreign Affairs* (September–October 2021).

"Case of Mosque Attack Registered." *News International,* May 3, 2016. https://www.thenews.com.pk/print/117032-Case-of-mosque-attack-registered.

Chalk, Peter, and Christine Fair. "Lashkar-e-Taiba Leads the Kashmiri Insurgency." *Jane's Intelligence Review* (December 2002).

Chang, Ailsa, Connor Donevan, and Amy Isackson. "A Kandahar Mosque Attack Exposes the Taliban's Security Challenges." October 15, 2021. https://www.npr.org/2021/10/15/1046519762/a-kandahar-mosque-attack-exposes-the-talibans-security-challenges.

"Chapter 6: Foreign Terrorist Organizations." Washington, DC: US State Department, May 30, 2013. https://2009-2017.state.gov/j/ct/rls/crt/45394.htm.

Chaudhry, Asif. "IS Cell Busted in Sialkot, Claim Officials." *Dawn,* December 29, 2015. https://www.dawn.com/news/1229341.

Chenoweth, Erica. "Democratic Competition and Terrorist Activity." *Journal of Politics* 72:1 (2010).

Chishti, Ali K. "The ISIS link." *Friday Times,* February 13, 2015. https://www.thefridaytimes.com/2015/02/13/the-isis-link.

Clark, James. "US Marines and Taliban Outside Kabul Airport Are So Close They Can Touch Each Other." August 25, 2021. https://taskandpurpose.com/news/video-marines-and-taliban-kabul-airport.

Clarke, Colin P. *After the Caliphate: The Islamic State & the Future Terrorist Diaspora.* Medford, MA: Polity Press, 2019.

Clarke, Colin, and Jonathan Schroden. "Brutally Ineffective: How the Taliban Are Failing in Their New Role As Counter-Insurgents." November 29, 2021. https://warontherocks.com/2021/11/brutally-ineffective-how-the-taliban-are-failing-in-their-new-role-as-counter-insurgents.

Clifford, Bennett, and Seamus Hughes. "Afghanistan and American Jihadists: More Inspiration, Less Destination." *Lawfare,* October 27, 2021. https://www.lawfareblog.com/afghanistan-and-american-jihadists-more-inspiration-less-destination.

Conrad, Justin, and Kevin Greene. "Competition, Differentiation, and the Severity of Terrorist Attacks." *Journal of Politics* 77:2 (2015).

———. "Differentiation and the Severity of Terrorist Attacks." *Journal of Politics* 77:2 (2015).

Constable, Patricia. "Taliban Vows Crackdown on ISIS." *New York Times,* April 22, 2022. https://www.washingtonpost.com/world/2022/04/22/afghanistan-isis-arrest -attacks-security.

Cragin, Kim, Peter Chalk, Sara Daly, and Brian Jackson. *Sharing the Dragon's Teeth: Terrorist Groups and the Exchange of New Technologies.* Santa Monica, CA: Rand, 2007.

Cruickshank, Paul. "A View from the CT Foxhole: Edmund Fitton-Brown, Coordinator, ISIL (Daesh)/al-Qaida/Taliban Monitoring Team, United Nations." *CTC Sentinel* 12:4 (2019).

Cullison, Alan. "Inside the Hidden War Between the Taliban and ISIS." *Wall Street Journal,* August 26, 2021. https://www.wsj.com/articles/isis-taliban-afghanistan -bombing-11630014684.

"Daesh Caused the Most Harm to Islam: JuD." *Khyber News,* January 4, 2016. https://khybernews.tv/daesh-caused-the-most-harm-to-islam-jud/?amp.

"Daesh Families Arrive in Kunar's Sarkano District: Syedkhel." *Pajhwok Afghan News,* March 25, 2016. https://pajhwok.com/en/2016/03/25/daesh-families-arrive -kunar%E2%80%99s-sarkano-district-syedkhel.

Davis, Anthony. "Foreign Combatants in Afghanistan." *Jane's Intelligence Review* (July 1993).

"The Day the Believers will Rejoice: Part 1." Video message. Wilayat Khorasan Media Office, May 31, 2015.

"Deadly Blasts Hit Afghan Capital Kabul." *Al-Jazeera,* December 10, 2021. https:// www.aljazeera.com/news/2021/12/10/bomb-blast-kills-two-civilians-on -minibus-in-afghanistans-kabul.

"Deadly Suicide Attack and Gun Battle Near Airport in Afghanistan." March 6, 2019. https://www.france24.com/en/20190306-eastern-afghanistan-jalalabad -suicide-bomb-attack-gun-explosion-airport.

Dearden, Lizzie. "Isis 'Kills at Least Six Red Cross' Aid Workers in Afghanistan." *The Independent,* February 8, 2017. https://www.independent.co.uk/news/world /middle-east/isis-islamic-state-afghanistan-wilayat-khorasan-red-cross-aid -workers-killed-shot-gunmen-massacre-a7568791.html.

Delong-Bas, Natana J. *Wahhabi Islam: From Revival and Reform to Global Jihad.* Oxford: Oxford University Press, 2008.

"Department of Defense Press Briefing by General Nicholson via Teleconference from Afghanistan." Washinton, DC, July 28, 2016. https://www.defense.gov /News/Transcripts/Transcript/Article/879392/department-of-defense-press -briefing-by-general-nicholson-via-teleconference-fr.

Desiderio, Andrew, and Lara Seligman. "U.S. Intensifies Talks to Use Russian Bases for Afghan Counterterrorism Ops." *Politico,* September 29, 2019. https:// www.politico.com/news/2021/09/29/us-russia-bases-afghan-counterterrorism -514743.

"Did the Security Agencies Break the Terrorist Network?" *Ling News,* May 7, 2021. https://www.lingnews24.com/did-the-security-agencies-break-the-terrorist -network-in-north-sindh.

Dodwell, Brian, Daniel Milton, and Don Rassler. *Then and Now: Comparing the Flow of Foreign Fighters to AQI and the Islamic State.* New York: Combating Terrorism Center at West Point, 2016.

"Dozens Killed in Kabul Ceremony Attack Claimed by ISIL." *Al-Jazeera,* March 6, 2020. https://www.aljazeera.com/news/2020/3/6/dozens-killed-in-kabul -ceremony-attack-claimed-by-isil.

Dreazen, Yochi. "The Taliban's New Number 2 Is a Mix of Tony Soprano and Che Guevara." *Foreign Policy*, July 31, 2015.

Dressler, Jeffrey. *The Haqqani Network: From Pakistan to Afghanistan*. Washington, DC: Institute for the Study of War, 2010.

Dunya News. "Sindh IS head Ujmar Kathiwer arrested." *Dunya News*, January 3, 2016. https://dunyanews.tv/en/Pakistan/315911-Sindh-IS-head-Ujmar-Kathiwer-arrested.

Dwyer, Colin. "At Least 25 People Dead After Hours-Long Attack on Sikh Complex in Kabul." March 25, 2020. https://www.npr.org/2020/03/25/821428292/at-least-25-people-dead-after-hours-long-attack-on-sikh-complex-in-kabul.

D'Souza, Shanthie Mariet, and Bibhu Prasad Routray. "Jihad in Jammu and Kashmir: actors, agendas and expanding benchmarks." *Small Wars & Insurgencies* 27:4 (2016).

Elms, Victoria. "Is IS Really a Threat in Kashmir?" September 27, 2018. https://www.orfonline.org/expert-speak/is-is-really-a-threat-in-kashmir-44547.

"Enhancing Security and Stability in Afghanistan." Washington, DC: US Department of Defense, December 20, 2017. https://dod.defense.gov/Portals/1/Documents/pubs/1225-Report-Dec-2017.pdf.

Eqbal, Saqalain. "Taliban Orders Kandahar City Transportation to Not Transport Women Without a Male Chaperone." May 30, 2022. https://www.khaama.com/taliban-orders-kandahar-city-transportation-to-not-transport-women-without-a-male-chaperone474384.

———. "Taliban's Highest-Ranking Army Officer Heads to Northern Afghanistan; Clash Between the Taliban and Mawlawi Mujahid Possible at 'Any Moment.'" June 24, 2022. https://www.khaama.com/talibans-highest-ranking-army-officer-heads-to-northern-afghanistan-clash-between-the-taliban-and-mawlawi-mujahid-possible-at-any-moment-44732.

Erfanyar, Ahmad S. "Afghan, US Forces Destroy Daesh Stronghold in Nangarhar." *Pajhwok Afghan News*, July 8, 2018. https://pajhwok.com/2018/07/08/afghan-us-forces-destroy-daesh-stronghold-nangarhar.

Esposito, John L. *Islam and Politics*. Syracuse: Syracuse University Press, 1984.

Fahim, Zeerak. "In Nangarhar, Daesh Strengthens Its Chokehold on Achin." *Pajhwok Afghan News*, September 16, 2015. https://pajhwok.com/2015/09/16/nangarhar-daesh-strengthens-its-chokehold-achin.

Fahim, Zeerak. "Daesh Fighters Torch Taliban Leaders' Homes." *Pajhwok Afghan News*, June 3, 2015.

———. "Daesh Has Imprisoned 127 People in Nangarhar's Achin: Official." *Pajhwok Afghan News*, September 10, 2015. https://pajhwok.com/2015/09/10/daesh-has-imprisoned-127-people-nangarhars-achin-official.

———. "Islamic State Has Started Recruiting in Kunar: Waziri." *Pajhwok Afghan News*, November 9, 2015. https://pajhwok.com/2015/11/09/islamic-state-has-started-recruiting-kunar-waziri.

———. "Kunar Province Likely to Be Daesh Next Hideout." *Pajhwok Afghan News*, March 17, 2016. https://pajhwok.com/2016/03/17/kunar-province-likely-be-daesh-next-hideout/.

———. "Up to 100 Daesh Militants Killed in Achin Offensive." *Pajhwok Afghan News*, September 30, 2015. https://pajhwok.com/2015/09/30/100-daesh-militants-killed-achin-offensive.

Faiez, Rahim, and Amir Shah. "Islamic State Attacks Afghan Intelligence Compound in Kabul." December 18, 2017. https://www.militarytimes.com/2017 /12/18/islamic-state-attacks-afghan-intelligence-compound-in-kabul.

Fair, C. Christine. *In Their Own Words: Understanding Lashkar-e-Tayyaba.* Oxford: Oxford University Press, 2018.

Farivar, Masood. "Afghan Fighting Season Ushers in Anti-Taliban Groups." *Voice of America,* April 27, 2022. https://www.voanews.com/a/afghan-fighting-season -ushers-in-new-anti-taliban-groups/6542148.html.

Farrall, Leah, and Mustafa Haamid. *The Arabs at War in Afghanistan.* London: Hurst, 2015.

Farrell, Theo. "Unbeatable: Social Resources, Military Adaptation, and the Afghan Taliban." *Texas National Security Review* 1:3 (2018).

Fazl-e-Haider, Syed. "Pakistani Separatists Turn Their Sights on China." *The Interpreter,* May 16, 2022. https://www.lowyinstitute.org/the-interpreter/pakistani -separatists-turn-their-sights-china.

"Female Suicide Bomber Kills Eight in Northwest Pakistan." Reuters, July 21, 2019. https://www.reuters.com/article/us-pakistan-attack/female-suicide-bomber-kills -eight-in-northwest-pakistan-idUSKCN1UG08J.

Feng, Emily. "China Taliban Afghanistan Uyghurs." October 15, 2021. https://www .npr.org/2021/10/15/1042399659/china-taliban-afghanistan-uyghurs.

Fernandez, Alberto M. *Here to Stay and Growing: Combating ISIS Propaganda Networks.* Washington, DC: Brookings Institution, 2015.

"FIA Arrests 60 Money Changers in Peshawar for Funding Daesh." *Khyber News,* January 14, 2016. https://khybernews.tv/fia-arrests-60-money-changers-in -peshawar-for-funding-daesh.

"FIA Raid: 60 Money Changers Arrested From Currency Market." *Express Tribune,* January 14, 2016. https://tribune.com.pk/story/1027629/fia-raid-60-money -changers-arrested-from-currency-market.

"Fighting Terrorism." *The Nation,* January 15, 2021. https://nation.com.pk/15 -Jan-2021/fighting-terrorism.

Fine, Glenn A., Steve A. Linick, and Ann Alvaresi Barr. *Operation Freedom's Sentinel: Lead Inspector General Quarterly Report to the United States Congress, July 1, 2018–September 30, 2018.* Alexandria, VA: US Department of Defense, Office of the Inspector General, 2018.

Firdous, Iftikhar. "Da'ish Peshawar Network Dismantled, 24 Arrested." *Express Tribune,* April 7, 2017. https://tribune.com.pk/story/1377453/daish-peshawar -network-dismantled-24-arrested.

Fitton-Brown, Edmund. "The Persistent Threat from the Islamic State and al-Qaeda: The View from the UN." February 6, 2020. https://www.washingtoninstitute .org/policy-analysis/persistent-threat-islamic-state-and-al-qaeda-view-un.

"Five Militants Arrested in Karachi." *Pakistan Today,* April 15, 2019. https:// archive.pakistantoday.com.pk/2019/04/15/five-militants-arrested-in-karachi.

"Five Rockets Hit US Airbase in Afghanistan." *Al-Jazeera,* April 9, 2020. https:// www.aljazeera.com/news/2020/4/9/five-rockets-hit-us-airbase-in-afghanistan.

Forsythe, Amy. "Special Forces Soldiers Help Afghan Forces Defeat ISIS in Eastern Afghanistan." *Army News,* August 10, 2018. https://www.army.mil/article /209723/special_forces_soldiers_help_afghan_forces_defeat_isis_in_eastern _afghanistan.

Foulkes, John. "Aslam Farooqi: Head of Islamic State-Khorasan Arrested." *Militant Leadership Monitor* 11:4 (2020).

Gabol, Imran. "42 IS Supporters Arrested in Punjab: Rana Sanaullah—Pakistan." *Dawn*, January 4, 2016. https://www.dawn.com/news/1230719.

Gad, Z. "International Cooperation Among Terrorist Groups." In *On Terrorism and Combating Terrorism: Proceedings of an International Seminar*, Tel Aviv, 1979, ed. Ariel Merari. Frederick, MD: University Publications of America, 1985.

Gall, Carlotta. *The Wrong Enemy: America in Afghanistan, 2001–2014*. New York: Houghton Mifflin Harcourt, 2014.

Ganguly, Sumit, and Feisal Al-Istrabadi. *The Future of ISIS: Regional and International Implications*. Washington, DC: Brookings Institution, 2018.

Gannon, Kathy. "Power Struggle Seen Within Surging Islamic State in Afghanistan." *Military Times*, June 7, 2017. https://www.militarytimes.com/news/pentagon-congress/2017/06/07/power-struggle-seen-within-surging-islamic-state-in-afghanistan.

Gannon, Kathy, and Tameem Akhgar. "US Blames Brutal Attack on Afghan Maternity Hospital on IS." May 15, 2020. https://apnews.com/article/europe-religion-islamic-state-group-eebcd4af6c821e5530f3795352542f9f.

George, Susannah, and Aziz Tassal. "Inside the Taliban's secret war in the Panjshir Valley." *Washington Post*, June 8, 2020. https://www.washingtonpost.com/world/2022/06/08/afghanistan-panjshir-valley-taliban-resistance/.

George, Susannah, and Sharif Hassan. "Blasts Disrupt Afghan President Ashraf Ghani's Swearing-In Ceremony amid a Deepening Political Crisis." *Washington Post*, March 9, 2020. https://www.washingtonpost.com/world/asia_pacific/dueling-presidential-inaugurations-planned-in-kabul/2020/03/09/f3b71a14-61ba-11ea-8a8e-5c5336b32760_story.html.

Ghazi, Zabihullah. "IS Radio Expands Reach in Afghanistan." *Voice of America*, January 27, 2016. https://www.voanews.com/a/islamic-state-radio-expands-reach-afghanistan/3165478.html.

Ghazi, Zabihullah, and Mujib Mashal. "29 Dead After ISIS Attack on Afghan Prison." *New York Times*, August 3, 2020. https://www.nytimes.com/2020/08/03/world/asia/afghanistan-prison-isis-taliban.html.

Gibbons-Neff, Thomas, and Wali Arian. "ISIS Bomber Kills Dozens at Shiite Mosque in Northern Afghanistan." *New York Times*, October 8, 2021. https://www.nytimes.com/2021/10/08/world/asia/afghanistan-mosque-attack.html.

Gibbons-Neff, Thomas, and Fatima Faizi. "Gunmen Storm Kabul University." *New York Times*, November 2, 2020. https://www.nytimes.com/2020/11/02/world/asia/kabul-university-attack.html.

Gibbons-Neff, Sami Sahak, and Taimoor Shah. "Dozens Killed in ISIS Attack on Military Hospital." *New York Times*, November 2, 2021. https://www.nytimes.com/2021/11/02/world/asia/afghanistan-kabul-hospital-attack.html#:~:text=At%20least%2025%20people%20were,the%20city%20into%20the%20afternoon.

Gishkori, Zahid. "Daesh Gradually Gaining Ground in Pakistan." *The News International*, March 3, 2017. https://www.thenews.com.pk/print/189914-Daesh-gradually-gaining-ground-in-Pakistan.

Ghanizada, Ahmad Shah. "Taliban Appoints First Shia Hazara As Shadow District." *Khaama Press*, April 28, 2020. https://www.khaama.com/taliban-appoints-first-shia-hazara-as-shadow-district-chief-of-the-group-04734.

———. "Taliban Appoints New Leader in Military Leadership Following Recent Upheavals." *Khaama Press*, May 10 2020. https://www.khaama.com/taliban-appoints-new-leader-in-military-leadership-following-recent-upheavals-07791.

Giustozzi, Antonio. *The Islamic State in Khorasan: Afghanistan, Pakistan, and the New Central Asian Jihad.* London: Hurst, 2018.

———. *Koran Kalashnikov and Laptop: The Neo-Taliban Insurgency in Afghanistan, 2002–2007.* London: Hurst, 2009.

———. "Shifting Ground: Competition Intensifies Between the Islamic State and al-Qaida for Central Asian Support." *Jane's Terrorism and Insurgency Monitor,* April 25, 2017.

———. "Taliban and Islamic State: Enemies or Brothers in Jihad?" December 14, 2017. https://www.crpaweb.org/single-post/2017/12/15/Enemies-or-Jihad -Brothers-Relations-Between-Taliban-and-Islamic-State.

———. "The Transformation of the Haqqani Network." *Jane's Terrorism and Insurgency Monitor,* November 2, 2017.

Giustozzi, Antonio, and Silab Mangal. "Taking Shape: The Islamic State Expands into Pakistan with Tehrik-e-Khilfat." *Jane's Terrorism and Insurgency Monitor,* January 30, 2015.

Glinski, Stefanie. "Afghanistan's Forests Are Turning a Profit for the Islamic State." *Foreign Policy,* July 15, 2019. https://foreignpolicy.com/2019/07/15/afghanistans -forests-are-turning-a-profit-for-the-islamic-state.

Global Terrorism Index 2019: Measuring the Impact of Terrorism. Sydney: Institute for Economics and Peace, November 2019. https://www.visionofhumanity.org /wp-content/uploads/2020/11/GTI-2019-web.pdf.

Global Witness. *At Any Price We Will Take the Mines: The Islamic State, the Taliban, and Afghanistan's White Talc Mountains.* London: Global Witness, 2018. https://www.kpsrl.org/sites/default/files/2018-06/AfghanistanTalcInvestigation _May2018.pdf.

Gohel, Sajjan. "The Taliban Are Far Closer to the Islamic State Than They Claim." *Foreign Policy,* August 26, 2021. https://foreignpolicy.com/2021/08/26 /afghanistan-kabul-airport-attack-taliban-islamic-state.

Goldman, Adam, and Eric Schmitt. "One by One, ISIS Social Media Experts Are Killed As Result of F.B.I. Program." *New York Times,* November 24, 2016. https://www.nytimes.com/2016/11/24/world/middleeast/isis-recruiters-social -media.html.

Gonzales, Richard. "U.S. Officials Confirm Death of Senior ISIS Leader in Afghanistan and Pakistan." August 12, 2016. https://www.npr.org/sections /thetwo-way/2016/08/12/489830363/u-s-officials-confirm-death-of-senior-isis -leader-in-afghanistan-and-pakistan.

"The Guarantors [Taliban] Are in Panic." Al-Azaim Foundation for Media Production, November 2021.

Gul, Ayaz. "Bus Bombing Kills Afghan Journalist." *IFJ News,* November 16, 2021. https://www.ifj.org/media-centre/news/detail/category/press-releases/article /afghanistan-former-ariana-television-journalist-killed-in-explosion.html.

"Gunmen Kill Many Hazara Shia Coal Miners." *Al-Jazeera,* January 3, 2021. https://www.aljazeera.com/news/2021/1/3/gunmen-kill-at-least-11-from-shia -minority-in-south-west-pakistan.

Gupta, Shishir. "Taliban to Act Against Pak LeT/JeM Terrorists in Afghanistan on Specific Intel." *Hindustan Times,* June 10, 2022. https://www.hindustantimes .com/world-news/taliban-to-act-against-pak-let-jem-terrorists-in-afghanistan -on-specific-indian-101654831818094.html.

Habibzada, Mohammad. "IS, Lashkar-e-Islam Clash in Eastern Afghanistan." *Voice of America,* February 11, 2018. https://www.voanews.com/a/is-lashkar-e-islam -clash-in-eastern-afghanistan/4249009.html.

Hafez, Mohammed. "Jihad After Iraq: Lessons from the Arab Afghans Phenomenon." *CTC Sentinel* 1:4 (2008).

Haidar, Suhasini, and Vijaita Singh. "India Unlikely to Allow Return of 4 Kerala Women." *The Hindu,* June 12, 2021. https://www.thehindu.com/news/national /india-unlikely-to-allow-4-kerala-women-who-joined-is-to-return/article 34792017.ece.

Hamid, Nafees. "The British Hacker Who Became the Islamic State's Chief Terror Cybercoach: A Profile of Junaid Hussain." *CTC Sentinel* 11:4 (2018).

Hamid, Tamim. "NDS Commander Gives Details of Daesh Leader's Arrest." *Tolo News,* April 5, 2020. https://tolonews.com/afghanistan/nds-commander-gives -details-daesh-leaders-arrest.

Hamming, Tore. *Al-Hazimiyya: The Ideological Conflict Destroying the Islamic State from Within.* The Hague: International Centre for Counter-Terrorism, 2021. https://icct.nl/publication/al-hazimiyya-islamic-state-ideological-conflict.

Harooni, Mirwais. "Islamic State Claims Responsibility for Attack on Iraqi Embassy in Kabul." Reuters, July 31, 2017. https://www.reuters.com/article/us -afghanistan-blast/islamic-state-claims-responsibility-for-attack-on-iraqi-embassy -in-kabul-idUSKBN1AG0OM.

———. "Islamic State Claims Responsibility for Kabul Attack, 80 Dead." Reuters, July 23, 2016. https://www.reuters.com/article/us-afghanistan-protests/islamic -state-claims-responsibility-for-kabul-attack-80-dead-idUSKCN1030GB.

———. "Over 30 killed As Gunmen Dressed As Medics Attack Afghan Military Hospital." Reuters, March 8, 2017. https://www.reuters.com/article/us-afghanistan -blast/over-30-killed-as-gunmen-dressed-as-medics-attack-afghan-military -hospital-idUSKBN16F0GP.

Harrison-Graham, Emma. "Two Suspected British Islamic State Recruits Seized by Taliban at Border." *The Guardian,* February 8, 2022. https://www.theguardian .com/world/2022/feb/08/two-suspected-british-islamic-state-recruits-seized-by -taliban-at-afghanistan-border.

"The Harvest of Wilayat Khorasan from 1 Rabi al-Awal untl 27 Rabii al-Awal." *Al-Naba* 311 (November 2021).

Hasan, Syed Shoaib. "Pakistan Bans Ahle Sunnah Wal Jamaat Islamist Group." BBC News, March 10, 2012. https://www.bbc.co.uk/news/world-asia-173 22095.

Hasan, Waheeda. "UNHCR: Half of Afghan Population Relies on Humanitarian Aid." *Tolo News,* May 28, 2022. https://tolonews.com/afghanistan-178213.

Hashemi, Sayed Z., Lolita C. Baldor, Kathy Gannon, and Ellen Knickmeyer. "American Forces Keep Up Airlift Under High Threat Warnings." *Associated Press News,* August 27, 2021. https://apnews.com/article/bombings-evacuations -kabul-bb32ec2b65b54ec24323e021c9b4a553.

Hashim, Asad. "Bomb and Gun Attack on Quetta Church Kills Eight." *Al-Jazeera,* December 17, 2017. https://www.aljazeera.com/news/2017/12/17/bomb-and -gun-attack-on-quetta-church-kills-eight.

———. "Pakistan's Unending Battle Over Balochistan." *Al-Jazeera,* April 16, 2013. https://www.aljazeera.com/features/2013/4/16/pakistans-unending-battle-over -balochistan.

Hasrat, Hussain. "Over a Century of Persecution: Massive Human Rights Violations Against Hazaras in Afghanistan." *Kabul Press,* May 15, 2019. https://www .kabulpress.org/article240586.html.

Hassan, Sharif. "Death Toll Rises in Suicide Bombing of Islamic Gathering in Kabul." *Washington Post,* November 21, 2018. https://www.washingtonpost

.com/world/asia_pacific/death-toll-rises-in-suicide-bombing-of-islamic
-gathering-in-kabul/2018/11/21/1e30b348-ed9c-11e8-8679-934a2b33be
52_story.html.

Hassan, Sharif, and Susannah George. "Brutal Attack on Mothers and Newborns
Prompts Afghanistan to Resume Offensive Operations against Taliban." *Washington Post*, May 12, 2020. https://www.washingtonpost.com/world/asia
_pacific/gunmen-storm-kabul-maternity-ward-killing-13-including-2-new
borns/2020/05/12/416a9174-9428-11ea-87a3-22d324235636_story.html.

Hassan, Zaheerul. "Quetta Church Attack Planned by Daesh and BNA." *Asian Tribune*,
December 18, 2017.

Haykel, Bernard. "On the Nature of Salafi Thought and Action." In *Global Islam's
New Religious Movement*, ed. Bernard Haykel. New York: Columbia University Press, 2009.

"Herat Mosque Blast: IS Says It Was Behind Afghanistan Attack." BBC News,
August 2, 2017. https://www.bbc.com/news/world-asia-40802572.

"Hizbul Mujahideen Chief Calls for Truce." *Times Now News*, June 30, 2019.
https://www.timesnownews.com/india/article/hizbul-mujahideen-chief-calls
-for-truce-as-infighting-among-terror-groups-in-kashmir-continues/445882.

Hughes, Seamus. "The Only Islamic State-Funded Plot in the U.S.: The Curious
Case of Mohamed Elshinawy." *Lawfare*, March 7, 2018. https://www
.lawfareblog.com/only-islamic-state-funded-plot-us-curious-case-mohamed
-elshinawy.

Human Rights Watch. "Afghanistan: Prosecute Head of ISIS-linked Group." April
6, 2020. https://www.hrw.org/news/2020/04/06/afghanistan-prosecute-head-isis
-linked-group.

Horowitz, Michael C., and Philip BK Potter. "Allying to Kill: Terrorist Intergroup
Cooperation and the Consequences for Lethality." *Journal of Conflict Resolution*
58:2 (2014).

Hussain, Safdar. *Pakistan's Achievements in War on Terror but at What Cost? A Special
Review of the Current Decade*. Islamabad: Pak Institute for Peace Studies, 2019.

Ibrahimi, Niamatullah, and Shahram Akbarzadeh. "Intra-Jihadist Conflict and Cooperation: Islamic State–Khorasan Province and the Taliban in Afghanistan." *Studies
in Conflict & Terrorism* 43:12 (2020).

"IMU Pledges Allegiance to IS Leader Abu Bakr al-Baghdadi." SITE Intelligence
Group, August 6, 2015.

Ingram, Haroro. *The Charismatic Leadership Phenomenon in Radical and Militant
Islamism*. Farnham: Ashgate Publishing, 2016.

Ingram, Haroro. *The Long Jihad: The Islamic State's Method of Insurgency—Control,
Meaning, & Occupation of Mosul in Context*. Washington, DC: Program on
Extremism at George Washington University, 2021.

Ingram, Haroro, and Andrew Mines. "The Islamic State's Second Global Pledge
Campaign: New Challenges in an Era of Great Power Competition." *Nexus*,
April 28, 2022. https://extremism.gwu.edu/islamic-state%E2%80%99s-second
-global-pledge-campaign.

Ingram, Haroro, Andrew Mines, and Amira Jadoon. "Islamic State Leader Killed in
US Raid: Where Does This Leave the Terrorist Group?" *The Conversation*,
February 3, 2022. https://theconversation.com/islamic-state-leader-killed-in-us
-raid-where-does-this-leave-the-terrorist-group-176410.

Ingram, Haroro J., Craig Whiteside, and Charlie Winter. *The ISIS Reader: Milestone
Texts of the Islamic State Movement*. Oxford: Oxford University Press, 2020.

————. "The Routinization of the Islamic State's Global Enterprise." Hudson Institute, April 5, 2021. https://www.hudson.org/node/43763.

"Interim National Security Strategic Guidance." March 3, 2021. https://www.whitehouse.gov/briefing-room/statements-releases/2021/03/03/interim-national-security-strategic-guidance.

"Internal Clash Between Taliban in Takhar Leaves 6 Dead and 2 Injured." *Hasht-e-Subh Daily*, July 12, 2022. https://8am.af/eng/internal-clash-between-taliban-in-takhar-leaves-6-dead-and-2-injured.

International Crisis Group. *Beyond Emergency Relief: Averting Afghanistan's Humanitarian Catastrophe*. Brussels, 2021.

————. *Pakistan: Countering Militancy in PATA*. Brussels, January 15, 2013.

International Federation of Journalists. "Afghanistan: Former Ariana television journalist killed in explosion." *IFJ News*, November 16, 2021. https://www.ifj.org/media-centre/news/detail/category/press-releases/article/afghanistan-former-ariana-television-journalist-killed-in-explosion.html.

"Interview with the Wali of Khorasan Shaykh Hafidh Sa'id Khan." *Dabiq* 13, January 2016.

"Investigators Find Held 'IS Men' Sent Funds to Afghanistan." *Dawn*, October 20, 2018. https://www.dawn.com/news/1440056.

Iqbal, Khuram. "Evolving Wave of Terrorism and Emergence of Daesh in Pakistan." In *Countering Daesh Extremism: European and Asian Responses*, ed. Rohan Gunaratna. Singapore: Konrad Adenauer Stiftung and S. Rajaratnam School of International Studies, 2016.

"IS Footprints Growing in Pakistan: Report." *Dawn*, November 9, 2014. https://www.dawn.com/news/1143272.

"ISIS Attack Kills Dozens at Mazari Ceremony in Kabul." *Salaam Times*, March 6, 2020. https://afghanistan.asia-news.com/en_GB/articles/cnmi_st/features/2020/03/06/feature-02.

"ISIS Claims Attack on Power Lines That Plunged Kabul into Darkness." *Agence France-Presse*, October 23, 2021. https://www.ndtv.com/world-news/isis-claims-attack-on-power-lines-that-plunged-kabul-into-darkness-2584868.

"ISIS Claims Killing of 3 Women." *The World*, March 3, 2021. https://theworld.org/stories/2021-03-03/isis-claims-killing-3-women-media-workers-afghanistan.

"ISIS Commander Killed in Afghanistan." *Khaama Press*, March 16, 2015. https://www.khaama.com/isis-commander-killed-in-afghanistan-3014.

"IS Khorasan Province Fighter Rallies Colleagues, Promotes Support of 'Caliphate' Video." SITE Intelligence Group, June 3, 2015. https://ent.siteintelgroup.com/Multimedia/fighter-in-is-khorasan-province-rallies-colleagues-promotes-support-of-caliphate-in-video.html.

"IS Regional Leader Sheikh Khorasani 'Arrested in Afghanistan.'" BBC News, May 11, 2020. https://www.bbc.com/news/world-asia-52623291.

"IS Reveals Rare Details of Ties with Pakistani Militant Group Lashkar-e-Jhangvi." *BBC Monitoring South Asia*, September 10, 2018.

"IS Supporters Create Kashmir Group to Step Up Presence in India." *Hindustan Times*, July 18, 2017. https://www.hindustantimes.com/india-news/islamic-state-supporters-create-kashmir-group-to-step-up-presence-in-india-give-instructions-on-nice-like-attack/story-5DMUzpbw8ge7EB1pIIKJYO.html.

"IS Video Promotes Afghanistan As Option for Immigration, Features Foreign Children and Adults." SITE Intelligence Group, March 6, 2018. https://ent.siteintel

group.com/Multimedia/is-video-promotes-afghanistan-as-option-for-immigration
-features-foreign-children-and-adults.html.

"IS-K Territorially Defeated in Afghanistan: MoI." *Reporterly,* November 10, 2019.
https://reporterly.net/live/newsfeed/sunday-november-10/is-k-territorially
-defeated-in-afghanistan-moi.

"The ISIS Files." 2020. https://isisfiles.gwu.edu/concern/reports/rv042t04f?locale=en.

"ISIS Radio Destroyed in US Drone Strike in East of Afghanistan." July 14, 2016.
https://www.khaama.com/isis-radio-destroyed-in-us-drone-strike-in-east-of
-afghanistan-01482.

"ISKP: A Threat Assessment." August 2021. https://public-assets.extrac.io/reports
/ExTrac_ISKP_0920.pdf.

"Islamic Movement of Uzbekistan (IMU)." Mackenzie Institute, January 7, 2016.
https://mackenzieinstitute.com/2016/01/islamic-movement-of-uzbekistan-imu.

"Islamic State Attacks on Taliban in Jalalabad, Wilayat Khorasan." September 19,
2021. https://aymennaltamimi.substack.com/p/islamic-state-attacks-on-taliban.

"Islamic State Claims Attack on State TV Station in Afghanistan." *France 24,* May
17, 2017. https://www.france24.com/en/20170517-afghanistan-gunmen-tv
-station-jalalabad.

"Islamic State Claims Responsibility for Attack in Herat, Afghanistan." Reuters,
January 23, 2022. https://www.reuters.com/world/asia-pacific/islamic-state-claims
-responsibility-attack-heart-afghanistan-2022-01-23.

"Islamic State Claims Responsibility for Attack That Killed 11 in Pakistan." NBC
News, January 3, 2021. https://www.nbcnews.com/news/world/islamic-state
-claims-responsibility-attack-pakistan-11-killed-n1252691.

"Islamic State Claims Suicide Bombing Targeting Afghan Vice President, Amaq."
Reuters, July 22, 2018. https://www.reuters.com/article/us-afghanistan-dostum
-claim/islamic-state-claims-suicide-bombing-targeting-afghan-vice-president
-amaq-idUSKBN1KC0Q4.

"Islamic State Commander Arrested in Jammu." *India TV News,* April 4, 2021.
https://www.indiatvnews.com/news/india/isjk-terror-strike-averted-jammu
-kashmir-commander-arrested-latest-news-695487.

"Islamic State Group Claims Deadly Attack on Afghanistan Prison." BBC News,
August 3, 2020. https://www.bbc.co.uk/news/world-asia-53633450.

"Islamic State Group 'Defeated' in Key Afghan Province in Latest Blow to Militants."
The New Arab, November 10, 2019. https://english.alaraby.co.uk/news/defeated
-key-afghan-province-official.

Islamic State Khorasan. *Voice of the Caliphate,* radio episodes 43–112, March–June
2021 (provided by Abdul Sayed).

"Islamic State Module Busted in Jammu and Kashmir, Five Arrested." *New Indian
Express,* February 12, 2020. https://www.5dariyanews.com/news/301044-ISIS
-module-busted-in-Kashmir-five-arrested.

Islamic State Statement Released via *Amaq.* September 5, 2018. https://afghanistan
.liveuamap.com/en/2018/5-september-is-released-the-statement-about-clashes-with.

Jackson, Brian A., John C. Baker, Kim Cragin, John Parachini, Horacio R. Trujillo,
and Peter Chalk. *Aptitude for Destruction: Organizational Learning in Terrorist
Groups and Its Implications for Combating Terrorism.* Santa Monica, CA:
RAND Corporation, 2005.

Jackson, William Kesler. "A Subcontinent's Sunni Schism: The Deobandi-Barelvi
Rivalry and the Creation of Modern South Asia." 2013. https://surface.syr
.edu/cgi/viewcontent.cgi?article=1101&context=hst_etd.

Jadoon, Amira. *Allied & Lethal: Islamic State Khorasan's Network and Organizational Capacity in Afghanistan and Pakistan.* New York: Combating Terrorism Center at West Point, 2018.

———. *The Evolution and Potential Resurgence of the Tehrik-i-Taliban Pakistan.* Washington, DC: US Institute of Peace, 2021.

———. "Playing Dirty to Survive: The Vulnerability of Civilian Targets Within U.S. Military Aid Recipient States." *Small Wars and Insurgencies* 30:3 (2019).

———. "The Untenable TTP-Pakistan Negotiations." *South Asian Voices,* June 24, 2022. https://southasianvoices.org/the-untenable-ttp-pakistan-negotiations.

Jadoon, Amira, Nakissa Jahanbani, and Charmaine Willis. "Challenging the ISK Brand in Afghanistan-Pakistan: Rivalries and Divided Loyalties." *CTC Sentinel* 11:4 (2018).

Jadoon, Amira, and Daniel Milton. "Strength from the Shadows? How Shadow Economies Affect Terrorist Activities." *Studies in Conflict & Terrorism* 45:5–6 (October 2019).

Jadoon, Amira, and Andrew Mines. *Broken but Not Defeated: An Examination of State-Led Operations Against Islamic State Khorasan in Afghanistan and Pakistan (2015–2018).* New York: Combating Terrorism Center at West Point, 2020.

———. "Taking Aim: Islamic State Khorasan's Leadership Losses." *CTC Sentinel* 8:12 (September 2019).

———. "The Taliban Can't Take On the Islamic State Alone." *War on the Rocks,* October 14, 2021. https://warontherocks.com/2021/10/the-taliban-cant-take-on -the-islamic-state-alone.

———. "What Is ISIS-K? Two Terrorism Experts on the Group Behind the Deadly Kabul Airport Attack and Its Rivalry with the Taliban." *The Conversation,* August 26, 2021. https://theconversation.com/what-is-isis-k-two-terrorism -experts-on-the-group-behind-the-deadly-kabul-airport-attack-and-its-rivalry -with-the-taliban-166873.

Jadoon, Amira, Andrew Mines, and Abdul Sayed. "The Evolving Taliban-ISK Rivalry." September 7, 2021. https://www.lowyinstitute.org/the-interpreter/evolving-taliban -isk-rivalry.

———. "Smaller and Smarter: Defining a Narrower U.S. Counterterrorism Mission in the Afghanistan-Pakistan Region." February 11, 2021. https://newlinesinstitute .org/governance/smaller-and-smarter-defining-a-narrower-u-s-counterterrorism -mission-in-the-afghanistan-pakistan-region.

Jadoon, Amira, Abdul Sayed, and Andrew Mines. "The Islamic State Threat in Taliban Afghanistan: Tracing the Resurgence of Islamic State Khorasan." *CTC Sentinel* 15:1 (January 2022).

Jadoon, Amira, Andrew Mines, and Daniel Milton. "Targeting Quality or Quantity? The Divergent Effects of Targeting Upper Verses Lower-Tier Leaders of Militant Organizations." *Journal of Conflict Resolution.* September 2022.

"Jaish-e-Mohammed." Center for International Security and Cooperation, June 25, 2015. https://cisac.fsi.stanford.edu/mappingmilitants/profiles/jaish-e-mohammed.

Jalaluddin, Shaikh. "Why Are We Fighting Against the Taliban?" Khorasan Studio, August 2015.

Jamal, Arif. *Shadow War: The Untold Story of Jihad in Kashmir.* New York: Melville House, 2009.

Jamal, Asad. *Police Organisations in Pakistan.* Lahore: Human Rights Commission of Pakistan and Commonwealth Human Rights Initiative, 2010.

Jamal, Sana, and M. Ahsan. "TTP: Analyzing the Network of Terror." *International Relations Insights and Analysis* 6 (2015).

Jameel, Yusef. "3 ISIS Militants Killed in J&K's Anantnag Schools, Colleges Shut in Srinagar." *Deccan Chronicle,* March 12, 2018. https://www.deccanchronicle.com/nation/current-affairs/120318/3-terrorists-killed-jk-anantnag-encounter-schools-shut-protests.html.

Jendruck, Evan. "Pakistani Militant Groups Form New TTP Coalition." *Jane's Terrorism and Insurgency Monitor,* March 13, 2015.

Jibran, Ahmed, and Kay Johnson. "Linked to Taliban and ISIS, Pakistani Group Seizes Notoriety with Bomb in Park." Reuters, March 28, 2016. https://www.reuters.com/article/us-pakistan-blast-militants/linked-to-taliban-and-isis-pakistani-group-seizes-notoriety-with-bomb-in-park-idUKKCN0WU1F4.

"Jihadi Movement Is Galvanized by Taliban's Takeover in Afghanistan, Expert Says." August 18, 2021. https://www.npr.org/2021/08/18/1028712064/jihadi-movement-is-galvanized-by-talibans-takeover-in-afghanistan-expert-says.

Johnson, Casey G. *The Rise and Stall of the Islamic State in Afghanistan.* Washington, DC: US Institute of Peace, 2016.

Johnson, Casey Garret, Masood Karokhail, and Rahmatullah Amiri. "The Islamic State in Afghanistan." *US Institute of Peace,* April 7, 2016. https://www.usip.org/sites/default/files/PB202-The-Islamic-State-in-Afghanistan-Assessing-the-Threat.pdf.

Johnston, Patrick B. "Does Decapitation Work? Assessing the Effectiveness of Leadership Targeting in Counterinsurgency Campaigns." *International Security* 36:4 (2012).

Jones, Seth G. "Countering a Resurgent Terrorist Threat in Afghanistan." *Council on Foreign Relations*, April 14, 2022. https://www.cfr.org/report/countering-resurgent-terrorist-threat-afghanistan.

Jones, Seth, and Christine Fair. *Counterinsurgency in Pakistan.* Santa Monica, CA: RAND Corporation, 2010.

Jordan, Jenna. "Attacking the Leader, Missing the Mark: Why Terrorist Groups Survive Decapitation Strikes." *International Security* 38:4 (2014).

———. *Leadership Decapitation: Strategic Targeting of Terrorist Organizations.* Stanford, CA: Stanford University Press, 2019.

———. "When Heads Roll: Assessing the Effectiveness of Leadership Decapitation." *Security Studies* 18:4 (2009).

Joscelyn, Thomas. "Pakistani Taliban Rejects Islamic State's Self-Professed Caliphate." *FDD's Long War Journal,* May 27, 2015. https://www.longwarjournal.org/archives/2015/05/pakistani-taliban-rejects-islamic-states-self-professed-caliphate.php.

———. "Twenty Years After 9/11: Taliban and al-Qaeda Remain Inseparable." September 10, 2021. https://www.fdd.org/in_the_news/2021/09/10/twenty-years-after-911-taliban-and-al-qaeda-remain-inseparable.

Joscelyn, Thomas, and Bill Roggio. "The Taliban's New Leadership Is Allied with al-Qaeda." *FDD's Long War Journal,* July 31, 2015. https://www.longwarjournal.org/archives/2015/07/the-talibans-new-leadership-is-allied-with-al-qaeda.php.

"Jundallah." *Jane's Intelligence Report,* March 24, 2016.

"Jundullah Vows Allegiance to Islamic State." *Express Tribune,* November 18, 2014. https://tribune.com.pk/story/792872/jundullah-vows-allegiance-to-islamic-state.

"Kabul Blast: Minivan Blown Up in Shiite Area of Kabul." *The National,* November 13, 2021. https://www.thenationalnews.com/world/asia/2021/11/13/kabul-blast-minivan-blown-up-in-shiite-area-of-kabul.

Kalin, Stephen. "Last Letters: From Mosul Schoolboys to Islamic State 'Martyrs.'" Reuters, February 27, 2017. https://www.reuters.com/article/us-islamic-state-recruits-insight/last-letters-from-mosul-schoolboys-to-islamic-state-martyrs-idUSKBN166181.

Karmon, Ely. *Coalitions Between Terrorist Organizations: Revolutionaries, Nationalists, and Islamists.* Leiden: Nijhoff, 2005.

"Kashmir Was Shaken by This Dangerous Organization." *Daily India,* July 13, 2022. https://dailyindia.net/kashmir-was-shaken-by-this-dangerous-organization-security-agencies-got-sleepless/14879.

"Kashmiri Group Pledges Allegiance to Islamic State." *BBC Urdu,* December 26, 2017.

Kermani, Secunder. "Afghanistan: Policing Faces, Bodies, and Beards on Kabul Streets." BBC News, May 22, 2022. https://www.bbc.co.uk/news/world-asia-61480248.

"'Key' Daesh Leaders Arrested in Kabul: NDS." *TOLO News,* May 11, 2020. https://tolonews.com/afghanistan/key-daesh-leaders-arrested-kabul-nds.

Khalid, Sakhi. "An Estimated 70 Families from Andarab Forcibly Displaced by the Taliban." *Hasht-e Subh Daily,* May 29, 2022. https://8am.af/eng/an-estimated-70-families-from-andarab-forcibly-displaced-by-the-taliban.

Khan, Faraz. "Daesh Money Trail Traced in Pakistan." *The News,* October 18, 2018. https://www.thenews.com.pk/print/382259-daesh-money-trail-traced-in-pakistan.

Khan, Hafiz Saeed. "Come Join Up with the Caliphate." ISK audio message, August 5, 2015.

———. "Message to Our People in Khorasan." ISK audio message, July 2015.

Khan, Ilyas. "Pakistan Shia Mosque Blast in Shikarpur Kills Dozens." BBC News, January 30, 2015. https://www.bbc.com/news/world-asia-31056086.

Khan, Javed Aziz. "14 Days Before Elections, ANP's Haroon Bilour Killed in Blast." *News International,* July 11, 2018. https://www.thenews.com.pk/print/340248-14-days-before-elections-anp-s-haroon-bilour-killed-in-blast.

Khan, Sahar. "Double Game: Why Pakistan Supports Militants and Resists U.S. Pressure to Stop." September 20, 2018. https://www.cato.org/policy-analysis/double-game-why-pakistan-supports-militants-resists-us-pressure-stop.

Khan, Tahir. "TTP Bajahur Declares Allegiance to Islamic State." *Express Tribune,* April 9, 2015. https://tribune.com.pk/story/867113/ttp-bajaur-declares-allegiance-to-islamic-state.

Khattak, Daud. "Mangal Bagh and LI Marginalized in Khyber Agency." *CTC Sentinel* 5:4 (2012).

Krishnankutty, Pia. "Help from Pakistan Taliban?" *The Print,* February 5, 2022. https://theprint.in/world/help-from-pakistan-taliban-what-lies-behind-unprecedented-attacks-by-baloch-liberation-army/822207.

Lalzoy, Najibullah. "US State Department Offers $10M Reward." February 8, 2022. https://www.khaama.com/us-state-department-offers-10m-reward-for-kabul-airport-bomber-897685.

Landay, Jonathan. "U.N. Envoy Says Islamic State Now Appears Present in All Afghan Provinces." Reuters, November 17, 2021. https://www.reuters.com/world/asia-pacific/un-envoy-says-islamic-state-now-appears-present-all-afghan-provinces-2021-11-17.

Lamothe, Dan. "Meet the Shadowy Figure Recruiting for the Islamic State." *Washington Post,* January 13, 2015. https://www.washingtonpost.com/news/checkpoint/wp/2015/01/13/meet-the-shadowy-figure-recruiting-for-the-islamic-state-in-afghanistan.

"Lashkar Says ISIS a Terrorist Group." *Kashmir Observer,* May 10, 2017. https:// kashmirobserver.net/2017/05/10/lashkar-says-isis-a-terrorist-group/.

"Lashkar-e-Islam Claims Killing 19 Islamic State Militants in Nangarhar." *Islamic Theology of Counter Terrorism,* October 7, 2018.

"Lashkar-e-Islami / Mangal Bagh Afridi." August 15, 2012. https://www.global security.org/military/world/para/lei.htm.

Lateef, Samaan. "IS Claims Zakura Attack." November 19, 2017. https://www .tribuneindia.com/news/archive/j-k/is-claims-zakura-attack-500289.

Lawrence, J. P. "ISIS Attack Targets US Troops at Bagram Airfield in Third Such Incident Since Taliban Peace Deal." *Stars and Stripes,* March 23, 2020. https:// www.stripes.com/news/isis-attack-targets-us-troops-at-bagram-airfield-in -third-such-incident-since-taliban-peace-deal-1.623420.

"LEAs Arrest Varsity Professor, Niece for ISIS links." *Pakistan Today,* May 22, 2017. https://archive.pakistantoday.com.pk/2017/05/22/leas-arrest-varsity-professor -niece-for-isis-links.

"LeJ 'Collaborated with ISIS' for Quetta attack." *The Nation,* October 26, 2016. http://nation.com.pk/national/26-Oct-2016/lej-collaborated-with-isis-for -quetta- attack.

"Letter from the Taliban to Abu Bakr al-Baghdadi From the Head of the Shura Council, Islamic Emirate of Afghanistan." June 16, 2015. http://jihadology.net /2015/06/16/new-release-from-the-islamic-emirate-of-afghanistan-to-abu-bakr -al-baghdadi-from-the-head-of-the-shura-council.

Liebermann, Oren, and Ellie Kaufman. "US Military Releases Videos of August Drone Strike That Killed 10 Afghan Civilians." CNN, January 19, 2022. https:// www.cnn.com/2022/01/19/politics/military-releases-videos-august-drone -strike-killed-civilians/index.html.

Lubold, Gordon. "U.S. Clears Path to Target Islamic State in Afghanistan." *Wall Street Journal,* January 19, 2016. https://www.wsj.com/articles/u-s-clears-path -to-target-islamic-state-in-afghanistan-1453251754.

Luce, Mark D. *Frontier as Process: Umayyad Khurāsān.* PhD dissertation, University of Chicago, 2009.

Macander, Michelle. "Examining Extremism: Lashkar-e-Taiba." Center for Strategic and International Studies, October 28, 2021. https://www.csis.org/blogs/examining -extremism/examining-extremism-lashkar-e-taiba.

Maher, Shiraz. *Salafi-Jihadism: The History of an Idea.* Oxford: Oxford University Press, 2016.

"Makers of Epic Battles Series: Khorasan Province." Islamic State video, July 2021.

"Malik Ishaq: Pakistan Sunni Militant Chief Killed by Police." BBC News, July 29, 2015. https://www.bbc.com/news/world-asia-33699133. https://www.bbc.com /news/world-asia-33699133.

"Mapping Militant Organizations: Haqqani Network." Center for International Security and Cooperation, November 8, 2017. https://web.stanford.edu/group /mappingmilitants/cgi-bin/groups/print_view/363.

Marszal, Andrew. "ISIL 'Took Part' in Quetta Attack, Says Pakistani Terror Group Ally." *The Telegraph,* October 26, 2016. https://www.telegraph.co.uk/news /2016/10/26/isil-took-part-in-quetta-attack-says-pakistani-terror-group-ally.

Marty, Franz J. "The Peculiar Presence of the Islamic State in Kunar." *The Diplomat,* May 14, 2019. https://thediplomat.com/2019/05/the-peculiar-presence-of -the-islamic-state-in-kunar.

Mashal, Mujib, and Fahim Abed. "From Maternity Ward to Cemetery." *New York Times,* May 12, 2020. https://www.nytimes.com/2020/05/12/world/asia/afghanistan -violence-kabul-nangarhar.html.

———. "Terror Attack Strikes Afghan Capital As Another City Is Locked Down for Coronavirus." *New York Times,* March 25, 2020. https://www.nytimes.com /2020/03/25/world/asia/afghanistan-sikh-kabul.html.

Mashal, Mujib, and Najim Rahim. "Deadly Explosion Hits Kabul Tutoring Center." *New York Times,* October 24, 2020. https://www.nytimes.com/2020/10/24 /world/asia/kabul-afghanistan-bombing-school.html.

"Mastung Bomber Identified, Peshawar Blast Suspect Arrested." *Daily Pakistan Today,* July 20, 2018. https://archive.pakistantoday.com.pk/2018/07/19/mastung -bomber-identified-peshawar-blast-suspect-arrested.

"Mawlawi Mehdi Coherences His Forces in Balkhab to Fight Against Taliban." *Hasht-e-Subh Daily,* July 6, 2022. https://8am.af/eng/mawlawi-mehdi-coherences -his-forces-in-balkhab-sar-e-pol.

McCormick, Gordon. "Terrorist Decision Making." *Annual Review of Political Science* 6:1 (2003).

McKelvey, Tara. "A Return to Hell in Swat." *Foreign Policy,* March 3, 2011. https:// foreignpolicy.com/2011/03/03/a-return-to-hell-in-swat.

McKenzie, Kenneth. "Posture Statement." US Central Command, March 15, 2022. https://www.armed-services.senate.gov/imo/media/doc/USCENTCOM%20 Written%20Posture%20Statement%20-%20SASC.pdf.

McKinnell, Jamie. "Isaac El Matari Jailed for Seven Years for Preparing Terrorist Attack in Australia." *ABC News,* October 11, 2021. https://www.abc .net.au/news/2021-10-11/isaac-el-matari-jailed-preparing-terrorist-attack /100530130.

Mehl, Damon. "The Islamic Movement of Uzbekistan Opens a Door to the Islamic State." *CTC Sentinel* 8:6 (June 2015).

Meleagrou-Hitchens, Alexander, and Seamus Hughes. "The Threat to the United States from the Islamic State's Virtual Entrepreneurs." *CTC Sentinel* 10:3 (2017).

Mellen, Ruby. "The Shocking Speed of The Taliban's Advance: A Visual Timeline." *Washington Post,* August 16, 2021. https://www.washingtonpost.com/world /2021/08/16/taliban-timeline.

Merhdad, Ezzatullah, Helier Cheung, and Susannah George. "Suicide Bombers Hit Shiite Mosque in Afghanistan Killing Dozens: The Second Such Attack in a Week." *Washington Post,* October 15, 2021. https://www.washingtonpost.com /world/2021/10/15/afghanistan-kandahar-mosque-explosion.

"Message from Dr Shahab al-Muhajir: The New Wali of Khorasan." Black Flags Media Center, July 3, 2021.

Miller, Nicholas, and Doug Rutzen. "US Counterterrorism Measures May Block Aid to Afghans." August 23, 2021. https://www.justsecurity.org/77966/us-counter terrorism-measures-may-block-aid-to-afghans.

Mir, Asfandyar. *Afghanistan's Terrorism Challenge: The Political Trajectories of al-Qaeda, the Afghan Taliban, and the Islamic State.* Washington, DC: Middle East Institute, October 2020. https://www.mei.edu/sites/default/files/2020-10 /Afghanistan%27s%20Terrorism%20Challenge.pdf.

———. "Biden Didn't See the ISIS-K Threat in Afghanistan Until Too Late." *New York Times,* August 31, 2021. https://www.nytimes.com/2021/08/31/opinion /biden-isis-k.html.

————. "What Explains Counterterrorism Effectiveness? Evidence from the U.S. Drone War in Pakistan." *International Security* 43:2 (2018).

Mir, Asfandyar, and Tricia Bacon. "India's Gamble in Afghanistan." *Foreign Affairs*, July 11, 2022. https://www.foreignaffairs.com/articles/afghanistan/2022-07-11/indias-gamble-afghanistan.

Mogelson, Luke. "The Shattered Afghan Dream of Peace." *New Yorker*, October 21, 2019. https://www.newyorker.com/magazine/2019/10/28/the-shattered-afghan-dream-of-peace.

Moghadam, Assaf. *Nexus of Global Jihad: Understanding Cooperation Among Terrorist Actors* New York: Columbia University Press, 2017.

Moosakhail, Zabihullah. "ISIS Fundraising in Pakistan's Karachi: Police Looking for Network of Female Fundraisers." *Khaama Press*, December 22, 2015. https://www.khaama.com/isis-fundraising-in-karachi-police-looking-for-network-of-female-fundraisers-4410.

Mozul, James. "The Quetta Shura Taliban: An Overlooked Problem." *International Affairs Review*, November 11, 2003. http://www.iargwu.org/node/106.

"Mumbai Terror Attacks." CNN, September 9, 2013. https://www.cnn.com/2013/09/18/world/asia/mumbai-terror-attacks/index.html.

Nadim, Hussain. "The Quiet Rise of the Quetta Shura." *Foreign Policy*, July 14, 2012. https://foreignpolicy.com/2012/08/14/the-quiet-rise-of-the-quetta-shura.

Naqash, Rayan. "Adil Ahmad Dass Killing: Did Hizbul Mujahideen and LeT Lure Islamic State Militants into a Trap?" *Firstpost*, June 28, 2019. https://www.firstpost.com/india/adil-ahmad-dass-killing-did-hizbul-mujahideen-and-let-lure-islamic-state-militants-into-a-trap-6896981.html.

Nasar, Khudai Noor. "Afghanistan: Taliban Leaders in Bust-Up at Presidential Palace, Sources Say." BBC News, September 15, 2021. https://www.bbc.com/news/world-asia-58560923.

Nawaz, Shuja. *FATA-A Most Dangerous Place*. Washington, DC: Center for Strategic and International Studies, 2009.

Nazish, Kiran. "The Emergence of the Islamic State in Pakistan." November 12, 2014. https://en.qantara.de/content/the-emergence-of-islamic-state-in-pakistan-they-dont-negotiate-they-dont-make-partners.

Nemeth, Stephen. "The Effect of Competition on Terrorist Group Operations." *Journal of Conflict Resolution* 58:2 (2014).

Neuman, Scott. "ISIS Claims Responsibility for Deadly Attack Aimed at Afghan Hazaras." NPR, March 9, 2018. https://www.npr.org/sections/thetwo-way/2018/03/09/592210383/isis-claims-responsibility-for-deadly-attack-aimed-at-afghan-hazaras.

————. "Suicide Bombers Kill Nearly 50 at a Shiite Mosque in Afghanistan." NPR, October 15, 2021. https://www.npr.org/2021/10/15/1046287550/suicide-bombers-attack-mosque-afghanistan.

Neumann, Peter R., Ryan Evans, and Raffaello Pantucci. "Locating al-Qaeda's Center of Gravity: The Role of Middle Managers." *Studies in Conflict and Terrorism* 34:11 (2011).

News Desk. "Sindh Daesh Emir Kathiyo, Islamabad Emir Amir arrested." *The News*, January 4, 2016. https://www.thenews.com.pk/print/86284-Sindh-Daesh-Emir-Kathiyo-Islamabad-Emir-Amir-arrested.

Nicholson, John. "Department of Defense Press Briefing by General Nicholson in the Pentagon Briefing Room." December 2, 2016. https://www.defense.gov/News/Transcripts/Transcript/Article/1019029/department-of-defense-press-briefing-by-general-nicholson-in-the-pentagon-brief.

————. "Statement for the Record on the Situation in Afghanistan." Testimony before Senate Committee on Armed Services, February 9, 2017. https://www .armed-services.senate.gov/imo/media/doc/Nicholson_02-09-17.pdf.

Noorzai, Roshan. "Afghanistan to Discuss Fate of Foreign IS Prisoners with Their Countries." *Voice of America*, May 3, 2021. https://www.voanews.com/a/extremism -watch_afghanistan-discuss-fate-foreign-prisoners-their-countries/6205369.html.

Nordland, Rod, and Zabihullah Ghazi. "ISIS Leader in Afghanistan Is Killed in U.S. Airstrike." *New York Times*, April 9, 2018. https://www.nytimes.com/2018 /04/09/world/asia/afghanistan-isis-leader.html.

Nossiter, Adam, and Eric Schmitt. "U.S. Strikes Taliban Targets in a Show of Force in Afghanistan." *New York Times*, July 23, 2021. https://www.nytimes.com /2021/07/23/world/europe/us-airstrikes-afghanistan-taliban.html.

"Nothing to Do with IS: Lashkar." *Greater Kashmir News*, November 22, 2015. https://www.greaterkashmir.com/news/kashmir/nothing-to-do-with-is-lashkar /202246.html.

Ochab, Ewelina U. "Bombings Outside a School in Afghanistan Kill over 68 People, Mostly Children." *Forbes*, May 9, 2021. https://www.forbes.com/sites /ewelinaochab/2021/05/09/bombings-outside-a-school-in-afghanistan-kill-over -68-people-mostly-children/?sh=4af4af121f3a.

"Officials: Taliban, ISIL Coordinated Sar-e Pul Attack." *Al-Jazeera*, August 7, 2017. https://www.aljazeera.com/news/2017/8/7/officials-taliban-isil-coordinated -sar-e-pul-attack.

"Ohio Man Arrested and Charged with Attempting to Travel to Join ISIS." US Department of Justice, October 25, 2018. https://www.justice.gov/opa/pr/ohio -man-arrested-and-charged-attempting-travel-join-isis.

Olivetti, Vincenzo. *Terror's Source: The Ideology of Wahhabi-Salafism and Its Consequences.* Birmingham: Amadeus, 2002.

Osman, Borhan. "The Battle for Mamand: ISKP Under Strain, but Not Yet Defeated." *Afghanistan Analysts Network*, May 23, 2017. https://www.afghanistan-analysts .org/en/reports/war-and-peace/the-battle-for-mamand-iskp-under-strain-but -not-yet-defeated.

————. *Bourgeois Jihad: Why Young Middle-Class Afghans Join the Islamic State.* Washington, DC: US Institute of Peace, 2020.

————. "Descent into Chaos: Why Did Nangarhar Turn into an IS Hub?" *Afghanistan Analysts Network*, September 27, 2016. https://www.afghanistan -analysts.org/en/reports/war-and-peace/descent-into-chaos-why-did-nangarhar -turn-into-an-is-hub.

————. "ISKP's Battle for Minds: What Are Its Main Messages and Who Do They Attract?" *Afghanistan Analysts Network*, December 12, 2016. https://www .afghanistan-analysts.org/iskps-battle-for-minds-what-are-their-main-messages -and-who-do-they.attract.

————. "The Islamic State in 'Khorasan': How It Began and Where It Stands Now in Nangarhar." *Afghanistan Analysts Network*, July 27, 2016. https://www .afghanistan-analysts.org/en/reports/war-and-peace/the-islamic-state-in -khorasan-how-it-began-and-where-it-stands-now-in-nangarhar.

————. "The Shadows of 'Islamic State' in Afghanistan: What Threat Does It Hold?" *Afghanistan Analysts Network*, February 12, 2015. https://www.afghanistan -analysts.org/en/reports/war-and-peace/the-shadows-of-islamic-state-in -afghanistan-what-threat-does-it-hold.

————. "With an Active Cell in Kabul, ISKP Tries to Bring Sectarianism to the Afghan War." *Afghanistan Analysts Network*, October 19, 2016. https://www

.afghanistan-analysts.org/en/reports/war-and-peace/with-an-active-cell-in
-kabul-iskp-tries-to-bring-sectarianism-to-the-afghan-war.

Osman, Borhan, Kate Clark, and Martine van Biljert. "Mother of All Bombs Dropped on ISKP: Assessing the Aftermath." *Afghanistan Analysts Network,* April 15, 2017. https://www.afghanistan-analysts.org/en/reports/war-and -peace/mother-of-all-bombs-dropped-on-iskp-assessing-the-aftermath.

"Outrage Grows over Government's Inaction to Stop Daesh Radio." *TOLO News,* January 26, 2016. https://tolonews.com/afghanistan/outrage-grows-over-govts -inaction-stop-daesh-radio.

"Pakistan: At Least 60 Killed, over 110 Injured in Quetta Police Academy Attack; ISIS Claims Responsibility." *International Business Times India,* October 25, 2016. https://www.ibtimes.co.in/pakistan-least-44-killed-over-100-injured-quetta -police-academy-attack-701085.

"Pakistan Coal Miners Kidnapped." BBC News, January 3, 2021. https://www.bbc .com/news/world-asia-55522830.

"Pakistan: Dawat-e-Haq Posts Images of Pro-ISIL Graffiti." Government Open-Source Enterprise, April 2015.

"Pakistan Gunmen Kill 45 on Karachi Ismaili Shia Bus." BBC News, May 13, 2020. https://www.bbc.com/news/world-asia-32717321.

"Pakistan Hospital Bomb Attack Kills Dozens in Quetta." BBC News, August 8, 2016. https://www.bbc.com/news/world-asia-37007661.

"Pakistan: IS Attack on Sufi Shrine in Sindh Kills Dozens." BBC News, February 17, 2017. https://www.bbc.com/news/world-asia-38994318.

"Pakistan: Security Assessment 2017." January 2018. https://www.picss.net/6654-2.

"Pakistani Taliban Splinter Group Again Pledges Allegiance to Islamic State." *FDD'S Long War Journal,* January 13, 2015. https://www.longwarjournal .org/archives/2015/01/video_pakistani_tali_2.php.

Panucci, Raffaello. "Indians and Central Asians Are the New Face of the Islamic State." *Foreign Policy,* October 8, 2020. https://foreignpolicy.com/2020/10/08 /isis-indian-kyrgyzstan-tajikistan-uzbekistan-central-asians-are-the-new-face -of-islamic-state.

Parvez, Tariq, and Mehwish Rani. *An Appraisal of Pakistan's Anti-Terrorism Act.* Washington, DC: US Institute of Peace, August 2015.

"Pathankot: Kashmir-Based Militant Coalition Claims Attack." BBC News, January 4, 2016. https://www.bbc.com/news/world-asia-india-35216716.

Pazir, Gul. "TTP Warns Against Playing Music, Women Going Out Alone in Miran-shah." *Dawn,* August 1, 2019. https://www.dawn.com/news/1497395/ttp-warns -against-playing-music-women-going-out-alone-in-miramshah.

Pettyjohn, Stacie. "Over-the-Horizon Does Not Have to Mean Next Door." *Lawfare,* November 7, 2021. https://www.lawfareblog.com/over-horizon-does-not-have -mean-next-door.

Phillips, Brian. "Enemies With Benefits? Violent Rivalry and Terrorist Group Longevity." *Journal of Peace Research* 52:1 (2014).

———. "Terrorist Group Cooperation and Longevity." *International Studies Quarterly* 58:2 (2014).

"Polling Station Attack Marks Bloody Election Day in Pakistan." *CBS News,* July 25, 2018. https://www.cbsnews.com/news/pakistan-election-violence-dozens -killed-quetta-polling-station-attack.

Popalzai, Ehsan, Ayub Farhat, and Joshua Berlinger. "4 Killed in ISIS Attack on Save the Children in Afghanistan." CNN, January 24, 2018. https://

www.cnn.com/2018/01/24/asia/afghanistan-save-the-children-bombing-intl
/index.html.

Popalzai, Ehsan, Jennifer Hansler, and Mohammed Tawfeeq. "Afghanistan Foils
ISIS Plan to Assassinate the Top US Envoy to Kabul." CNN, January 13, 2021.
https://www.cnn.com/2021/01/13/middleeast/isis-assassination-attempt-us-intl
/index.html.

Popalzai, Masoud, and Saleem Mehsud. "ISIS Militant Bomber on Motorbike Kills
33 at Bank in Afghanistan." CNN, April 19, 2015. https://www.cnn.com/2015
/04/18/asia/afghanistan-violence/index.html.

Popalzai, Ehsan, and Chandrika Narayan. "20 Dead in Suicide Blast Outside Afghan
Supreme Court in Kabul." CNN, February 8, 2017. https://www.cnn.com
/2017/02/07/world/afghanistan-explosion/index.html.

Price, Bryan C. "Targeting Top Terrorists: How Leadership Decapitation Con-
tributes to Counterterrorism." *International Security* 4:36 (2012).

Program on Extremism at George Washington University. "Mosul and the Islamic
State: Bonus Content Episode." August 17, 2021. https://extremism.gwu
.edu/mosul-and-the-islamic-state.

———. "Mosul and the Islamic State: Episode 2, Part 1: Opportunities Lost, Democracy." August 4, 2021. https://extremism.gwu.edu/mosul-and-the-islamic-state.

———. "Mosul and the Islamic State: Episode 4, Part 2: Never Again, Silence."
August 4, 2021. https://extremism.gwu.edu/mosul-and-the-islamic-state.

"Pro-IS Eid Message Calls on Taliban Members to Join Its Ranks." *BBC Monitoring,*
July 14, 2022.

Puri, Luv. "The Past and Future of Deobandi Islam." *CTC Sentinel* 2:11 (November
2009).

Purkiss, Jessica, and Emran Feroz. "CIA-Backed Afghan Unit Accused of Atrocities
Is Able to Call in Air Strikes." *Bureau of Investigative Journalism,* August 2,
2019. https://www.thebureauinvestigates.com/stories/2019-02-08/cia-backed
-afghan-unit-atrocities.

Qadri, Azhar. "Kashmir Militant Releases Video." *The Tribune,* August 26, 2015.
https://www.tribuneindia.com/news/archive/features/kashmir-militant-releases
-video-vows-to-establish-caliphate-124897.

Qazi, Shereena. "Afghanistan's Taliban, US Sign Agreement Aimed at Ending War."
Al-Jazeera, February 29, 2020. https://www.aljazeera.com/news/2020/2/29
/afghanistans-taliban-us-sign-agreement-aimed-at-ending-war.

Qazizai, Fazelminallah. "The Special Units Leading the Taliban's Fight Against the
Islamic State." *Newlines Magazine,* September 3, 2021. https://newlinesmag
.com/reportage/the-special-units-leading-the-talibans-fight-against-the-islamic
-state.

"Quarterly Report, July 1, 2021–September 30, 2021, to the United States Congress."
November 16, 2021. https://www.dodig.mil/Reports/Lead-Inspector-General
-Reports/Article/2844712/lead-inspector-general-for-operation-freedoms
-sentinel-i-quarterly-report-to-th.

"Quarterly Report to the United States Congress." July 30, 2016. https://www
.sigar.mil/pdf/quarterlyreports/2016-07-30qr.pdf.

"Quetta Attack: Militants Kill Dozens at Balochistan Police College." BBC News,
October 25, 2016. https://www.bbc.com/news/world-asia-37757914.

Quilty, Andrew. "'Faint Lights Twinkling Against the Dark': Reportage from the
Fight Against ISKP in Nangarhar." *Afghanistan Analysts Newtork,* February 19,
2019. https://www.afghanistan-analysts.org/en/reports/war-and-peace/faint

-lights-twinkling-against-the-dark-reportage-from-the-fight-against-iskp
-in-nangrahar.

Qutb, Sayyid. *Milestones*. Beirut: Holy Koran, 1978.

"The Rafidah from Ibn Saba' to the Dajjal." *Dabiq* 13 (January 19, 2016).

"The Rafidah Project in Khorasan and the Efforts of the Caliphate Soldiers to Foil It: Part 1." *Al-Naba* 118 (February 2018).

Rafiq, Arif. "Will the Islamic State Spread Its Tentacles to Pakistan?" *The Diplomat*, July 28, 2014. https://thediplomat.com/2014/07/will-the-islamic-state-spread-its-tentacles-to-pakistan.

Raghavan, Sudarsan. "The Islamic State is Making These Afghans Long for the Taliban." *Washington Post*, October 13, 2015. https://www.washingtonpost.com/world/asia_pacific/a-new-age-of-brutality-how-islamic-state-rose-up-in-one-afghan-province/2015/10/13/a6dbed67-717b-41e3-87a5-01c81384f34c_story.html.

Raghavan, Sudarsan, and Ellen Francis. "ISIS-K Claims Mosque Blast in Kunduz, Afghanistan, That Killed Nearly 50, Injured Dozens." *Washington Post*, October 8, 2021. https://www.washingtonpost.com/world/2021/10/08/afghanistan-explosion-mosque-kunduz.

Rahim, Nakim, and Rod Nordland. "Are ISIS Fighters Prisoners or Honored Guests of the Afghan Government?" *New York Times*, August 4, 2018. https://www.nytimes.com/2018/08/04/world/asia/islamic-state-prisoners-afghanistan.html.

Rahimzoy, Ashiqullah, and Ibrahim Nasar. "Islamic State Running Prisons Inside Afghanistan." *Voice of America*, September 9, 2015. https://www.voanews.com/a/islamic-state-running-prisons-inside-afghanistan/2954886.html.

Rasa, Mohammad Shaker. "NRF: Taliban Deploys 30,000 Special Fighters in Panjshir, Baghlan and Takhar." *Hasht-e Subh Daily*, June 3, 2022. https://8am.af/eng/taliban-deploys-30000-special-fighters-in-panjshir-baghlan-and-takhar.

———. "Taliban Disrupts Women's Protest in Kabul," *Hasht-e Subh Daily*, May 29, 2022. https://8am.af/eng/taliban-disrupts-womens-protest-in-kabul.

Rasmussen, Sune E. "Isis Claims Responsibility for Kabul Bomb Attack on Hazara Protesters." *The Guardian*, July 24, 2016. https://www.theguardian.com/world/2016/jul/23/hazara-minority-targeted-by-suicide-bombs-at-kabul-protest.

———. "Kabul: At Least 90 Killed by Massive Car Bomb in Diplomatic Quarter." *The Guardian*, May 31, 2017. https://www.theguardian.com/world/2017/may/31/huge-explosion-kabul-presidential-palace-afghanistan.

Rassler, Don. *The Islamic State and Drones: Supply, Scale, and Future Threats*. New York: Combating Terrorism Center at West Point, 2018.

———. "Situating the Emergence of the Islamic State of Khorasan." *CTC Sentinel* 8:3 (March 2015).

"The Realities of Jihad in Kashmir and Role of Pakistani Agencies." *Al-Qaraar*, January 2018.

Reed, Alastair. *Al-Qaeda in the Indian Subcontinent: A New Frontline in the Global Jihadist Movement?* The Hague: International Centre for Counter-Terrorism, May 2015.

Rehman, Zia Ur. "Killing of Top ISIS Leaders in Sindh Seen As Major Blow to Group." *Pakistan Forward*, March 4, 2019. https://pakistan.asia-news.com/en/GB/articles/cnmi_pf/features/2019/03/04/feature-03.

———. "A Profile of Ahrar-ul-Hind and Ansar-ul-Mujahidin in Pakistan." *CTC Sentinel* 7:5 (2014).

Rempfer, Kyle. "Inside a Fatal Ranger Raid That Killed An ISIS-K Emir in Afghanistan." *Army Times*, August 13, 2020. https://www.armytimes.com/news

/your-army/2020/08/13/inside-a-fatal-ranger-raid-that-killed-an-isis-k-emir-in
-afghanistan.

"Revisiting Counter-Terrorism Strategies in Pakistan: Opportunities and Pitfalls."
Crisis Group, July 22, 2015. https://www.crisisgroup.org/asia/south-asia/pakistan
/revisiting-counter-terrorism-strategies-pakistan-opportunities-and-pitfalls.

Roel Meijer, ed. *Introduction to Global Islam's New Religious Movement.* New
York: Columbia University Press, 2009.

Roggio, Bill. "Ansarul Muhajideen Suicide Bomber Kills 2 Pakistani Troops."
FDD's Long War Journal, November 20, 2013. https://www.longwarjournal
.org/tags/ansarul-mujahideen.

———. "IMU Announces Death of Emir, Announces New Leader." *FDD's Long
War Journal,* August 4, 2012. https://www.longwarjournal.org/archives/2012
/08/imu_announces_death_1.php.

———. "Pakistani Taliban Name Mullah Fazlullah As New Emir." *FDD's Long War
Journal,* November 7, 2013. https://www.longwarjournal.org/archives/2013/11
/pakistani_taliban_na_1.php.

———. "US Kills Islamic State's Deputy." *FDD's Long War Journal,* February 9,
2015. https://www.longwarjournal.org/archives/2015/02/us_kills_islamic_sta
_1.php.

———. "US State Department Lists Jamaat-ul-Ahrar As Terrorist Group." *FDD's
Long War Journal,* August 3, 2016. https://www.longwarjournal.org/archives
/2016/08/us-state-department-lists-jamaat-ul-ahrar-as-terrorist-group.php.

Roggio, Bill, and Caleb Weiss. "Islamic Movement of Uzbekistan Faction Emerges
After Group's Collapse." *FDD's Long War Journal,* June 14, 2016. https://
www.longwarjournal.org/archives/2016/06/islamic-movement-of-uzbekistan
-faction-emerges-after-groups-collapse.php.

Ross, Jamie, Justin Rohrlich, Sami Yousafzai, and Noor Ibrahim. "Sheer Chaos: At
Least 13 U.S. Troops Killed As Blasts Rock Kabul Airport." *Yahoo News,*
August 26, 2021. https://news.yahoo.com/large-explosion-reported-outside
-kabul-134937587.html.

Roul, Animesh. "Islamic State Hind Province's Kashmir Campaign." *Terrorism
Monitor* 18:22 (2020).

Safdar, Hussain. *Pakistan's Achievements in War on Terror but at What Cost? A
Special Review of the Current Decade.* Islamabad: Pakistan Institute for Peace
Studies, 2019.

Safi, Michael. "Kashmir Militant Leader Announced As Head of New al-Qaida-
Linked Cell." *The Guardian,* July 27, 2017. https://www.theguardian.com
/world/2017/jul/27/kashmir-militant-leader-announced-as-head-of-new-al
-qaida-linked-cell-zakir-musa.

Sahi, Nokhaiz. "Balochistan Police Facing Paucity of Senior Cops." *The Nation,*
September 13, 2019. https://nation.com.pk/13-Sep-2019/balochistan-police
-facing-paucity-of-senior-cops.

Saifi, Sophia, Syed A. Shah, and Juliet Perry. "Quetta Attack Survivor: 'We Were
Sleeping When Terrorists Attacked.'" CNN, October 25, 2016. https://www.cnn
.com/2016/10/24/world/pakistan-police-academy-attack/index.html.

Salahuddin, Sayed. "Islamic State Suicide Bomber Strikes Meeting of Afghan Clerics
Who Had Just Condemned Terrorism." *Washington Post,* June 5, 2018. https://
www.washingtonpost.com/world/asia_pacific/suicide-bomber-hits-meeting
-of-afghan-religious-figures-condemning-terrorism-killing-14/2018/06/04/00c
2b53e-67d9-11e8-bea7-c8eb28bc52b1_story.html.

Salam, Abdul, and Saleem Shahid. "128 Perish As Savage Attack on Mastung Rally Stuns Nation." *Dawn,* July 14, 2018. https://www.dawn.com/news /1419972.

Salarzai, Khan W. "Hundreds of Daesh Rebels Emerge in Kunar: Police Chief." *Pajhwok Afghan News,* July 5, 2017. https://pajhwok.com/2017/07/05/hundreds -daesh-rebels-emerge-kunar-police-chief.

"Sanaullah Ghafari, Rewards for Justice; United States Department of State, Rewards for Justice." February 7, 2022. https://rewardsforjustice.net/terrorist -rewards/sanaullah-ghafari.

Sands, Leo, and Malu Cursino. "Afghan Earthquake: At Least 1,000 People Killed and 1,500 Injured." BBC News, June 22, 2022. https://www.bbc.com/news /world-asia-61890804.

Sarkar, Saurav. "The Islamic State's Increasing Focus on India." *The Diplomat,* March 30, 2020. https://thediplomat.com/2020/03/the-islamic-states-increasing -focus-on-india.

Sayed, Abdul. "Daesh Khorasan: Who Is Dr. Shahab Al-Muhajir and Has He Been Chosen As the New Head of IS Khorasan?" *BBC Urdu,* August 21, 2020.

———. "The Dynamics of the Upcoming Battle Between the Taliban AND Daesh-K." *TRT World,* September 13, 2021. https://www.trtworld.com/opinion/the -dynamics-of-the-upcoming-battle-between-the-taliban-and-daesh-k-49928.

———. "Islamic State Khorasan Province's Peshawar Seminary Attack and War Against Afghan Taliban Hanafis." *Terrorism Monitor* 18:21 (2020).

———. "The Mysterious Case of Shaikh Abdul Rahim Muslim Dost: The Founder of IS-K." *Militant Leadership Monitor* 12:1 (2021).

———. "The Taliban's Persistent War on Salafists in Afghanistan." *Terrorism Monitor* 19:8 (2021).

———. "Who Is the New Leader of Islamic State-Khorasan Province?" *Lawfare,* September 2, 2020. https://www.lawfareblog.com/who-new-leader-islamic-state -khorasan-province.

———. "Why Islamic State Khurasan Poses an Indigenous Threat to the Afghan Taliban." *Nexus,* May 9, 2022. https://extremism.gwu.edu/ISK-poses-indigenous -threat-to-Afghan-Taliban.

Sayed, Abdul, and Colin Clarke. "With Haqqanis at the Helm, the Taliban Will Grow Even More Extreme." *Foreign Policy,* November 4, 2021. https:// foreignpolicy.com/2021/11/04/haqqani-network-taliban-relationship-afghanistan -pakistan-terrorism.

Sayed, Abdul, and Tore Hamming. "The Revival of the Pakistani Taliban." *CTC Sentinel* 14:4 (April–May 2021).

Schlein, Lisa. "UN Says Record Number of Afghans Face Acute Hunger." *Voice of America,* May 11, 2022. https://www.voanews.com/a/un-says-record-number -of-afghans-face-acute-hunger-/6566730.html.

Schmitt, Eric. "U.S. Military Focusing on ISIS Cell Behind Attack at Kabul Airport." *New York Times,* January 1, 2022. https://www.nytimes.com/2022/01/01/us /politics/afghan-war-isis-attack.html.

Schroden, Jonathan. "Afghanistan's Security Forces Versus the Taliban: A Net Assessment." *CTC Sentinel* 14:1 (2021).

Schroden, Jonathan. "Lessons from the Collapse of Afghanistan's Security Forces." *CTC Sentinel* 14:8 (2021).

———. "New Ideas for Over-the-Horizon Counterterrorism in Afghanistan." *Lawfare,* May 8, 2022. https://www.lawfareblog.com/new-ideas-over-horizon-counter terrorism-afghanistan.

Secunder Kermani, Sami Yousafzai, and Ishtiaq Mehsud. "Kabul Taliban: Spies, Militants, and a Mysterious Assassination." BBC News, February 7, 2020. https://www.bbc.com/news/world-asia-51356940.

"Security Council ISIL (Da'esh) and al-Qaida Sanctions Committee Adds One Name to Its Sanctions List." August 18, 2017. https://www.un.org/press/en /2017/sc12962.doc.htm.

Sediqi, Abdul Q., Hamid Shalizi, and Ahmad Sultan. "Newborns Among 16 Dead in Kabul Hospital Attack; 24 Killed in Funeral Bombing." Reuters, May 12, 2020. https://www.reuters.com/article/us-afghanistan-attacks/newborns -among-16-dead-in-kabul-hospital-attack-24-killed-in-funeral-bombing -idUSKBN22O0RS.

Seir, Ahmad, Rahim Faiez, Tameem Akhgar, and Jon Gambell. "Taliban Sweep into Afghan Capital after Government Collapses." *Associated Press News*, August 15, 2021. https://apnews.com/article/afghanistan-taliban-kabul-bagram-e1ed 33fe0c665ee67ba132c51b8e32a5.

Semple, Michael. *The Taliban Movement: An Appraisal.* Barcelona: Barcelona Centre for International Affairs, November 2014. https://www.cidob.org/en/publications /publication_series/project_papers/stap_rp/policy_research_papers/the_pakistan _taliban_movement_an_appraisal.

Shah, Saeed. "Al Qaeda Linked Group Claims Kabul Suicide Attacks on Shia Pilgrims." *The Guardian*, December 6, 2011. https://www.theguardian.com/world /2011/dec/06/al-qaida-kabul-attack-shia-pilgrims.

———. "Pakistan Militant Group Jamaat-ul-Ahrar Threatens Fresh Wave of Violence." *Wall Street Journal*, March 29, 2016. https://www.wsj.com/articles/pakistan -militant-group-jamaat-ul-ahrar-threatens-fresh-wave-of-violence-1459270788.

Shah, Saeed, and Syed Shoaib Hasan. "In Pakistan, Extremist Group Expands Its Reach." *Wall Street Journal*. https://www.wsj.com/articles/in-pakistan-extremist -group-expands-its-reach-1438300910.

Shah, Wasseem Ahmad. "Malakand Announces Nizam-e-Adl Implementation." *Dawn*, April 15, 2009. https://www.dawn.com/news/457515/malakand-announces -nizam-e-adl-implementation.

Shahid, Saleem, and Abdul Salam. "128 Perish As Savage Attack on Mastung Rally Stuns Nation." *Dawn*, July 14, 2018. https://www.dawn.com/news/1419972.

Shaikh, Ubaidullah. "At Least 60 Killed in Blast at Shikarpur Imambargah." *Dawn*, January 30, 2015. https://www.dawn.com/news/1160444.

Sharifi, Shoaib, and Louise Adamou. "Taliban 'Threaten 70% of Afghanistan.'" BBC News, January 31, 2018. https://www.bbc.com/news/world-asia-42863116.

Sharipzhan, Merhat. "IMU Declares It Is Now Part of the Islamic State." *Radio Free Europe Radio Liberty*, August 6, 2015. https://www.rferl.org/a/imu-islamic -state/27174567.html.

Sherazi, Zahir Shah. "'Anti-Drone' Militant Group Claims Parachinar Twin Blasts." *Dawn*, July 27, 2013. https://www.dawn.com/news/1032326.

Sherzad, Rafiq. "Afghan Blast Kills 33; President Blames Islamic State." Reuters, April 18, 2015. https://www.reuters.com/article/us-afghanistan-blast/afghan -blast-kills-33-president-blames-islamic-state-idUSKBN0N904620150419.

———. "Islamic State Claims Suicide Attack on Pakistani Consulate in Afghan City." Reuters, January 13, 2016. https://www.reuters.com/article/us-afghanistan -blast-battle/islamic-state-claims-suicide-attack-on-pakistani-consulate-in -afghan-city-idUSKCN0UR0HU20160113.

Shinkman, Paul D. "ISIS in Afghanistan Could Attack U.S. Within 6 Months: U.S. Intelligence." *U.S. News*, October 26, 2021. https://www.usnews.com/news

/national-news/articles/2021-10-26/isis-in-afghanistan-could-attack-us-within -6-months-us-intelligence.

Shinwari, Ibrahim. "Eight Militants Killed in New Khyber Operation." *Dawn,* July 18, 2017. https://www.dawn.com/news/1346011.

Shire, Mohammed I. "How Do Leadership Decapitation and Targeting Error Affect Suicide Bombings? The Case of al-Shabaab." *Studies in Conflict & Terrorism* (June 2020).

Shivaram, Deepa, and Sharon Pruitt-Young. "The Attack Outside Kabul Airport Pushes the U.S. Exit into Deeper Disarray." NPR, August 26, 2021. https://www .npr.org/2021/08/26/1031428645/the-attacks-outside-kabul-airport-pushes-the-u -s-exit-into-deeper-disarray.

Siddique, Abubaker. "The Quetta Shura: Understanding the Afghan Taliban's Leader-ship." Jamestown Foundation, February 21, 2014. https://jamestown.org/program /the-quetta-shura-understanding-the-afghan-talibans-leadership.

"Sipah-e-Sahaba Pakistan." May 5, 2022. https://www.satp.org/satporgtp/countries /pakistan/terroristoutfits/ssp.htm.

"Sirajuddin Jallaloudine Haqqani." September 13, 2007. https://www.un.org/security council/sanctions/1988/materials/summaries/individual/sirajuddin-jallaloudine -haqqani.

Smith, Greg. "The Tangled Web of Taliban and Associated Movements." *Journal of Strategic Security* 2:4 (2010).

Snow, Shawn, Leo Shane III, and Joe Gould. "Afghan Special Operators Partnering with US Forces More Often, Still Reliant on American Support." *Military Times,* February 5, 2020. https://www.militarytimes.com/flashpoints/2020/02 /05/afghan-special-operators-partnering-with-us-forces-more-often-still-reliant -on-american-support.

Soliev, Nodirbek. "The April 2020 Islamic State Terror Plot Against U.S. and NATO Military Bases in Germany: The Tajik Connection." *CTC Sentinel* 14:1 (2021).

Special Inspector General for Afghanistan Reconstruction. *October 30, 2016 Quarterly Report to the United States Congress.* Arlington: Special Inspector General for Afghanistan Reconstruction, 2016.

Starr, Barbara, and Ryan Browne. "US Officials Warn ISIS' Afghanistan Branch Poses a Major Threat." CNN, February 19, 2019. https://www.cnn.com/2019 /02/19/politics/isis-afghanistan-threat/index.html.

Steffens, Nilas K., Kim Peters, S. A. Haslam, and Rolf van Dick. "Dying for Charisma: Leaders' Inspirational Appeal Increases Post-Mortem." *Leadership Quarterly* 28:4 (2017).

Steinberg, Guido. "Jihadi Salafism and the Shi'is: Remarks About the Intellectual Roots of Anti-Shi'ism." In *Global Salafism: Islam's New Religious Movement,* ed. Roel Meijer. New York: Columbia University Press, 2009.

Subrahmanian, V. S., Aaron Mannes, Amy Sliva, Jana Shakarian, and John P. Dick-erson. *Computational Analysis of Terrorist Groups: Lashkar-e-taiba.* New York: Springer, 2013.

"Suicide Bomber Targets Afghan Military Training Centre in Kabul." *Al-Jazeera,* May 30, 2019. https://www.aljazeera.com/news/2019/5/30/suicide-bomber-targets -afghan-military-training-centre-in-kabul.

"Suicide Bombing at Afghanistan's Kunduz Mosque Kills at Least 55 Worshippers." *South China Morning Post,* October 8, 2021. https://www.scmp.com/news /world/russia-central-asia/article/3151716/blast-afghanistans-kunduz-mosque -kills-least-50.

Sukhanyar, Jawad, and Mujib Mashal. "Twin Mosque Attacks Kill Scores in One of Afghanistan's Deadliest Weeks." *New York Times*, October 20, 2017. https://www.nytimes.com/2017/10/20/world/asia/afghanistan-kabul-attack-mosque.html.

Sultan, Ahmad. "Islamic State Say They Have Captured Afghanistan's Tora Bora Caves." Reuters, June 15, 2017. https://www.reuters.com/article/us-afghanistan-islamic-state/islamic-state-say-they-have-captured-afghanistans-tora-bora-caves-idUSKBN1960Z6.

Swami, Praveen. "Al-Qaeda Sets Up Valley Wing with Chandigarh College Dropout As Chief." *Indian Express*, July 28, 2017. https://indianexpress.com/article/india/al-qaeda-sets-up-valley-wing-with-chandigarh-college-dropout-as-chief-4770684.

———. "Islamic State Threatens to Expand to Kashmir." *Indian Express*, February 3, 2016. https://indianexpress.com/article/india/india-news-india/islamic-state-threatens-to-expand-to-kashmir.

Syed, Azaz. "Govt Bans Jundullah, Notification Issued." *News International*, February 14, 2018. https://www.thenews.com.pk/print/280698-govt-bans-jundullah-notification-issued.

Syed, Baqir S. "Top IS Leadership Targeted in Mastung Operation." *Dawn*, June 4, 2017. https://www.dawn.com/news/1337339.

Takeyh, Ray, and Nikolas Gvosdev. "Do Terrorist Networks Need a Home?" *Washington Quarterly* 25:3 (2002).

"Taliban Captures Afghan Provincial Capital Zaranj." *Al-Jazeera*, August 6, 2021. https://www.aljazeera.com/news/2021/8/6/taliban-capture-afghan-provincial-capital-zaranj-nimruz.

"Taliban Condemns 'Brutal' ISIS Video of Afghan Prisoners Being Murdered." *The Guardian*, August 11, 2015. https://www.theguardian.com/world/2015/aug/11/taliban-condemns-brutal-isis-video-afghan-prisoners-murdered.

"Taliban Fighters Divert to ISIS." *Khaama Press*, February 1, 2015. https://www.khaama.com/taliban-fighters-divert-to-isis-nbc-news-28099.

"Taliban Leader Mullah Akhtar Mansour Killed." BBC News, May 22, 2016. https://www.bbc.com/news/world-asia-36352559.

Tankel, Stephen. *Storming the World Stage: The Story of Lashkar-e-Taiba*. London: Oxford University Press, 2013.

Tarzi, Amin. "Islamic State-Khurasan Province." In *The Future of ISIS: Regional and International Implications*, eds. Feisal al-Istrabadi and Sumit Ganguly. Washington, DC: Brookings Institution, 2018.

Taylor, Jack. "Afghanistan: The Taliban Had Promised 'Amnesty for All'—But They Are Responsible for Most Violence Against Civilians." *Sky News*, June 16, 2022. https://news.sky.com/story/afghanistan-the-taliban-had-promised-amnesty-for-all-but-they-are-responsible-for-most-violence-against-civilians-12628906.

Tellis, Ashley. "The Menace That Is Lashkar-e-Taiba." Carnegie Endowment for International Peace, March 2012. https://carnegieendowment.org/files/LeT_menace.pdf.

"13 Key ISIS Leaders Killed in MOAB Bombing in East of Afghanistan." *Khaama Press*, April 19, 2017. https://www.khaama.com/13-key-isis-leaders-killed-in-moab-bombing-in-east-of-afghanistan-02600.

"Three 'Militants' Held for Plotting Attack on Shrine." *Dawn*, October 20, 2018. https://www.dawn.com/news/1440056.

"Three Suspected IS Militants Arrested." *Dawn*, November 7, 2017. https://www.dawn.com/news/1368805.

"Three Women Linked to al-Qaeda, Islamic State Arrested in Karachi." *Dunya News,* December 20, 2015. https://dunyanews.tv/en/Pakistan/313764-Three -women-linked-to-AlQaeda-Islamic-State-arre.

Tominaga, Yasutaka. "Killing Two Birds with One Stone? Examining the Diffusion Effect of Militant Leadership Decapitation." *International Studies Quarterly* 62:1 (2018).

"Top Leader of Jundullah, ISIS-Affiliated Militant Group, Killed in Kunduz Air Strike." *Afghan Zariza.* August 25, 2015.

Trofimov, Yaroslav. "Left Behind after U.S. Withdrawal, Some Former Afghan Spies and Soldiers Turn to Islamic State." *Wall Street Journal,* October 31, 2021. https://www.wsj.com/articles/left-behind-after-u-s-withdrawal-some-former -afghan-spies-and-soldiers-turn-to-islamic-state-11635691605.

"The TTP Statement Against the Unjust UN Report About the TTP." *Umar Media,* July 29, 2020.

Tunio, Hafeez. "Two High-Profile Da'esh Terrorists Killed in an Encounter." *Express Tribune,* March 1, 2019. https://tribune.com.pk/story/1920633/1-two -high-profile-daesh-terrorists-killed-encounter.

"Two Suspected British Daesh Members Arrested.in Afghanistan." *Arab News,* February 8, 2022. https://www.arabnews.com/node/2020711/world.

"United Jihad Council." *Janes World Insurgency and Terrorism Report,* June 24, 2013.

United Nations Assistance Mission in Afghanistan. "Protection of Civilians in Armed Conflict: Election-Related Attacks and Abuses During the Initial Voter Registration Period." May 10, 2018. https://reliefweb.int/sites/reliefweb.int /files/resources/protection_of_civilians_-_special_report_-_election-related _attacks_and_abuses_may_2018_english.pdf.

"U.S. Airstrike Hit ISIS Suicide Training Camp in Afghanistan Leaving 40 Dead." *Khaama Press,* October 22, 2017. https://www.khaama.com/us-airstrike-hit -isis-suicide-training-camp-in-afghanistan-leaving-40-dead-03691.

US Director of National Intelligence. "Hezb-E-Islami Gulbuddin (HIG)." [accessed June 7, 2022] https://www.dni.gov/nctc/groups/hezb_e_islami.html.

US Department of Defense, Office of Inspector General. *Lead Inspector General for Operation Freedom's Sentinel, Quarterly Report, July 1, 2021–September 30, 2021, to the United States Congress.* Alexandria, VA, 2021.

———. *Lead Inspector General for Operation Freedom's Sentinel and Operation Enduring Sentinel: Quarterly Report to the United States Congress, October 1, 2021–December 31, 2021.* Alexandria, VA, 2022.

Valle, Ricardo. "Islamic State Khurasan Province Threatens Uzbekistan, Central Asia, and Neighboring Countries." *Geopolitical Report* 19:4 (2022).

Valle, Riccardo, and Firdous Ifthikar. "Islamic State Khorasan Propaganda Targets New Audience with Release of Pashto Magazine Khurasan Ghag." *Terrorism Monitor* 20:12 (June 16, 2022).

Valle, Ricardo, and Lucas Webber. "The Growth and Internationalization of Islamic State Khurasan Province's Media Operations." *Militant Wire,* February 17, 2022. https://www.militantwire.com/p/the-growth-and-internationalization?s=r.

———. "ISKP's Uzbekistan-Directed Attack Bolsters Rhetoric with Deeds." *Eurasianet,* April 25, 2022. https://eurasianet.org/perspectives-iskps-uzbekistan -directed-attack-bolsters-rhetoric-with-deeds.

Varshalomidze, Tamila, Usaid Siddiqui, and Ted Regencia. "US, Allies Warn of 'High Terror Threat' at Kabul Airport." *Al-Jazeera,* August 25, 2021. https://

www.aljazeera.com/news/2021/8/25/afghans-race-to-flee-taliban-as-us-keeps
-airlift-deadline-live.

"Virtue and Vice Ministry Reject Claims of Ordering Gender Segregation in Restaurants." *Ariana News,* May 15, 2022. https://www.ariananews.af/virtue-and
-vice-ministry-reject-claims-of-ordering-gender-segregation-in-restaurants.

"Wali Saqib, Head of Salafi Scholars, Mysteriously Killed in Kabul." *Hasht-e-Subh Daily,* July 14, 2022. https://8am.af/eng/wali-saqeb-head-of-salafi-scholars
-mysteriously-killed-in-kabul.

Ward, Alex. "Terrorists Just Tried to Assassinate Defense Secretary Jim Mattis in Afghanistan." Vox, September 27, 2017. https://www.vox.com/world/2017/9
/27/16374772/mattis-afghanistan-kabul-airport-attack-taliban-isis.

Watkins, Andrew. "Afghanistan on the Edge? Elections, Elites, and Ethnic Tensions." *War on the Rocks,* October 31, 2019. https://warontherocks.com/2019
/10/afghanistan-on-the-edge-elections-elites-and-ethnic-tensions.

———. "An Assessment of Taliban Rule at Three Months." *CTC Sentinel* 14:9 (2021).

———. *Taliban Fragmentation: Fact, Fiction, and Future.* Washington, DC: US Institute of Peace, 2020.

Wazir, Dilawar. "Pamphlet Warns Police to Leave S. Waziristan in Three Days Pamphlet." *Dawn,* April 23, 2019. https://www.dawn.com/news/1477791/pamphlet
-warns-police-to-leave-s-waziristan-in-three-days.

Webber, Lucas. "Islamic State in Afghanistan Promises Attacks on Chinese and Iranian Cities, Threatens Uzbekistan and Tajikistan." *Militant Wire,* June 20, 2022. https://www.militantwire.com/p/islamic-state-in-afghanistan-promises.

———. "The Islamic State's Global Campaign of 'Economic War' Targeting Infrastructure: An Interview with Jihad Analytics." *Militant Wire,* December 8, 2021. https://www.militantwire.com/p/the-islamic-states-global-campaign
?s=r.

———. "Islamic State's Threat to Foreign Commercial Activity in Afghanistan." *Terrorism Monitor* 20:12 (June 16, 2022). https://jamestown.org/program
/islamic-states-threat-to-foreign-commercial-activity-in-afghanistan.

———. "Voice of Khorasan Magazine and the Internationalization of Islamic State's Anti-Taliban Propaganda." *Terrorism Monitor* 20:9 (May 6, 2022). https://
jamestown.org/program/voice-of-khorasan-magazine-and-the-internationalization
-of-islamic-states-anti-taliban-propaganda.

Wellman, Phillip W. "Afghan Official: Death Toll from Massive US Bomb Rises to 94, Including 4 ISIS Commanders." *Stars and Stripes,* April 15, 2017. https://
www.stripes.com/theaters/middle_east/afghan-official-death-toll-from-massive
-us-bomb-rises-to-94-including-4-isis-commanders-1.463677.

"What Works in Policing? Counterterrorism Strategies." June 2022. https://cebcp
.org/evidence-based-policing/what-works-in-policing/research-evidence-review
/counterterrorism-strategies.

"What's Next for Afghans Fleeing the Taliban?" Human Rights Watch, September 9, 2021. https://www.hrw.org/news/2021/09/09/whats-next-afghans-fleeing
-taliban.

Whiteside, Craig. *Nine Bullets for the Traitors, One for the Enemy: The Slogans and Strategy Behind the Islamic State's Campaign to Defeat the Sunni Awakening (2006–2017).* The Hague: International Centre for Counter-Terrorism, September 2018. https://icct.nl/app/uploads/2018/09/ICCT-Whiteside-Nine
-Bullets-For-The-Traitors-September-2018.pdf.

"Who Are the Kashmiri Militants?" BBC News, August 1, 2012. https://www.bbc.com/news/world-asia-18738906.

"Why We Should Leave the Militant Groups in Kashmir." *Al-Qaraar,* February 2018.

Wiktorowicz, Quintan. "Anatomy of the Salafi Movement." *Studies in Conflict and Terrorism* 29:3 (2006).

Winter, Charlie. "Apocalypse Later: A Longitudinal Study of the Islamic State Brand." *Critical Studies in Media Communication* 35:1 (2018).

———. *Media Jihad: The Islamic State's Doctrine for Information Warfare.* London: International Centre for the Study of Radicalisation and Political Violence, 2017.

———. "Suicide Tactics and the Islamic State." International Centre for Counter-Terrorism—The Hague, January 10, 2017. https://icct.nl/publication/suicide-tactics-and-the-islamic-state.

———. *The Virtual "Caliphate": Understanding Islamic State's Propaganda Strategy.* London: Quilliam Foundation, 2015.

Withington, Sean. *Islamic State Wilayat Khorasan: Phony Caliphate or Bona Fide Province?* Kabul: Afghan Institute for Strategic Studies, 2020.

Yousaf, Kamran. "Peace Talks to Pre-empt 'TTP-Da'ish Nexus.'" *Express Tribune,* July 6, 2022. https://tribune.com.pk/story/2364901/peace-talks-to-pre-empt-ttp-daish-nexus.

Yusafzai, Gul. "Gunmen Kill Four Police in Pakistani City of Quetta." Reuters, July 13, 2017. https://www.reuters.com/article/us-pakistan-shooting/gunmen-kill-four-police-in-pakistani-city-of-quetta-idUSKBN19Y143.

———. "Islamic State Claims Attack on Pakistan Police Academy, 59 Dead." Reuters, October 24, 2016. https://www.reuters.com/article/us-pakistan-attack/islamic-state-claims-attack-on-pakistan-police-academy-59-dead-idUS KCN12O2M6.

———. "Suicide Bombing at Southwest Pakistan Shrine Kills 18." Reuters, October 5, 2017. https://www.reuters.com/article/us-pakistan-blast/suicide-bombing-at-southwest-pakistan-shrine-kills-18-idUSKBN1CA1MK.

Yusafzai, Sami, and Jibran Ahmad. "Afghan Taliban's New Chief Replaces 24 'Shadow' Officials." Reuters, January 27, 2017. https://www.reuters.com/article/us-afghanistan-taliban/afghan-talibans-new-chief-replaces-24-shadow-officials-idUSKBN15B1PN.

Yousafzai, Sami, and Tucker Reals. "ISIS-K Is Trying to Undermine Afghanistan's Taliban Regime, from Inside and Out—That's America's Problem, Too." *CBS News,* October 8, 2021. https://www.cbsnews.com/news/isis-k-taliban-afghanistan-regime.

Zafar, Mohammad. "Quetta Weeps Again: Islamic State, TTP-JA Claim Responsibility for Attack." *Express Tribune,* August 8, 2016. https://tribune.com.pk/story/1157855/explosion-firing-heard-near-civil-hospital-quetta.

———. "61 Killed, at Least 165 Injured As Militants Storm Police Training Centre in Quetta." *Express Tribune,* April 20, 2022. https://tribune.com.pk/story/1208735/militants-attack-police-training-centre-quetta.

Zahid, Farhan. "Counter Terrorism Policy Measures: A Critical Analysis of Pakistan's National Action Plan." Mackenzie Institute, July 19, 2016. https://mackenzieinstitute.com/2016/07/counter-terrorism-policy-measures-a-critical-analysis-of-pakistans-national-action-plan.

———. "Lashkar-e-Jhangvi al-Alami: A Pakistani Partner for Islamic State." *Terrorism Monitor* 15:2 (2017).

————. "The 'New' Militants." *Dawn,* March 4, 2015. https://www.dawn.com/news /1167235.

————. "Two New IS Wilayat in South Asia." *Terrorism Monitor* 17:1 (2019).

Zahid, Noor. "Son of Slain IMU Leader Promotes IS in Afghanistan." *Voice of America,* February 8, 2017. https://gandhara.rferl.org/a/son-of-imu-leader -promotes-is-in-afghanistan/28298506.html.

Zaidi, Syed Manzar Abbas. "The Role of Lashkar-i-Islam in Pakistan's Khyber Agency." *CTC Sentinel* 3:10 (2010).

Zarifi, Yousuf. "Anti-Daesh Uprising Force Springs Into Action in Nazian." *Pajhwok Afghan News,* November 7, 2018. https://pajhwok.com/2018/11/07/anti -daesh-uprising-force-springs-action-nazian/rising.

————. "Daesh Rebels Continue to Get Equipment: Achin Residents." *Pajhwok Afghan News,* November 25, 2017. https://pajhwok.com/2017/11/25/daesh -rebels-continue-get-equipment-achin-residents.

Zerai, Khalid. "ISIS, Other Militants Clash over Illegal Logging in Nangarhar." *Salaam Times,* April 5, 2018. https://afghanistan.asia-news.com/en_GB/articles /cnmi_st/features/2018/04/05/feature-01.

Index

237

About the Book

The deadly attack on Kabul's airport in August 2021 shocked the world and brought concentrated attention to the Islamic State Khorasan Province (ISK). New questions quickly arose: How did this ISIS affiliate become such a force in Afghanistan and Pakistan? And why is it now a lethal threat to the Taliban? Addressing these questions, Amira Jadoon and Andrew Mines draw on original data and newly available primary sources to dissect ISK's inner workings and explain its rise and resilience.

Amira Jadoon is assistant professor of political science at Clemson University and nonresident fellow at the Stimson Center. Previously, she was assistant professor in the Department of Political Science and the Combating Terrorism Center at the US Military Academy at West Point. **Andrew Mines** is research fellow in the Program on Extremism at George Washington University.